AMERICAN EDUCATION

Its Men,

Ideas,

and

Institutions

Advisory Editor

Lawrence A. Cremin
Frederick A. P. Barnard Professor of Education
Teachers College, Columbia University

AMERICAN EDUCATION: *Its Men, Ideas, and Institutions* presents selected works of thought and scholarship that have long been out of print or otherwise unavailable. Inevitably, such works will include particular ideas and doctrines that have been outmoded or superseded by more recent research. Nevertheless, all retain their place in the literature, having influenced educational thought and practice in their own time and having provided the basis for subsequent scholarship.

THE

AMERICAN WOMAN'S HOME:

OR,

PRINCIPLES OF DOMESTIC SCIENCE;

BEING

A GUIDE TO THE FORMATION AND MAINTENANCE OF ECONOMICAL,
HEALTHFUL, BEAUTIFUL, AND CHRISTIAN HOMES.

BY

CATHARINE E. BEECHER

AND

HARRIET BEECHER STOWE.

ARNO PRESS & THE NEW YORK TIMES
*New York * 1971*

Reprint Edition 1971 by Arno Press Inc.

Reprinted from a copy in
The University of Illinois Library

American Education:
  Its Men, Ideas, and Institutions - Series II
ISBN for complete set: 0-405-03600-0
See last pages of this volume for titles.

Manufactured in the United States of America

Library of Congress Cataloging in Publication Data

Beecher, Catharine Esther, 1800-1878.
    The American woman's home.
    (American education: its men, ideas, and
institutions. Series II)
    1. Home economics. I. Stowe, Harriet
Elizabeth (Beecher) 1811-1896, joint author.
II. Title. III. Series.
TX145.B415 1971   640   77-165703
ISBN 0-405-03692-2

THE

AMERICAN WOMAN'S HOME

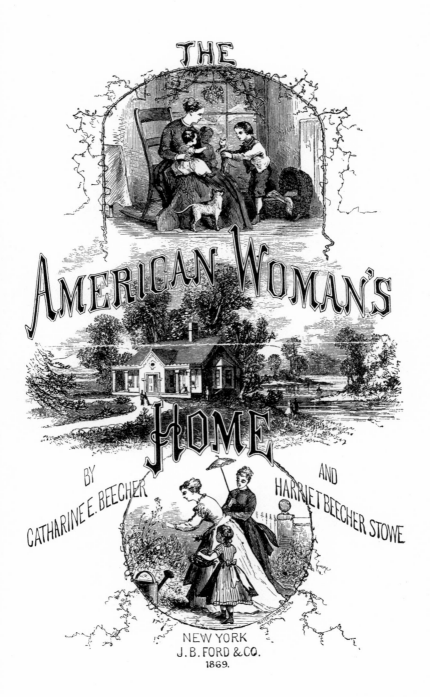

THE
AMERICAN WOMAN'S
HOME

BY
CATHARINE E. BEECHER
AND
HARRIET BEECHER STOWE

NEW YORK
J. B. FORD & CO.
1869.

THE

AMERICAN WOMAN'S HOME:

OR,

PRINCIPLES OF DOMESTIC SCIENCE;

BEING

A GUIDE TO THE FORMATION AND MAINTENANCE OF ECONOMICAL, HEALTHFUL, BEAUTIFUL, AND CHRISTIAN HOMES.

BY

CATHARINE E. BEECHER

AND

HARRIET BEECHER STOWE.

NEW-YORK:

J. B. FORD AND COMPANY.

BOSTON: H. A. BROWN & CO. PHILADELPHIA: CHAS. S. GREENE & CO.
CHICAGO: J. A. STODDARD & CO. CINCINNATI: HENRY HOWE.
SAN FRANCISCO: FRANCIS DEWING & CO.

—

1869.

UNIVERSITY PRESS: WELCH, BIGELOW, & CO.,
CAMBRIDGE.

TO

THE WOMEN OF AMERICA,

IN WHOSE HANDS REST THE REAL DESTINIES OF THE REPUBLIC, AS
MOULDED BY THE EARLY TRAINING AND PRESERVED
AMID THE MATURER INFLUENCES OF HOME,
THIS VOLUME IS

AFFECTIONATELY INSCRIBED.

TABLE OF CONTENTS.

VII.

THE CARE OF HEALTH.

VIII.

DOMESTIC EXERCISE.

IX.

HEALTHFUL FOOD.

XVI.

GOOD TEMPER IN THE HOUSEKEEPER.

XVII.

HABITS OF SYSTEM AND ORDER.

XVIII.

GIVING IN CHARITY.

The American Woman's Home.

INTRODUCTION.

The authors of this volume, while they sympathize with every honest effort to relieve the disabilities and sufferings of their sex, are confident that the chief cause of these evils is the fact that the honor and duties of the family state are not duly appreciated, that women are not trained for these duties as men are trained for their trades and professions, and that, as the consequence, family labor is poorly done, poorly paid, and regarded as menial and disgraceful.

To be the nurse of young children, a cook, or a house-maid, is regarded as the lowest and last resort of poverty, and one which no woman of culture and position can assume without loss of caste and respectability.

It is the aim of this volume to elevate both the honor and the remuneration of all the employments that sustain the many difficult and sacred duties of the family state, and thus to render each department of woman's true profession as much desired and respected as are the most honored professions of men.

When the other sex are to be instructed in law, medicine, or divinity, they are favored with numerous institutions richly endowed, with teachers of the highest talents and acquirements, with extensive libraries, and abundant and costly apparatus. With such advantages they devote nearly ten of the best years of life to preparing themselves for their profession ; and to secure the public from unqualified members of these professions, none can enter them until examined by a competent body, who certify to their due preparation for their duties.

Woman's profession embraces the care and nursing of the body in the critical periods of infancy and sickness, the training of the human mind in the most impressible period of childhood, the instruction and control of servants, and most of the government and economies of the family state. These duties of woman are as sacred and important as any ordained to man ; and yet no such advantages for preparation have been accorded to her, nor is there any qualified body to certify the public that a woman is duly prepared to give proper instruction in her profession.

This unfortunate want, and also the questions frequently asked concerning the domestic qualifications of both the authors of this work, who have formerly written upon such topics, make it needful to give some account of the advantages they have enjoyed in preparation for the important office assumed as teachers of woman's domestic duties.

The sister whose name is subscribed is the eldest of nine children by her own mother, and of four by her step-mother ; and having a natural love for children, she found it a pleasure as well as a duty to aid in the care of infancy and childhood. At sixteen, she was deprived of a mother, who was remarkable not only for intelligence and culture, but for a natural taste and skill in domestic handicraft. Her place was awhile filled by an aunt remarkable for her habits of neatness and order, and especially for her economy. She was, in the course of time, replaced by a step-mother, who had been accustomed to a superior style of housekeeping, and was an expert in all departments of domestic administration.

Under these successive housekeepers, the writer learned not only to perform in the most approved manner all the manual employments of domestic life, but to honor and enjoy these duties.

At twenty-three, she commenced the institution which ever since has flourished as " The Hartford Female Seminary," where, at the age of twelve, the sister now united with her in the authorship of this work became her pupil, and, after a few years, her associate. The removal of the family to the West, and failure of health, ended a connection with the Hartford Seminary, and originated a similar one in Cincinnati, of which the younger authoress of this work was associate principal till her marriage.

At this time, the work on *Domestic Economy*, of which this volume may be called an enlarged edition, although a great portion of it is entirely new, embodying the latest results of science, was prepared by the writer as a part of the *Massachusetts School Library*, and has since been extensively introduced as a text-book into public schools and higher female seminaries. It was followed by its sequel, *The Domestic Receipt-Book*, widely circulated by the Harpers in every State of the Union.

These two works have been entirely remodeled, former topics rewritten, and many new ones introduced, so as to include all that is properly embraced in a complete Encyclopedia of Domestic Economy.

In addition to the opportunities mentioned, the elder sister, for many years, has been studying the causes and the remedies for the decay of constitution and loss of health so increasingly prevalent among American women, aiming to promote the establishment of *endowed* institutions, in which women shall be properly trained for their profession, as both housekeepers and health-keepers. What advantages have thus been received and the results thus obtained will appear in succeeding pages.

During the upward progress of the age, and the advance of a more enlightened Christianity, the writers of this volume have gained more elevated views of the true mission of woman—of the dignity and importance of her distinctive duties, and of the true happiness which will be the reward of a right appreciation of this mission, and a proper performance of these duties.

There is at the present time an increasing agitation of the public mind, evolving many theories and some crude speculations as to woman's rights and duties. That there is a great social and moral power in her keeping, which is now seeking expression by organization, is manifest, and that resulting plans and efforts will involve some mistakes, some collisions, and some failures, all must expect.

But to intelligent, reflecting, and benevolent women—whose faith rests on the character and teachings of Jesus Christ—there are great principles revealed by Him, which in the end will secure the grand result which He taught and suffered to achieve. It is hoped that in the following pages these principles will be so exhibited and illustrated as to aid in securing those rights and advantages which Christ's religion aims to provide for all, and especially for the most weak and defenseless of His children.

Catharine E. Beecher.

1.

THE CHRISTIAN FAMILY.

It is the aim of this volume to elevate both the honor and the remuneration of all employments that sustain the many difficult and varied duties of the family state, and thus to render each department of woman's profession as much desired and respected as are the most honored professions of men.

What, then, is the end designed by the family state which Jesus Christ came into this world to secure?

It is to provide for the training of our race to the highest possible intelligence, virtue, and happiness, by means of the self-sacrificing labors of the wise and good, and this with chief reference to a future immortal existence.

The distinctive feature of the family is self-sacrificing labor of the stronger and wiser members to raise the weaker and more ignorant to equal advantages. The father undergoes toil and self-denial to provide a home, and then the mother becomes a self-sacrificing laborer to train its inmates. The useless, troublesome infant is served in the humblest offices; while both parents unite in training it to an equality with themselves in every advantage. Soon the older children become helpers to raise the younger to a level with their own. When any are sick, those who are well become self-sacrificing ministers. When the parents are old and useless, the children become their self-sacrificing servants.

Thus the discipline of the family state is one of daily self-devotion of the stronger and wiser to elevate and support the weaker members. Nothing could be more contrary to its first principles than for the older and more capable children to combine to secure to themselves the highest advantages, enforcing the drudgeries on the younger, at the sacrifice of their equal culture.

Jesus Christ came to teach the fatherhood of God and consequent brotherhood of man. He came as the "firstborn Son" of God and the Elder Brother of man, to teach by example the self-sacrifice by which the great family of man is to be raised to equality of advantages as children of God. For this end, he "humbled himself" from the highest to the lowest place. He chose for his birthplace the most despised village; for his parents the lowest in rank; for his trade, to labor with his hands as a carpenter being "subject to his parents" thirty years. And, what is very significant, his trade was that which prepares the family home, as if he would teach that the great duty of man is labor—to provide for and train weak and ignorant creatures. Jesus Christ worked with his hands nearly thirty years, and preached less than three. And he taught that his kingdom is exactly opposite to that of the world, where all are striving for the highest positions. " Whoso will be great shall be your minister, and whoso will be chiefest shall be servant of all."

The family state then, is the aptest earthly illustration of the heavenly kingdom, and in it woman is its chief minister. Her great mission is self-denial, in training its members to self-sacrificing labors for the ignorant and weak : if not her own children, then the neglected children of her Father in heaven. She is to rear all under her care to lay up treasures, not on earth, but in heaven. All the pleasures of this life end here ; but those who train immortal minds are to reap the fruit of their labor through eternal ages.

To man is appointed the out-door labor—to till the earth, dig the mines, toil in the foundries, traverse the ocean, transport merchandise, labor in manufactories, construct houses, conduct civil, municipal, and state affairs, and all the heavy work, which, most of the day, excludes him from the comforts of a home. But the great stimulus to all these toils, implanted in the heart of every true man, is the desire for a home of his own, and the hopes of paternity. Every man who truly lives for immortality responds to the beatitude, " Children are a heritage from the Lord : blessed is the man that hath his quiver full of them !" The more a father and mother live under the influence of that " immortality which Christ hath brought to light," the more is the blessedness of rearing a family understood and appreciated. Every child trained aright is to dwell forever in exalted bliss with those that gave it life and trained it for heaven.

The blessed privileges of the family state are not confined to those who rear children of their own. Any woman who can earn a livelihood, as every woman should be trained to do, can take a properly qualified female associate, and institute a family of her own, receiving to its heavenly influences the orphan, the sick, the homeless, and the sinful, and by motherly devotion train them to follow the self-denying example of Christ, in educating his earthly children for true happiness in this life and 'for his eternal home.

And such is the blessedness of aiding to sustain a truly Christian home, that no one comes so near the pattern of the All-perfect One as those who might hold what men call a higher place, and yet humble themselves to the lowest in order to aid in training the young, "not as men-pleasers, but as servants to Christ, with good-will doing service as to the Lord, and not to men." Such are preparing for high places in the kingdom of heaven. " Whosoever will be chiefest among you, let him be your servant."

It is often the case that the true humility of Christ is not understood. It was not in having a low opinion of his own character and claims, but it was in taking a low place in order to raise others to a higher. The worldling seeks to raise himself and family to an equality with others, or, if possible, a superiority to them. The true follower of Christ comes down in order to elevate others.

The maxims and institutions of this world have ever been antagonistic to the teachings and example of Jesus Christ. Men toil for wealth, honor, and power, not as means for raising others to an equality with themselves, but mainly for earthly, selfish advantages. Although the experience of this life shows that children brought up to labor have the fairest chance for a virtuous and prosperous life, and for hope of future eternal blessedness, yet it is the aim of most parents who can do so, to lay up wealth that their children need not labor with the hands as Christ did.

And although exhorted by our Lord not to lay up treasure on earth, but rather the imperishable riches which are gained in toiling to train the ignorant and reform the sinful, as yet a large portion of the professed followers of Christ, like his first disciples, are "slow of heart to believe."

Not less have the sacred ministries of the family state been undervalued and warred upon in other directions; for example, the Romish Church has made celibacy a prime virtue, and given its highest honors to those who forsake the family state as ordained by God. Thus came great communities of monks and nuns, shut out from the love and labors of a Christian home; thus, also, came the monkish systems of education, collecting the young in great establishments away from the watch and care of parents, and the healthful and self-sacrificing labors of a home. Thus both religion and education have conspired to degrade the family state.

Still more have civil laws and social customs been opposed to the principles of Jesus Christ. It has ever been assumed that the learned, the rich, and the powerful are not to labor with the hands, as Christ did, and as Paul did when he would "not eat any man's bread for naught, but wrought with labor, not because we have not power" [to live without hand-work,] "but to make ourselves an example." (2 Thess. 3.)

Instead of this, manual labor has been made dishonorable and unrefined by being forced on the ignorant and poor. Especially has the most important of all hand-labor, that which sustains the family, been thus disgraced; so that to nurse young children, and provide the food of a family by labor, is deemed the lowest of all positions in honor and profit, and the last resort of poverty. And so our Lord, who himself took the form of a servant, teaches, "How hardly shall they that have riches enter the kingdom of heaven!"—that kingdom in which all are toiling to raise the weak, ignorant, and sinful to such equality with themselves as the children of a loving family enjoy. One mode in which riches have led to antagonism with the true end of the family state is in the style of living, by which the hand-labor, most important to health, comfort, and beauty, is confined to the most ignorant and neglected members of society, without any effort being made to raise them to equal advantages with the wise and cultivated.

And, the higher civilization has advanced, the mor-have children been trained to feel that to labor, as did Christ and Paul, is disgraceful, and to be made the portion of a degraded class. Children of the rich grow up with the feeling that servants are to work for them, and they themselves are not to work. To the minds of most children and servants, "to be a lady," is almost synonymous with "to be waited on, and do no work." It is the earnest desire of the authors of this volume to make plain the falsity of this growing popular feeling, and to show how much happier and more efficient family life will become when it is strengthened, sustained, and adorned by family work.

II

A CHRISTIAN HOUSE.

In the Divine Word it is written, "The wise woman buildeth her house." To be "wise," is "to choose the best
means for accomplishing the best end." It has been shown
that the best end for a woman to seek is the training of
God's children for their eternal home, by guiding them to
intelligence, virtue, and true happiness. When, therefore,
the wise woman seeks a home in which to exercise this

ministry, she will aim to secure a house so planned that it will provide in the best manner for health, industry, and economy, those cardinal requisites of domestic enjoyment and success. To aid in this, is the object of the following drawings and descriptions, which will illustrate a style of living more conformed to the great design for which the family is instituted than that which ordinarily prevails among those classes which take the lead in forming the customs of society. The aim will be to exhibit modes of economizing labor, time, and expenses, so as to secure health, thrift, and domestic happiness to persons of limited means, in a measure rarely attained even by those who possess wealth.

At the head of this chapter is a sketch of what may be properly called a Christian house; that is, a house contrived for the express purpose of enabling every member of a family to labor with the hands for the common good, and by modes at once healthful, economical, and tasteful

Of course, much of the instruction conveyed in the fol lowing pages is chiefly applicable to the wants and habits of those living either in the country or in such suburban vicinities as give space of ground for healthful outdoor occupation in the family service, although the general principles of house-building and house-keeping are of ne- cessity universal in their application—as true in the busy confines of the city as in the freer and purer quietude of the country. So far as circumstances can be made to yield the opportunity, it will be assumed that the family state demands some outdoor labor for all. The cultiva- tion of flowers to ornament the table and house, of fruits and vegetables for food, of silk and cotton for clothing, and the care of horse, cow, and dairy, can be so divided that each and all of the family, some part of the day, can take exercise in the pure air, under the magnetic and healthful rays of the sun. Every head of a family should seek a soil and climate which will afford such opportunities. Railroads, enabling men toiling in cities to rear families in the country, are on this account a special blessing. So, also, is the opening of the South to free labor, where, in the pure and mild climate of the uplands, openair labor can proceed most of the year, and women and children labor out of doors as well as w thin.

In the following drawings are presented modes of economizing time, labor, and expense by the close packing of conveniences. By such methods, small and economical houses can be made to secure most of the comforts and many of the refinements of large and expensive ones. The cottage at the head of this chapter is projected on a plan which can be adapted to a warm or cold climate with little change. By adding another story, it would serve a large family.

Fig. 1 shows the ground-plan of the first floor. On the inside it is forty-three feet long and twenty-five wide, excluding conservatories and front and back projections. Its inside height from floor to ceiling is ten feet. The piazzas each side of the front projection have sliding-windows to the floor, and can, by glazed sashes, be made green-houses in winter. In a warm climate, piazzas can be made at the back side also.

In the description and arrangement, the leading aim is to show how time, labor, and expense are saved, not only in the building but in furniture and its arrangement. With this aim, the ground-floor and its furniture will first be shown, then the second story and its furniture, and then the basement and its conveniences. The conservatories are appendages not necessary to housekeeping, but useful in many ways pointed out more at large in other chapters.

The entry has arched recesses behind the front doors, (Fig. 2,) furnished with hooks for over-clothes in both—a box for over-shoes in one, and a stand for umbrellas in the other. The roof of the recess is for statuettes, busts, or

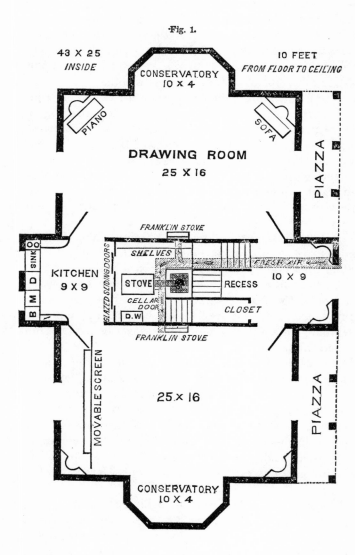

·Fig. 1.

43 X 25
INSIDE

CONSERVATORY
10 X 4

10 FEET
FROM FLOOR TO CEILING

PIANO

SOFA

DRAWING ROOM
25 X 16

PIAZZA

FRANKLIN STOVE

SHELVES

GLAZED SLIDING DOORS

FRESH AIR

KITCHEN
9 X 9

SINK

B M D

STOVE

RECESS

10 X 9

CELLAR
DOOR

D.W

CLOSET

FRANKLIN STOVE

MOVABLE SCREEN

25 X 16

PIAZZA

CONSERVATORY
10 X 4

flowers. The stairs turn twice with broad steps, making a recess at the lower landing, where a table is set with a

Fig. 2.

vase of flowers, (Fig. 3.) On one side of the recess is a closet, arched to correspond with the arch over the stairs. A bracket over the first broad stair, with flowers or statuettes, is visible from the entrance, and pictures can be hung as in the illustration.

The large room on the left can be made to serve the purpose of several rooms by means of a *movable screen.* By shifting this rolling screen from one part of the room to another, two apartments are always available, of any desired size within the limits of the large room. One side of the screen fronts what may be used as the parlor or sitting-room ; the other side is arranged for bedroom conveniences. Of this, Fig. 4 shows the front side ; covered first with strong canvas, stretched and nailed on. Over this is pasted panel-paper, and the upper part is made to resemble an ornamental cornice by fresco-paper. Pictures can be hung in the panels, or be pasted on and varnished with white varnish. To

Fig. 3.

CLOSET   RECESS   STAIR LANDING

prevent the absorption of the varnish, a wash of gum isinglass (fish-glue) must be applied twice.

Fig. 4.

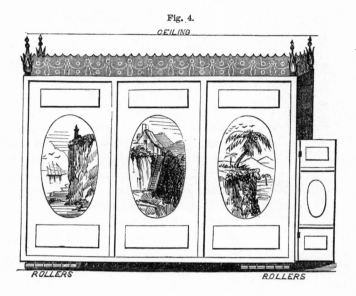

Fig. 5 shows the back or inside of the movable screen, toward the part of the room used as the bedroom. On one side, and at the top and bottom, it has shelves with *shelf-boxes*, which are cheaper and better than drawers, and much preferred by those using them. Handles are cut in the front and back side, as seen in Fig. 6. Half an inch space must be between the box and the shelf over it, and as much each side, so that it can be taken out and put in easily. The central part of the screen's interior is a wardrobe.

This screen must be so high as nearly to reach the ceiling, in order to prevent it from overturning. It is to fill the width of the room, except two feet on each side. A projecting cleat or strip, reaching nearly to the top of

the screen, three inches wide, is to be screwed to the front
sides, on which light frame doors are to be hung, covered

Fig 5.

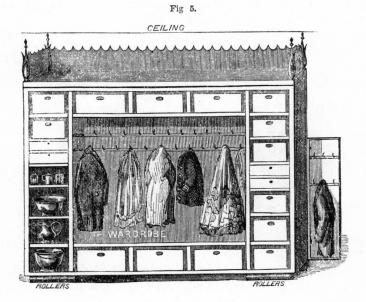

with canvas and panel-paper like the front of the screen.
The inside of these doors is furnished with hooks for clothing, for which the projection makes room.   The whole
screen is to be eighteen inches deep at the top and two

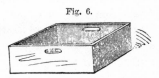

Fig. 6.

feet deep at the base, giving a
solid foundation.   It is moved
on four wooden rollers, one
foot long and four inches in
diameter.   The pivots of the
rollers and the parts where
there is friction must be rubbed with hard soap, and then
a child can move the whole easily.

A curtain is to be hung across the whole interior of the

screen by rings, on a strong wire. The curtain should be
in three parts, with lead or large nails in the hems to
keep it in place. The wood-work must be put together
with screws, as the screen is too large to pass through a
door.

At the end of the room, behind the screen, are two
couches, to be run one under the other, as in Fig. 7. The

Fig. 7.

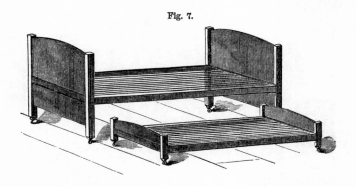

upper one is made with four posts, each three feet high
and three inches square, set on casters two inches high.
The frame is to be fourteen inches from the floor, seven
feet long, two feet four inches wide, and three inches in
thickness. At the head, and at the foot, is to be screwed
a notched two-inch board, three inches wide, as in Fig. 8.

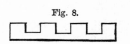

Fig. 8.

The mortises are to be one inch
wide and deep, and one inch apart,
to receive slats made of ash, oak,
or spruce, one inch square, placed
lengthwise of the couch. The slats being small, and so
near together, and running lengthwise, make a better
spring frame than wire coils. If they warp, they can be
turned. They must not be fastened at the ends, except
by insertion in the notches. Across the posts, and of equal
height with them, are to be screwed head and foot-boards.

The under couch is like the upper, except these dimensions: posts, nine inches high, including castors; frame, six feet two inches long, two feet four inches wide. The frame should be as near the floor as possible, resting on the casters.

The most healthful and comfortable mattress is made by a case, open in the centre and fastened together with buttons, as in Fig. 9; to be filled with oat

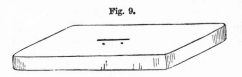

Fig. 9.

straw, which is softer than wheat or rye. This can be adjusted to the figure, and often renewed.

Fig. 10 represents the upper couch when covered, with the under couch put beneath it. The coverlid should match the curtain of the screen; and the pillows, by day, should have a case of the same.

Fig. 10.   Fig. 11.

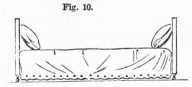

Fig. 11 is an ottoman, made as a box, with a lid on hinges. A cushion is fastened to this lid by strings at each corner, passing through holes in the box lid and tied inside. The cushion to be cut square, with side pieces; stuffed with hair, and stitched through like a mattress. Side handles are made by cords fastened inside with knots. The box must be two inches larger at the bottom than at the top, and the lid and cushion the same size as the bottom, to give it a tasteful shape. This ottoman is set on casters, and is a great convenience for holding articles, while serving also as a seat.

The expense of the screen, where lumber averages $4 a hundred, and carpenter labor $3 a day, would be about $30, and the two couches about $6. The material for covering might be cheap and yet pretty. A woman with these directions, and a son or husband who would use plane and saw, could thus secure much additional room, and also what amounts to two bureaus, two large trunks, one large wardrobe, and a wash-stand, for less than $20—the mere cost of materials. The screen and couches can be so arranged as to have one room serve first as a large and airy sleeping-room; then, in the morning, it may be used as sitting-room one side of the screen, and breakfast-room the other; and lastly, through the day it can be made a large parlor on the front side, and a sewing or retiring-room the other side. The needless spaces usually devoted to kitchen, entries, halls, back-stairs, pantries, store-rooms, and closets, by this method would be used in adding to the size of the large room, so variously used by day and by night.

Fig. 12 is an enlarged plan of the kitchen and stove-room. The chimney and stove-room are contrived to ventilate the whole house, by a mode exhibited in another chapter.

Between the two rooms glazed sliding-doors, passing each other, serve to shut out heat and smells from the kitchen. The sides of the stove-room must be lined with shelves; those on the side by the cellar stairs, to be one foot wide, and eighteen inches apart; on the other side, shelves may be narrower, eight inches wide and nine inches apart. Boxes with lids, to receive stove utensils, must be placed near the stove.

On these shelves, and in the closet and boxes, can be placed every material used for cooking, all the table and cooking utensils, and all the articles used in house work, and yet much spare room will be left. The cook's galley in a steamship has every article and utensil used in cook-

Fig. 12.

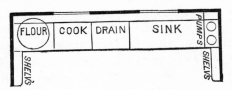

KITCHEN
9 × 9

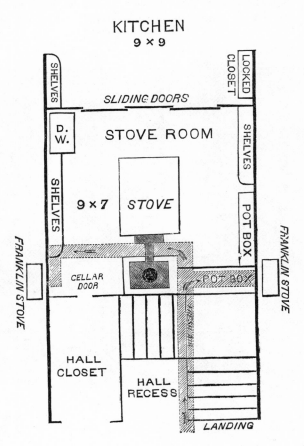

ing for two hundred persons, in a space not larger than this stove-room, and so arranged that with one or two steps the cook can reach all he uses.

In contrast to this, in most large houses, the table furniture, the cooking materials and utensils, the sink, and the eating-room, are at such distances apart, that half the time and strength is employed in walking back and forth to collect and return the articles used.

Fig. 13.

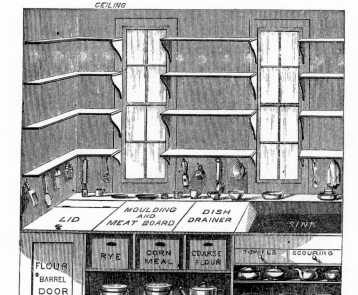

Fig. 13 is an enlarged plan of the sink and cooking-form. Two windows make a better circulation of air in warm weather, by having one open at top and the other at the bottom, while the light is better adjusted for working, in case of weak eyes.

The flour-barrel just fills the closet, which has a door for admission, and a lid to raise when used. Beside it, is the form for cooking, with a moulding-board laid on it; one side used for preparing vegetables and meat, and the other for moulding bread. The sink has two pumps, for well and for rain-water—one having a forcing power to throw water into the reservoir in the garret, which supplies the water-closet and bath-room. On the other side of the sink is the dish-drainer, with a ledge on the edge next the sink, to hold the dishes, and grooves cut to let the water drain into the sink. It has hinges, so that it can either rest on the cook-form or be turned over and cover the sink. Under the sink are shelf-boxes placed on two shelves run into grooves, with other grooves above and below, so that one may move the shelves and increase or diminish the spaces between. The shelf-boxes can be used for scouring-materials, dish-towels, and dish-cloths; also to hold bowls for bits of butter, fats, etc. Under these two shelves is room for two pails, and a jar for soap-grease.

Under the cook-form are shelves and shelf-boxes for unbolted wheat, corn-meal, rye, etc. Beneath these, for white and brown sugar, are wooden can-pails, which are the best articles in which to keep these constant necessities. Beside them is the tin molasses-can with a tight, movable cover, and a cork in the spout. This is much better than a jug for molasses, and also for vinegar and oil, being easier to clean and to handle. Other articles and implements for cooking can be arranged on or under the shelves at the side and front.

A small cooking-tray, holding pepper, salt, dredging-box, knife and spoon, should stand close at hand by the stove, (Fig. 14.)

Fig. 14.

The articles used for setting tables are to be placed on the shelves at the front and side of the sink. Two tumbler-trays, made of pasteboard, covered with varnished fancy papers and divided by wires, (as shown in Fig. 15,) save many steps in setting and clearing table. Similar trays, (Fig. 16,) for

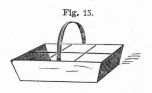

Fig. 15.

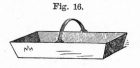

Fig. 16.

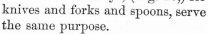

knives and forks and spoons, serve the same purpose.

The sink should be three feet long and three inches deep, its width matching the cook-form.

Fig. 17 is the second or attic story. The main objection to attic rooms is their warmth in summer, owing to the heated roof. This is prevented by so enlarging the closets each side that their walls meet the ceiling under the garret floor, thus excluding all the roof. In the bed-chambers, corner dressing-tables, as Fig. 18, instead of projecting bureaus, save much space for use, and give a handsome form and finish to the room. In the bath-room must be the opening to the garret, and a step-ladder to reach it. A reservoir in the garret, supplied by a forcing-pump in the cellar or at the sink, must be well supported by timbers, and the plumbing must be well done, or much annoyance will ensue.

Fig. 18.

The large chambers are to be lighted by large windows or glazed sliding-doors, opening upon the balcony. A roof can be put over the balcony and its sides inclosed by win-

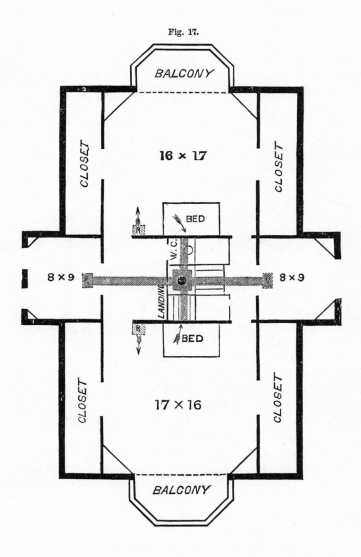

Fig. 17.

dows, and the chamber extend into it, and be thus much enlarged.

The water-closets must have the latest improvements for safe discharge, and there will be no trouble. They cost no more than an out-door building, and save from the most disagreeable house-labor.

A great improvement, called *earth-closets*, will probably take the place of water-closets to some extent; though at present the water is the more convenient. A description of the earth-closet will be given in another chapter relating to tenement-houses for the poor in large cities.

The method of ventilating all the chambers, and also the cellar, will be described in another chapter.

Fig. 19 represents a shoe-bag, that can be fastened to the side of a closet or closet-door.

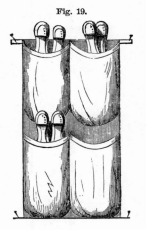

Fig. 19.

Fig. 20 represents a piece-bag, and is a very great labor and space-saving invention. It is made of calico, and fastened to the side of a closet or a door, to hold all the bundles that are usually stowed in trunks and drawers. India-rubber or elastic tape drawn into hems to hold the contents of the bag is better than tape-strings. Each bag should be labeled with the name of its contents, written with indelible ink on white tape sewed on to the bag. Such systematic arrangement saves much time and annoyance. Drawers or trunks to hold these articles can not be kept so easily in good order, and moreover, occupy spaces saved by this contrivance.

Fig. 21 is the basement. It has the floor and sides plastered, and is lighted with glazed doors. A form is raised close by the cellar stairs, for baskets, pails, and tubs.

Here, also, the refrigerator can be placed, or, what is better, an ice-closet can be made, as designated in the illustration. The floor of the basement must be an inclined plane toward a drain, and be plastered with water-lime. The wash-tubs have plugs in the bottom to let off water, and cocks and pipes over them bringing cold water from the reservoir in the garret and hot water from the laundry stove. This saves much heavy labor of emptying tubs and carrying water.

The laundry closet has a stove for heating irons, and also a kettle on top for heating water. Slides or clothes-

Fig. 20.

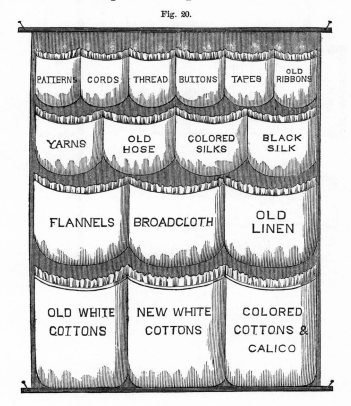

Fig. 21.

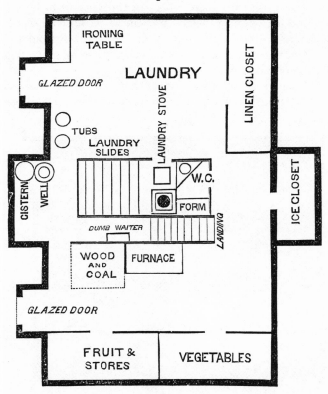

frames are made to draw out to receive wet clothes, and then run into the closet to dry. This saves health as well as time and money, and the clothes are as white as when dried outdoors.

The wood-work of the house, for doors, windows, etc., should be oiled chestnut, butternut, whitewood, and pine. This is cheaper, handsomer, and more easy to keep clean than painted wood.

In Fig. 1 are planned two conservatories, and few understand their value in the training of the young. They provide soil, in which children, through the winter months, can be starting seeds and plants for their gardens and raising valuable, tender plants. Every child should cultivate flowers and fruits to sell and to give away, and thus be taught to learn the value of money and to practice both economy and benevolence.

According to the calculation of a house-carpenter, in a place where the *average* price of lumber is $4 a hundred, and carpenter work $3 a day, such a house can be built for $1600. For those practicing the closest economy, two small families could occupy it, by dividing the kitchen, and yet have room enough. Or one large room and the chamber over it can be left till increase of family and means require enlargement.

A strong horse and carryall, with a cow, garden, vineyard, and orchard, on a few acres, would secure all the substantial comforts found in great establishments, without the trouble of ill-qualified servants.

And if the parents and children were united in the daily labors of the house, garden, and fruit culture, such thrift, health, and happiness would be secured as is but rarely found among the rich.

Let us suppose a colony of cultivated and Christian people, having abundant wealth, who now are living as the wealthy usually do, emigrating to some of the beautiful Southern uplands, where are rocks, hills, valleys, and

mountains as picturesque as those of New-England, where
the thermometer but rarely reaches 90° in summer, and
in winter as rarely sinks below freezing-point, so that out-
door labor goes on all the year, where the fertile soil is
easily worked, where rich tropical fruits and flowers
abound, where cotton and silk can be raised by children
around their home, where the produce of vineyards and
orchards finds steady markets by railroads ready made;
suppose such a colony, with a central church and school-
room, library, hall for sports, and a common laundry, (taking the most trying part of domestic labor from each
house,)—suppose each family to train the children to
labor with the hands as a healthful and honorable duty;
suppose all this, which is perfectly practicable, would not
the enjoyment of this life be increased, and also abundant
treasures be laid up in heaven, by using the wealth thus
economized in diffusing similar enjoyments and culture
among the poor, ignorant, and neglected ones in desolated
sections where many now are perishing for want of such
Christian example and influences?

III.

A HEALTHFUL HOME.

WHEN " the wise woman buildeth her house," the first consideration will be the health of the inmates. The first and most indispensable requisite for health is pure air, both by day and night.

If the parents of a family should daily withhold from their children a large portion of food needful to growth and health, and every night should administer to each a small dose of poison, it would be called murder of the most hideous character. But it is probable that more than one half of this nation are doing that very thing. The murderous operation is perpetrated daily and nightly, in our parlors, our bed-rooms, our kitchens, our school-rooms; and even our churches are no asylum from the barbarity. Nor can we escape by our railroads, for even there the same dreadful work is going on.

The only palliating circumstance is the ignorance of those who commit these wholesale murders. As saith the Scripture, "The people do perish for lack of knowledge." And it is this lack of knowledge which it is woman's special business to supply, in first training her household to intelligence as the indispensable road to virtue and happiness.

The above statements will be illustrated by some account of the manner in which the body is supplied with healthful nutriment. There are two modes of nourishing the body, one is by food and the other by air. In the stomach the food is dissolved, and the nutritious portion is absorbed by the blood, and then is carried by blood-vessels to the lungs, where it receives oxygen from the air we breathe. This oxygen is as necessary to the nourishment of the body as the food for the stomach. In a full-grown man weighing one hundred and fifty-four pounds, one hundred and eleven pounds consists of oxygen, obtained chiefly from the air we breathe. Thus the lungs feed the body with oxygen, as really as the stomach supplies the other food required.

Fig. 22.

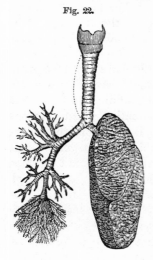

The lungs occupy the upper portion of the body from the collar-bone to the lower ribs, and between their two lobes is placed the heart.

Fig. 22 shows the position of the lungs, though not the exact shape. On the right hand is the exterior of one of the lobes, and on the left hand are seen the branching tubes of the interior, through which the air we breathe passes to the exceedingly minute air-cells of which the lungs chiefly consist. Fig. 23 shows the outside of a cluster of these air-cells, and

Fig. 23.

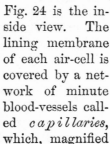

Fig. 24 is the inside view. The lining membrane of each air-cell is covered by a network of minute blood-vessels called *capillaries*, which, magnified

Fig. 24.

several hundred times, appear in the microscope as at Fig. 25. Every air-cell has a blood-vessel that brings blood from the heart,

Fig. 25.

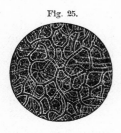

which meanders through its capillaries till it reaches another blood-vessel that carries it back to the heart, as seen in Fig. 26. In this passage of the blood through these capillaries, the air in the air-cell imparts its oxygen to the blood, and receives in exchange carbonic acid and watery vapor. These latter are expired at every breath into the atmosphere.

Fig. 26.

Artery.

Vein.

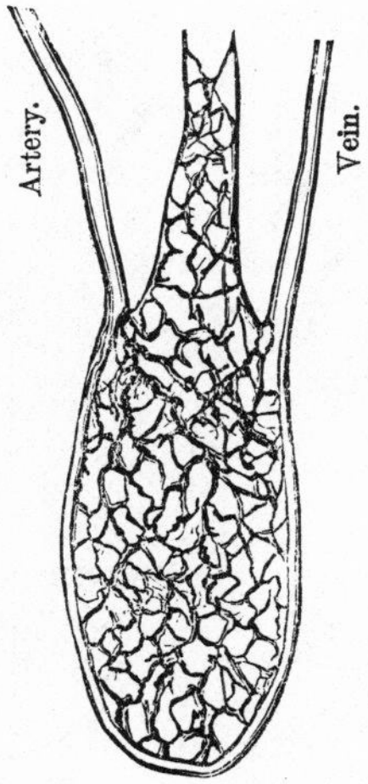

By calculating the number of air cells in a small portion of the lungs, under a miscroscope, it is ascertained that there are no less than eighteen million of these wonderful little purifiers and feeders of the body. By their ceaseless ministries, every grown person receives, each day, thirty-three hogsheads of air into the lungs to nourish and vitalize every part of the body, and also to carry off its impurities.

But the heart has a most important agency in this operation. Fig. 27 is a diagram of the heart, which is placed between the two lobes of the lungs. The right side of the heart receives the dark and impure blood, which is loaded with carbonic acid. It is brought from every point of the body by branching veins that unite in the upper and the lower *vena cava*, which discharge into the right side of the heart. This impure blood passes to the capillaries of the air-cells in the lungs, where it gives off carbonic acid, and, taking oxygen from the air, then returns to the left side of the heart, from whence it is sent out through the *aorta* and its myriad branching arteries to every part of the body.

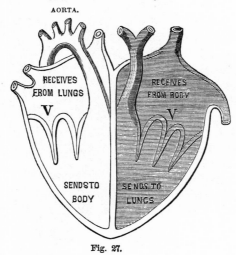

AORTA.

RECEIVES FROM LUNGS

V

RECEIVES FROM BODY

V

SENDS TO BODY

SENDS TO LUNGS

Fig. 27.

When the upper portion of the heart contracts, it forces both the pure blood from the lungs, and the impure blood from the body, through the valves marked V, V, into the lower part. When the lower portion contracts, it closes the valves and forces the impure blood into the lungs on one side, and also on the other side forces the purified blood through the aorta and arteries to all parts of the body.

As before stated, the lungs consist chiefly of air-cells, the walls of which are lined with minute blood-vessels; and we know that in every man these air-cells number *eighteen millions.*

Now every beat of the heart sends two ounces of blood into the minute, hair-like blood-vessels, called capillaries, that line these air-cells, where the air in the air-cells gives its oxygen to the blood, and in its place receives carbonic acid. This gas is then expired by the lungs into the surrounding atmosphere.

Thus, by this powerful little organ, the heart, no less than twenty-eight pounds of blood, in a common-sized man, is sent three times every hour through the lungs, giving out carbonic acid and watery vapor, and receiving the life-inspiring oxygen.

Whether all this blood shall convey the nourishing and invigorating oxygen to every part of the body, or return unrelieved of carbonic acid, depends entirely on the pureness of the atmosphere that is breathed.

Every time we think or feel, this mental action dissolves some particles of the brain and nerves, which pass into the blood to be thrown out of the body through the lungs and skin. In like manner, whenever we move any muscle, some of its particles decay and pass away. It is in the capillaries, which are all over the body, that this change takes place. The blood-vessels that convey the pure blood from the heart, divide into myriads of little branches that terminate in capillary vessels like those lining the air-cells of the lungs. The blood meanders through these minute capillaries, depositing the oxygen taken from the lungs and the food of the stomach, and receiving in return the decayed matter, which is chiefly carbonic acid.

This carbonic acid is formed by the union of oxygen with *carbon* or *charcoal*, which forms a large portion of the body. Watery vapor is also formed in the capillaries by the union of oxygen with the hydrogen contained in the food and drink that nourish the body.

During this process in the capillaries, the bright red blood of the arteries changes to the purple blood of the veins, which is carried back to the heart, to be sent to the lungs as before described. A portion of the oxygen received in the lungs unites with the dissolved food sent from the stomach into the blood, and no food can nourish the body till it has received a proper supply of oxygen in the lungs. At every breath a half-pint of blood receives its needed oxygen in the lungs, and at the same time gives out an equal amount of carbonic acid and water.

Now, this carbonic acid, if received into the lungs, undiluted by sufficient air, is a fatal poison, causing

certain death. When it is mixed with only a small portion of air, it is a slow poison, which imperceptibly undermines the constitution.

We now can understand how it is that all who live in
houses where the breathing of inmates has deprived the
air of oxygen, and loaded it with carbonic acid, may truly
be said to be poisoned and starved; poisoned with carbonic
acid, and starved for want of oxygen.

Whenever oxygen unites with carbon to form carbonic
acid, or with hydrogen to form water, heat is generated
Thus it is that a kind of combustion is constantly going
on in the capillaries all over the body. It is this burning
of the decaying portions of the body that causes animal
heat. It is a process similar to that which takes place
when lamps and candles are burning. The oil and tallow,
which are chiefly carbon and hydrogen, unite with the
oxygen of the air and form carbonic acid and watery
vapor, producing heat during the process. So in the capillaries all over the body, the carbon and hydrogen supplied to the blood by the stomach, unite with the oxygen
gained in the lungs, and cause the heat which is diffused
all over the body.

The skin also performs an office, similar to that of the
lungs. In the skin of every adult there are no less than
seven million minute perspirating tubes, each one fourth
of an inch long. If all these were united in one length,
they would extend twenty-eight miles. These minute
tubes are lined with capillary blood-vessels, which are
constantly sending out not only carbonic acid, but other
gases and particles of decayed matter. The skin and
lungs together, in one day and night, throw out three
quarters of a pound of charcoal as carbonic acid, beside
other gases and water.

While the bodies of men and animals are filling the
air with the poisonous carbonic acid, and using up the
life-giving oxygen, the trees and plants are performing an

exactly contrary process; for they are absorbing carbonic acid and giving out oxygen. Thus, by a wonderful arrangement of the beneficent Creator, a constant equilibrium is preserved. What animals use is provided by vegetables, and what vegetables require is furnished by animals; and all goes on, day and night, without care or thought of man.

The human race in its infancy was placed in a mild and genial clime, where each separate family dwelt in tents, and breathed, both day and night, the pure air of heaven. And when they became scattered abroad to colder climes, the open fire-place secured a full supply of pure air. But civilization has increased economies and conveniences far ahead of the knowledge needed by the common people for their healthful use. Tight sleeping-rooms, and close, air-tight stoves, are now starving and poisoning more than one half of this nation. It seems impossible to make people know their danger. And the remedy for this is the light of knowledge and intelligence which it is woman's special mission to bestow, as she controls and regulates the ministries of a home.

The poisoning process is thus exhibited in Mrs. Stowe's "House and Home Papers," and can not be recalled too often:

"No other gift of God, so precious, so inspiring, is treated with such utter irreverence and contempt in the calculations of us mortals as this same air of heaven. A sermon on oxygen, if we had a preacher who understood the subject, might do more to repress sin than the most orthodox discourse to show when and how and why sin came. A minister gets up in a crowded lecture-room, where the mephitic air almost makes the candles burn blue, and bewails the deadness of the church—the church the while, drugged by the poisoned air, growing sleepier and sleepier, though they feel dreadfully wicked for being so.

"Little Jim, who, fresh from his afternoon's ramble in

the fields, last evening said his prayers dutifully, and lay down to sleep in a most Christian frame, this morning sits up in bed with his hair bristling with crossness, strikes at his nurse, and declares he won't say his prayers—that he don't want to be good. The simple difference is, that the child, having slept in a close box of a room, his brain all night fed by poison, is in a mild state of moral insanity. Delicate women remark that it takes them till eleven or twelve o'clock to get up their strength in the morning. Query, Do they sleep with closed windows and doors, and with heavy bed-curtains?

" The houses built by our ancestors were better ventilated in certain respects than modern ones, with all their improvements. The great central chimney, with its open fire-places in the different rooms, created a constant current which carried off foul and vitiated air. In these days, how common is it to provide rooms with only a flue for a stove! This flue is kept shut in summer, and in winter opened only to admit a close stove, which burns away the vital portion of the air quite as fast as the occupants breathe it away. The sealing up of fire-places and introduction of air-tight stoves may, doubtless, be a saving of fuel; it saves, too, more than that; in thousands and thousands of cases it has saved people from all further human wants, and put an end forever to any needs short of the six feet of narrow earth which are man's only inalienable property. In other words, since the invention of air-tight stoves, thousands have died of slow poison.

" It is a terrible thing to reflect upon, that our northern winters last from November to May, six long months, in which many families confine themselves to one room, of which every window-crack has been carefully calked to make it air-tight, where an air-tight stove keeps the atmosphere at a temperature between eighty and ninety; and the inmates, sitting there with all their winter clothes on, become enervated both by the heat and by the poisoned

air, for which there is no escape but the occasional opening of a door.

" It is no wonder that the first result of all this is such
a delicacy of skin and lungs that about half the inmates
are obliged to give up going into the open air during the
six cold months, because they invariably catch cold if they
do so. It is no wonder that the cold caught about the first
of December has by the first of March become a fixed consumption, and that the opening of the spring, which ought
to bring life and health, in so many cases brings death.

" We hear of the lean condition in which the poor bears
emerge from their six months' wintering, during which
they subsist on the fat which they have acquired the previous summer. Even so, in our long winters, multitudes
of delicate people subsist on the daily waning strength
which they acquired in the season when windows and
doors were open, and fresh air was a constant luxury. No
wonder we hear of spring fever and spring biliousness, and
have thousands of nostrums for clearing the blood in the
spring. All these things are the pantings and palpita
tions of a system run down under slow poison, unable to
get a step further.

" Better, far better, the old houses of the olden time,
with their great roaring fires, and their bed-rooms where
the snow came in and the wintry winds whistled. Then,
to be sure, you froze your back while you burned your
face, your water froze nightly in your pitcher, your breath
congealed in ice-wreaths on the blankets, and you could
write your name on the pretty snow-wreath that had sifted
in through the window-cracks. But you woke full of life
and vigor, you looked out into the whirling snow-storms
without a shiver, and thought nothing of plunging through
drifts as high as your head on your daily way to school.
You jingled in sleighs, you snow-balled, you lived in snow
like a snow-bird, and your blood coursed and tingled, in
full tide of good, merry, real life, through your veins—

none of the slow-creeping, black blood which clogs the brain and lies like a weight on the vital wheels!"

To illustrate the effects of this poison, the horrors of "the Black Hole of Calcutta" are often referred to, where one hundred and forty-six men were crowded into a room only eighteen feet square with but two small windows, and in a hot climate. After a night of such horrible torments as chill the blood to read, the morning showed a pile of one hundred and twenty-three dead men and twenty-three half dead that were finally recovered only to a life of weakness and suffering.

In another case, a captain of the steamer Londonderry, in 1848, from sheer ignorance of the consequences, in a storm, shut up his passengers in a tight room without windows. The agonies, groans, curses, and shrieks that followed were horrible. The struggling mass finally burst the door, and the captain found seventy-two of the two hundred already dead; while others, with blood starting from their eyes and ears, and their bodies in convulsions, were restored, many only to a life of sickness and debility.

It is ascertained by experiments that breathing bad air tends so to reduce all the processes of the body, that less oxygen is demanded and less carbonic acid sent out. This, of course, lessens the vitality and weakens the constitution; and it accounts for the fact that a person of full health, accustomed to pure air, suffers from bad air far more than those who are accustomed to it. The body of strong and healthy persons demands more oxygen, and throws off more carbonic acid, and is distressed when the supply fails. But the one reduced by bad air feels little inconvenience, because all the functions of life are so slow that less oxygen is needed, and less carbonic acid thrown out. And the sensibilities being deadened, the evil is not felt. This provision of nature prolongs many lives, though it turns vigorous constitutions into feeble ones. Were it not for this change in the constitution, thousands in badly ventilated rooms and houses would come to a speedy death. One of the results of unventilated rooms is *scrofula.* A distinguished French physician, M. Baudeloque, states that: "The repeated respiration of the same atmosphere is *the* cause of scrofula. If there be entirely pure air, there may be bad food, bad clothing, and want of personal cleanliness, but scrofulous disease can not exist. This disease *never* attacks persons who pass their lives in the open air, and *always* manifests itself when they abide in air which is unrenewed. *Invariably* it will be found that a tru.y scrofulous disease is caused by vitiated air; and it is not necessary that there should be a prolonged stay in such an atmosphere. Often, several hours each day is sufficient. Thus persons may live in the most healthy country, pass most of the day in the open air, and yet become scrofulous by sleeping in a close room where the air is not renewed. This is the case with many shepherds who pass their nights in small huts with no opening but a door closed tight at night."

The same writer illustrates this by the history of a French village where the inhabitants all slept in close, unventilated houses. Nearly all were seized with scrofula, and many families became wholly extinct, their last members dying "rotten with scrofula." A fire destroyed a large part of this village. Houses were then built to secure pure air, and scrofula disappeared from the part thus rebuilt.

We are informed by medical writers that defective ventilation is one great cause of diseased joints, as well as of diseases of the eyes, ears, and skin.

Foul air is the leading cause of tubercular and scrofulous consumption, so very common in our country. Dr. Guy, in his examination before public health commissioners in Great Britain, says: "Deficient ventilation I believe to be more fatal than *all other causes* put together." He

states that consumption is twice as common among trades-
men as among the gentry, owing to the bad ventilation of
their stores and dwellings.

Dr. Griscom, in his work on Uses and Abuses of Air,
says:

" Food carried from the stomach to the blood can not become *nutritive* till it is properly oxygenated in the lungs;
so that a small quantity of food, even if less wholesome,
may be made nutritive by pure air as it passes through
the lungs. But the best of food can not be changed into
nutritive blood till it is vitalized by pure air in the lungs."

And again:

" To those who have the care and instruction of the rising generation—the future fathers and mothers of men—
this subject of ventilation commends itself with an interest surpassing every other. Nothing can more convincingly establish the belief in the existence of something vital-
ly wrong in the habits and circumstances of civilized life
than the appalling fact that *one fourth* of all who are born
die before reaching the fifth year, and *one half* the deaths
of mankind occur under the twentieth year. Let those
who have these things in charge answer to their own con-
sciences how they discharge their duty in supplying to the
young a *pure atmosphere*, which is the *first* requisite for
healthy bodies and *sound minds*."

On the subject of infant mortality the experience of savages should teach the more civilized. Professor Brewer,
who traveled extensively among the Indians of our western
territories, states: " I have rarely seen a sick boy among
the Indians." Catlin, the painter, who resided and traveled
so much among these people, states that infant mortality is
very small among them, the reason, of course, being abundant exercise and pure air.

Dr. Dio Lewis, whose labors in the cause of health are
well known, in his very useful work, *Weak Lungs, and
How to Make them Strong*, says:

"As a medical man I have visited thousands of sick-rooms, and have not found in *one in a hundred* of them a pure atmosphere. I have often returned from church doubting whether I had not committed a sin in exposing myself so long to its poisonous air. There are in our great cities churches costing $50,000, in the construction of which not fifty cents were expended in providing means for ventilation. Ten thousand dollars for ornament, but not ten cents for pure air!

"Unventilated parlors, with gas-burners, (each consuming as much oxygen as several men,) made as tight as possible, and a party of ladies and gentlemen spending half the night in them! In 1861, I visited a legislative hall, the legislature being in session. I remained half an hour in the most impure air I ever breathed. Our school-houses are, some of them, so vile in this respect, that I would prefer to have my son remain in utter ignorance of books rather than to breathe, six hours every day, such a poisonous atmosphere. Theatres and concert-rooms are so foul that only reckless people continue to visit them. Twelve hours in a railway-car exhausts one, not by the journeying, but because of the devitalized air. While crossing the ocean in a Cunard steamer, I was amazed that men who knew enough to construct such ships did not know enough to furnish air to the passengers. The distress of sea-sickness is greatly intensified by the sickening air of the ship. Were carbonic acid *only black*, what a contrast there would be between our hotels in their elaborate ornament!

"Some time since I visited an establishment where one hundred and fifty girls, in a single room, were engaged in needle-work. Pale-faced, and with low vitality and feeble circulation, they were unconscious that they were breathing air that at once produced in me dizziness and a sense of suffocation. If I had remained a week with them, I should, by reduced vitality, have become unconscious of the vileness of the air!"

There is a prevailing prejudice against *night air* as unhealthful to be admitted into sleeping-rooms, which is owing wholly to sheer ignorance. In the night every body necessarily breathes night air and no other. When admitted from without into a sleeping-room it is colder, and therefore heavier, than the air within, so it sinks to the bottom of the room and forces out an equal quantity of the impure air, warmed and vitiated by passing through the lungs of inmates. Thus the question is, Shall we shut up a chamber and breathe night air vitiated with carbonic acid or night air that is pure? The only real difficulty about night air is, that usually it is damper, and therefore colder and more likely to chill. This is easily prevented by sufficient bed-clothing.

One other very prevalent mistake is found even in books written by learned men. It is often thought that carbonic acid, being heavier than common air, sinks to the floor of sleeping-rooms, so that the low trundle-beds for children should not be used. This is all a mistake; for, as a fact, in close sleeping-rooms the purest air is below and the most impure above. It is true that carbonic acid is heavier than common air, when pure; but this it rarely is except in chemical experiments. It is the property of all gases, as well as of the two (oxygen and nitrogen) composing the atmosphere, that when brought together they always are entirely mixed, each being equally diffused exactly as it would be if alone. Thus the carbonic acid from the skin and lungs, being warmed in the body, rises as does the common air, with which it mixes, toward the top of a room; so that usually there is more carbonic acid at the top than at the bottom of a room.* Both common air and carbonic acid expand and become lighter in the same proportions; that is, for every

---

* Prof. Brewer, of the Yale Scientific School, says: "As a fact, often demonstrated by analysis, there is generally more carbonic acid near the ceiling than near the floor."

degree of added heat they expand at the rate of $\frac{1}{480}$ of their bulk.

Here, let it be remembered, that in ill-ventilated rooms the carbonic acid is not the only cause of disease. Experiments seem to prove that other matter thrown out of the body, through the lungs and skin, is as truly excrement and in a state of decay as that ejected from the bowels, and as poisonous to the animal system. Carbonic acid has no odor; but we are warned by the disagreeable effluvia of close sleeping-rooms of the other poison thus thrown into the air from the skin and lungs. There is one provision of nature that is little understood, which saves the lives of thousands living in unventilated houses; and that is, the passage of pure air inward and impure air outward through the pores of bricks, wood, stone, and mortar. Were such dwellings changed to tin, which is not thus porous, in less than a week thousands and tens of thousands would be in danger of perishing by suffocation.

These statements give some idea of the evils to be remedied. But the most difficult point is *how* to secure the remedy. For often the attempt to secure pure air by one class of persons brings chills, colds, and disease on another class, from mere ignorance or mismanagement.

To illustrate this, it must be borne in mind that those who live in warm, close, and unventilated rooms are much more liable to take cold from exposure to draughts and cold air than those of vigorous vitality accustomed to breathe pure air.

Thus the strong and healthy husband, feeling the want of pure air in the night, and knowing its importance, keeps windows open and makes such draughts that the wife, who lives all day in a close room and thus is low in vitality, can not bear the change, has colds, and sometimes perishes a victim to wrong modes of ventilation.

So, even in health-establishments, the patients will pass most of their days and nights in badly-ventilated rooms.

But at times the physician, or some earnest patient, insists on a mode of ventilation that brings more evil than good to the delicate inmates.

The grand art of ventilating houses is by some method that will empty rooms of the vitiated air and bring in a supply of pure air *by small and imperceptible currents.*

But this important duty of a Christian woman is one that demands more science, care, and attention than almost any other; and yet, to prepare her for this duty has never been any part of female education. Young women are taught to draw mathematical diagrams and to solve astronomical problems; but few, if any, of them are taught to solve the problem of a house constructed to secure pure and moist air by day and night for all its inmates.

The heating and management of the air we breathe is one of the most complicated problems of domestic economy, as will be farther illustrated in the succeeding chapter; and yet it is one of which most American women are profoundly ignorant.

IV.

WE have seen in the preceding pages the process through which the air is rendered unhealthful by close rooms and want of ventilation. Every person inspires air about twenty times each minute, using half a pint each time. At this rate, every pair of lungs vititates one hogshead of air every hour. The membrane that lines the multitudinous air-cells of the lungs in which the capillaries are, should it be united in one sheet, would cover the floor of a room twelve feet square. Every breath brings a surface of air in contact with this extent of capillaries, by which the air inspired gives up most of its oxygen and receives carbonic acid in its stead. These facts furnish a guide for the proper ventilation of rooms. Just in proportion to the number of persons in a room or a house, should be the amount of air brought in and carried out by arrangements for ventilation. But how rarely is this rule regarded in building houses or in the care of families by housekeepers!

The evils resulting from the substitution of stoves instead of the open fireplace, have led scientific and benevolent men to contrive various modes of supplying pure air to both public and private houses. But as yet little has been accomplished, except for a few of the more intelligent and wealthy. The great majority of the American people, owing to sheer ignorance, are, for want of pure air, being poisoned and starved; the result being weakened constitutions, frequent disease, and shortened life.

Whenever a family-room is heated by an open fire, it is duly ventilated, as the impure air is constantly passing off through the chimney, while, to supply the vacated space, the pure air presses in through the cracks of doors, windows, and floors. No such supply is gained for rooms warmed by stoves. And yet, from mistaken motives of economy, as well as from ignorance of the resulting evils, multitudes of householders are thus destroying health and shortening life, especially in regard to women and children who spend most of their time within-doors.

The most successful modes of making "a healthful home" by a full supply of pure air to every inmate, will now be described and illustrated.

It is the common property of both air and water to expand, become lighter and rise, just in proportion as they are heated; and therefore it is the invariable law that cool air sinks, thus replacing the warmer air below. Thus, whenever cool air enters a warm room, it sinks downward and takes the place of an equal amount of the warmer air, which is constantly tending upward and outward. This principle of all fluids is illustrated by the following experiment:

Take a glass jar about a foot high and three inches in diameter, and with a wire to aid in placing it aright, sink a small bit of lighted candle so as to stand in the centre at the bottom. (Fig. 28.) The candle will heat the air of the jar, which will rise a little on one side, while the colder air without will begin falling on the other side. These two currents will so conflict as finally to cease, and then the candle, having no supply of oxygen from fresh air, will begin to go out. Insert a bit of stiff paper so as to divide the mouth of the jar, and instantly the cold and warm air are not in conflict as before, because a current is formed each side of the paper; the cold air descending on one side and the warm air ascending the other side, as indicated by the arrows. As long as the paper remains, the candle will burn, and as soon as it is removed, it will begin to go out, and can be restored by again inserting the paper.

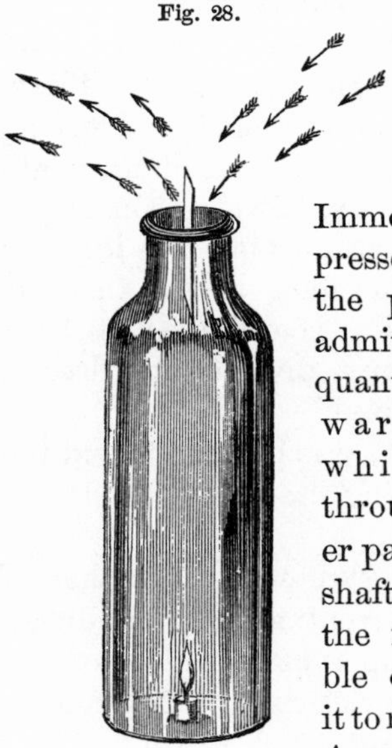

This illustrates the mode by which coal-mines are ventilated when filled with carbonic acid. A shaft divided into two passages, (Fig. 29,) is let down into the mine, where the air is warmer than the outside air. Immediately the colder air outside presses down into the mine, through the passage which is highest, being admitted by the escape of an equal quantity of the warmer air, which rises through the lower passage of the shaft, this being the first available opening for it to rise through. A current is thus created, which continues as long as the inside air is warmer than that without the mine, and no longer. Sometimes a fire is kindled in the mine, in order to continue or increase the warmth, and consequent upward current of its air.

Fig. 28.

Fig. 29.

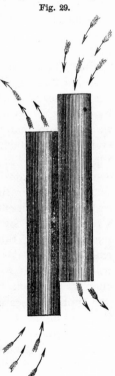

This illustrates one of the cases where a " wise woman that buildeth her house" is greatly needed   For, owing to the ignorance of architects, house-builders, and men in general, they have been building schoolhouses, dwelling-houses, churches, and colleges, with the most absurd and senseless contrivances for ventilation, and all from not applying this simple principle of science. On this point, Prof. Brewer, of the Scientific School of Yale College, writes thus :

" I have been in public buildings, (I have one in mind now, filled with dormitories,) which cost half a million, where they attempted to ventilate every room by a flue, long and narrow, built into partition walls, and extending up into the capacious garret of the fifth story. Every room in the building had one such flue, with an opening into it at the floor and at the ceiling. It is needless to say that the whole concern was entirely useless. Had these flues been of proper proportions, and properly divided, the desired ventilation would have been secured."

And this piece of ignorant folly was perpetrated in the midst of learned professors, teaching the laws of fluids and the laws of health.

A learned physician also thus wrote to the author of this chapter : " The subject of the ventilation of our dwelling-houses is one of the most important questions of our times. How many thousands are victims to a slow suicide and murder, the chief instrument of which is want of ventilation! How few are aware of the fact that every person, every day, vitiates thirty-three hogsheads of the air, and that each inspiration takes one fifth of the oxygen, and returns as much carbonic acid, from every pair of lungs in a room! How few understand that after air has received ten per cent of this fatal gas, if drawn into the lungs, it can no longer take carbonic acid from the capillaries! No wonder there is so much impaired nervous and muscular energy, so much scrofula, tubercles, catarrhs, dyspepsia, and typhoid diseases. I hope you can do much to remedy the poisonous air of thousands and thousands of stove-heated rooms."

In a cold climate and wintry weather, the grand impediment to ventilating rooms by opening doors or win dows is the dangerous currents thus produced, which are so injurious to the delicate ones that for their sake it can not be done. Then, also, as a matter of economy, the poor can not afford to practice a method which carries off the heat generated by their stinted store of fuel. Even in a warm season and climate, there are frequent periods when the air without is damp and chilly, and yet at nearly the same temperature as that in the house. At such times, the opening of windows often has little effect in emptying a room of vitiated air. The ventilating-flues, such as are used in mines, have, in such cases, but little influence; for it is only when outside air is colder that a current can be produced within by this method.

The most successful mode of ventilating a house is by creating a current of warm air in a flue, into which an opening is made at both the top and the bottom of a room, while a similar opening for outside air is made at the opposite side of the room. This is the mode employed in chemical laboratories for removing smells and injurious gases.

The laboratory-closet is closed with glazed doors, and has an opening to receive pure air through a conductor from without. The stove or furnace within has a pipe which joins a larger cast-iron chimney-pipe, which is warmed by the smoke it receives from this and other fires. This cast-iron pipe is surrounded by a brick flue, through which air passes from below to be warmed by the pipe, and thus an upward current of warm air is created. Openings are then made at the top and bottom of the laboratory-closet into the warm-air flue, and the gases and smells are pressed by the colder air into this flue, and are carried off in the current of warm air.

The same method is employed in the dwelling-house shown in a preceding chapter. A cast-iron pipe is made in sections, which are to be united, and the whole fastened at top and bottom in the centre of the warm-air flue by ears extending to the bricks, and fastened when the flue is in process of building. Projecting openings to receive the pipes of the furnace, the laundry stove, and two stoves in each story, should be provided, which must be closed when not in use. A large opening is to be made into the warm-air flue, and through this the kitchen stove-pipe is to pass, and be joined to the cast-iron chimney-pipe. Thus the smoke of the kitchen stove will warm the iron chimney-pipe, and this will warm the air of the flue, causing a current upward, and this current will draw the heat and smells of cooking out of the kitchen into the opening of the warm-air flue. Every room surrounding the chimney has an opening at the top and bottom into the warm-air flue for ventilation, as also have the bath-room and water-closets.

Fig. 30.

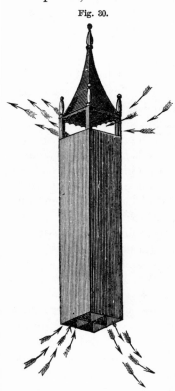

The writer has examined the methods most employed at the present time, which are all modifications of the two modes here described. One is that of Robinson, patented by a Boston company, which is a modification of the mining mode. It consists of the two ventilating tubes, such as are employed in mines, united in one shaft with a roof to keep out rain, and a valve to regulate the entrance and exit of air, as illustrated in Fig. 30. This method works well in certain circumstances, but fails so often as to prove very unreliable. Another mode is that of Ruttan, which is effected by heating air. This also has certain advantages and disadvantages. But the mode adopted for the preceding cottage plan is free from the difficulties of both the above methods, while it will surely ventilate every room in the house, both by day and night, and at all seasons, without any risk to health, and requiring no attention or care from the family.

By means of a very small amount of fuel in the kitchen stove, to be described hereafter, the whole house can be ventilated, and all the cooking done both in warm and cold weather. This stove will also warm the whole house, in the Northern States, eight or nine months in the year. Two Franklin stoves, in addition, will warm the whole house during the three or four remaining coldest months.

In a warm climate or season, by means of the non-conducting castings, the stove will ventilate the house and do all the cooking, without imparting heat or smells to any part of the house except the stove-closet.

At the close of this volume, drawings, prepared by Mr. Lewis Leeds, are given, more fully to illustrate this mode of warming and ventilation, and in so plain and simple a form that any intelligent woman who has read this work can see that the plan is properly executed, even with workmen so entirely ignorant on this important subject as are most house-builders, especially in the newer territories. In the same article, directions are given as to the best modes of ventilating houses that are already built without any arrangements for ventilation.

THE CONSTRUCTION AND CARE OF STOVES, FURNACES, AND CHIMNEYS.

IF all American housekeepers could be taught how to select and manage the most economical and convenient apparatus for cooking and for warming a house, many millions now wasted by ignorance and neglect would be saved. Every woman should be taught the scientific principles in regard to heat, and then their application to practical purposes, for her own benefit, and also to enable her to train her children and servants in this important duty of home life on which health and comfort so much depend.

The laws that regulate the generation, diffusion, and preservation of heat as yet are a sealed mystery to thousands of young women who imagine they are completing a suitable education in courses of instruction from which most that is practical in future domestic life is wholly excluded. We therefore give a brief outline of some of the leading scientific principles which every housekeeper should understand and employ, in order to perform successfully one of her most important duties.

Concerning the essential nature of heat, and its intimate relations with the other great natural forces, light, electricity, etc., we shall not attempt to treat, but shall, for practical purposes, assume it to be a separate and independent force.

Heat or caloric, then, has certain powers or principles. Let us consider them :

First, we find *Conduction*, by which heat passes from one particle to another next to it; as when one end of a poker is warmed by placing the other end in the fire. The bodies which allow this power free course are called conductors, and those which do not are named non-conductors. Metals are good conductors; feathers, wool, and furs are poor conductors; and water, air, and gases are non-conductors.

Another principle of heat is *Convection*, by which water, air, and gases are warmed. This is, literally, the process of *conveying* heat from one portion of a fluid body to another by currents resulting from changes of temperature. It is secured by bringing one portion of a liquid or gas into contact with a heated surface, whereby it becomes lighter and expanded in volume. In consequence, the cooler and heavier particles above pressing downward, the lighter ones rise upward, when the former, being heated, rise in their turn, and give place to others again descending from above. Thus a constant motion of currents and interchange of particles is produced until, as in a vessel of water, the whole body comes to an equal temperature. Air is heated in the same way. In case of a hot stove, the air that touches it is heated, becomes lighter, and rises, giving place to cooler and heavier particles, which, when heated, also ascend. It is owing to this process that the air of a room is warmest at the top and coolest at the bottom.

It is owing to this principle, also, that water and air can not be heated by fire from above. For the particles of these bodies, being non-conductors, do not impart heat to each other; and when the warmest are at the top, they can not take the place of cooler and heavier ones below.

Another principle of heat (which it shares with light) is *Radiation*, by which all things send out heat to surrounding cooler bodies. Some bodies will absorb radiated heat, others will reflect it, and others allow it to pass through them without either absorbing or reflecting Thus, black and rough substances absorb heat, (or light,) colored and smooth articles reflect it, while air allows it to pass through without either absorbing or reflecting. It is owing to this, that rough and black vessels boil water sooner than smooth and light-colored ones.

Another principle is *Reflection*, by which heat radiated to a surface is turned back from it when not absorbed or allowed to pass through; just as a ball rebounds from a wall; just as sound is thrown back from a hill, making echo; just as rays of light are reflected from a mirror.

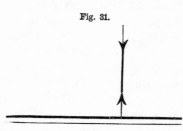

Fig. 31.

And, as with light, the rays of heat are always reflected from a surface in an angle exactly corresponding to the direction in which it strikes that surface. Thus, if heated air comes to an object perpendicularly— that is, at right angles, it will be reflected back in the same line. If it strikes obliquely, it is reflected obliquely, at an angle with the surface precisely the same as the angle with which it first struck. And, of course, if it moves toward the surface and comes upon it in a line having so small an angle with it as to be almost parallel with it, the heated air is spread wide and diffused

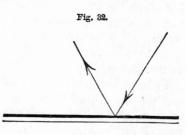

Fig. 32.

through a larger space than when the angles are greater and the width of reflection less.

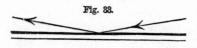

Fig. 33.

The simplest mode of warming a house and cooking food

is by radiated heat from fires; but this is the most wasteful method, as respects time, labor, and expense. The most convenient, economical, and labor-saving mode of employing heat is by convection, as applied in stoves and furnaces. But for want of proper care and scientific knowledge this method has proved very destructive to health. When warming and cooking were done by open fires, houses were well supplied with pure air, as is rarely the case in rooms heated by stoves. For such is the prevailing ignorance on this subject that, as long as stoves save labor and warm the air, the great majority of people, especially among the poor, will use them in ways that involve debilitated constitutions and frequent disease.

The most common modes of cooking, where open fires are relinquished, are by the range and the cooking-stove. The range is inferior to the stove in these respects: it is less economical, demanding much more fuel; it endangers the dress of the cook while standing near for various operations; it requires more stooping than the stove while cooking; it will not keep a fire all night, as do the best stoves; it will not burn wood and coal equally well; and lastly, if it warms the kitchen sufficiently in winter, it is too warm for summer. Some prefer it because the fumes of cooking can be carried off; but stoves properly arranged accomplish this equally well.

After extensive inquiry and many personal experiments, the author has found a cooking-stove constructed on true scientific principles, which unites convenience, comfort, and economy in a remarkable manner. Of this stove, drawings and descriptions will now be given, as the best mode of illustrating the practical applications of these principles to the art of cooking, and to show how much American women have suffered and how much they have been imposed upon for want of proper knowledge in this branch of their profession. And every woman can understand what follows with much less effort than young girls at high-schools give to the first problems of Geometry—for which they will never have any practical use, while attention to this problem of home affairs will cultivate the intellect quite as much as the abstract reasonings of Algebra and Geometry.

Fig. 34.

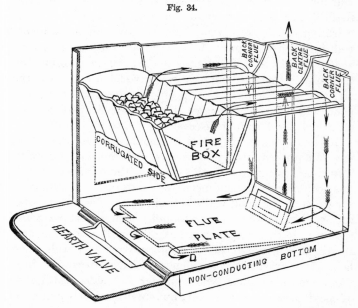

Fig. 34 represents a portion of the interior of this cooking-stove. First, notice the fire-box, which has corrugated (literally, wrinkled) sides, by which space is economized, so that as much heating surface is secured as if they were one third larger; as the heat radiates from every part of the undulating surface, which is one third greater in superficial extent than if it were plane. The shape of the fire-box also secures more heat by having oblique sides— which radiate more effectively into the oven beneath than if they were perpendicular, as illustrated below—while also it is sunk into the oven, so as to radiate from three instead of from two sides, as in most other stoves, the

front of whose fire-boxes with their grates are built so as
to be the front of the stove itself.

The oven is the space under and around the back and

Fig. 35.

Model Stove.

front sides of the fire-box.
The oven-bottom is not
introduced in the dia-
gram, but it is a horizontal plate between the fire-
box and what is represen-
ted as the "flue-plate,"

Fig. 36.

Ordinary Stove.

which separates the oven from the bottom of the stove.
The top of the oven is the horizontal corrugated plate
passing from the rear edge of the fire-box to the back flues.
These are three in number—the back centre-flue, which
is closed to the heat and smoke coming over the oven from
the fire-box by a damper—and the two back corner-flues.
Down these two corner-flues passes the current of hot air
and smoke, having first drawn across the corrugated oven-
top. The arrows show its descent through these flues,
from which it obliquely strikes and passes over the flue-
plate, then under it, and then out through the centre back-
flue, which is open at the bottom, up into the smoke-pipe.

The flue-plate is placed obliquely, to accumulate heat by
forcing and compression; for the back space where the
smoke enters from the corner-flues is largest, and decreases
toward the front, so that the hot current is compressed in a
narrow space, between the oven-bottom and the flue-plate
at the place where the bent arrows are seen. Here again
it enters a wider space, under the flue-plate, and proceeds
to another narrow one, between the flue-plate and the
bottom of the stove, and thus is compressed and retained longer than if not impeded by these various contrivances. The heat and smoke also strike the plate
obliquely, and thus, by reflection from its surface, impart
more heat than if the passage was a horizontal one.

The external radiation is regulated by the use of non-conducting plaster applied to the flue-plate and to the sides of the corner-flues, so that the heat is prevented from radiating in any direction except toward the oven. The doors, sides, and bottom of the stove are lined with tin casings, which hold a stratum of air, also a non-conductor. These are so arranged as to be removed whenever the weather becomes cold, so that the heat may then radiate into the kitchen. The outer edges of the oven are also similarly protected from loss of heat by tin casings and air-spaces, and the oven-doors opening at the front of the store are provided with the same economical savers of heat. High tin covers placed on the top prevent the heat from radiating above the stove. These are exceedingly useful, as the space under them is well heated and arranged for baking, for heating irons, and many other incidental necessities. Cake and pies can be baked on the top, while the oven is used for bread or for meats. When all the casings and covers are on, almost all the heat is confined within the stove, and whenever heat for the room is wanted, opening the front oven-doors turns it out into the kitchen.

Another contrivance is that of ventilating-holes in the front doors, through which fresh air is brought into the oven. This secures several purposes : it carries off the fumes of cooking meats, and prevents the mixing of flavors when different articles are cooked in the oven ; it drives the heat that accumulates between the fire-box and front doors down around the oven, and equalizes its heat, so that articles need not be moved while baking ; and lastly, as the air passes through the holes of the fire-box, it causes the burning of gases in the smoke, and thus increases heat. When wood or bituminous coal is used, perforated metal linings are put in the fire-box, and the result is the burning of smoke and gases that otherwise would pass into the chimney. This is a great discovery in the economy of fuel, which can be applied in many ways.

Heretofore, most cooking-stoves have had dumping-grates,

which are inconvenient from the dust produced, are uneco-
nomical in the use of fuel, and disadvantageous from too
many or too loose joints. But recently this stove has been
provided with a dumping-grate which also will sift ashes,
and can be cleaned without dust and the other objectionable features of dumping-grates. A further account of this
stove, and the mode of purchasing and using it, will be
given at the close of the book.

Those who are taught to manage the stove properly
keep the fire going all night, and equally well with wood
or coal, thus saving the expense of kindling and the trouble
of starting a new fire. When the fuel is of good quality,
all that is needed in the morning is to draw the back-
damper, shake the grate, and add more fuel.

Another remarkable feature of this stove is the extension-
top, on which is placed a water reservoir, constantly heated
by the smoke as it passes from the stove, through one or two
uniting passages, to the smoke-pipe. Under this is placed
a closet for warming and keeping hot the dishes, vegetables,
meats, etc., while preparing for dinner. It is also very
useful in drying fruit ; and when large baking is required,
a small appended pot for charcoal turns it into a fine large
oven, that bakes as nicely as a brick oven.

Another useful appendage is a common tin oven, in
which roasting can be done in front of the stove, the oven-
doors being removed for the purpose. The roast will be
done as perfectly as by an open fire.

This stove.is furnished with pipes for heating water, like
the water-back of ranges, and these can be taken or left
out at pleasure. So also the top covers, the baking-stool
and pot, and the summer-back, bottom, and side-casings
can be used or omitted as preferred.

Fig. 37 exhibits the stove completed, with all its appendages, as they might be employed in cooking for a large
number

Its capacity, convenience, and economy as a stove may

be estimated by the following fact : With proper management of dampers, one ordinary-sized coal-hod of anthracite
coal will, for twenty-four hours, keep the stove running,
keep seventeen gallons of water hot at all hours, bake pies

Fig. 37.

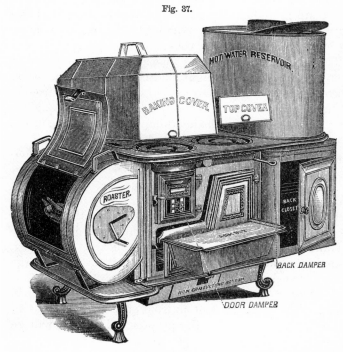

and puddings in the warm closet, heat flat-irons under the
back cover, boil tea-kettle and one pot under the front
cover, bake bread in the oven, and cook a turkey in the
tin roaster in front. The author has numerous friends,
who, after trying the best ranges, have dismissed them for
this stove, and in two or three years cleared the whole expense by the saving of fuel.

The remarkable durability of this stove is another economic feature. For in addition to its fine castings and

nice-fitting workmanship, all the parts liable to burn out are so protected by linings, and other contrivances easily renewed, that the stove itself may pass from one generation to another, as do ordinary chimneys. The writer has visited in families where this stove had been in constant use for eighteen and twenty years, and was still as good as new. In most other families the stoves are broken, burnt-out, or thrown aside for improved patterns every four, five, or six years, and sometimes, to the knowledge of the writer, still oftener.

Another excellent point is that, although it is so complicated in its various contrivances as to demand intelligent management in order to secure all its advantages, it also can be used satisfactorily even when the mistress and maid are equally careless and ignorant of its distinctive merits. To such it offers all the advantages of ordinary good stoves, and is extensively used by those who take no pains to understand and apply its peculiar advantages.

But the writer has managed the stove herself in all the details of cooking, and is confident that any housekeeper of common sense, who is instructed properly, and who also aims to have her kitchen affairs managed with strict economy, can easily train any servant who is willing to learn, so as to gain the full advantages offered. And even without any instructions at all, except the printed directions sent with the stove, an intelligent woman can, by due attention, though not without, both manage it, and teach her children and servants to do likewise. And whenever this stove has failed to give the highest satisfaction, it has been, either because the housekeeper was not apprized of its peculiarities, or because she did not give sufficient attention to the matter, or was not able or willing to superintend and direct its management.

The consequence has been that, in families where this stove has been understood and managed aright, it has saved nearly one half of the fuel that would be used in ordinary stoves, constructed with the usual disregard of scientific and economic laws. And it is because we know this particular stove to be convenient, reliable, and economically efficient beyond ordinary experience, in the important housekeeping element of kitchen labor, that we devote to it so much space and pains to describe its advantageous points.

CHIMNEYS.

One of the most serious evils in domestic life is often found in chimneys that will not properly draw the smoke of a fire or stove. Although chimneys have been building for a thousand years, the artisans of the present day seem strangely ignorant of the true method of constructing them so as always to carry smoke upward instead of downward. It is rarely the case that a large house is built in which there is not some flue or chimney which "will not draw." One of the reasons why the stove described as excelling all others is sometimes cast aside for a poorer one is, that it requires a properly constructed chimney, and multitudes of women do not know how to secure it. The writer in early life shed many a bitter tear, drawn forth by smoke from an ill-constructed kitchen-chimney, and thousands all over the land can report the same experience.

The following are some of the causes and the remedies for this evil.

The most common cause of poor chimney draughts is too large an opening for the fireplace, either too wide or too high in front, or having too large a throat for the smoke. In a lower story, the fireplace should not be larger than thirty inches wide, twenty-five inches high, and fifteen deep. In the story above, it should be eighteen inches square and fifteen inches deep.

Another cause is too short a flue, and the remedy is to lengthen it. As a general rule, the longer the flue the stronger the draught. But in calculating the length of a flue, reference must be had to side-flues, if any open into it. Where this is the case, the length of the main flue is to be considered as extending only from the bottom to the point where the upper flue joins it, and where the lower will receive air from the upper flue. If a smoky flue can not be increased in length, either by closing an upper flue or lengthening the chimney, the fireplace must be contracted so that all the air near the fire will be heated and thus pressed upward.

If a flue has more than one opening, in some cases it is impossible to secure a good draught. Sometimes it will work well and sometimes it will not. The only safe rule is to have a separate flue to each fire.

Another cause of poor draughts is too tight a room, so that the cold air from without can not enter to press the warm air up the chimney. The remedy is to admit a small current of air from without.

Another cause is two chimneys in one room, or in rooms opening together, in which the draught in one is much stronger than in the other. In this case, the stronger draught will draw away from the weaker. The remedy is, for each room to have a proper supply of outside air; or, in a single room, to stop one of the chimneys.

Another cause is the too close vicinity of a hill or buildings higher than the top of the chimney, and the remedy for this is to raise the chimney.

Another cause is the descent, into unused fireplaces, of smoke from other chimneys near. The remedy is to close the throat of the unused chimney.

Another cause is a door opening toward the fireplace, on the same side of the room, so that its draught passes along the wall and makes a current that draws out the smoke. The remedy is to change the hanging of the door so as to open another way.

Another cause is strong winds. The remedy is a turn-cap on top of the chimney.

Another cause is the roughness of the inside of a chimney, or projections which impede the passage of the smoke. Every chimney should be built of equal dimensions from bottom to top, with no projections into it, with as few bends as possible, and with the surface of the inside as smooth as possible.

Another cause of poor·draughts is openings into the chimney of chambers for stove-pipes. The remedy is to close them, or insert stove-pipes that are in use.

Another cause is the falling out of brick in some part of the chimney so that outer air is admitted. The remedy is to close the opening.

The draught of a stove may be affected by most of these causes. It also demands that the fireplace have a tight fire-board, or that the throat be carefully filled. For neglecting this, many a good stove has been thrown aside and a poor one taken in its place.

If all young women had committed to memory these causes of evil and their remedies, many a badly-built chimney might have been cured, and many smoke-drawn tears, sighs, ill-tempers, and irritating words avoided.

But there are dangers in this direction which demand special attention. Where one flue has two stoves or fireplaces, in rooms one above the other, in certain states of the atmosphere, the lower room, being the warmer, the colder air and carbonic acid in the room above will pass down into the lower room through the opening for the stove or the fireplace.

This occurred not long since in a boarding-school, when the gas in a room above flowed into a lower one, and suffocated several to death. This room had no mode of ventilation, and several persons slept in it, and were thus stifled. Professor Brewer states a similar case in the family of a relative. An anthracite stove was used in the upper room ; and on one still, close night, the gas from this stove descended through the flue and the opening into a room below, and stifled two persons to insensibility, though, by proper efforts, their lives were saved. Many such cases have occurred where rooms have been thus filled with poisonous gases, and servants and children destroyed, or their constitutions injured, simply because housekeepers are not properly instructed in this important branch of their profession.

FURNACES.

There is no improved mechanism in the economy of domestic life requiring more intelligent management than furnaces. Let us then consider some of the principles involved.

The earth is heated by radiation from the sun. The air is not warmed by the passage of the sun's heat through it, but by convection from the earth, in the same way that it is warmed by the surfaces of stoves. The lower stratum of air is warmed by the earth and by objects which have been warmed by radiated heat from the sun. The particles of air thus heated expand, become lighter, and rise, being replaced by the descent of the cooler and heavier particles from above, which, on being warmed also rise, and give place to others. Owing to this process, the air is warmest nearest the earth, and grows cooler as height increases.

The air has a strong attraction for water, and always holds a certain quantity as invisible vapor. The warmer the air, the more moisture it demands, and it will draw it from all objects within reach. The air holds water according to its temperature. Thus, at fifty-two degrees, Fahrenheit's thermometer, it holds half the moisture it can sustain; but at thirty-six degrees, it will hold only one eighty-sixth part. The earth and all plants and trees are constantly sending out moisture; and when the air has received all it can hold, without depositing it as dew, it is said to be *saturated*, and the point of temperature at which dew begins to form, by condensation, upon the surface of the earth and its vegetation, is called the *dew-point.* When air, at a given temperature, has only forty per cent of the moisture it requires for saturation, it is said to be dry. In a hot summer day, the air will hold far more moisture than in cool days. In summer, out-door air rarely holds less than half its volume of water. In 1838, at Cambridge, Massachusetts, and New-Haven, Connecticut, at seventy degrees, Fahrenheit, the air held eighty per cent of moisture.

In New-Orleans, the air often retains ninety per cent of the moisture it is capable of holding; and in cool days at the North, in foggy weather, the air is sometimes wholly saturated.

When air holds all the moisture it can, without depositing dew, its moisture is called 100. When it holds three fourths of this, it is said to be at seventy-five per cent. When it holds only one half, it is at fifty per cent. When it holds only one fourth, it is at twenty-five per cent, etc.

Sanitary observers teach that the proper amount of moisture in the air ranges from forty to seventy per cent of saturation.

Now, furnaces, which are of course used only in winter, receive outside air at a low temperature, holding little moisture; and heating it greatly increases its demand for moisture. This it sucks up, like a sponge, from the walls and furniture of a house. If it is taken into the human lungs, it draws much of its required moisture from the body, often causing dryness of lips and throat, and painfully affecting the lungs. Prof. Brewer, of the Scientific School of New-Haven, who has experimented extensively on this subject, states that, while forty per cent of moisture is needed in air to make it healthful, most stoves and furnaces do not, by any contrivances, supply one half of this, or not twenty per cent. He says most furnace-heated air is dryer than is ever breathed in the hottest deserts of Sahara.

Thus, for want of proper instruction, most American housekeepers not only poison their families with carbonic acid and starve them for want of oxygen, but also diminish health and comfort for want of a due supply of moisture in the air. And often when a remedy is sought, by evaporating water in the furnace, it is without knowing that the amount evaporated depends, not on the quantity of water in the vessel, but on the extent of evaporating surface exposed to the air. A quart of water in a wide shallow pan will give more moisture than two gallons with a small surface exposed to heat.

There is also no little wise economy in expense attained by keeping a proper supply of moisture in the air. For it is found that the body radiates its heat less in moist than in dry air, so that a person feels as warm at a lower temperature when the air has a proper supply of moisture, as in a much higher temperature of dry air. Of course, less fuel is needed to warm a house when water is evaporated in stove and furnace-heated rooms. It is said by those who have experimented, that the saving in fuel is twenty per cent when the air is duly supplied with moisture.

There is a very ingenious instrument, called the hygrodeik, which indicates the exact amount of moisture in the air. It consists of two thermometers side by side, one of which has its bulb surrounded by floss-silk wrapping, which is kept constantly wet by communication with a cup of water near it. The water around the bulb evaporates just in proportion to the heat of the air around it. The changing of water to vapor draws heat from the nearest object, and this being the bulb of the thermometer, the mercury is cooled and sinks. Then the difference between the two thermometers shows the amount of moisture in the air by a pointer on a dial-plate constructed by simple mechanism for this purpose.

There is one very important matter in regard to the use of furnaces, which is thus stated by Professor Brewer:

"I think it is a well-established fact that carbonic oxide will pass through iron. It is always formed in great abundance in any *anthracite* fire, but especially in anthracite stoves and furnaces. Moreover, furnaces *always* leak, more or less; how much they leak depending on the care and skill with which they are managed. Carbonic oxide is much more poisonous than carbonic acid. Doubtless some carbonic oxide finds its way into all furnace-heated houses, especially where anthracite is used; the amount varying with the kind of furnace and its management. As to how much escapes into a room, and its specific effect upon the health of its occupants, we have no accurate data, no analysis to show the quantity, and no observati ns to show the relation between the quantity inhaled and the health of those exposed; all is mere conjecture upon this point; but the inference is very strong that it has a very injurious effect, producing headaches, weariness, and other similar symptoms.

"Recent pamphlets lay the blame of all the bad effects of anthracite furnaces and stoves to the carbonic oxide mingled in the air. I think these pamphlets have a bad influence. *Excessive dryness* also has bad effects. So also the excessive heat in the evenings and coolness in the mornings has a share in these evils. But how much in addition is owing to carbonic oxide, we can not know, until we know something of the actual amount of this gas in rooms, and as yet we know absolutely nothing definite. In fact, it will be a difficult thing to *prove*."

There are other difficulties connected with furnaces which should be considered. It is necessary to perfect health that an equal circulation of the blood be preserved. The greatest impediment to this is keeping the head warmer than the feet. This is especially to be avoided in a nation where the brain is by constant activity drawing the blood from the extremities. And nowhere is this more important than in schools, churches, colleges, lecture and recitation-rooms, where the brain is called into active exercise. And yet, furnace-heated rooms always keep the feet in the coldest air, on cool floors, while the head is in the warmest air.

Another difficulty is the fact that all bodies tend to radiate their heat to each other, till an equal temperature exists. Thus, the human body is constantly radiating its heat to the walls, floors, and cooler bodies around. At the same time, a thermometer is affected in the same way, radiating its heat to cooler bodies around, so that it always marks a lower degree of heat than actually exists in the warm air around it. Owing to these facts, the injected air of a furnace is always warmer than is good for the lungs, and much warmer than is ever needed in rooms warmed by radiation from fires or heated surfaces. The cooler the air we inspire, the more oxygen is received, the faster the blood circulates, and the greater is the vigor imparted to brain, nerves, and muscles.

Scientific men have been contriving various modes of meeting these difficulties, and at the close of this volume some results will be given to aid a woman in selecting and managing the most healthful and economical furnace, or in providing some better method of warming a house. Some account will also be given of the danger involved in gas-stoves, and some other recent inventions for cooking and heating.

VI.

Having duly arranged for the physical necessities of a healthful and comfortable home, we next approach the important subject of *beauty* in reference to the decoration of houses. For while the æsthetic element must be subordinate to the requirements of physical existence, and, as a matter of expense, should be held of inferior consequence to means of higher moral growth; it yet holds a place of great significance among the influences which make home happy and attractive, which give it a constant and wholesome power over the young, and contributes much to the education of the entire household in refinement, intellectual development, and moral sensibility.

Here we are met by those who tell us that of course they want their houses handsome, and that, when they get money enough, they intend to have them so, but at present they are too poor, and because they are poor they dismiss the subject altogether, and live without any regard to it.

We have often seen people who said that they could not afford to make their houses beautiful, who had spent upon them, outside or in, an amount of money which did not produce either beauty or comfort, and which, if judiciously applied, might have made the house quite charming.

For example, a man, in building his house, takes a plan of an architect. This plan includes, on the outside, a number of what Andrew Fairservice called " curlywurlies" and "whigmaliries," which make the house neither prettier nor more comfortable, and which take up a good deal of money. We would venture to say that we could buy the chromo of Bierstadt's "Sunset in the Yo Semite Valley," and four others like it, for half the sum that we have sometimes seen laid out on a very ugly, narrow, awkward porch on the outside of a house. The only use of this porch was to cost money, and to cause every body who looked at it to exclaim as they went by, "What ever induced that man to put a thing like that on the outside of his house?"

Then, again, in the inside of houses, we have seen a dwelling looking very bald and bare, when a sufficient sum of money had been expended on one article to have made the whole very pretty: and it has come about in this way.

We will suppose the couple who own the house to be in the condition in which people generally are after they have built a house—having spent more than they could afford on the building itself, and yet feeling themselves under the necessity of getting some furniture.

"Now," says the housewife, "I must at least have a parlor-carpet. We must get that to begin with, and other things as we go on." She goes to a store to look at carpets. The clerks are smiling and obliging, and sweetly complacent. The storekeeper, perhaps, is a neighbor or a friend, and after exhibiting various patterns, he tells her of a Brussels carpet he is selling wonderfully cheap—actually a dollar and a quarter less a yard than the usual price or Brussels, and the reason is that it is an unfashionable pattern, and he has a good deal of it, and wishes to close it off.

She looks at it and thinks it is not at all the kind of carpet she meant to buy, but then it is Brussels, and so cheap! And as she hesitates, her friend tells her that she will find it "cheapest in the end—that one Brussels carpet will outlast three or four ingrains," etc., etc.

The result of all this is, that she buys the Brussels carpet, which, with all its reduction in price, is one third dearer than the ingrain would have been, and not half so pretty. When she comes home, she will find that she has spent, we will say eighty dollars, for a very homely carpet whose greatest merit it is an affliction to remember—namely, that it will outlast three ordinary carpets. And because she has bought this carpet she can not afford to paper the walls or put up any window-curtains, and can not even begin to think of buying any pictures.

Now let us see what eighty dollars could have done for that room. We will suppose, in the first place, she invests in thirteen rolls of wall-paper of a lovely shade of buff, which will make the room look sunshiny in the day-time, and light up brilliantly in the evening. Thirteen rolls of good satin paper, at thirty-seven cents a roll, expends four dollars and eighty-one cents. A maroon bordering, made in imitation of the choicest French style, which can not at a distance be told from it, can be bought for six cents a yard. This will bring the paper to about five dollars and a half; and our friends will give a day of their time to putting it on. The room already begins to look furnished.

Then, let us cover the floor with, say, thirty yards of good matting, at fifty cents a yard. This gives us a carpet for fifteen dollars. We are here stopped by the prejudice that matting is not good economy, because it wears out so soon. We humbly submit that it is precisely the thing for a parlor, which is reserved for the reception-room of friends, and for our own dressed leisure hours. Matting is not good economy in a dining-room or a hard-worn sitting-room; but such a parlor as we are describing is precisely the place where it answers to the very best advantage.

We have in mind one very attractive parlor which has been, both for summer and winter, the daily sitting-room for the leisure hours of a husband and wife, and family of children, where a plain straw matting has done service for seven years. That parlor is in a city, and these friends are in the habit of receiving visits from people who live upon velvet and Brusssls; but they prefer to spend the money which such carpets would cost on other modes of embellishment; and this parlor has often been cited to us as a very attractive room.

And now our friends, having got thus far, are requested to select some one tint or color which shall be the prevailing one in the furniture of the room. Shall it be green? Shall it be blue? Shall it be crimson? To carry on our illustration, we will choose green, and we proceed with it to create furniture for our room. Let us imagine that on one side of the fireplace there be, as there is often, a recess about six feet long and three feet deep. Fill this recess with a rough frame with four stout legs, one foot high, and upon the top of the frame have an elastic rack of slats. Make a mattress for this, or, if you wish to avoid that trouble, you can get a nice mattress for the sum of two dollars, made of cane-shavings or husks. Cover this with a green English furniture print. The glazed English comes at about twenty-five cents a yard, the glazed French at seventy-five cents a yard, and a nice article of yard-wide French twill (very strong) is from seventy-five to eighty cents a yard.

With any of these cover your lounge. Make two large, square pillows of the same substance as the mattress, and set up at the back. If you happen to have one or two feather pillows that you can spare for the purpose, shake them down into a square shape and cover them with the same print, and you will then have four pillows for your lounge—one at each end, and two at the back, and you will find it answers for all the purposes of a sofa.

It will be a very pretty thing, now, to cut out of the same material as your lounge, sets of lambrequins (or, as they are called, *lamberkins*,) a kind of pendent curtain-top, as shown in the illustration, to put over the windows, which are to be embellished with white muslin curtains. The cornices to your windows can be simply strips of wood covered with paper to match the bordering of your

Fig. 38.

room, and the lambrequins, made of chintz like the lounge, can be trimmed with fringe or gimp of the same color. The patterns of these can be varied according to fancy, but simple designs are usually the prettiest. A tassel at the lowest point improves the appearance.

The curtains can be made of plain white muslin, or some of the many styles that come for this purpose. If plain muslin is used, you can ornament them with hems an inch in width, in which insert a strip of gingham or chambray of the same color as your chintz. This will wash with the curtains without losing its color, or should it fade, it can easily be drawn out and replaced.

The influence of white-muslin curtains in giving an air of grace and elegance to a room is astonishing. White curtains really create a room out of nothing. No matter how coarse the muslin, so it be white and hang in graceful folds, there is a charm in it that supplies the want of multitudes of other things.

Very pretty curtain-muslin can be bought at thirty-seven cents a yard. It requires six yards for a window.

Let your men-folk knock up for you, out of rough, un-planed boards, some ottoman frames, as described in Chapter II. ; stuff the tops with just the same material as the lounge, and cover them with the self-same chintz.

Now you have, suppose your selected color to be green, a green lounge in the corner and two green ottomans; you have white muslin curtains, with green lambrequins

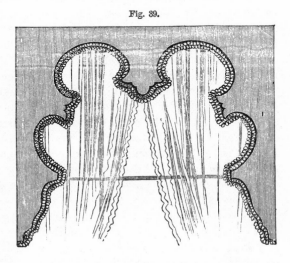

Fig. 39.

and borders, and your room already looks furnished. If you have in the house any broken-down arm-chair, reposing in the oblivion of the garret, draw it out—drive a nail here and there to hold it firm—stuff and pad, and stitch the padding through with a long upholsterer's needle, and cover it with the chintz like your other furniture. Presto—you create an easy-chair.

Thus can broken and disgraced furniture reappear, and, being put into uniform with the general suit of your room, take a new lease of life.

If you want a centre-table, consider this—that any kind of table, well concealed beneath the folds of *handsome drapery, of a color corresponding to the general hue of the room,* will look well. Instead of going to the cabinet-maker and paying from thirty to forty dollars upon a little, narrow, cold, marble-topped stand, that gives just room enough to hold a lamp and a book or two, reflect within yourself what a centre-table is made for. If you have in your house a good, broad, generous-topped table, take it, cover it with an ample cloth of green broadcloth. Such a cover, two and a half yards square, of fine green broadcloth, figured with black and with a pattern-border of grape-leaves, has been bought for ten dollars. In a room we wot of, it covers a cheap pine table, such as you may buy for four or five dollars any day; but you will be astonished to see how handsome an object this table makes under its green drapery. Probably you could make the cover more cheaply by getting the cloth and trimming its edge with a handsome border, selected for the purpose; but either way, it will be an economical and useful ornament. We set down our centre-table, therefore, as consisting mainly of a nice broadcloth cover, matching our curtains and lounge.

We are sure that any one with "a heart that is humble" may command such a centre-table and cloth for fifteen dollars or less, and a family of five or six may all sit and work, or read, or write around it, and it is capable of entertaining a generous allowance of books and knick-knacks.

You have now for your parlor the following figures:

Wall-paper and border,...................................	$5 50
Thirty yards matting,.....................................	15 00
Centre-table and cloth,...................................	15 00
Muslin for three windows,................................	6 75
Thirty yards green English chintz, at 25 cents,..............	7 50
Six chairs, at $2 each,....................................	12 00
Total,.......................................	$61 75

Subtracted from eighty dollars, which we set down as the price of the cheap, ugly Brussels carpet, we have our whole room papered, carpeted, curtained, and furnished, and we have nearly twenty dollars remaining for pictures.

As a little suggestion in regard to the selection, you can get Miss Oakley's charming little cabinet picture of

"The Little Scrap-Book Maker" for........................ $7 50
Eastman Johnson's "Barefoot Boy,"..................(Prang) 5 00
Newman's "Blue-fringed Gentians,"..................(Prang) 6 00
Bierstadt's "Sunset in the Yo Semite Valley,".........(Prang) 12 00

Here are thirty dollars' worth of really admirable pictures of some of our best American artists, from which you can choose at your leisure. By sending to any leading picture-dealer, lists of pictures and prices will be forwarded to you. These chromos, being all varnished, can wait for frames until you can afford them. Or, what is better, because it is at once cheaper and a means of educating the ingenuity and the taste, you can make for yourselves pretty rustic frames in various modes. Take a very

Fig. 40.

thin board, of the right size and shape, for the foundation or "mat;" saw out the inner oval or rectangular form to suit the picture. Nail on the edge a rustic frame made of branches of hard, seasoned wood, and garnish the corners with some pretty device; such, for instance, as a cluster of acorns; or, in place of the branches of trees, fasten on with glue small pine cones, with larger ones for corner ornaments. Or use the mosses of the wood or ocean shells for this purpose. It may be more convenient to get the mat or inner moulding from a framer, or have it made by your carpenter, with a groove behind to hold a glass. Here are also picture-frames of pretty effect, and very simply made. The one in Fig. 42

Fig. 41.

is made of either light or dark wood, neat, thin, and not very wide, with the ends simply broken off, or cut so as to resemble a rough break. The other

Fig. 42.

is white pine, sawn into simple form, well smoothed, and marked with a delicate black tracery, as suggested in Fig. 43. This should also be varnished, then it will take a rich, yellow tinge, which harmonizes admirably with chromos, and lightens up engravings to singular advantage. Besides the American and the higher range of German and English chromos, there are very many pretty little French chromos, which can be had at prices from $1 to $5, including black walnut frames.

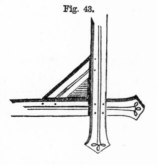

Fig. 43.

We have been through this calculation merely to show our readers how much beautiful effect may be produced by a wise disposition of color and skill in arrangement. If any of our friends should ever carry it out, they will find that the buff paper, with its dark, narrow border; the green chintz repeated in the lounge, the ottomans, and lambrequins; the flowing, white curtains; the broad, generous centre-

table, draped with its ample green cloth, will, when arranged together, produce an effect of grace and beauty
far beyond what any one piece or even half a dozen pieces
of expensive cabinet furniture could. The great, simple
principle of beauty illustrated in this room is *harmony of
color*.

You can, in the same way, make a red room by using
Turkey red for your draperies; or a blue room by using
blue chintz. Let your chintz be of a small pattern, and
one that is decided in color.

We have given the plan of a room with matting on the
floor because that is absolutely the cheapest cover. The
price of thirty yards plain, good ingrain carpet, at $1.50
per yard, would be forty-five dollars; the difference be
tween forty-five and fifteen dollars would *furnish* a room
with pictures such as we have instanced. However, the
same programme can be even better carried out with a
green ingrain carpet as the foundation of the color of the
room.

Our friends, who lived seven years upon matting, contrived to give their parlor in winter an effect of warmth
and color by laying down, in front of the fire, a large
square of carpeting, say three breadths, four yards long.
This covered the gathering-place around the fire where the
winter circle generally sits, and gave an appearance of
warmth to the room.

If we add this piece of carpeting to the estimates for
our room, we still leave a margin for a picture, and make
the programme equally adapted to summer and winter.

Besides the chromos, which, when well selected and of the
best class, give the charm of color which belongs to expensive paintings, there are engravings which finely reproduce
much of the real spirit and beauty of the celebrated pictures of the world. And even this does not exhaust the
resources of economical art; for there are few of the
renowned statues, whether of antiquity or of modern times,

that have not been accurately copied in plaster casts; and a few statuettes, costing perhaps five or six dollars each, will give a really elegant finish to your rooms—providing always that they are selected with discrimination and taste.

The educating influence of these works of art can hardly be over-estimated. Surrounded by such suggestions of the beautiful, and such reminders of history and art, children are constantly trained to correctness of taste and refinement of thought, and stimulated—sometimes to efforts at artistic imitation, always to the eager and intelligent inquiry about the scenes, the places, the incidents represented.

Just here, perhaps, we are met by some who grant all that we say on the subject of decoration by works of art, and who yet impatiently exclaim, " But I have *no* money to spare for any thing of this sort. I am condemned to an absolute bareness, and beauty in my case is not to be thought of."

Are you sure, my friend? If you live in the country, or can get into the country, and have your eyes opened and your wits about you, your house need not be condemned to an absolute bareness. Not so long as the woods are full of beautiful ferns and mosses, while every swamp shakes and nods with tremulous grasses, need you feel yourself an utterly disinherited child of nature, and deprived of its artistic use.

For example: Take an old tin pan condemned to the retired list by reason of holes in the bottom, get twenty-five cents' worth of green paint for this and other purposes, and paint it. The holes in the bottom are a recommendation for its new service. If there are no holes, you must drill two or three, as drainage is essential. Now put a layer one inch deep of broken charcoal and potsherds over the bottom, and then soil, in the following proportions :

Two fourths wood-soil, such as you find in forests, under trees.

One fourth clean sand.

One fourth meadow-soil, taken from under fresh turf. Mix with this some charcoal dust.

In this soil plant all sorts of ferns, together with some few swamp-grasses; and around the edge put a border of money-plant or periwinkle to hang over. This will need to be watered once or twice a week, and it will grow and thrive all summer long in a corner of your room. Should you prefer, you can suspend it by wires and make a hanging-basket. Ferns and wood-grasses need not have sunshine—they grow well in shadowy places.

On this same principle you can convert a salt-box or an old drum of figs into a hanging-basket. Tack bark and pine-cones and moss upon the outside of it, drill holes and pass wires through it, and you have a woodland hanging-basket, which will hang and grow in any corner of your house.

We have been into rooms which, by the simple disposition of articles of this kind, have been made to have an air

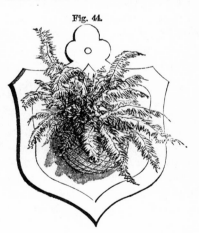

Fig. 44.

so poetical and attractive that they seemed more like a nymph's cave than any thing in the real world.

Another mode of disposing of ferns is this: Take a flat piece of board sawed out something like a shield, with a hole at the top for hanging it up.

Upon the board nail a wire pocket made of an ox-muzzle flattened on one side; or make something of the kind with stiff wire. Line this with a sheet of close moss, which appears green behind the wire

net-work. Then you fill it with loose, spongy moss, such
as you find in swamps, and plant therein great plumes
of fern and various swamp-grasses ; they will continue to
grow there, and hang gracefully over. When watering,
set a pail under for it to drip into. It needs only to keep
this moss always damp, and to sprinkle these ferns occasionally with a whisk-broom, to have a most lovely ornament for your room or hall.

The use of ivy in decorating a room is beginning to be
generally acknowledged. It needs to be planted in the
kind of soil we have described, in a well-drained pot or
box, and to have its leaves thoroughly washed once or
twice a year in strong suds made with soft-soap, to free it
from dust and scale-bug; and an ivy will live and thrive
and wind about in a room, year in and year out, will grow
around pictures, and do almost any thing to oblige you that
you can suggest to it. For instance, in a March number of
*Hearth and Home,** there is a picture of the most delightful
library-window imaginable, whose chief charm consists in
the running vines that start from a longitudinal box at the
bottom of the window, and thence clamber up and about
the casing and across the rustic frame-work erected for its
convenience. On the opposite page we present another
plain kind of window, ornamented with a variety of these
rural economical adornings.

In the centre is a Ward's case. On one side is a pot of
Fuchsia. On the other side is a Calla Lily. In the hanging-baskets and on the brackets are the ferns and flowers
that flourish in the deep woods, and around the window is
the ivy, running from two boxes; and, in case the window
has some sun, a *Nasturtion* may spread its bright blossoms
among the leaves. Then, in the winter, when there is less
sun, the *Striped Spider-wort,* the *Smilax* and the *Saxifraga*

* A beautifully illustrated agricultural and family weekly paper, edited
by Donald G. Mitchell (Ik Marvel) and Mrs. H. B. Stowe.

Fig. 45.

Samentosa (or *Wandering Jew*) may be substituted. Pretty brackets can be made of common pine, ornamented with odd-growing twigs or mosses or roots, scraped and varnished, or in their native state.

A beautiful ornament for a room with pictures is German ivy. Slips of this will start without roots in bottles of water. Slide the bottle behind the picture, and the ivy will seem to come from fairyland, and hang its verdure in all manner of pretty curves around the picture. It may then be trained to travel toward other ivy, and thus aid in forming green cornice along the ceiling. We have seen some rooms that had an ivy cornice around the whole, giving the air of a leafy bower.

There are some other odd devices to ornament a room. For example, a sponge, kept wet by daily immersion, can be filled with flax-seed and suspended by a cord, when it will ere long be covered with verdure and afterward with flowers.

A sweet potato, laid in a bowl of water on a bracket, or still better, suspended by a knitting-needle, run through or laid across the bowl half in the water, will, in due time, make a beautiful verdant ornament. A large carrot, with the smallest half cut off, scooped out to hold water and then suspended with cords, will send out graceful shoots in rich profusion.

Half a cocoa-nut shell, suspended, will hold earth or water for plants and make a pretty hanging-garden.

It may be a very proper thing to direct the ingenuity and activity of children into the making of hanging-baskets and vases of rustic work. The best foundations are the cheap wooden bowls, which are quite easy to get, and the walks of children in the woods can be made interesting by their bringing home material for this rustic work. Different colored twigs and sprays of trees, such as the bright scarlet of the dog-wood, the yellow of the willow, the black of the birch, and the silvery gray of the poplar, may be combined in fanciful net-work. For this sort of work, no other investment is needed than a hammer and an assortment of different-sized tacks, and beautiful results will be produced.

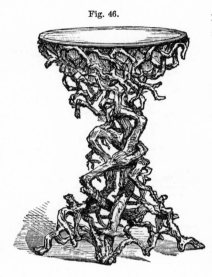

Fig. 46.

Fig. 46 is a stand for flowers, made of roots, scraped and varnished.

But the greatest and cheapest and most delightful fountain of beauty is a " Ward case."

Now, immediately all our economical friends give up in despair. Ward's cases sell all the way along from eighteen to fifty dollars, and are, like every thing else in this lower world, regarded as the sole perquisites of the rich.

Let us not be too sure. Plate-glass, and hot-house plants, and rare patterns, *are* the especial inheritance of the rich; but any family may command all the requisites of a Ward case for a very small sum. Such a case is a small glass closet over a well-drained box of soil. You make a Ward case on a small scale when you turn a tumbler over a plant. The glass keeps the temperature moist and equable, and preserves the plants from dust, and the soil being well drained, they live and thrive accordingly. The requisites of these are the glass top and the bed of well-drained soil.

Suppose you have a common cheap table, four feet long and two wide. Take off the top boards of your table, and with them board the bottom across tight and firm; then line it with zinc, and you will have a sort of box or sink on legs. Now make a top of common window-glass such as you would get for a cucumber-frame; let it be two and a half feet high, with a ridge-pole like a house, and a slant-

Fig. 47.

ing roof of glass resting on this ridge-pole ; on one end let there be a door two feet square.

We have seen a Ward case made in this way, in which the capabilities for producing ornamental effect were greatly beyond many of the most elaborate ones of the shops. It was large, and roomy, and cheap. Common window-sash and glass are not dear, and any man with moderate ingenuity could fashion such a glass closet for his wife ; or a woman, not having such a husband, can do it herself.

The sink or box part must have in the middle of it a hole of good size for drainage. In preparing for the reception of plants, first turn a plant-saucer over this hole, which may otherwise become stopped. Then, as directed for the other basket, proceed with a layer of broken charcoal and potsherds for drainage, two inches deep, and prepare the soil as directed above, and add to it some pounded charcoal, or the scrapings of the charcoal-bin. In short, more or less charcoal and charcoal-dust is *always* in order in the treatment of these moist subjects, as it keeps them from fermenting and growing sour.

Now for filling the case.

Our own native forest-ferns have a period in the winter months when they cease to grow. They are very particular in asserting their right to this yearly nap, and will not, on any consideration, grow for you out of their appointed season.

Nevertheless, we shall tell you what we have tried ourselves, because greenhouse ferns are expensive, and often great cheats when you have bought them, and die on your hands in the most reckless and shameless manner. If you make a Ward case in the spring, your ferns will grow beautifully in it all summer; and in the autumn, though they stop growing, and cease to throw out leaves, yet the old leaves will remain fresh and green till the time for starting the new ones in the spring.

But, supposing you wish to start your case in the fall, out of such things as you can find in the forest; by searching carefully the rocks and clefts and recesses of the forest, you can find a quantity of beautiful ferns whose leaves the frost has not yet assailed. Gather them carefully, remembering that the time of the plant's sleep has come, and that you must make the most of the leaves it now has, as you will not have a leaf more from it till its waking-up time in February or March. But we have succeeded, and you will succeed, in making a very charming and picturesque collection. You can make in your Ward case lovely little grottoes with any bits of shells, and minerals, and rocks you may have; you can lay down, here and there, fragments of broken looking-glass for the floor of your grottoes, and the effect of them will be magical. A square of looking-glass introduced into the back side of your case will produce charming effects.

The trailing arbutus or May-flower, if cut up carefully in sods, and put into this Ward case, will come into bloom there a month sooner than it otherwise would, and gladden your eyes and heart.

In the fall, if you can find the tufts of eye-bright or houstonia cerulia, and mingle them in with your mosses, you will find them blooming before winter is well over.

But among the most beautiful things for such a case is the partridge-berry, with its red plums. The berries swell and increase in the moist atmosphere, and become intense in color, forming an admirable ornament.

Then the ground pine, the princess pine, and various nameless pretty things of the woods, all flourish in these little conservatories. In getting your sod of trailing arbutus, remember that this plant forms its buds in the fall. You must, therefore, examine your sod carefully, and see if the buds are there; otherwise you will find no blossoms in the spring.

There are one or two species of violets, also, that form their buds in the fall, and these too, will blossom early for you.

We have never tried the wild anemones, the crowfoot, etc.; but as they all do well in moist, shady places, we recom mend hopefully the experiment of putting some of them in.

A Ward case has this recommendation over common house-plants, that it takes so little time and care. If well made in the outset, and thoroughly drenched with water when the plants are first put in, it will after that need only to be watered about once a month, and to be ventilated by occasionally leaving open the door for a half-hour or hour when the moisture obscures the glass and seems in excess.

To women embarrassed with the care of little children, yet longing for the refreshment of something growing and beautiful, this indoor garden will be an untold treasure. The glass defends the plant from the inexpedient intermeddling of little fingers; while the little eyes, just on a level with the panes of glass, can look through and learn to enjoy the beautiful, silent miracles of nature.

For an invalid's chamber, such a case would be an inde-
scribable comfort.   It is, in fact, a fragment of the green
woods brought in and silently growing; it will refresh
many a weary hour to watch it.

VII.

THE CARE OF HEALTH.

THERE is no point where a woman is more liable to suffer from a want of knowledge and experience than in reference to the health of a family committed to her care. Many a young lady who never had any charge of the sick; who never took any care of an infant; who never obtained information on these subjects from books, or from the experience of others; in short, with little or no preparation, has found herself the principal attendant in dangerous sickness, the chief nurse of a feeble infant, and the responsible guardian of the health of a whole family.

The care, the fear, the perplexity of a woman suddenly called to these unwonted duties, none can realize till they themselves feel it, or till they see some young and anxious novice first attempting to meet such responsibilities. To a woman of age and experience these duties often involve a measure of trial and difficulty at times deemed almost insupportable; how hard, then, must they press on the heart of the young and inexperienced!

There is no really efficacious mode of preparing a woman to take a rational care of the health of a family, except by communicating that knowledge in regard to the construction of the body and the laws of health which is the basis of the medical profession. Not that a woman should undertake the minute and extensive investigation requisite for a physician; but she should gain a general knowledge of first principles, as a guide to her judgment in emergencies when she can rely on no other aid.

With this end in view, in the preceding chapters some portions of the organs and functions of the human body have been presented, and others will now follow in connection with the practical duties which result from them.

On the general subject of health, one recent discovery of science may here be introduced as having an important relation to every organ and function of the body, and as being one to which frequent reference will be made ; and that is, the nature and operation of *cell-life*.

By the aid of the microscope, we can examine the minute construction of plants and animals, in which we discover contrivances and operations, if not so sublime, yet more wonderful and interesting, than the vast systems of worlds revealed by the telescope.

By this instrument it is now seen that the first formation, as well as future changes and actions, of all plants and animals are accomplished by means of small cells or bags containing various kinds of liquids. These cells are so minute that, of the smallest, some hundreds would not cover the dot of a printed *i* on this page. They are of diverse shapes and contents, and perform various different operations.

The first formation of every animal is accomplished by the agency of cells, and may be illustrated by the egg of any bird or fowl. The exterior consists of a hard shell for protection, and this is lined with a tough skin, to which is fastened the yelk, (which means the *yellow*,) by fibrous strings, as seen at *a*, *a*, in the diagram. In the yelk floats the germ-cell, *b*, which is the point where the formation of the future animal commences. The yelk, being lighter than the white, rises upward, and the germ being still lighter, rises in the yelk. This is to bring both nearer to the vitalizing warmth of the brooding mother.

Fig. 48.

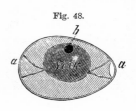

New cells are gradually formed from the nourishing yelk around the germ, each being at first roundish in shape, and having a spot near the centre, called the nucleus. The reason why cells increase must remain a mystery, until we can penetrate the secrets of vital force —probably forever. But the mode in which they multiply is as follows: The first change noticed in a cell, when warmed into vital activity, is the appearance of a second nucleus within it, while the cell gradually becomes oval in form, and then is drawn inward at the middle, like an hour-glass, till the two sides meet. The two portions then divide, and two cells appear, each containing its own germinal nucleus. These both divide again in the same manner, proceeding in the ratio of 2, 4, 8, 16, and so on, until most of the yelk becomes a mass of cells.

The central point of this mass, where the animal itself commences to appear, shows, first, a round-shaped figure, which soon assumes form like a pear, and then like a violin. Gradually the busy little cells arrange themselves to build up heart, lungs, brain, stomach, and limbs, for which the yelk and white furnish nutriment. There is a small bag of air fastened to one end inside of the shell; and when the animal is complete, this air is taken into its lungs, life begins, and out walks little chick, all its powers prepared, and ready to run, eat, and enjoy existence. Then, as soon as the animal uses its brain to think and feel, and its muscles to move, the cells which have been made up into these parts begin to decay, while new cells are formed from the blood to take their place. Thus with life commences the constant process of decay and renewal all over the body.

The liquid portion of the blood consists of material formed from food, air, and water. From this material the cells of the blood are formed: first, the white cells, which are incomplete in formation; and then the red cells, which are completed by the addition of the oxygen received from

air in the lungs. Fig. 49 represents part of a magnified
blood-vessel, *a, a,* in which the round cells are the white,
and the oblong the red cells,
floating in the blood. Surrounding the blood-vessels
are the cells forming the adjacent membrane, *b b,* each
having a nucleus in its centre.

Cells have different powers
of selecting and secreting
diverse materials from the
blood. Thus, some secrete
bile to carry to the liver,
others secrete saliva for the
mouth, others take up the
tears, and still others take
material for the brain, mus-
cles, and all other organs. Cells also have a converting
power, of taking one kind of matter from the blood, and
changing it to another kind. They are minute chemical
laboratories all over the body, changing materials of one
kind to another form in which they can be made useful.

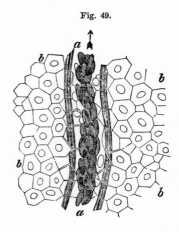

Fig. 49.

Both animal and vegetable substances are formed of
cells. But the vegetable cells take up and use unorgan-
ized or simple, natural matter ; whereas the animal cell
only takes substances already organized into vegetable or
animal life, and then changes one compound into another
of different proportions and nature.

These curious facts in regard to cell-life have important
relations to the general subject of the care of health, and
also to the cure of disease, as will be noticed in following
chapters.

THE NERVOUS SYSTEM.

There is another portion of the body, which is so intimately connected with every other that it is placed in this

chapter as also having reference to every department in the general subject of the care of health.

The body has no power to move itself, but is a collection of instruments to be used by the mind in securing various kinds of knowledge and enjoyment. The organs through which the mind thus operates are the *brain* and *nerves*. The drawing (Fig. 50) represents them.

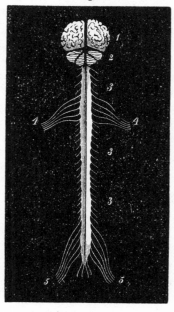

Fig. 50.

The brain lies in the skull, and is divided into the large or upper brain, marked 1, and the small or lower brain, marked 2. From the brain runs the spinal marrow through the spine or backbone. From each side of the spine the large nerves run out into innumerable smaller branches to every portion of the body. The drawing shows only some of the larger branches. Those marked 3 run to the neck and organs of the chest; those marked 4 go to the arms; those below the arms, marked 3, go to the trunk; and those marked 5 go to the legs.

The brain and nerves consist of two kinds of nervous matter—the *gray*, which is supposed to be the portion that originates and controls a nervous fluid which imparts power of action; and the *white*, which seems to conduct this fluid to every part of the body.

The brain and nervous system are divided into distinct portions, each having different offices to perform, and each acting independently of the others; as, for example, one portion is employed by the mind in thinking, and in feeling pleasurable or painful mental emotions; another in moving the muscles; while the nerves that run to the nose, ears, eyes, tongue, hands, and surface generally, are employed in seeing, hearing, smelling, tasting, and feeling all physical sensations.

The *back* portion of the spinal marrow and the nerves that run from it are employed in *sensation*, or the *sense of feeling*. These nerves extend over the whole body, but are largely developed in the network of nerves in the skin. The *front* portion of the spinal marrow and its branches are employed in moving those muscles in all parts of the body which are controlled by the *will* or *choice* of the mind. These are called the *nerves of motion*.

The nerves of sensation and nerves of motion, although they start from different portions of the spine, are united in the same *sheath* or *cover*, till they terminate in the muscles. Thus, every muscle is moved by nerves of motion; while alongside of this nerve, in the same sheath, is a nerve of sensation. All the nerves of motion and sensation are connected with those portions of the brain used when we think, feel, and choose. By this arrangement the mind *knows* what is wanted in all parts of the body by means of the nerves of sensation, and then it *acts* by means of the nerves of motion.

For example, when we feel the cold air on the skin, the nerves of sensation report to the brain, and thus to the mind, that the body is growing cold. The mind thus knows that more clothing is needed, and *wills* to have the eyes look for it, and the hands and feet move to get it. This is done by the nerves of sight and of motion.

Next are the nerves of *involuntary motion*, which move all those parts of the head, face, and body that are used in breathing, and in other operations connected with it. By these we continue to breathe when asleep, and whether we will to do so or not. There are also some of the nerves of voluntary motion that are mixed with these, which enable the mind to stop respiration, or to regulate it to a certain extent. But the mind has no power to stop it for any great length of time.

There is another large and important system of nerves called the *sympathetic* or *ganglionic* system. It consists of small masses of gray and white nervous matter, that seem to be small brains with nerves running from them. These are called *ganglia*, and are arranged on each side of the spine, while small nerves from the spinal marrow run into them, thus uniting the sympathetic system with the nerves of the spine. These ganglia are also distributed around in various parts of the interior of the body, especially in the intestines, and all the different ganglia are connected with each other by nerves, thus making one system. It is the ganglionic system that carries on the circulation of the blood, the action of the capillaries, lymphatics, arteries, and veins, together with the work of secretion, absorption, and most of the internal working of the body, which goes forward without any knowledge or control of the mind.

Every portion of the body has nerves of sensation coming from the spine, and also branches of the sympathetic or ganglionic system. The object of this is to form a sympathetic communication between the several parts of the body, and also to enable the mind to receive, through the brain, some general knowledge of the state of the whole system. It is owing to this that, when one portion of the body is affected, other portions sympathize. For example, if one part of the body is diseased, the stomach may so sympathize as to lose all appetite until the disease is removed.

All the operations of the nervous system are performed by the influence of the nervous fluid, which is generated in the gray portions of the brain and ganglia. Whenever a nerve is cut off from its connection with these nervous centres, its power is gone, and the part to which it minis tered becomes lifeless and incapable of motion.

The brain and nerves can be overworked, and can also suffer for want of exercise, just as the muscles do. It is necessary for the perfect health of the brain and nerves that the several portions be exercised sufficiently, and that no part be exhausted by over-action. For example, the nerves of sensation may be very much exercised, and the nerves of motion have but little exercise. In this case, one will be weakened by excess of work, and the other by the want of it.

It is found by experience that the proper exercise of the nerves of motion tends to reduce any extreme susceptibility of the nerves of sensation. On the contrary, the neglect of such exercise tends to produce an excessive sensibility in the nerves of sensation.

Whenever that part of the brain which is employed in thinking, feeling, and willing, is greatly exercised by hard study, or by excessive care or emotion, the blood tends to the brain to supply it with increased nourishment, just as it flows to the muscles when they are exercised. Over-exercise of this portion of the brain causes engorgement of the blood-vessels. This is sometimes indicated by pain, or by a sense of fullness in the head; but oftener the result is a debilitating drain on the nervous system, which depends for its supply on the healthful state of the brain.

The brain has, as it were, a fountain of supply for the nervous fluid, which flows to all the nerves, and stimulates them to action. Some brains have a larger, and some a smaller fountain; so that a degree of mental activity that would entirely exhaust one, would make only a small and healthful drain upon another.

The excessive use of certain portions of the brain tends to withdraw the nervous energy from other portions; so that when one part is debilitated by excess, another fails by neglect. For example, a person may so exhaust the brain power in the excessive use of the nerves of motion by hard work, as to leave little for any other faculty. On the other hand, the nerves of feeling and thinking may be so used as to withdraw the nervous fluid from the nerves of motion, and thus debilitate the muscles.

Some animal propensities may be indulged to such excess as to produce a constant tendency of the blood to a certain portion of the brain, and to the organs connected with it, and thus cause a constant and excessive excitement, which finally becomes a disease. Sometimes a paralysis of this portion of the brain results from such an entire exhaustion of the nervous fountain and of the overworked nerves.

Thus, also, the thinking portion of the brain may be so overworked as to drain the nervous fluid from other portions, which become debilitated by the loss. And in this way, also, the overworked portion may be diseased or paralyzed by the excess.

The necessity for the *equal development* of all portions of the brain by an appropriate exercise of *all* the faculties of mind and body, and the influence of this upon happiness, is the most important portion of this subject, and will be more directly exhibited in another chapter.

VIII.

In a work which aims to influence women to train the young to honor domestic labor and to seek healthful exercise in home pursuits, there is special reason for explaining the construction of the muscles and their connection with the nerves, these being the chief organs of motion.

The muscles, as seen by the naked eye, consist of very fine fibres or strings, bound up in smooth, silky casings of thin membrane. But each of these visible fibres or strings the microscope shows to be made up of still finer strings, numbering from five to eight hundred in each fibre. And each of these microscopic fibres is a series or chain of elastic cells, which are so minute that one hundred thousand would scarcely cover a capital O on this page.

The peculiar property of the cells which compose the muscles is their elasticity, no other cells of the body having this property. At Fig. 51 is a diagram representing a microscopic muscular fibre, in which the cells are relaxed, as in the natural state of rest. But when the muscle contracts, each of its numberless cells in all its small fibres becomes widened, making each fibre of the muscle shorter and thicker, as at Fig. 52. This explains the cause of the swelling out of muscles when they act.

Fig. 51.
a

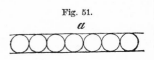

Fig. 52.
b

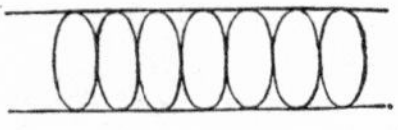

Every motion in every part of the body has a special

muscle to produce it, and many have other muscles to restore the part moved to its natural state. The muscles that
move or bend any part are called *flexors*, and those that restore the natural position are called *extensors.*

Fig. 53 represents the muscles of the arm after the skin

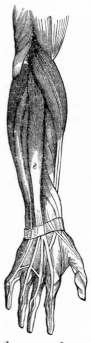

and flesh are removed. They are all in
smooth silky cases, laid over each other,
and separated both by the smooth membranes that encase them and by layers of
fat, so as to move easily without interfering with each other. They are fastened
to the bones by strong tendons and cartilages ; and around the wrist, in the drawing, is shown a band of cartilage to confine them in place. The muscle marked
8 is the extensor that straightens the fingers after they have been closed by a
flexor the other side of the arm. In like
manner, each motion of the arm and fingers has one muscle to produce it and
another to restore to the natural position.

The muscles are dependent on the
brain and nerves for power to move. It
has been shown that the gray matter of
the brain and spinal marrow furnishes
the stimulating power that moves the
muscles, and causes sensations of touch
on the skin, and the other sensations of
the several senses. The white part of the brain and spinal
marrow consists solely of conducting tubes to transmit this
influence. Each of the minute fibrils of the muscles has a
small conducting nerve connecting it with the brain or
spinal marrow, and in this respect each muscular fibril is
separate from every other.

When, therefore, the mind wills to move a flexor muscle
of the arm, the gray matter sends out the stimulus through

the nerves to the cells of each individual fibre of that muscle, and they contract. When this is done, the nerve of sensation reports it to the brain and mind. If the mind desires to return the arm to its former position, then follows the willing, and consequent stimulus sent through the nerves to the corresponding muscle; its cells contract, and the limb is restored.

When the motion is a compound one, involving the action of several muscles at the same time, a multitude of impressions are sent back and forth to and from the brain through the nerves. But the person acting thus is unconscious of all this delicate and wonderful mechanism. He wills the movement, and instantly the requisite nervous power is sent to the required cells and fibres, and they perform the motions required. Many of the muscles are moved by the sympathetic system, over which the mind has but little control.

Among the muscles and nerves so intimately connected, run the minute capillaries of the blood, which furnish nourishment to all.

Fig. 54 represents an artery at *a*, which brings pure blood to a muscle from the heart. After

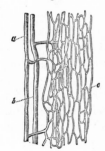

Fig. 54.

meandering through the capillaries at *c*, to distribute oxygen and food from the stomach, the blood enters the vein, *b*, loaded with carbonic acid and water taken up in the capillaries, to be carried to the lungs or skin, and thrown out into the air.

The manner in which the exercise of the muscles quickens the circulation of the blood will now be explained.

The veins abound in every part of every muscle, and the large veins have *valves* which prevent the blood from flowing backward. If the wrist is grasped tightly, the veins of the hand are immediately swollen.

This is owing to the fact that the blood is prevented from flowing toward the heart by this pressure, and by the vein-valves from returning into the arteries; while the arteries themselves, being placed deeper down, are not so compressed, and continue to send the blood into the hand, and thus it accumulates. As soon as this pressure is removed, the blood springs onward from the restraint with accelerated motion. This same process takes place when any of the muscles are exercised. The contraction of any muscle presses some of the veins, so that the blood can not flow the natural way, while the valves in the veins prevent its flowing backward. Meantime the arteries continue to press the blood along until the veins become swollen. Then, as soon as the muscle ceases its contraction, the blood flows faster from the previous accumulation.

If, then, we use a number of muscles, and use them strongly and quickly, there are so many veins affected in this way as to quicken the whole circulation. The heart receives blood faster, and sends it to the lungs faster. Then the lungs work quicker, to furnish the oxygen required by the greater amount of blood. The blood returns with greater speed to the heart, and the heart sends it out with quicker action through the arteries to the capillaries. In the capillaries, too, the decayed matter is carried off faster, and then the stomach calls for more food to furnish new and pure blood. Thus it is that exercise gives new life and nourishment to every part of the body.

It is the universal law of the human frame that *exercise* is indispensable to the health of the several parts. Thus, if a blood-vessel be tied up, so as not to be used, it shrinks, and becomes a useless string; if a muscle be condemned to inaction, it shrinks in size and diminishes in power; and thus it is also with the bones. Inactivity produces softness, debility, and unfitness for the functions they are designed to perform.

Now, the nerves, like all other parts of the body, gain

and lose strength according as they are exercised. If they have too much or too little exercise, they lose strength; if they are exercised to a proper degree, they gain strength. When the mind is continuously excited, by business, study, or the imagination, the nerves of emotion and sensation are kept in constant action, while the nerves of motion are unemployed. If this is continued for a long time, the nerves of sensation lose their strength from over-action, and the nerves of motion lose their power from inactivity. In consequence, there is a morbid excitability of the nervous, and a debility of the muscular system, which make all exertion irksome and wearisome.

The only mode of preserving the health of these systems is to keep up in them an equilibrium of action. For this purpose, occupations must be sought which exercise the muscles and interest the mind; and thus the equal action of both kinds of nerves is secured. This shows why exercise is 'so much more healthful and invigorating when the mind is interested, than when it is not. As an illustration, let a person go shopping with a friend, and have nothing to do but look on. How soon do the continuous walking and standing weary! But, suppose one, thus wearied, hears of the arrival of a very dear friend: she can instantly walk off a mile or two to meet her, without the least feeling of fatigue. By this is shown the importance of furnishing, for young persons, exercise in which they will take an interest. Long and formal walks, merely for exercise, though they do some good, in securing fresh air, and some exercise of the muscles, would be of triple benefit if changed to amusing sports, or to the cultivation of fruits and flowers, in which it is impossible to engage without acquiring a great interest.

It shows, also, why it is far better to trust to useful domestic exercise at home than to send a young person out to walk for the mere purpose of exercise. Young girls can seldom be made to realize the value of health, and the need of exercise to secure it, so as to feel much interest in walking abroad, when they have no other object. But, if they are brought up to minister to the comfort and enjoyment of themselves and others, by performing domestic duties, they will constantly be interested and cheered in their exercise by the feeling of usefulness and the consciousness of having performed their duty.

There are few young persons, it is hoped, who are brought up with such miserable habits of selfishness and indolence that they can not be made to feel happier by the consciousness of being usefully employed. And those who have never been accustomed to think or care for any one but themselves, and who seem to feel little pleasure in making themselves useful, by wise and proper influences can often be gradually awakened to the new pleasure of benevolent exertion to promote the comfort and enjoyment of others. And the more this sacred and elevating kind of enjoyment is tasted, the greater is the relish induced. Other enjoyments often cloy; but the heavenly pleasure secured by virtuous industry and benevolence, while it satisfies at the time, awakens fresh desires for the continuance of so ennobling a good.

IX.

HEALTHFUL FOOD.

THE person who decides what shall be the food and drink of a family, and the modes of its preparation, is the one who decides, to a greater or less extent, what shall be the health of that family. It is the opinion of most medical men, that intemperance in eating is one of the most fruitful of all causes of disease and death. If this be so, the woman who wisely adapts the food and cooking of her family to the laws of health removes one of the greatest risks which threatens the lives of those under her care. But, unfortunately, there is no other duty that has been involved in more doubt and perplexity. Were one to believe all that is said and written on this subject, the conclusion probably would be, that there is not one solitary article of food on God's earth which it is healthful to eat. Happily, however, there are general principles on this subject which, if understood and applied, will prove a safe guide to any woman of common sense; and it is the object of the following chapter to set forth these principles.

All material things on earth, whether solid, liquid, or gaseous, can be resolved into sixty-two simple substances, only fourteen of which are in the human body; and these, in certain proportions, in all mankind.

Thus, in a man weighing 154 lbs. are found, 111 lbs. oxygen gas, and 14 lbs. hydrogen gas, which, united, form water; 21 lbs. carbon; 3 lbs. 8 oz. nitrogen gas; 1 lb. 12 oz. 190 grs. phosphorus; 2 lbs. calcium, the chief ingredient of bones; 2 oz. fluorine; 2 oz. 219 grs. sulphur; 2 oz

47 grs. chlorine; 2 oz. 116 grs. sodium; 100 grs. iron; 290 grs. potassium; 12 grs. magnesium; and 2 grs. silicon.

These simple substances are constantly passing out of the body through the lungs, skin, and other excreting organs.

It is found that certain of these simple elements are used for one part of the body, and others for other parts, and this in certain regular proportions. Thus, carbon is the chief element of fat, and also supplies the fuel that combines with oxygen in the capillaries to produce animal heat. The nitrogen which we gain from our food and the air is the chief element of muscle; phosphorus is the chief element of brain and nerves; and calcium or lime is the hard portion of the bones. Iron is an important element of blood, and silicon supplies the hardest parts of the teeth, nails, and hair.

Water, which is composed of the two gases, oxygen and hydrogen, is the largest portion of the body, forming its fluids; there is four times as much of carbon as there is of nitrogen in the body; while there is only two per cent as much phosphorus as carbon. A man weighing one hundred and fifty-four pounds, who leads an active life, takes into his stomach daily from two to three pounds of solid food, and from five to six pounds of liquid. At the same time he takes into his lungs, daily, four or five thousand gallons of air. This amounts to three thousand pounds of nutriment received through stomach and lungs, and then expelled from the body, in one year; or about twenty times the man's own weight.

The change goes on in every minute point of the body, though in some parts much faster than in others; as set forth in the piquant and sprightly language of Dr. O. W Holmes,* who, giving a vivid picture of the constant decay and renewal of the body, says:

---

* *Atlantic Almanac,* 1869, p. 40.

" *Every organized being always lives immersed in a strong solution of its own elements.*"

" Sometimes, as in the case of the air-plant, the solution contains all its elements ; but in higher plants, and in animals generally, some of the principal ones only. Take our own bodies, and we find the atmosphere contains the oxygen and the nitrogen, of which we are so largely made up, as its chief constituents ; the hydrogen, also, in its watery vapor ; the carbon, in its carbonic acid. What our air-bath does not furnish us, we must take in the form of nourishment, supplied through the digestive organs. But the first food we take, after we have set up for ourselves, is air, and the last food we take is air also. We are all chameleons in our diet, as we are all salamanders in our *habitats*, inasmuch as we live always in the fire of our own smouldering combustion ; a gentle but constant flame, fanned every day by the same forty hogsheads of air which furnish us not with our daily bread, which we can live more than a day without touching, but with our momentary, and oftener than momentary, aliment, without which we can not live five minutes."

" We are perishing and being born again at every instant. We do literally enter over and over again into the womb of that great mother, from whom we get our bones, and flesh, and blood, and marrow. ' I die daily ' is true of all that live. If we cease to die, particle by particle, and to be born anew in the same proportion, the whole movement of life comes to an end, and swift, universal, irreparable decay resolves our frames into the parent elements."

" The products of the internal fire which consumes us over and over again every year, pass off mainly in smoke and steam from the lungs and the skin. The smoke is only invisible, because the combustion is so perfect. The steam is plain enough in our breaths on a frosty morning ; and an over-driven horse will show us, on a larger scale, the cloud that is always arising from own bodies."

" Man walks, then, not only in a vain show, but wrapped

in an uncelestial aureole of his own material exhalations. A great mist of gases and of vapor rises day and night from the whole realm of living nature. The water and the carbonic acid which animals exhale become the food of plants, whose leaves are at once lungs and mouths. The vegetable world reverses the breathing process of the animal creation, restoring the elements which that has combined and rendered effete for its own purposes, to their original condition. The salt-water ocean is a great aquarium. The air ocean in which we live is a 'Wardian case,' of larger dimensions."

It is found that the simple elements will not nourish the body in their natural state, but only when organized, either as vegetable or animal food; and, to the dismay of the Grahamite or vegetarian school, it is now established by chemists that animal and vegetable food contain the same elements, and in nearly the same proportions.

Thus, in animal food, carbon predominates in fats, while in vegetable food it shows itself in sugar, starch, and vegetable oils. Nitrogen is found in animal food in the albumen, fibrin, and caseine; while in vegetables it is in gluten, albumen, and caseine.

It is also a curious fact that, in all articles of food, the elements that nourish diverse parts of the body are divided into separable portions, and also that the proportions correspond in a great degree to the wants of the body. For example, a kernel of wheat contains all the articles demanded for every part of the body. Fig. 55 represents, upon an enlarged scale, the position and proportions of the chief elements required. The white central part is the largest in quantity, and is chiefly carbon in the form of starch, which supplies fat and fuel for the capillaries. The shaded outer portion is chiefly nitrogen, which nourishes the muscles, and the dark spot at the bottom is principally phosphorus, which nourishes the brain and

Fig. 55.

nerves. And these elements are in due proportion to the demands of the body. A portion of the outer covering of a wheat-kernel holds lime, silica, and iron, which are needed by the body, and which are found in no other part of the grain. The woody fibre is not digested, but serves by its bulk and stimulating action to facilitate digestion. It is therefore evident that bread made of unbolted flour is more healthful than that made of superfine flour. The process of bolting removes all the woody fibre; the lime needed.for the bones; the silica for hair, nails, and teeth; the iron for the blood; and most of the nitrogen and phosphorus needed for muscles, brain, and nerves.

Experiments on animals prove that fine flour alone, which is chiefly carbon, will not sustain life more than a month, while unbolted flour furnishes all that is needed for every part of the body. There are cases where persons can not use such coarse bread, on account of its irritating action on inflamed coats of the stomach. For such, a kind of wheaten grit is provided, containing all the kernel of the wheat, except the outside woody fibre.

When the body requires a given kind of diet, specially demanded by brain, lungs, or muscles, the appetite will crave food for it until the necessary amount of this article is secured. If, then, the food in which the needed aliment abounds is not supplied, other food will be taken in larger quantities than needed until that amount is gained. For all kinds of food have supplies for every want of the body, though in different proportions. Thus, for example, if the muscles are worked a great deal, food in which nitrogen abounds is required, and the appetite will continue until the requisite amount of nitrogen is secured. If, then, food is taken which has not the requisite quantity, the consequence is, that more is taken than the system can use, while the vital powers are needlessly taxed to throw off the excess.

These facts were ascertained by Liebig, a celebrated German chemist and physicist, who, assisted by his government, conducted experiments on a large scale in prisons, in armies, and in hospitals. Among other results, he states that those who use potatoes for their principal food eat them in very much larger quantities than their bodies would demand if they used also other food. The reason is, that the potato has a very large proportion of starch that supplies only fuel for the capillaries and very little nitrogen to feed the muscles. For this reason lean meat is needed with potatoes.

In comparing wheat and potatoes we find that in one hundred parts wheat there are fourteen parts nitrogen for muscle, and two parts phosphorus for brain and nerves. But in the potato there is only one part in one hundred for muscle, and nine tenths of one part of phosphorus for brain and nerves.

The articles containing most of the three articles needed generally in the body are as follows: for fat and heat-making—butter, lard, sugar, and molasses; for muscle-making—lean meat, cheese, peas, beans, and lean fishes; for brain and nerves—shell-fish, lean meats, peas, beans, and very active birds and fishes who live chiefly on food in which phosphorus abounds. In a meat diet, the fat supplies carbon for the capillaries and the lean furnishes nutriment for muscle, brain, and nerves. Green vegetables, fruits, and berries furnish the acid and water needed.

In grains used for food, the proportions of useful elements are varied; there is in some more of carbon and in others more of nitrogen and phosphorus. For example, in oats there is more of nitrogen for the muscles, and less carbon for the lungs, than can be found in wheat. In the corn of the North, where cold weather demands fuel for lungs and capillaries, there is much more carbon to supply it than is found in the Southern corn.

From these statements it may be seen that one of the chief mistakes in providing food for families has been in changing the proportions of the elements nature has fitted for our food. Thus, fine wheat is deprived by bolting of some of the most important of its nourishing elements, leaving carbon chiefly, which, after supplying fuel for the capillaries, must, if in excess, be sent out of the body; thus needlessly taxing all the excreting organs. So milk, which contains all the elements needed by the body, has the cream taken out and used for butter, which again is chiefly carbon. Then, sugar and molasses, cakes and candies, are chiefly carbon, and supply but very little of other nourishing elements, while to make them safe much exercise in cold and pure air is necessary. And yet it is the children of the rich, housed in chambers and school-rooms most of their time, who are fed with these dangerous dainties, thus weakening their constitutions, and inducing fevers, colds, and many other diseases.

The proper digestion of food depends on the wants of the body, and on its power of appropriating the aliment supplied. The best of food can not be properly digested when it is not needed. All that the system requires will be used, and the rest will be thrown out by the several excreting organs, which thus are frequently over-taxed, and vital forces are wasted. Even food of poor quality may digest well if the demands of the system are urgent. The way to increase digestive power is to increase the demand for food by pure air and exercise of the muscles, quickening the blood, and arousing the whole system to a more rapid and vigorous rate of life.

Rules for persons in full health, who enjoy pure air and exercise, are not suitable for those whose digestive powers are feeble, or who are diseased. On the other hand, many rules for invalids are not needed by the healthful, while rules for one class of invalids will not avail for other classes. Every weak stomach has its peculiar wants, and can not furnish guidance for others.

We are now ready to consider intelligently the following

general principles in regard to the proper selection of food:

Vegetable and animal food are equally healthful if apportioned to the given circumstances.

In cold weather, carbonaceous food, such as butter, fats, sugar, molasses, etc., can be used more safely than in warm weather. And they can be used more safely by those who exercise in the open air than by those of confined and sedentary habits.

Students who need food with little carbon, and women who live in the house, should always seek coarse bread, fruits, and lean meats, and avoid butter, oils, sugar, and molasses, and articles containing them.

Many students and women using little exercise in the open air, grow thin and weak, because the vital powers are exhausted in throwing off excess of food, especially of the carbonaceous. The liver is especially taxed in such cases, being unable to remove all the excess of carbonaceous matter from the blood, and thus "biliousness" ensues, particularly on the approach of warm weather, when the air brings less oxygen than in cold.

It is found, by experiment, that the supply of gastric juice, furnished from the blood by the arteries of the stomach, is proportioned, not to the amount of food put into the stomach, but to the wants of the body; so that it is possible to put much more into the stomach than can be digested. To guide and regulate in this matter, the sensation called *hunger* is provided. In a healthy state of the body, as soon as the blood has lost its nutritive supplies, the craving of hunger is felt, and then, if the food is suitable, and is taken in the proper manner, this sensation ceases as soon as the stomach has received enough to supply the wants of the system. But our benevolent Creator, in this, as in our other duties, has connected enjoyment with the operation needful to sustain our bodies. In addition to the allaying of hunger, the gratification of the palate is secured by the immense variety of food, some articles of which are far more agreeable than others.

This arrangement of Providence, designed for our happiness, has become, either through ignorance, or want of self-control, the chief cause of the many diseases and sufferings which afflict those classes who have the means of seeking a variety to gratify the palate. If mankind had only one article of food, and only water to drink, though they would have less enjoyment in eating, they would never be tempted to put any more into the stomach than the calls of hunger require. But the customs of society, which present an incessant change, and a great variety of food, with those various condiments which stimulate appetite, lead almost every person very frequently to eat merely to gratify the palate, after the stomach has been abundantly supplied, so that hunger has ceased.

When too great a supply of food is put into the stomach, the gastric juice dissolves only that portion which the wants of the system demand. Most of the remainder is ejected, in an unprepared state; the absorbents take portions of it into the system; and all the various functions of the body, which depend on the ministries of the blood, are thus gradually and imperceptibly injured. Very often, intemperance in eating produces immediate results, such as colic, headaches, pains of indigestion, and vertigo.

But the more general result is a gradual undermining of all parts of the human frame; thus imperceptibly shortening life, by so weakening the constitution, that it is ready to yield, at every point, to any uncommon risk or exposure. Thousands and thousands are passing out of the world, from diseases occasioned by exposures which a healthy constitution could meet without any danger. It is owing to these considerations, that it becomes the duty of every woman, who has the responsibility of providing food for a family, to avoid a variety of tempting dishes. It is a much safer rule, to have only one kind of healthy food, for each meal,

than the too abundant variety which is often met at the
tables of almost all classes in this country.   When there is
to be any variety of dishes, they ought not to be successive,
but so arranged as to give the opportunity of selection.
How often is it the case, that persons, by the appearance
of a favorite article, are tempted to eat merely to gratify
the palate, when the stomach is already adequately supplied.
All such intemperance wears on the constitution, and
shortens life.   It not unfrequently happens that excess in
eating produces a morbid appetite, which must constantly
be denied.

But the organization of the digestive organs demands,
not only that food should be taken in proper quantities,
but that it be taken at proper times.

Fig. 56 shows one
important feature of
the digestive organs
relating to this point.
The part marked L M
shows the muscles of
the inner coat of the
stomach, which run
in one direction, and
C M shows the mus-
cles of the outer coat,
running in another
direction.

Fig. 56.

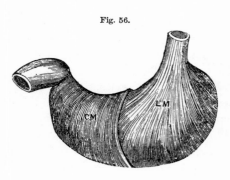

As soon as the food enters the stomach, the muscles are
excited by the nerves, and the *peristaltic motion* commences.
This is a powerful and constant exercise of the muscles of
the stomach, which continues until the process of digestion
is complete.   During this time the blood is withdrawn from
other parts of the system, to supply the demands of the
stomach, which is laboring hard with all its muscles.
When this motion ceases, and the digested food has gradually passed out, nature requires that the stomach should

have a period of repose. And if another meal be eaten immediately after one is digested, the stomach is set to work again before it has had time to rest, and before a sufficient supply of gastric juice is provided.

The general rule, then, is, that three hours be given to the stomach for labor, and two for rest; and in obedience to this, five hours, at least, ought to elapse between every two regular meals. In cases where exercise produces a flow of perspiration, more food is needed to supply the loss; and strong laboring men may safely eat as often as they feel the want of food. So, young and healthy children, who gambol and exercise much and whose bodies grow fast, may have a more frequent supply of food. But, as a general rule, meals should be five hours apart, and eating between meals avoided. There is nothing more unsafe, and wearing to the constitution, than a habit of eating at any time merely to gratify the palate. When a tempting article is presented, every person should exercise sufficient self-denial to wait till the proper time for eating arrives. Children, as well as grown persons, are often injured by eating between their regular meals, thus weakening the stomach by not affording it any time for rest.

In deciding as to *quantity* of food, there is one great difficulty to be met by a large portion of the community. The exercise of every part of the body is necessary to its health and perfection. The bones, the muscles, the nerves, the organs of digestion and respiration, and the skin, all demand exercise, in order properly to perform their functions. When the muscles of the body are called into action, all the blood-vessels entwined among them are frequently compressed. As the veins have valves so contrived that the blood can not run back, this compression hastens it forward toward the heart; which is immediately put in quicker motion, to send it into the lungs; and they, also, are thus stimulated to more rapid action, which is the cause of that panting which active exercise always occasions. The blood thus courses with greater celerity through the body, and sooner loses its nourishing properties. Then the stomach issues its mandate of hunger, and a new supply of food must be furnished.

Thus it appears, as a general rule, that the quantity of food actually needed by the body depends on the amount of muscular exercise taken. A laboring man, in the open fields, probably throws off from his skin and lungs a much larger amount than a person of sedentary pursuits. In consequence of this, he demands a greater amount of food and drink.

Those persons who keep their bodies in a state of health by sufficient exercise can always be guided by the calls of hunger. They can eat when they feel hungry, and stop when hunger ceases; and thus they will calculate exactly right. But the difficulty is, that a large part of the community, especially women, are so inactive in their habits that they seldom feel the calls of hunger. They habitually eat, merely to gratify the palate. This produces such a state of the system that they lose the guide which Nature has provided. They are not called to eat by hunger, nor admonished, by its cessation, when to stop. In consequence of this, such persons eat what pleases the palate, till they feel no more inclination for the article. It is probable that three fourths of the women in the wealthier circles sit down to each meal without any feeling of hunger, and eat merely on account of the gratification thus afforded them. Such persons find their appetite to depend almost solely upon the kind of food on the table. This is not the case with those who take the exercise which Nature demands. They approach their meals in such a state that almost any kind of food is acceptable.

The question then arises, How are persons, who have lost the guide which Nature has provided, to determine as to the proper amount of food they shall take ?

The best method is for several days to take their

ordinary exercise and eat only one or two articles of simple food, such as bread and milk, or bread and butter with cooked fruit, or lean meat with bread and vegetables, and at the same time eat less than the appetite demands. Then on the following two days, take just enough to satisfy the appetite, and on the third day notice the quantity which satisfies. After this, decide before eating that only this amount of simple food shall be taken.

Persons who have a strong constitution, and take much exercise, may eat almost any thing with apparent impunity; but young children who are forming their constitutions, and persons who are delicate, and who take but little exercise, are very dependent for health on a proper selection of food.

It is found that there are some kinds of food which afford nutriment to the blood, and do not produce any other effect on the system. There are other kinds, which are not only nourishing, but *stimulating*, so that they quicken the functions of the organs on which they operate. The condiments used in cookery, such as pepper, mustard, and spices, are of this nature. There are certain states of the system when these stimulants may be beneficial; such cases can only be pointed out by medical men.

Persons in perfect health, and especially young children, never receive any benefit from such kind of food; and just in proportion as condiments operate to quicken the labors of the internal organs, they tend to wear down their powers. A person who thus keeps the body working under an unnatural excitement, *live faster* than Nature designed, and the constitution is worn out just so much the sooner. A woman, therefore, should provide dishes for her family which are free from these stimulating condiments.

It is also found, by experience, that the lean part of animal food is more stimulating than vegetable. This is the reason why, in cases of fevers or inflammations, medical men forbid the use of meat. A person who lives chiefly on animal food is under a higher degree of stimulus than if his food was chiefly composed of vegetable substances. His blood will flow faster, and all the functions of his body will be quickened. This makes it important to secure a proper proportion of animal and vegetable diet. Some medical men suppose that an exclusively vegetable diet is proved, by the experience of many individuals, to be fully sufficient to nourish the body ; and bring, as evidence, the fact that some of the strongest and most robust men in the world are those who are trained, from infancy, exclusively on vegetable food. From this they infer that life will be shortened just in proportion as the diet is changed to more stimulating articles ; and that, all other things being equal, children will have a better chance of health and long life if they are brought up solely on vegetable food.

But, though this is not the common opinion of medical men, they all agree that, in America, far too large a portion of the diet consists of animal food. As a nation, the Americans are proverbial for the gross and luxurious diet with which they load their tables; and there can be no doubt that the general health of the nation would be increased by a change in our customs in this respect. To take meat but once a day, and this in small quantities, compared with the common practice, is a rule, the observance of which would probably greatly reduce the amount of fevers, eruptions, headaches, bilious attacks, and the many other ailments which are produced or aggravated by too gross a diet.

The celebrated Roman physician, Baglivi, (who, from practicing extensively among Roman Catholics, had ample opportunities to observe,) mentions that, in Italy, an unusual number of people recover their health in the forty days of Lent, in consequence of the lower diet which is required as a religious duty. An American physician remarks, "For every reeling drunkard that disgraces our country, it contains one hundred gluttons—persons, I mean, who eat to excess, and suffer in consequence." Another distinguished physician says, " I believe that every stomach, not actually impaired by organic disease, will perform its functions, if it receives reasonable attention; and when we perceive the manner in which diet is generally conducted, both in regard to *quantity* and *variety* of articles of food and drink, which are mixed up in one heterogeneous mass—instead of being astonished at the prevalence of indigestion, our wonder must rather be that, in such circumstances, any stomach is capable of digesting at all."

In regard to articles which are the most easily digested, only general rules can be given. Tender meats are digested more readily than those which are tough, or than many kinds of vegetable food. The farinaceous articles, such as rice, flour, corn, potatoes, and the like, are the most nutritious, and most easily digested. The popular notion, that meat is more nourishing than bread, is a great mistake. Good bread contains more nourishment than butcher's meat. The meat is more *stimulating*, and for this reason is more readily digested.

A perfectly healthy stomach can digest almost any healthful food; but when the digestive powers are weak, every stomach has its peculiarities, and what is good for one is hurtful to another. In such cases, experiment alone can decide which are the most digestible articles of food. A person whose food troubles him must deduct one article after another, till he learns, by experience, which is the best for digestion. Much evil has been done, by assuming that the powers of one stomach are to be made the rule in regulating every other.

The most unhealthful kinds of food are those which are made so by bad cooking; such as sour and heavy bread, cakes, pie-crust, and other dishes consisting of fat mixed and cooked with flour. Rancid butter and high-seasoned food are equally unwholesome. The fewer mixtures there are in cooking, the more healthful is the food likely to be.

There is one caution as to the *mode* of eating which seems peculiarly needful to Americans. It is indispensable to good digestion, that food be well chewed and taken slowly. It needs to be thoroughly chewed and mixed with saliva, in order to prepare it for the action of the gastric juice, which, by the peristaltic motion, will be thus brought into contact with every one of the minute portions. It has been found that a solid lump of food requires much more time and labor of the stomach for digestion than divided substances.

It has also been found, that as each bolus, or mouthful, enters the stomach, the latter closes, until the portion received has had some time to move around and combine with the gastric juice, and that the orifice of the stomach resists the entrance of any more till this is accomplished. But, if the eater persists in swallowing fast, the stomach yields; the food is then poured in more rapidly than the organ can perform its duty of preparative digestion; and evil results are sooner or later developed. This exhibits the folly of those hasty meals, so common to travelers and to men of business, and shows why children should be taught to eat slowly.

After taking a full meal, it is very important to health that no great bodily or mental exertion be made till the labor of the stomach is over. Intense mental effort draws the blood to the head, and muscular exertions draw it to the muscles; and in consequence of this, the stomach loses the supply which it requires when performing its office. When the blood with its stimulating effects is thus withdrawn from the stomach, the adequate supply of gastric juice is not afforded, and indigestion is the result. The heaviness which follows a full meal is the indication which Nature gives of the need of quiet. When the meal is moderate, a sufficient quantity of gastric juice is exuded in an hour, or an hour and a half; after which, labor of body and mind may safely be resumed.

When undigested food remains in the stomach, and is at last thrown out into the bowels, it proves an irritating substance, producing an inflamed state in the lining of the stomach and other organs.

It is found that the stomach has the power of gradually accommodating its digestive powers to the food it habitually receives. Thus, animals which live on vegetables can gradually become accustomed to animal food; and the reverse is equally true. Thus, too, the human stomach can eventually accomplish the digestion of some kinds of food, which, at first, were indigestible.

But any changes of this sort should be gradual; as those which are sudden are trying to the powers of the stomach, by furnishing matter for which its gastric juice is not prepared.

Extremes of heat or cold are injurious to the process of digestion. Taking hot food or drink, habitually, tends to debilitate all the organs thus needlessly excited. In using cold substances, it is found that a certain degree of warmth in the stomach is indispensable to their digestion; so that, when the gastric juice is cooled below this temperature, it ceases to act. Indulging in large quantities of cold drinks, or eating ice-creams, after a meal, tends to reduce the temperature of the stomach, and thus to stop digestion. This shows the folly of those refreshments, in convivial meetings, where the guests are tempted to load the stomach with a variety such as would require the stomach of a stout farmer to digest; and then to wind up with ice-creams, thus lessening whatever ability might otherwise have existed to digest the heavy load. The fittest temperature for drinks, if taken when the food is in the digesting process, is blood heat. Cool drinks, and even ice, can be safely taken at other times, if not in excessive quantity. When the thirst is excessive, or the body weakened by fatigue, or when in a state of perspiration, large quantities of cold drinks are injurious.

Fluids taken into the stomach are not subject to the slow process of digestion, but are immediately absorbed and carried into the blood. This is the reason why liquid nourishment, more speedily than solid food, restores from exhaustion.

The minute vessels of the stomach absorb its fluids, which are carried into the blood, just as the minute extremities of the arteries open upon the inner surface of the stomach, and there exude the gastric juice from the blood.

When food is chiefly liquid, (soup, for example,) the fluid part is rapidly absorbed. The solid parts remain, to be acted on by the gastric juice. In the case of St. Martin,* in fifty minutes after taking soup, the fluids were absorbed, and the remainder was even thicker than is usual after eating solid food. This is the reason why soups are deemed bad for weak stomachs; as this residuum is more difficult of digestion than ordinary food.

Highly-concentrated food, having much nourishment in a small bulk, is not favorable to digestion, because it can not be properly acted on by the muscular contractions of the stomach, and is not so minutely divided as to enable the gastric juice to act properly. This is the reason why a certain *bulk* of food is needful to good digestion; and why those people who live on whale-oil and other highly nourishing food, in cold climates, mix vegetables and even sawdust with it to make it more acceptable and digestible. So in civilized lands, fruits and vegetables are mixed with more highly concentrated nourishment. For this reason also, soups, jellies, and arrow-root should have bread or crackers mixed with them. This affords another reason why coarse bread, of unbolted wheat, so often proves beneficial. Where, from inactive habits or other causes, the bowels become con-

---

* The individual here referred to—Alexis St. Martin—was a young Canadian, eighteen years of age, of a good constitution and robust health, who, in 1822, was accidentally wounded by the discharge of a musket which carried away a part of the ribs, lacerated one of the lobes of the lungs, and perforated the stomach, making a large aperture, which never closed; and which enabled Dr. Beaumont (a surgeon of the American army, stationed at Michilimackinac, under whose care the patient was placed) to witness all the processes of digestion and other functions of the body for several years.

stipated and sluggish, this kind of food proves the appropriate remedy.

One fact on this subject is worthy of notice. In England, under the administration of William Pitt, for two years or more there was such a scarcity of wheat that, to make it hold out longer, Parliament passed a law that the army should have all their bread made of unbolted flour. The result was, that the health of the soldiers improved so much as to be a subject of surprise to themselves, the officers, and the physicians. These last came out publicly and declared that the soldiers never before were so robust and healthy; and that disease had nearly disappeared from the army. The civic physicians joined and pronounced it the healthiest bread; and for a time schools, families, and public institutions used it almost exclusively. Even the nobility, convinced by these facts, adopted it for their common diet, and the fashion continued a long time after the scarcity ceased, until more luxurious habits resumed their sway.

We thus see why children should not have cakes and candies allowed them between meals. Besides being largely carbonaceous, these are highly concentrated nourishments, and should be eaten with more bulky and less nourishing substances. The most indigestible of all kinds of food are fatty and oily substances, if heated. It is on this account that pie-crust and articles boiled and fried in fat or butter are deemed not so healthful as other food.

The following, then, may be put down as the causes of a debilitated constitution from the misuse of food. Eating *too much*, eating *too often*, eating *too fast*, eating food and condiments that are *too stimulating*, eating food that is *too warm* or *too cold*, eating food that is *highly concentrated*, without a proper admixture of less nourishing matter, and eating hot food that is *difficult of digestion*.

X

HEALTHFUL DRINKS.

THERE is no direction in which a woman more needs both scientific knowledge and moral force than in using her influence to control her family in regard to stimulating beverages.

It is a point fully established by experience that the full development of the human body and the vigorous exercise of all its functions can be secured without the use of stimulating drinks. It is, therefore, perfectly safe to bring up children never to use them, no hazard being incurred by such a course.

It is also found by experience that there are two evils incurred by the use of stimulating drinks. The first is, their positive effect on the human system. Their peculiarity consists in so exciting the nervous system that all the functions of the body are accelerated, and the fluids are caused to move quicker than at their natural speed. This increased motion of the animal fluids always produces an agreeable effect on the mind. The intellect is invigorated, the imagination is excited, the spirits are enlivened; and these effects are so agreeable that all mankind, after having once experienced them, feel a great desire for their repetition.

But this temporary invigoration of the system is always followed by a diminution of the powers of the stimulated organs; so that, though in all cases this reaction may not be perceptible, it is invariably the result. It may be set down as the unchangeable rule of physiology, that stimulating drinks deduct from the powers of the constitution in exactly the proportion in which they operate to produce temporary invigoration.

The second evil is the temptation which always attends the use of stimulants. Their effect on the system is so agreeable, and the evils resulting are so imperceptible and distant, that there is a constant tendency to increase such excitement both in frequency and power. And the more the system is thus reduced in strength, the more craving is the desire for that which imparts a temporary invigoration. This process of increasing debility and increasing craving for the stimulus that removes it, often goes to such an extreme that the passion is perfectly uncontrollable, and mind and body perish under this baleful habit.

In this country there are three forms in which the use of such stimulants is common; namely, *alcoholic drinks, opium mixtures*, and *tobacco*. These are all alike in the main peculiarity of imparting that extra stimulus to the system which tends to exhaust its powers.

Multitudes in this nation are in the habitual use of some one of these stimulants; and each person defends the indulgence by certain arguments:

First, that the desire for stimulants is a natural propensity implanted in man's nature, as is manifest from the universal tendency to such indulgences in every nation. From this, it is inferred that it is an innocent desire, which ought to be gratified to some extent, and that the aim should be to keep it within the limits of temperance, instead of attempting to exterminate a natural propensity.

This is an argument which, if true, makes it equally proper for not only men, but women and children, to use opium, brandy, or tobacco as stimulating principles, provided they are used temperately. But if it be granted that perfect health and strength can be gained and secured without these stimulants, and that their peculiar effect is to diminish the power of the system in exactly the same proportion as they stimulate it, then there is no such thing as a temperate u unless they are so diluted as to destroy any stimulating power; and in this form they are seldom desired.

The other argument for their use is, that they are among the good things provided by the Creator for our gratification ; that, like all other blessings, they are exposed to abuse and excess ; and that we should rather seek to regulate their use than to banish them entirely.

This argument is based on the assumption that they are, like healthful foods and drinks, necessary to life and health, and injurious only by excess. But this is not true; for whenever they are used in any such strength as to be a gratification, they operate to a greater or less extent as stimulants; and to just such extent they wear out the powers of the constitution ; and it is abundantly proved that they are not, like food and drink, necessary to health. Such articles are designed for medicine and not for common use. There can be no argument framed to defend the use of one of them which will not justify women and children in most dangerous indulgences.

There are some facts recently revealed by the microscope in regard to alcoholic drinks, which every woman should understand and regard. It has been shown in a previous chapter that every act of mind, either by thought, feeling, or choice, causes the destruction of certain cells in the brain and nerves. It now is proved by microscopic science[*] that the kind of nutrition furnished to the brain by the blood to a certain extent decides future feelings, thoughts, and volitions. The cells of the brain not only abstract from the blood the healthful nutrition, but also are affected in shape, size, color, and action by unsuitable elements in the blood. This is especially the case when alcohol is taken into the stomach, from whence it is always carried to the brain. The consequence is, that it affects the nature and action of the

---

[*] For these statements the writer is indebted to Maudsley, a recent writer on Microscopic Physiology.

brain-cells, until a habit is formed which is *automatic;* that is, the mind loses the power of controlling the brain in its development of thoughts, feelings, and choices as it would in the natural state, and is itself controlled by the brain. In this condition a real disease of the brain is created, called *oino-mania,* (see *Glossary,*) and the only remedy is total abstinence, and that for a long period, from the alcoholic poison. And what makes the danger more fearful is, that the brain-cells never are so renewed but that this pernicious stimulus will bring back the disease in full force, so that a man once subject to it is never safe except by maintaining perpetual and total abstinence from every kind of alcoholic drink. Dr. Day, who for many years has had charge of an inebriate asylum, states that he witnessed the dissection of the brain of a man once an inebriate, but for many years in practice of total abstinence, and found its cells still in the weak and unnatural state produced by earlier indulgences.

There has unfortunately been a difference of opinion among medical men as to the use of alcohol. Liebig, the celebrated writer on animal chemistry, having found that both sugar and alcohol were heat-producing articles of food, framed a theory that alcohol is burnt in the lungs, giving off carbonic acid and water, and thus serving to warm the body. But modern science has proved that it is in the capillaries that animal heat is generated, and it is believed that alcohol lessens instead of increasing the power of the body to bear the cold. Sir John Ross, in his Arctic voyage, proved by his own experience and that of his men that cold-water drinkers could bear cold longer and were stronger than any who used alcohol.

Carpenter, a standard writer on physiology, says the objection to a habitual use of even small quantities of alcoholic drinks is, that "they are universally admitted to possess a poisonous character," and "tend to produce a morbid condition of body;" while "the capacity for enduring extremes of heat and cold, or of mental or bodily labor, is diminished rather than increased by their habitual employment."

Prof. J. Bigelow, of Harvard University, says, "Alcohol is highly stimulating, heating, and intoxicating, and its effects are so fascinating that when once experienced there is danger that the desire for them may be perpetuated."

Dr. Bell and Dr. Churchill, both high medical authorities, especially in lung disease, for which whisky is often recommended, come to the conclusion that " the opinion that alcoholic liquors have influence in preventing the deposition of tubercle is destitute of any foundation ; on the contrary, their use predisposes to tubercular deposition." And "where tubercle exists, alcohol has no effect in modifying the usual course, neither does it modify the morbid effects on the system."

Prof. Youmans, of New-York, says : " It has been demonstrated that alcoholic drinks prevent the natural changes in the blood, and obstruct the nutritive and reparative functions." He adds, " Chemical experiments have demonstrated that the action of alcohol on the digestive fluid is to destroy its active principle, the *pepsin*, thus confirming the observations of physiologists, that its use gives rise to serious disorders of the stomach and malignant aberration of the whole economy."

We are now prepared to consider the great principles of science, common sense, and religion, which should guide every woman who has any kind of influence or responsibility on this subject.

It is allowed by all medical men that pure water is perfectly healthful and supplies all the liquid needed by the body; and also that by proper means, which ordinarily are in the reach of all, water can be made sufficiently pure.

It is allowed by all that milk, and the juices of fruits, when taken into the stomach, furnish water that is always pure, and that our bread and vegetable food also supply it in large quantities. There are besides a great variety of agreeable and healthful beverages, made from the juices of fruit, containing no alcohol, and agreeable drinks, such as milk, cocoa, and chocolate, that contain no stimulating principles, and which are nourishing and healthful.

As one course, then, is perfectly safe and another involves great danger, it is wrong and sinful to choose the path of danger. There is no peril in drinking pure water, milk, the juices of fruits, and infusions that are nourishing and harmless. But there is great danger to the young, and to the commonwealth, in patronizing the sale and use of alcoholic drinks. The religion of Christ, in its distinctive feature, involves generous self-denial for the good of others, especially for the weaker members of society. It is on this principle that St. Paul sets forth his own example, " If meat make n.y brother to offend, I will eat no flesh while the world standeth, lest I make my brother to offend." And again he teaches, "We, then, that are strong ought to bear the infirmities of the weak, and not to please ourselves."

This Christian principle also applies to the common drinks of the family, tea and coffee.

It has been shown that the great end for which Jesus Christ came, and for which he instituted the family state, is the training of our whole race to virtue and happiness, with chief reference to an immortal existence. In this mission, of which woman is chief minister, as before stated, the distinctive feature is self-sacrifice of the wiser and stronger members to save and to elevate the weaker ones. The children and the servants are these weaker members, who by ignorance and want of habits of self-control are in most danger. It is in this aspect that we are to consider the expediency of using tea and coffee in a family.

These drinks are a most extensive cause of much of the nervous debility and suffering endured by American women; and relinquishing them would save an immense amount of such suffering. Moreover, all housekeepers will allow that

they can not regulate these drinks in their kitchens, where
the ignorant use them to excess.   There is little probability
that the present generation will make so decided a change
in their habits as to give up these beverages ; but the subject is presented rather in reference to forming the habits
of children.

It is a fact that tea and coffee are at first seldom or never
agreeable to children.   It is the mixture of milk, sugar, and
water, that reconciles them to a taste, which in this manner
gradually becomes agreeable.   Now suppose that those who
provide for a family conclude that it is not *their* duty to
give up entirely the use of stimulating drinks, may not the
case appear different in regard to teaching their children to
love such drinks ?   Let the matter be regarded thus : The
experiments of physiologists all prove that stimulants are
not needful to health, and that, as the general rule, they tend
to debilitate the constitution.   Is it right, then, for a parent
to tempt a child to drink what is not needful, when there
is a probability that it will prove, to some extent, an undermining drain on the constitution ?   Some constitutions can
bear much less excitement than others ; and in every family
of children, there is usually one or more of delicate organization, and consequently peculiarly exposed to dangers from
this source.   It is this child who ordinarily becomes the victim to stimulating drinks.   The tea and coffee which the
parents and the healthier children can use without immediate injury, gradually sap the energies of the feebler child,
who proves either an early victim or a living martyr to all
the sufferings that debilitated nerves inflict.   Can it be right
to lead children where all allow that there is some danger,
and where in many cases disease and death are met, when
another path is known to be perfectly safe ?

The impression common in this country, that *warm drinks*,
especially in winter, are more healthful than cold, is not
warranted by any experience, nor by the laws of the physical
system.   At dinner, cold drinks are universal, and no one

deems them injurious. It is only at the other two meals that they are supposed to be hurtful.

There is no doubt that *warm* drinks are healthful, and more agreeable than cold, at certain times and seasons; but it is equally true that drinks above blood-heat are not healthful. If a person should bathe in warm water every day, debility would inevitably follow ; for the frequent application of the stimulus of heat, like all other stimulants, eventually causes relaxation and weakness. If, therefore, a person is in the habit of drinking hot drinks twice a day, the teeth, throat, and stomach are gradually debilitated. This, most probably, is one of the causes of an early decay of the teeth, which is observed to be much more common among American ladies, than among those in European countries.

It has been stated to the writer, by an intelligent traveler who had visited Mexico, that it was rare to meet an individual with even a tolerable set of teeth, and that almost every grown person he met in the street had merely remnants of teeth. On inquiry into the customs of the country, it was found that it was the universal practice to take their usual beverage at almost the boiling-point ; and this doubtless was the chief cause of the almost entire want of teeth in that country. In the United States, it can not be doubted that much evil is done in this way by hot drinks. Most tea-drinkers consider tea as ruined if it stands until it reaches the healthful temperature for drink.

The following extract, from Dr. Andrew Combe, presents the opinion of most intelligent medical men on this subject.*

" *Water* is a safe drink for all constitutions, provided it be resorted to in obedience to the dictates of natural thirst

---

* The writer would here remark, in reference to extracts made from various authors, that, for the sake of abridging, she has often left out parts of a paragraph, but never so as to modify the meaning of the author. Some ideas, not connected with the subject in hand, are omitted, but none are altered.

only, and not of habit. Unless the desire for it is felt, there is no occasion for its use during a meal."

"The primary effect of all distilled and fermented liquors is to *stimulate the nervous system and quicken the circulation*. In infancy and childhood, the circulation is rapid and easily excited; and the nervous system is strongly acted upon even by the slightest external impressions. Hence, slight causes of irritation readily excite febrile and convulsive disorders. In youth, the natural tendency of the constitution is still to excitement, and consequently, as a general rule, the stimulus of fermented liquors is injurious."

These remarks show that parents, who find that stimulating drinks are not injurious to themselves, may mistake in inferring from this that they will not be injurious to their children.

Dr. Combe continues thus : "In mature age, when digestion is good, and the system in full vigor, if the mode of life be not too exhausting, the nervous functions and general circulation are in their best condition, and require no stimulus for their support. The bodily energy is then easily sustained by nutritious food and a regular regimen, and consequently artificial excitement only increases the wasting of the natural strength."

It may be asked, in this connection, why the stimulus of animal food is not to be regarded in the same light as that of stimulating drinks. In reply, a very essential difference may be pointed out. Animal food furnishes nutriment to the organs which it stimulates, but stimulating drinks excite the organs to quickened action without affording any nourishment.

It has been supposed by some that tea and coffee have, at least, a degree of nourishing power. But it is proved that it is the milk and sugar, and not the main portion of the drink, which imparts the nourishment. Tea has not one particle of nourishing properties ; and what little exists in the coffee-berry is lost by roasting it in the usual mode. All that these articles do, is simply *to stimulate without nourishing.*

Although there is little hope of banishing these drinks, there is still a chance that something may be gained in attempts to regulate their use by the rules of temperance. If, then, a housekeeper can not banish tea and coffee entirely, she may use her influence to prevent excess, both by her instructions, and by the power of control committed more or less to her hands.

It is important for every housekeeper to know that the health of a family very much depends on the *purity* of water used for cooking and drinking. There are three causes of impure and unhealthful water. One is, the existence in it of vegetable or animal matter, which can be remedied by filtering through sand and charcoal. Another cause is, the existence of mineral matter, especially in limestone countries, producing diseases of the bladder. This is remedied in a measure by boiling, which secures a deposit of the lime on the vessel used. The third cause is, the corroding of zinc and lead used in pipes and reservoirs, producing oxides that are slow poisons. The only remedy is prevention, by having supply-pipes made of iron, like gas-pipe, instead of zinc and lead ; or the lately invented lead pipe lined with tin, which metal is not corrosive. The obstacle to this is, that the trade of the plumbers would be greatly diminished by the use of reliable pipes. When water must be used from supply-pipes of lead or zinc, it is well to let the water run some time before drinking it and to use as little as possible, taking milk instead ; and being further satisfied for inner necessities by the water supplied by fruits and vegetables. The water in these is always pure. But in using milk as a drink, it must be remembered that it is also rich food, and that less of other food must be taken when milk is thus used, or bilious troubles will result from excess of food.

The use of opium, especially by women, is usually caused at first by medical prescriptions containing it. All that has been stated as to the effect of alcohol in the brain is true of opium; while, to break a habit thus induced is almost hopeless. Every woman who takes or who administers this drug, is dealing as with poisoned arrows, whose wounds are without cure.

The use of tobacco in this country, and especially among young boys, is increasing at a fearful rate. On this subject, we have the unanimous opinion of all medical men; the following being specimens.

A distinguished medical writer thus states the case: "Every physician knows that the agreeable sensations that tempt to the use of tobacco are caused by *nicotine*, which is a rank poison, as much so as prussic acid or arsenic. When smoked, the poison is absorbed by the blood of the mouth, and carried to the brain. When chewed, the nicotine passes to the blood through the mouth and stomach. In both cases, the whole nervous system is thrown into abnormal excitement to expel the poison, and it is this excitement that causes agreeable sensations. The excitement thus caused is invariably followed by a diminution of nervous power, in exact proportion to the preceding excitement to expel the evil from the system."

Few will dispute the general truth and effect of the above statement, so that the question is one to be settled on the same principle as applies to the use of alcoholic drinks. Is it, then, according to the generous principles of Christ's religion, for those who are strong and able to bear this poison, to tempt the young, the ignorant, and the weak to a practice not needful to any healthful enjoyment, and which leads multitudes to disease, and often to vice? For the use of tobacco tends always to lessen nerve-power, and probably every one out of five that indulges in its use awakens a morbid craving for increased stimulus, lessens the power of self-control, diminishes the strength of the constitution; and sets an example that influences the weak to the path of danger and of frequent ruin.

The great danger of this age is an increasing, intense

worldliness, and disbelief in the foundation principle of the religion of Christ, that we are to reap through everlasting ages the consequences of habits formed in this life. In the light of his word, they only who are truly wise " shall shine as the firmament, and they that turn many to righteousness, as the stars, forever and ever."

It is increased *faith* or *belief* in the teachings of Christ's religion, as to the influence of this life upon the *life to come,* which alone can save our country and the world from that inrushing tide of sensualism and worldliness, now seeming to threaten the best hopes and prospects of our race.

And woman, as the chief educator of our race, and the prime minister of the family state, is bound in the use of meats and drinks to employ the powerful and distinctive motives of the religion of Christ in forming habits of temperance and benevolent self-sacrifice for the good of others.

XI.

CLEANLINESS.

BOTH the health and comfort of a family depend, to a great extent, on cleanliness of the person and the family surroundings. True cleanliness of person involves the scientific treatment of the skin. This is the most complicated organ of the body, and one through which the health is affected more than through any other; and no persons can or will be so likely to take proper care of it as those by whom its construction and functions are understood.

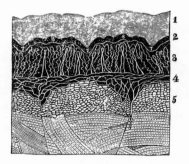

Fig. 57.

Fig. 57 is a very highly magnified portion of the skin. The layer marked 1 is the outside, very thin skin, called the *cuticle* or *scarf skin*. This consists of transparent layers of minute cells, which are constantly decaying and being renewed, and the white scurf that passes from the skin to the clothing is a decayed portion of these cells. This part of the skin has neither nerves nor blood-vessels.

The dark layer, marked 2, 7, 8, is that portion of the true skin which gives the external color marking diverse races. In the portion of the dark layer marked 3, 4, is seen a network of nerves which run from two branches of the nervous trunks coming from the spinal marrow. These are nerves of sensation, by which the sense of touch or feeling is performed. Fig. 58 represents the

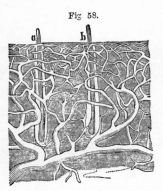

Fig. 58.

blood-vessels, (intermingled with the nerves of the skin,) which divide into minute capillaries, that act like the capillaries of the lungs, taking oxygen from the air, and giving out carbonic acid. At *a* and *b* are seen the roots of two hairs, which abound in certain parts of the skin, and are nourished by the blood of the capillaries.

At Fig. 59 is a magnified view of another set of vessels, called the *lymphatics* or *absorbents*. These are extremely minute vessels that interlace with the nerves and blood-vessels of the skin. Their office is to aid in collecting the use-

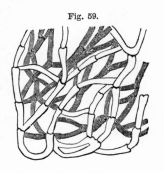

Fig. 59.

less, injurious, or decayed matter, and carry it to certain reservoirs, from which it passes into some of the large veins, to be thrown out through the lungs, bowels, kidneys, or skin. These *absorbent* or *lymphatic vessels* have mouths opening on the surface of the true skin, and, though covered by the cuticle, they can absorb both liquids and solids that are placed in close contact with the skin. In proof of this, one of the main trunks of the lymphatics in the hand can be cut off from all communication with other portions, and tied up: and if the hand is immersed in milk a given time, it will be found that the milk has been absorbed through the cuticle and fills the lymphatics. In this way, long-con-

tinued blisters on the skin will introduce the blistering matter into the blood through the absorbents, and then the kidneys will take it up from the blood passing through them to
carry it out of the body, and thus become irritated and inflamed by it.

There are also oil-tubes, imbedded in the skin, that draw
off oil from the blood. This issues on the surface and spreads
over the cuticle to keep it soft and moist.

Fig. 60.

But the most curious part of the skin
is the system of innumerable minute
perspiration-tubes. Fig. 60 is a drawing of one very greatly magnified.
These tubes open on the cuticle, and
the openings are called pores of the
skin. They descend into the true skin,
and there form a coil, as is seen in the
drawing. These tubes are hollow, like
a pipe-stem, and their inner surface
consists of wonderfully minute capillaries filled with the impure venous
blood. And in these small tubes the
same process is going on as takes place
when the carbonic acid and water of
the blood are exhaled from the lungs.
The capillaries of these tubes through
the whole skin of the body are thus
constantly exhaling the noxious and decayed particles of
the body, just as the lungs pour them out through the
mouth and nose.

It has been shown that the perspiration-tubes are coiled
up into a ball at their base. The number and extent of
these tubes are astonishing. In a square inch on the palm
of the hand have been counted, through a microscope, thirty-five hundred of these tubes. Each one of them is about
a quarter of an inch in length, including its coils. This
makes the united lengths of these little tubes to be seventy-

three feet to a square inch. Their united length over the whole body is thus calculated to be equal to *twenty-eight miles.* What a wonderful apparatus this ! And what mischiefs must ensue when the drainage from the body of such an extent as this becomes obstructed !

But the inside of the body also has a skin, as have all its organs. The interior of the head, the throat, the gullet, the lungs, the stomach, and all the intestines, are lined with a skin. This is called the *mucous membrane,* because it is constantly secreting from the blood a slimy substance called *mucus.* When it accumulates in the lungs, it is called *phlegm.* This inner skin also has nerves, blood-vessels, and lymphatics. The outer skin joins to the inner at the mouth, the nose, and other openings of the body, and there is a constant sympathy between the two skins, and thus between the inner organs and the surface of the body.

SECRETING ORGANS.

Those vessels of the body which draw off certain portions of the blood and change it into a new form, to be employed for service or to be thrown out of the body, are called *secreting organs.* The skin in this sense is a secreting organ, as its perspiration-tubes secrete or separate the bad portions of the blood, and send them off.

Of the internal secreting organs, the *liver* is the largest. Its chief office is to secrete from the blood all matter not properly supplied with oxygen. For this purpose, a set of veins carries the blood of all the lower intestines to the liver, where the imperfectly oxidized matter is drawn off in the form of *bile,* and accumulated in a reservoir called the *gall-bladder.* Thence it passes to the place where the smaller intestines receive the food from the stomach, and there it mixes with this food. Then it passes through the long intestines, and is thrown out of the body through the rectum. This shows how it is, that want of pure and cool air and exercise causes excess of bile, from lack of oxygen. The liver also has arterial blood sent to nourish it, and corresponding veins to return this blood to the heart. So there are two sets of blood-vessels for the liver—one to secrete the bile, and the other to nourish the organ itself.

The kidneys secrete from the arteries that pass through them all excess of water in the blood, and certain injurious substances. These are carried through small tubes to the bladder, and thence thrown out of the body.

The *pancreas*, a whitish gland, situated in the abdomen below the stomach, secretes from the arteries that pass through it the pancreatic juice, which unites with the bile from the liver, in preparing the food for nourishing the body.

There are certain little glands near the eyes that secrete the tears, and others near the mouth that secrete the saliva, or spittle.

These organs all have arteries sent to them to nourish them, and also veins to carry away the impure blood. At the same time, they secrete from the arterial blood the peculiar fluid which it is their office to supply.

All the food that passes through the lower intestines which is not drawn off by the lacteals or by some of these secreting organs, passes from the body through a passage called the rectum.

Learned men have made very curious experiments to ascertain how much the several organs throw out of the body, It is found that the skin throws off five out of eight pounds of the food and drink, or probably about three or four pounds a day. The lungs throw off one quarter as much as the skin, or about a pound a day. The remainder is carried off by the kidneys and lower intestines.

There is such a sympathy and connection between all the organs of the body, that when one of them is unable to work, the others perform the office of the feeble one. Thus, if the skin has its perspiration-tubes closed up by a chill, then all the poisonous matter that would have been thrown out through them must be emptied out either by the lungs, kidneys, or bowels.

When all these organs are strong and healthy, they can bear this increased labor without injury. But if the lungs are weak, the blood sent from the skin by the chill engorges the weak blood-vessels, and produces an inflammation of the lungs. Or it increases the discharge of a slimy mucous substance, that exudes from the skin of the lungs. This fills up the air-vessels, and would very soon end life, were it not for the spasms of the lungs, called *coughing*, which throw off this substance.

If, on the other hand, the bowels are weak, a chill of the skin sends the blood into all the blood-vessels of the intestines, and produces inflammation there, or else an excessive secretion of the mucous substance, which is called a *diarrhea*. Or if the kidneys are weak, there is an increased secretion and discharge from them, to an unhealthy and injurious extent.

This connection between the skin and internal organs is shown, not only by the internal effects of a chill on the skin; but by the sympathetic effect on the skin when these internal organs suffer. For example, there are some kinds of food that will irritate and influence the stomach or the bowels; and this, by sympathy, will produce an immediate eruption on the skin. Some persons, on eating strawberries, will immediately be affected with a nettle-rash. Others can not eat certain shell-fish without being affected in this way. Many humors on the face are caused by a diseased state of the internal organs with which the skin sympathizes.

This short account of the construction of the skin, and of its intimate connection with the internal organs, shows the philosophy of those modes of medical treatment that are addressed to this portion of the body.

It is on this powerful agency that the steam-doctors rely, when, by moisture and heat, they stimulate all the innu merable perspiration-tubes and lymphatics to force out from the body a flood of unnaturally excited secretions; while it is "kill or cure," just as the chance may meet or oppose the demands of the case. It is the skin also that is the chief basis of medical treatment in the Water Cure, whose slow processes are as much safer as they are slower.

At the same time it is the ill-treatment or neglect of the skin which, probably, is the cause of disease and decay to an incredible extent. The various particulars in which this may be seen will now be pointed out. In the management and care of this wonderful and complex part of the body, many mistakes have been made.

The most common one is the misuse of the bath, especially since cold water cures have come into use. This mode of medical treatment originated with an ignorant peasant, amid a population where outdoor labor had strengthened nerves and muscles and imparted rugged powers to every part of the body. It was then introduced into England and America without due consideration or knowledge of the diseases, habits, or real condition of patients, especially of women. The consequence was a mode of treatment too severe and exhausting; and many practices were spread abroad not warranted by true medical science.

But in spite of these mistakes and abuses, the treatment of the skin for disease by the use of cold water has become an accepted doctrine of the most learned medical practitioners. It is now held by all such that fevers can be detected in their distinctive features by the thermometer, and that all fevers can be reduced by cold baths and packing in the wet sheet, in the mode employed in all water-cures. Directions for using this method will be given in another place.

It has been supposed that large bath-tubs for immersing the whole person are indispensable to the proper cleaning of the skin. This is not so. A wet towel, applied every morning to the skin, followed by friction in pure air, is all that is absolutely needed; although a full bath is a great luxury.

Access of air to every part of the skin when its perspiratory tubes are cleared and its blood-vessels are filled by friction is the best ordinary bath.

In early life, children should be washed all over, every night or morning, to remove impurities from the skin. But in this process, careful regard should be paid to the peculiar constitution of a child. Very nervous children sometimes revolt from cold water, and like a tepid bath. Others prefer a cold bath; and nature should be the guide. It must be remembered that the skin is the great organ of sensation, and in close connection with brain, spine, and nerve-centres: so that what a strong nervous system can bear with advantage is too powerful and exhausting for another. As age advances, or as disease debilitates the body, great care should be taken not to overtax the nervous system by sudden shocks, or to diminish its powers by withdrawing animal heat to excess. Persons lacking robustness should bathe or use friction in a warm room ; and if very delicate, should expose only a portion of the body at once to cold air.

Johnson, a celebrated writer on agricultural chemistry, tells of an experiment by friction on the skin of pigs, whose skins are like that of the human race. He treated six of these animals with a curry-comb seven weeks, and left three other pigs untouched. The result was a gain of thirty-three pounds more of weight, with the use of five bushels less of food for those curried, than for the neglected ones. This result was owing to the fact that all the functions of the body were more perfectly performed when, by friction, the skin was kept free from filth and the blood in it exposed to the air. The same will be true of the human skin. A calculation has been made on this fact, by which it is estimated that a man, by proper care of his skin, would save over thirty-one dollars in food yearly, which is the interest on over five hundred dollars. If men will give as much care to their own skin as they give to currying a horse, they will gain both health and wealth.

XII.

THERE is no duty of those persons having control of a family where principle and practice are more at variance than in regulating the dress of young girls, especially at the most important and critical period of life. It is a difficult duty for parents and teachers to contend with the power of fashion, which at this time of a young girl's life is frequently the ruling thought, and when to be out of the fashion, to be odd and not dress as all her companions do, is a mortification and grief that no argument or instructions can relieve. The mother is often so overborne that, in spite of her better wishes, the daughter adopts modes of dress alike ruinous to health and to beauty.

The greatest protection against such an emergency is to train a child to understand the construction of her own body and to impress upon her, in early days, her obligations to the invisible Friend and Guardian of her life, the "Former of her body and the Father of her spirit," who has committed to her care so precious and beautiful a casket. And the more she can be made to realize the skill and beauty of construction shown in her earthly frame, the more will she feel the obligation to protect it from injury and abuse.

It is a singular fact that the war of fashion has attacked most fatally what seems to be the strongest foundation and defense of the body, the bones. For this reason, the construction and functions of this part of the body will now receive attention.

The bones are composed of two substances, one animal.

and the other mineral. The animal part is a very fine network, called *cellular membrane.* In this are deposited the harder mineral substances, which are composed principally of carbonate and phosphate of lime. In very early life, the bones consist chiefly of the animal part, and are then soft and pliant. As the child advances in age, the bones grow harder, by the gradual deposition of the phosphate of lime, which is supplied by the food, and carried to the bones by the blood. In old age, the hardest material preponderates; making the bones more brittle than in earlier life.

The bones are covered with a thin skin or membrane, filled with small blood-vessels which convey nourishment to them.

Where the bones unite with others to form joints, they are covered with *cartilage*, which is a smooth, white, elastic substance. This enables the joints to move smoothly, while its elasticity prevents injuries from sudden jars.

The joints are bound together by strong, elastic bands called *ligaments*, which hold them firmly and prevent dislocation.

Between the ends of the bones that unite to form joints are small sacks or bags, that contain a soft lubricating fluid. This answers the same purpose for the joints as oil in making machinery work smoothly, while the supply is constant and always in exact proportion to the demand.

If you will examine the leg of some fowl, you can see the cartilage that covers the ends of the bones at the joints, and the strong white ligaments that bind the joints together.

The health of the bones depends on the proper nourishment and exercise of the body as much as that of any other part. When a child is feeble and unhealthy, or when it grows up without exercise, the bones do not become firm and hard as they are when the body is healthfully developed by exercise. The size as well as the strength of the bones, to a certain extent, also depend upon exercise and good health.

The chief supporter of the body is the spine, which consists of twenty-four small bones, interlocked or hooked into each other, while between them are elastic cushions of cartilage which aid in preserving the upright, natural position. Fig. 61 shows three of the spinal bones, hooked into each other, the dark spaces showing the disks or flat circular plates of cartilage between them.

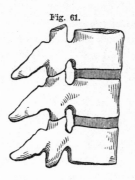

Fig. 61.

The spine is held in its proper position, partly by the ribs, partly by muscles, partly by aid of the elastic disks, and partly by the close packing of the intestines in front of it.

The upper part of the spine is often thrown out of its proper position by constant stooping of the head over books or work. This affects the elastic disks so that they grow thick at the back side and thinner at the front side by such constant pressure. The result is the awkward projection of the head forward which is often seen in schools and colleges.

Another distortion of the spine is produced by tight dress around the waist. The liver occupies the right side of the body and is a solid mass, while on the other side is the larger part of the stomach, which is often empty. The consequence of tight dress around the waist is a constant pressure of the spine toward the unsupported part where the stomach lies. Thus the elastic disks again are compressed; till they become thinner on one side than the other, and harden into that condition. This produces what is called the *lateral curvature of the spine*, making one shoulder higher than the other.

The compression of the lower part of the waist is especially dangerous at the time young girls first enter society and are tempted to dress according to the fashion. Many a school-girl, whose waist was originally of a proper and healthful size, has gradually pressed the soft bones of youth until the lower ribs that should rise and fall with every breath, become entirely unused. Then the abdominal breathing, performed by the lower part of the lungs, ceases; the whole system becomes reduced in strength; the abdominal muscles that hold up the interior organs become weak, and the upper ones gradually sink upon the lower.

This pressure of the upper interior organs upon the lower ones, by tight dress, is increased by the weight of clothing resting on the hips and abdomen. Corsets, as usually worn, have no support from the shoulders, and consequently all the weight of dress resting upon or above them presses upon the hips and abdomen, and this in such a way as to throw out of use and thus weaken the most important supporting muscles of the abdomen, and impede abdominal breathing.

The diaphragm is a kind of muscular floor, extending across the centre of the body, on which the heart and lungs rest. Beneath it are the liver, stomach, and the abdominal viscera, or intestines, which are supported by the abdominal muscles, running upward, downward, and crosswise. When these muscles are thrown out of use, they lose their power, the whole system of organs mainly resting on them for support can not continue in their naturally snug, compact, and rounded form, but become separated, elongated, and unsupported. The *stomach* begins to draw from above instead of resting on the viscera beneath. This in some cases causes dull and wandering pains, a sense of pulling at the centre of the chest, and a drawing downward at the pit of the stomach. Then as the support beneath is really *gone,* there is what is often called " a feeling of *goneness.*" This is sometimes relieved by food, which, so long as it remains in a solid form, helps to hold up the falling superstructure.

This displacement of the stomach, liver, and spleen interrupts their healthful functions, and dyspepsia and biliary difficulties not unfrequently are the result.

As the stomach and its appendages fall downward, the *diaphragm*, which holds up the heart and lungs, must descend also. In this state of things, the inflation of the lungs is less and less aided by the abdominal muscles, and is confined chiefly to their upper portion. Breathing sometimes thus becomes quicker and shorter on account of the elongated or debilitated condition of the assisting organs. Consumption not unfrequently results from this cause.

The *heart* also feels the evil. "Palpitations," "flutterings," "sinking feelings," all show that, in the language of Scripture, "the heart trembleth, and is moved out of its place."

But the *lower intestines* are the greatest sufferers from this dreadful abuse of nature. Having the weight of all the unsupported organs above pressing them into unnatural and distorted positions, the passage of the food is interrupted, and inflammations, indurations, and constipation are the frequent result. Dreadful ulcers and cancers may be traced in some instances to this cause.

Although these internal displacements are most common among women, some foolish members of the other sex are adopting customs of dress, in girding the central portion of the body, that tend to similar results.

But this distortion brings upon woman peculiar distresses. The pressure of the whole superincumbent mass on the pelvic or lower organs induces sufferings proportioned in acuteness to the extreme delicacy and sensitiveness of the parts thus crushed. And the intimate connection of these organs with the brain and whole nervous system renders injuries thus inflicted the causes of the most extreme anguish, both of body and mind. This evil is becoming so common, not only among married women, but among young girls, as to be a just cause for universal alarm.

How very common these sufferings are, few but the medical profession can realize, because they are troubles that must be concealed. Many a woman is moving about in uncomplaining agony who, with any other trouble involving equal suffering, would be on her bed surrounded by sympathizing friends.

The terrible sufferings that are sometimes thus induced can never be conceived of, or at all appreciated from, any use of language. Nothing that the public can be made to believe on this subject will ever equal the reality. Not only mature persons and mothers, but fair young girls sometimes, are shut up for months and years as helpless and suffering invalids from this cause. This may be found all over the land. And there frequently is a horrible extremity of suffering in certain forms of this evil, which no woman of feeble constitution can ever be certain may not be her doom. Not that in all cases this extremity is involved, but none can say who will escape it.

In regard to this, if one must choose for a friend or a child, on the one hand, the horrible torments inflicted by savage Indians or cruel inquisitors on their victims, or, on the other, the protracted agonies that result from such deformities and displacements, sometimes the former would be a merciful exchange.

And yet this is the fate that is coming to meet the young as well as the mature in every direction. And tender parents are unconsciously leading their lovely and hapless daughters to this awful doom.

There is no excitement of the imagination in what is here indicated. If the facts and details could be presented, they would send a groan of terror all over the land. For it is not one class, or one section, that is endangered. In every part of our country the evil is progressing.

And, as if these dreadful ills were not enough, there have been added methods of medical treatment at once useless, torturing to the mind, and involving great liability to immoralities.

In hope of abating these evils, drawings are given (Fig. 62 and Fig. 63) of the front and back of a jacket that will

Fig. 62.

preserve the advantages of the corset without its evils. This jacket may at first be fitted to the figure with corsets underneath it, just like the waist of a dress. Then, delicate whalebones can be used to stiffen the jacket, so that it will take the proper shape, when the corset may be dispensed with. The buttons below are to hold all articles of dress below the waist by button-holes. By this method, the bust is supported as well as by corsets, while the shoulders support from above, as they should do, the weight of the dress below. No stiff bone should be allowed to press in front, and the jacket should be so loose that a full breath can be inspired with ease, while in a sitting position.

The proper way to dress a young girl is to have a cotton or flannel close-fitting jacket next the body, to which the drawers should be buttoned. Over this, place the chemise; and over that, such a jacket as the one here drawn, to which should be buttoned the hoops and other skirts. Thus every article of dress will be supported by the shoulders. The sleeves of the jacket can be omitted, and in that case a strong lining, and also a tape binding, must surround the arm-hole, which should be loose.

Fig. 63.

It is hoped that increase of intelligence and moral power among mothers, and a combination among them to regulate fashions, may banish the pernicious practices that have prevailed. If a school-girl dress without corsets and without tight belts could be established as a fashion, it would be one step gained in the right direction. Then if mothers could secure daily domestic exercise in chambers, eating-rooms and parlors in loose dresses, a still farther advance would be secured.

A friend of the writer informs her that her daughter had her wedding outfit made up by a fashionable milliner in Paris, and every dress was beautifully fitted to the form, and yet was not compressing to any part. This was done too without the use of corsets, the stiffening being delicate and yielding whalebones.

Not only parents but all having the care of young girls, especially those at boarding-schools, have a fearful responsibility resting upon them in regard to this important duty.

In regard to the dressing of young children, much discretion is needed to adapt dress to circumstances and peculiar constitutions. The leading fact must be borne in mind that the skin is made strong and healthful by exposure to light and pure air, while cold air, if not excessive, has a tonic influence. If the skin of infants is rubbed with the hand till red with blood, and then exposed naked to sun and air in a well-ventilated room, it will be favorable to health.

There is a constitutional difference in the skin of different children in regard to retaining the animal heat manufactured within, so that some need more clothing than others for comfort. Nature is a safe guide to a careful nurse and mother, and will indicate by the looks and actions of a child when more clothing is needful. As a general rule, it is safe for a healthful child to wear as little clothing as suffices to keep it from complaining of cold. Fifty years ago, it was not common for children to wear as much under-clothing as they now do. The writer well remembers how even girls, though not of strong constitutions, used to play for hours in the snow-drifts without the protection of drawers, kept warm by exercise and occasional runs to an open fire. And multitudes of children grew to vigorous maturity through similar exposures to cold air-baths, and without the frequent colds and sicknesses so common among children of the present day, who are more carefully housed and warmly dressed. But care was taken that the feet should be kept dry and warmly clad, because, circulation being feebler in the extremities, this precaution was important.

It must also be considered that age brings with it decrease in vigor of circulation, and the consequent generation of heat, so that more warmth of air and clothing is needed at an advanced period of life than is suitable for the young.

These are the general principles which must be applied with modification to each individual case. A child of delicate constitution must have more careful protection from cold air than is desirable for one more vigorous, while the leading general principle is retained that cold air is a healthful tonic for the skin whenever it does not produce an uncomfortable chilliness.

XIII.

GOOD COOKING.

THERE are but a few things on which health and happiness depend more than on the manner in which food is cooked. You may make houses enchantingly beautiful, hang them with pictures, have them clean and airy and convenient; but if the stomach is fed with sour bread and burnt meats, it will raise such rebellions that the eyes will see no beauty anywhere. The abundance of splendid material we have in America is in great contrast with the style of cooking most prevalent in our country. How often, in journeys, do we sit down to tables loaded with material, originally of the very best kind, which has been so spoiled in the treatment that there is really nothing to eat! Green biscuits with acrid spots of alkali; sour yeast-bread; meat slowly simmered in fat till it seemed like grease itself, and slowly congealing in cold grease; and above all, that unpardonable enormity, strong butter! How one longs to show people what might have been done with the raw material out of which all these monstrosities were concocted!

There is no country where an ample, well-furnished table is more easily spread, and for that reason, perhaps, none where the bounties of Providence are more generally neglected. Considering that our resources are greater than those of any other civilized people, our results are comparatively poorer.

It is said that a list of the summer vegetables which are exhibited on New-York hotel-tables being shown to a French *artiste*, he declared that to serve such a dinner properly

would take till midnight.   A traveler can not but be struck
with our national plenteousness, on returning from a Con-
tinental tour, and going directly from the ship to a New-
York hotel, in the bounteous season of autumn.   For
months habituated to neat little bits of chop or poultry,
garnished with the inevitable cauliflower or potato, which
seemed to be the sole possibility after the reign of green
peas was' over; to sit down all at once to such a carnival ! to
such ripe, juicy tomatoes, raw or cooked; cucumbers in brittle
slices; rich, yellow sweet-potatoes; broad lima-beans, and
beans of other and various names; tempting ears of Indian-
corn steaming in enormous piles ; great smoking tureens of
the savory succotash, an Indian gift to the table for which
civilization need not blush; sliced egg-plant in delicate frit-
ters; and marrow-squashes, of creamy pulp and sweetness;
a rich variety, embarrassing to the appetite, and perplexing
to the choice.

Verily, the thought must often occur that the vegetarian
doctrine preached in America leaves a man quite as much
as he has capacity to eat or enjoy, and that in the midst of
such tantalizing abundance he has really lost the apology,
which elsewhere bears him out in preying upon his less gifted
and accomplished animal neighbors.

But with all this, the American table, taken as a whole,
is inferior to that of England or France.   It presents a fine
abundance of material, carelessly and poorly treated.   The
management of food is nowhere in the world, perhaps,
more slovenly and wasteful.   Every thing betokens that want
of care that waits on abundance; there are great capabilities and poor execution.   A tourist through England can
seldom fail, at the quietest country-inn, of finding himself
served with the essentials of English table-comfort—his
mutton-chop done to a turn, his steaming little private apparatus for concocting his own tea, his choice pot of marmalade
or slice of cold ham, and his delicate rolls and creamy butter, all served with care and neatness. In France, one never

asks in vain for delicious *café-au-lait*, good bread and butter, a nice omelet, or some savory little portion of meat with a French name. But to a tourist taking like chance in American country-fare, what is the prospect? What is the coffee? what the tea? and the meat? and above all, the butter?

In writing on cooking, the main topics should be first, bread; second, butter; third, meat; fourth, vegetables; and fifth, tea—by which last is meant, generically, all sorts of warm, comfortable drinks served out in tea-cups, whether they be called tea, coffee, chocolate, broma, or what not.

If these five departments are all perfect, the great ends of domestic cookery are answered, so far as the comfort and well-being of life are concerned. There exists another department, which is often regarded by culinary amateurs and young aspirants as the higher branch and very collegiate course of practical cookery; to wit, confectionery, by which is designated all pleasing and complicated compounds of sweets and spices, devised not for health and nourishment, and strongly suspected of interfering with both—mere tolerated gratifications of the palate, which we eat, not with the expectation of being benefited, but only with the hope of not being injured by them. In this large department rank all sorts of cakes, pies, preserves, etc., whose excellence is often attained by treading under foot and disregarding the five grand essentials.

There is many a table garnished with three or four kinds of well-made cake, compounded with citron and spices and all imaginable good things, where the meat was tough and greasy, the bread some hot preparation of flour, lard, saleratus, and acid, and the butter unutterably detestable, where, if the mistress of the feast had given the care, time, and labor to preparing the simple items of bread, butter, and meat, that she evidently had given to the preparation of these extras, the lot of her guests and family might be much more comfortable.

But she does not think of these common articles as consti
tuting a good table. So long as she has puff pastry, rich
black cake, clear jelly and preserves, she considers that
such unimportant matters as bread, butter, and meat may
take care of themselves. It is the same inattention to common things as that which leads people to build houses with
stone fronts, and window-caps and expensive front-door
trimmings, without bathing-rooms or fireplaces, or venti-
lators.

Those who go into the country looking for summer board
in farm-houses know perfectly well that a table where the
butter is always fresh, the tea and coffee of the best kinds and
well made, and the meats properly kept, dressed, and served,
is the one table of a hundred, the fabulous enchanted island.
It seems impossible to get the idea into the minds of many
people that what is called common food, carefully prepared,
becomes, in virtue of that very care and attention, a delicacy,
superseding the necessity of artificially compounded dainties.

To begin, then, with the very foundation of a good table
—*Bread :* What ought it to be ?

It should be light, sweet, and tender. This matter
of lightness is the distinctive line between savage and
civilized bread. The savage mixes simple flour and water into balls of paste, which he throws into boiling
water, and which come out solid, glutinous masses, of which
his common saying is, "Man eat dis, he no die," which a
facetious traveler who was obliged to subsist on it inter-
preted to mean, "Dis no kill you, nothing will." In short,
it requires the stomach of a wild animal or of a savage to
digest this primitive form of bread, and of course more or
less attention in all civilized modes of bread-making is giv-
en to producing lightness. By lightness is meant simply
that in order to facilitate digestion the particles are to be
separated from each other by little holes or air-cells ; and
all the different methods of making light bread are neither
more nor less than the formation of bread with these air
cells.

So far as we know, there are four practicable methods of aerating bread; namely, by fermentation; by effervescence of an acid and an alkali; by aerated egg, or egg which has been filled with air by the process of beating; and lastly, by pressure of some gaseous substance into the paste, by a process much resembling the impregnation of water in a soda-fountain. All these have one and the same object— to give us the cooked particles of our flour separated by such permanent air-cells as will enable the stomach more readily to digest them.

A very common mode of aerating bread in America is by the effervescence of an acid and an alkali in the flour. The carbonic acid gas thus formed produces minute air-cells in the bread, or, as the cook says, makes it light. When this process is performed with exact attention to chemical laws, so that the acid and alkali completely neutralize each other, leaving no overplus of either, the result is often very palatable. The difficulty is, that this is a happy conjunction of circumstances which seldom occurs. The acid most commonly employed is that of sour milk, and, as milk has many degrees of sourness, the rule of a certain quantity of alkali to the pint must necessarily produce very different results at different times. As an actual fact where this mode of making bread prevails, as we lament to say it does to a great extent in this country, one finds five cases of failure to one of success.

It is a woeful thing that the daughters of our land have abandoned the old respectable mode of yeast-brewing and bread-raising for this specious substitute, so easily made, and so seldom well made. The green, clammy, acrid substance, called biscuit, which many of our worthy republicans are obliged to eat in these days, is wholly unworthy of the men and women of the republic. Good patriots ought not to be put off in that way—they deserve better fare.

As an occasional variety, as a household convenience for obtaining bread or biscuit at a moment's notice, the process of effervescence may be retained ; but we earnestly entreat American housekeepers, in scriptural language, to stand in the way and ask for the old paths, and return to the good yeast-bread of their sainted grandmothers.

If acid and alkali must be used, by all means let them be mixed in due proportions. No cook should be left to guess and judge for herself about this matter. There are articles made by chemical rule which produce very perfect results, and the use of them obviates the worst dangers in making bread by effervescence.

Of all processes of aeration in bread-making, the oldest and most time-honored mode is by fermentation. That this was known in the days of our Saviour is evident from the forcible simile in which he compares the silent permeating force of truth in human society to the very familiar household process of raising bread by a little yeast.

There is, however, one species of yeast, much used in some parts of the country, against which protest should be made. It is called salt-risings, or milk-risings, and is made by mixing flour, milk, and a little salt together, and leaving them to ferment. The bread thus produced is often very attractive, when new and made with great care. It is white and delicate, with fine, even air-cells. It has, however, when kept, some characteristics which remind us of the terms in which our old English Bible describes the effect of keeping the manna of the ancient Israelites, which we are informed, in words more explicit than agreeable, " stank, and bred worms." If salt-rising bread does not fulfill the whole of this unpleasant description, it certainly does emphatically a part of it. The smell which it has in baking, and when more than a day old, suggests the inquiry, whether it is the saccharine or the putrid fermentation with which it is raised. Whoever breaks a piece of it after a day or two, will often see minute filaments or clammy strings drawing out from the fragments, which, with the unmistakable smell, will cause him to pause before consummating a nearer acquaintance.

The fermentation of flour by means of brewer's or distiller's yeast produces, if rightly managed, results far more palatable and wholesome. The only requisites for success in it are, first, good materials, and, second, great care in small things. There are certain low-priced or damaged kinds of flour which can never by any kind of domestic chemistry be made into good bread; and to those persons whose stomachs forbid them to eat gummy, glutinous paste, under the name of bread, there is no economy in buying these poor brands, even at half the price of good flour.

But good flour and good yeast being supposed, with a temperature favorable to the development of fermentation, the whole success of the process depends on the thorough diffusion of the proper proportion of yeast through the whole mass, and on stopping the subsequent fermentation at the precise and fortunate point. The true housewife makes her bread the sovereign of her kitchen—its behests must be attended to in all critical points and moments, no matter what else be postponed.

She who attends to her bread only when she has done this, and arranged that, and performed the other, very often finds that the forces of nature will not wait for her. The snowy mass, perfectly mixed, kneaded with care and strength, rises in its beautiful perfection till the moment comes for filling the air-cells by baking. A few minutes now, and the acetous fermentation will begin, and the whole result be spoiled. Many bread-makers pass in utter carelessness over this sacred and mysterious boundary. Their oven has cake in it, or they are skimming jelly, or attending to some other of the so-called higher branches of cookery, while the bread is quickly passing into the acetous stage. At last, when they are ready to attend to it, they find that it has been going its own way,—it is so sour that the pungent smell is plainly perceptible. Now the saleratus-bottle is handed down, and a quantity of the dissolved alkali mixed with the paste—an expedient sometimes making itself too manifest by greenish streaks or small acrid spots in the bread. As the result, we have a beautiful article spoiled —bread without sweetness, if not absolutely sour.

In the view of many, lightness is the only property required in this article. The delicate refined sweetness which exists in carefully kneaded bread, baked just before it passes to the extreme point of fermentation, is something of which they have no conception ; and thus they will even regard this process of spoiling the paste by the acetous fermentation, and then rectifying that acid by effervescence with an alkali, as something positively meritorious. How else can they value and relish bakers' loaves, such as some are, drugged with ammonia and other disagreeable things ; light indeed, so light that they seem to have neither weight nor substance, but with no more sweetness or taste than so much cotton wool ?

Some persons prepare bread for the oven by simply mixing it in the mass, without kneading, pouring it into pans, and suffering it to rise there. The air-cells in bread thus prepared are coarse and uneven ; the bread is as inferior in delicacy and nicety to that which is well kneaded as a raw servant to a perfectly educated and refined lady. The process of kneading seems to impart an evenness to the minute air-cells, a fineness of texture, and a tenderness and pliability to the whole substance, that can be gained in no other way.

The divine principle of beauty has its reign over bread as well as over all other things ; it has its laws of æsthetics ; and that bread which is so prepared that it can be formed into separate and well-proportioned loaves, each one carefully worked and moulded, will develop the most beautiful results. After being moulded, the loaves should stand usually not over ten minutes, just long enough to allow the fermentation going on in them to expand each little air-cell to the point at which it stood before it was worked down, and then they should be immediately put into the oven.

Many a good thing, however, is spoiled in the oven. We can not but regret, for the sake of bread, that our old steady brick ovens have been almost universally superseded by those of ranges and cooking-stoves, which are infinite in their caprices, and forbid all general rules. One thing, however, may be borne in mind as a principle—that the excellence of bread in all its varieties, plain or sweetened, depends on the perfection of its air-cells, whether produced by yeast, egg, or effervescence; that one of the objects of baking is to fix these air-cells, and that the quicker this can be done through the whole mass, the better will the result be. When cake or bread is made heavy by baking too quickly, it is because the immediate formation of the top crust hinders the exhaling of the moisture in the centre, and prevents the air-cells from cooking. The weight also of the crust pressing down on the doughy air-cells below destroys them, producing that horror of good cooks, a heavy streak. The problem in baking, then, is the quick application of heat rather below than above the loaf, and its steady continuance till all the air-cells are thoroughly dried into permanent consistency. Every housewife must watch her own oven to know how this can be best accomplished.

Bread-making can be cultivated to any extent as a fine art—and the various kinds of biscuit, tea-rusks, twists, rolls, into which bread may be made, are much better worth a housekeeper's ambition than the getting-up of rich and expensive cake or confections. There are also varieties of material which are rich in good effects. Unbolted flour, altogether more wholesome than the fine wheat, and when properly prepared more palatable—rye-flour and corn-meal, each affording a thousand attractive possibilities—all of these come under the general laws of bread-stuffs, and are worth a careful attention.

A peculiarity of our American table, particularly in the Southern and Western States, is the constant exhibition of various preparations of hot bread. In many families of the

South and West, bread in loaves to be eaten cold is an article quite unknown. The effect of this kind of diet upon the health has formed a frequent subject of remark among travelers; but only those know the full mischiefs of it who have been compelled to sojourn for a length of time in families where it is maintained. The unknown horrors of dyspepsia from bad bread are a topic over which we willingly draw a vail.

Next to Bread comes *Butter*—on which we have to say, that, when we remember what butter is in civilized Europe, and compare it with what it is in America, we wonder at the forbearance and lenity of travelers in their strictures on our national commissariat.

Butter, in England, France, and Italy, is simply solidified cream, with all the sweetness of the cream in its taste, freshly churned each day, and unadulterated by salt. At the present moment, when salt is five cents a pound and butter fifty, we Americans are paying, at high prices, for about one pound of salt to every ten of butter, and those of us who have eaten the butter of France and England do this with rueful recollections.

There is, it is true, an article of butter made in the American style with salt, which, in its own kind and way, has a merit not inferior to that of England and France. Many prefer it, and it certainly takes a rank equally respectable with the other. It is yellow, hard, and worked so perfectly free from every particle of buttermilk that it might make the voyage of the world without spoiling. It is salted, but salted with care and delicacy, so that it may be a question whether even a fastidious Englishman might not prefer its golden solidity to the white, creamy freshness of his own. But it is to be regretted that this article is the exception, and not the rule, on our tables.

America must have the credit of manufacturing and putting into market more bad butter than all that is made in all the rest of the world together. The varieties of bad tastes and smells which prevail in it are quite a study. This has a cheesy taste, that a mouldy, this is flavored with cabbage, and that again with turnip, and another has the strong, sharp savor of rancid animal fat. These varieties probably come from the practice of churning only at long intervals, and keeping the cream meanwhile in unventilated cellars or dairies, the air of which is loaded with the effluvia of vegetable substances. No domestic articles are so sympathetic as those of the milk tribe: they readily take on the smell and taste of any neighboring substance, and hence the infinite variety of flavors on which one mournfully muses who has late in autumn to taste twenty firkins of butter in hopes of finding one which will simply not be intolerable on his winter table.

A matter for despair as regards bad butter is, that at the tables where it is used it stands sentinel at the door to bar your way to every other kind of food. You turn from your dreadful half-slice of bread, which fills your mouth with bitterness, to your beef-steak, which proves virulent with the same poison; you think to take refuge in vegetable diet, and find the butter in the string-beans, and polluting the innocence of early peas; it is in the corn, in the succotash, in the squash; the beets swim in it, the onions have it poured over them. Hungry and miserable, you think to solace yourself at the dessert; but the pastry is cursed, the cake is acrid with the same plague. You are ready to howl with despair, and your misery is great upon you—especially if this is a table where you have taken board for three months with your delicate wife and four small children. Your case is dreadful, and it is hopeless, because long usage and habit have rendered your host perfectly incapable of discovering what is the matter. "Don't like the butter, sir? I assure you I paid an extra price for it, and it's the very best in the market. I looked over as many as a hundred tubs, and picked out this one." You are dumb, but not less despairing.

Yet the process of making good butter is a very simple one. To keep the cream in a perfectly pure, cool atmosphere, to churn while it is yet sweet, to work out the buttermilk thoroughly, and to add salt with such discretion as not to ruin the fine, delicate flavor of the fresh cream—all this is quite simple, so simple that one wonders at thousands and millions of pounds of butter yearly manufactured which are merely a hobgoblin bewitchment of cream into foul and loathsome poisons.

The third head of my discourse is that of *Meat*, of which America furnishes, in the gross material, enough to spread our tables royally, were it well cared for and served.

The faults in the meat generally furnished to us are, first, that it is too new. A beef steak, which three or four days of keeping might render palatable, is served up to us palpitating with freshness, with all the toughness of animal muscle yet warm.

In the next place, there is a woeful lack of nicety in the butcher's work of cutting and preparing meat. Who that remembers the neatly trimmed mutton-chop of an English inn, or the artistic little circle of lamb-chop fried in breadcrumbs coiled around a tempting centre of spinach which may always be found in France, can recognize any family resemblance to those dapper, civilized preparations, in these coarse, roughly-hacked strips of bone, gristle, and meat which are commonly called mutton-chop in America? There seems to be a large dish of something resembling meat, in which each fragment has about two or three edible morsels, the rest being composed of dry and burnt skin, fat, and ragged bone.

Is it not time that civilization should learn to demand somewhat more care and nicety in the modes of preparing what is to be cooked and eaten? Might not some of the refinement and trimness which characterize the preparations of the European market be with advantage introduced into our own? The housekeeper who wishes to garnish her ta ble with some of those nice things is stopped in the outset by the butcher. Except in our large cities, where some foreign travel may have created the demand, it seems impossible to get much in this line that is properly prepared.

If this is urged on the score of æsthetics, the ready reply will be, " Oh ! we can't give time here in America to go into niceties and French whim-whams !" But the French mode of doing almost all practical things is based on that true philosophy and utilitarian good sense which characterize that seemingly thoughtless people. Nowhere is economy a more careful study, and their market is artistically arranged to this end. The rule is so to cut their meats that no portion designed to be cooked in a certain manner shall have wasteful appendages which that mode of cooking will spoil. The French soup-kettle stands ever ready to receive the bones, the thin fibrous flaps, the sinewy and gristly portions, which are so often included in our roasts or broilings, which fill our plates with unsightly *débris*, and finally make an amount of blank waste for which we pay our butcher the same price that we pay for what we have eaten.

The dead waste of our clumsy, coarse way of cutting meats is immense. For example, at the beginning of the season, the part of a lamb denominated leg and loin, or hind-quarter, may sell for thirty cents a pound. Now this includes, besides the thick, fleshy portions, a quantity of bone, sinew, and thin fibrous substance, constituting full one third of the whole weight. If we put it into the oven entire, in the usual manner, we have the thin parts over-done, and the skinny and fibrous parts utterly dried up, by the application of the amount of heat necessary to cook the thick portion. Supposing the joint to weigh six pounds, at thirty cents, and that one third of the weight is so treated as to become perfectly useless, we throw away sixty cents. Of a piece of beef at twenty-five cents a pound, fifty cents' worth is often lost in bone, fat, and burnt skin.

The fact is, this way of selling and cooking meat in

large, gross portions is of English origin, and belongs to a country where all the customs of society spring from a class who have no particular occasion for economy. The practice of minute and delicate division comes from a nation which acknowledges the need of economy, and has made it a study. A quarter of lamb in this mode of division would be sold in three nicely prepared portions. The thick part would be sold by itself, for a neat, compact little roast; the rib-bones would be artistically separated, and all the edible matter would form those delicate dishes of lamb-chop, which, fried in bread-crumbs to a golden brown, are so ornamental and palatable a side-dish; the trimmings which remain after this division would be destined to the soup-kettle or stew-pan.

In a French market is a little portion for every purse, and the far-famed and delicately flavored soups and stews which have arisen out of French economy are a study worth a housekeeper's attention. Not one atom of food is wasted in the French modes of preparation; even tough animal cartilages and sinews, instead of appearing burned and blackened in company with the roast meat to which they happen to be related, are treated according to their own laws, and come out either in savory soups, or those fine, clear meat-jellies which form a garnish no less agreeable to the eye than palatable to the taste.

Whether this careful, economical, practical style of meat-cooking can ever to any great extent be introduced into our kitchens now is a question. Our butchers are against it; our servants are wedded to the old wholesale wasteful ways, which seem to them easier because they are accustomed to them. A cook who will keep and properly tend a soup-kettle which shall receive and utilize all that the coarse preparations of the butcher would require her to trim away, who understands the art of making the most of all these remains, is a treasure scarcely to be hoped for. If such things are to be done, it must be primarily through the educated brain of cultivated women who do not scorn to turn their culture and refinement upon domestic problems.

When meats have been properly divided, so that each portion can receive its own appropriate style of treatment, next comes the consideration of the modes of cooking. These may be divided into two great general classes: those where it is desired to keep the juices within the meat, as in baking, broiling, and frying—and those whose object is to extract the juice and dissolve the fibre, as in the making of soups and stews. In the first class of operations, the process must be as rapid as may consist with the thorough cooking of all the particles. In this branch of cookery, doing quickly is doing well. The fire must be brisk, the attention alert. The introduction of cooking-stoves offers to careless domestics facilities for gradually drying-up meats, and despoiling them of all flavor and nutriment— facilities which appear to be very generally accepted. They have almost banished the genuine, old-fashioned roast-meat from our tables, and left in its stead dried meats with their most precious and nutritive juices evaporated. How few cooks, unassisted, are competent to the simple process of broiling a beefsteak or mutton-chop! how very generally one has to choose between these meats gradually dried away, or burned on the outside and raw within! Yet in England these articles *never* come on the table done amiss; their perfect cooking is as absolute a certainty as the rising of the sun.

No one of these rapid processes of cooking, however, is so generally abused as frying. The frying-pan has awful sins to answer for. What untold horrors of dyspepsia have arisen from its smoky depths, like the ghost from witches' caldrons! The fizzle of frying meat is a warning knell on many an ear, saying, " Touch not, taste not, if you would not burn and writhe!"

Yet those who have traveled abroad remember that some of the lightest, most palatable, and most digestible preparations of meat have come from this dangerous source. But we fancy quite other rites and ceremonies inaugurated the process, and quite other hands performed its offices, than those known to our kitchens. Probably the delicate *côtelettes* of France are not flopped down into half-melted grease, there gradually to warm and soak and fizzle, while Biddy goes in and out on her other ministrations, till finally, when they are thoroughly saturated, and dinner-hour impends, she bethinks herself, and crowds the fire below to a roaring heat, and finishes the process by a smart burn, involving the kitchen and surrounding precincts in volumes of Stygian gloom. From such preparations has arisen the very current medical opinion that fried meats are indigestible. They are indigestible, if they are greasy; but French cooks have taught us that a thing has no more need to be greasy because emerging from grease than Venus had to be salt because she rose from the sea.

There are two ways of frying employed by the French cook. One is, to immerse the article to be cooked in *boiling* fat, with an emphasis on the present participle—and the philosophical principle is, so immediately to crisp every pore, at the first moment or two of immersion, as effectually to seal the interior against the intrusion of greasy particles; it can then remain as long as may be necessary thoroughly to cook it, without imbibing any more of the boiling fluid than if it were inclosed in an egg-shell. The other method is to rub a perfectly smooth iron surface with just enough of some oily substance to prevent the meat from adhering, and cook it with a quick heat, as cakes are baked on a griddle. In both these cases there must be the most rapid application of heat that can be made without burning, and by the adroitness shown in working out this problem the skill of the cook is tested. Any one whose cook attains this important secret will find fried things quite as digestible, and often more palatable, than any other.

In the second department of meat-cookery, to wit, the

slow and gradual application of heat for the softening and dissolution of its fibre and the extraction of its juices, common cooks are equally untrained. Where is the so-called cook who understands how to prepare soups and stews? These are precisely the articles in which a French kitchen excels. The soup-kettle, made with a double bottom, to prevent burning, is a permanent, ever-present institution, and the coarsest and most impracticable meats distilled through that alembic come out again in soups, jellies, or savory stews. The toughest cartilage, even the bones, being first cracked, are here made to give forth their hidden virtues, and to rise in delicate and appetizing forms.

One great law governs all these preparations : the application of heat must be gradual, steady, long protracted, never reaching the point of active boiling. Hours of quiet simmering dissolve all dissoluble parts, soften the sternest fibre, and unlock every minute cell in which Nature has stored away her treasures of nourishment. This careful and protracted application of heat and the skillful use of flavors constitute the two main points in all those nice preparations of meat for which the French have so many names—processes by which a delicacy can be imparted to the coarsest and cheapest food superior to that of the finest articles under less philosophic treatment.

French soups and stews are a study, and they would not be an unprofitable one to any person who wishes to live with comfort and even elegance on small means.

There is no animal fibre that will not yield itself up to long-continued, steady heat. But the difficulty with almost any of the common servants who call themselves cooks is, that they have not the smallest notion of the philosophy of the application of heat. Such a one will complacently tell you concerning certain meats, that the harder you boil them the harder they grow—an obvious fact which, under her mode of treatment by an indiscriminate galloping boil, has fre-

quently come under her personal observation. If you tell
her that such meat must stand for six hours in a heat just
below the boiling point, she will probably answer, " Yes,
ma'am," and go on her own way. Or she will let it stand
till it burns to the bottom of the kettle—a most common
termination of the experiment.

The only way to make sure of the matter is, either to obtain a French kettle, or to fit into an ordinary kettle a false
bottom, such as any tinman may make, that shall leave a
space of an inch or two between the meat and the fire.
This kettle may be maintained in a constant position on
the range, and into it the cook may be instructed to throw
all the fibrous trimmings of meat, all the gristle, tendons,
and bones, having previously broken up these last with a
mallet.   Such a kettle, the regular occupant of a French
cooking-stove. which they call the *pot au feu*, will furnish
the basis for clear, rich soups, or other palatable dishes. This
is ordinarily called " stock."

Clear soup consists of the dissolved juices of the meat
and gelatine of the bones, cleared from the fat and fibrous
portions by straining.   The grease, which rises to the top of
the fluid, may be easily removed when cold.

English and American soups are often heavy and hot
with spices.   There are appreciable tastes in them.   They
burn your mouth with cayenne, or clove, or allspice.   You
can tell at once what is in them, oftentimes to your sorrow.
But a French soup has a flavor which one recognizes at
once as delicious, yet not to be characterized as due to any
single condiment ; it is the just blending of many things.
The same remark applies to all their stews, ragouts, and
other delicate preparations.   No cook will ever study these
flavors; but perhaps many cooks' mistresses may, and thus
be able to impart delicacy and comfort to economy.

As to those things called hashes, commonly manufactured by unwatched, untaught cooks out of the remains of
yesterday's meal, let us not dwell too closely on their mem-

ory—compounds of meat, gristle, skin, fat, and burnt fibre, with a handful of pepper and salt flung at them, dredged with lumpy flour, watered from the spout of the tea-kettle, and left to simmer at the cook's convenience while she is otherwise occupied. Such are the best performances a housekeeper can hope for from an untrained cook.

But the cunningly devised minces, the artful preparations choicely flavored, which may be made of yesterday's repast —by these is the true domestic artist known. No cook untaught by an educated brain ever makes these, and yet economy is a great gainer by them.

As regards the department of *Vegetables*, their number and variety in America are so great that a table might almost be furnished by these alone. Generally speaking, their cooking is a more simple art, and therefore more likely to be found satisfactorily performed, than that of meats. If only they are not drenched with rancid butter, their own native excellence makes itself known in most of the ordinary modes of preparation.

There is, however, one exception. Our staunch old friend, the potato, is to other vegetables what bread is on the table. Like bread, it is held as a sort of *sine-qua-non;* like that, it may be made invariably palatable by a little care in a few plain particulars, through neglect of which it often becomes intolerable. The soggy, waxy, indigestible viand that often appears in the potato-dish is a downright sacrifice of the better nature of this vegetable.

The potato, nutritive and harmless as it appears, belongs to a family suspected of very dangerous traits. It is a family connection of the deadly-nightshade and other ill-reputed gentry, and sometimes shows strange proclivities to evil—now breaking out uproariously, as in the noted potato-rot, and now more covertly, in various evil affections. For this reason scientific directors bid us beware of the water in which potatoes are boiled—into which, it appears, the evil principle is drawn off; and they caution us not to shred them into stews without previously suffering the slices to lie for an hour or so in salt and water. These cautions are worth attention.

The most usual modes of preparing the potato for the table are by roasting or boiling. These processes are so simple that it is commonly supposed every cook understands them without special directions; and yet there is scarcely an uninstructed cook who can boil or roast a potato.

A good roasted potato is a delicacy worth a dozen compositions of the cook-book; yet when we ask for it, what burnt, shriveled abortions are presented to us! Biddy rushes to her potato-basket and pours out two dozen of different sizes, some having in them three times the amount of matter of others. These being washed, she tumbles them into her oven at a leisure interval, and there lets them lie till it is time to serve breakfast, whenever that may be. As a result, if the largest are cooked, the smallest are presented in cinders, and the intermediate sizes are withered and watery. Nothing is so utterly ruined by a few moments of overdoing. That which at the right moment was plump with mealy richness, a quarter of an hour later shrivels and becomes watery—and it is in this state that roast potatoes are most frequently served.

In the same manner we have seen boiled potatoes from an untaught cook coming upon the table like lumps of yellow wax—and the same article, under the directions of a skillful mistress, appearing in snowy balls of powdery whiteness. In the one case, they were thrown in their skins into water, and suffered to soak or boil, as the case might be, at the cook's leisure, and after they were boiled to stand in the water till she was ready to peel them. In the other case, the potatoes being first peeled were boiled as quickly as possible in salted water, which the moment they were done was drained off, and then they were gently shaken for a moment or two over the fire to dry them still more thoroughly. We have never yet seen the potato so depraved and given over to evil that it could not be reclaimed by this mode of treatment.

As to fried potatoes, who that remembers the crisp, golden slices of the French restaurant, thin as wafers and light as snow-flakes, does not speak respectfully of them ? What cousinship with these have those coarse, greasy masses of sliced potato, wholly soggy and partly burnt, to which we are treated under the name of fried potatoes in America ? In our cities the restaurants are introducing the French article to great acceptance, and to the vindication of the fair fame of this queen of vegetables.

Finally, we arrive at the last great head of our subject, to wit—*Tea*—meaning thereby, as before observed, what our Hibernian friend did in the inquiry, " Will y'r honor take ' tay tay ' or coffee tay ?"

We are not about to enter into the merits of the great tea-and-coffee controversy, further than in our general caution concerning them in the chapter on Healthful Drinks ; but we now proceed to treat of them as actual existences, and speak only of the modes of making the best of them.

The French coffee is reputed the best in the world ; and a thousand voices have asked, What is it about the French coffee ?

In the first place, then, the French coffee is coffee, and not chickory, or rye, or beans, or peas. In the second place, it is freshly roasted, whenever made—roasted with great care and evenness in a little revolving cylinder which makes part of the furniture of every kitchen, and which keeps in the aroma of the berry. It is never overdone, so as to destroy the coffee-flavor, which is in nine cases out of ten the fault of the coffee we meet with. Then it is ground, and placed in a coffee-pot with a filter through which, when it has yielded up its life to the boiling water poured upon it, the delicious extract percolates in clear drops, the coffee-pot standing on a heated stove to maintain the temperature. The nose of the coffee-pot is stopped up to prevent the escape of the aroma during this process.   The extract thus obtained is a perfectly clear, dark fluid, known as *café noir*, or black coffee.   It is black only because of its strength, being in fact almost the very essential oil of coffee.   A ta-ble-spoonful of this in boiled milk would make what is or-dinarily called a strong cup of coffee.   The boiled milk is prepared with no less care.   It must be fresh and new, not merely warmed or even brought to the boiling-point, but slowly simmered till it attains a thick, creamy richness.   The coffee mixed with this, and sweetened with that sparkling beet-root sugar which ornaments a French table, is the cele-brated *café-au-lait*, the name of which has gone round the world.

As we look to France for the best coffee, so we must look to England for the perfection of tea.   The tea-kettle is as much an English institution as aristocracy or the Prayer-Book ; and when one wants to know exactly how tea should be made, one has only to ask how a fine old English house-keeper makes it.

The first article of her faith is, that the water must not merely be hot, not merely *have boiled* a few moments since, but be actually *boiling* at the moment it touches the tea. Hence, though servants in England are vastly better trained than with us, this delicate mystery is seldom left to their hands.   Tea-making belongs to the drawing-room, and high-born ladies preside at " the bubbling and loud hissing urn," and see that all due rites and solemnities are properly per-formed—that the cups are hot, and that the infused tea waits the exact time before the libations commence.

Of late, the introduction of English breakfast-tea has raised a new sect among the tea-drinkers, reversing some of the old canons.   Breakfast-tea must be boiled !   Unlike the delicate article of olden time, which required only a momentary infusion to develop its richness, this requires a longer and severer treatment to bring out its strength— thus confusing all the established usages, and throwing the work into the hands of the cook in the kitchen. The faults of tea, as too commonly found at our hotels and boarding-houses, are, that it is made in every way the reverse of what it should be. The water is hot, perhaps, but not boiling; the tea has a general flat, stale, smoky taste, devoid of life or spirit; and it is served usually with thin milk, instead of cream. Cream is as essential to the richness of tea as of coffee. Lacking cream, boiled milk is better than cold.

Chocolate is a French and Spanish article, and one seldom served on American tables. We in America, however, make an article every way equal to any which can be imported from Paris, and he who buys the best vanilla-chocolate may rest assured that no foreign land can furnish any thing better. A very rich and delicious beverage may be made by dissolving this in milk, slowly boiled down after the French fashion.

A word now under the head of *Confectionery*, meaning by this the whole range of ornamental cookery—or pastry, ices, jellies, preserves, etc. The art of making all these very perfectly is far better understood in America than the art of common cooking. There are more women who know how to make good cake than good bread—more who can furnish you with a good ice-cream than a well-cooked mutton-chop; a fair charlotte-russe is easier to gain than a perfect cup of coffee; and you shall find a sparkling jelly to your dessert where you sighed in vain for so simple a luxury as a well-cooked potato.

Our fair countrywomen might rest upon their laurels in these higher fields, and turn their great energy and ingenuity to the study of essentials. To do common things perfectly is far better worth our endeavor than to do uncommon things respectably. We Americans in many things as yet have been a little inclined to begin making our shirt at the ruffle; but, nevertheless, when we set about it, we can make the shirt as nicely as any body; it needs only that we turn our attention to it, resolved that, ruffle or no ruffle, the shirt we will have.

A few words as to the prevalent ideas in respect to French cookery. Having heard much of it, with no very distinct idea of what it is, our people have somehow fallen into the notion that its *forte* lies in high spicing—and so when our cooks put a great abundance of clove, mace, nutmeg, and cinnamon into their preparations, they fancy that they are growing up to be French cooks. But the fact is, that the Americans and English are far more given to spicing than the French. Spices in our made dishes are abundant, and their taste is strongly pronounced. Living a year in France one forgets the taste of nutmeg, clove, and allspice, which abounds in so many dishes in America. The English and Americans deal in *spices*, the French in *flavors* — flavors many and fine, imitating often in their delicacy those subtle blendings which nature produces in high-flavored fruits. The recipes of our cookery-books are most of them of English origin, coming down from the times of our phlegmatic ancestors, when the solid, burly, beefy growth of the foggy island required the heat of fiery condiments, and could digest heavy sweets. Witness the national recipe for plum-pudding: which may be rendered: Take a pound of every indigestible substance you can think of, boil into a. cannon-ball, and serve in flaming brandy. So of the Christmas mince-pie, and many other national dishes. But in America, owing to our brighter skies and more fervid climate, we have developed an acute, nervous delicacy of temperament far more akin to that of France than of England.

Half of the recipes in our cook-books are mere murder to such constitutions and stomachs as we grow here. We require to ponder these things, and think how we, in our climate and under our circumstances, ought to live; and in doing so, we may, without accusation of foreign foppery, take some leaves from many foreign books.

XIV

EARLY RISING.

THERE is no practice which has been more extensively eulogized in all ages than early rising; and this universal impression is an indication that it is founded on true philosophy. For it is rarely the case that the common sense of mankind fastens on a practice as really beneficial, especially one that demands self-denial, without some substantial reason.

This practice, which may justly be called a domestic virtue, is one which has a peculiar claim to be styled American and democratic. The distinctive mark of aristocratic nations is a disregard of the great mass, and a disproportionate regard for the interests of certain privileged orders. All the customs and habits of such a nation are, to a greater or less extent, regulated by this principle. Now the mass of any nation must always consist of persons who labor at occupations which demand the light of day. But in aristocratic countries, especially in England, labor is regarded as the mark of the lower classes, and indolence is considered as one mark of a gentleman. This impression has gradually and imperceptibly, to a great extent, regulated their customs, so that, even in their hours of meals and repose, the higher orders aim at being different and distinct from those who, by laborious pursuits, are placed below them. From this circumstance, while the lower orders labor by day and sleep at night, the rich, the noble, and the honored sleep by day, and follow their pursuits and pleasures by night.

It will be found that the aristocracy of London breakfast

near midday, dine after dark, visit and go to Parliament be
tween ten and twelve at night, and retire to sleep toward
morning.   In consequence of this, the subordinate classes
who aim at gentility gradually fall into the same practice.
The influence of this custom extends across the ocean, and
here, in this democratic land, we find many who measure
their grade of gentility by the late hour at which they arrive
at a party.   And this aristocratic folly is growing upon us,
so that, throughout the nation, the hours for visiting and
retiring are constantly becoming later, while the hours for
rising correspond in lateness.

The question, then, is one which appeals to American
women, as a matter of patriotism and as having a bearing on
those great principles of democracy which we conceive to
be equally the principles of Christianity.   Shall we form
our customs on the assumption that labor is degrading and
indolence genteel ?   Shall we assume, by our practice, that
the interests of the great mass are to be sacrificed for the
pleasures and honors of a privileged few ?   Shall we ape the
customs of aristocratic lands, in those very practices which
result from principles and institutions that we condemn ?
Shall we not rather take the place to which we are entitled,
as the leaders, rather than the followers, in the customs of
society, turn back the tide of aristocratic inroads, and carry
through the whole, not only of civil and political but of
social and domestic life, the true principles of democratic
freedom and equality ?   The following considerations may
serve to strengthen an affirmative decision.

The first relates to the health of a family.   It is a universal law of physiology, that all living things flourish best
in the light.   Vegetables, in a dark cellar, grow pale and
spindling.   Children brought up in mines are always wan
and stunted, while men become pale and cadaverous who
live under ground.   This indicates the folly of losing the
genial influence which the light of day produces on all
animated creation.

Sir James Wylie, of the Russian imperial service, states that in the soldiers' barracks, three times as many were taken sick on the shaded side as on the sunny side; though both sides communicated, and discipline, diet, and treatment were the same. The eminent French surgeon, Dupuytren, cured a lady whose complicated diseases baffled for years his own and all other medical skill, by taking her from a dark room to an abundance of daylight.

Florence Nightingale writes: " Second only to fresh air in importance for the sick is *light*. Not only daylight but direct sunlight is necessary to speedy recovery, except in a small number of cases. Instances, almost endless, could be given where, in dark wards, or wards with only northern exposure, or wards with borrowed light, even when properly ventilated, the sick could not be, by any means, made speedily to recover."

In the prevalence of cholera, it was invariably the case that deaths were more numerous in shaded streets or in houses having only northern exposures than in those having sunlight. Several physicians have stated to the writer that, in sunny exposures, women after childbirth gained strength much faster than those excluded from sunlight. In the writer's experience, great nervous debility has been always immediately lessened by sitting in the sun, and still more by lying on the earth and in open air, a blanket beneath, and head and eyes protected, under the direct rays of the sun.

Some facts in physiology and natural philosophy have a bearing on this subject. It seems to be settled that the red color of blood is owing to iron contained in the red blood-cells, while it is established as a fact that the sun's rays are metallic, having " vapor of iron " as one element. It is also true that want of light causes a diminution of the red and an increase of the imperfect white blood-cells, and that this sometimes results in a disease called *leucoemia*, while all who live in the dark have pale and waxy skins, and flabby, weak muscles. Thus it would seem that it is the sun that imparts the iron and color to the blood. These things being so, the customs of society that bring sleeping hours into daylight, and working and study hours into the night, are direct violations of the laws of health. The laws of health are the laws of God, and "sin is the transgression of law."

To this we must add the great neglect of economy as well as health in substituting unhealthful gaslight, poisonous, anthracite warmth, for the life-giving light and warmth of the sun. Millions and millions would be saved to this nation in fuel and light, as well as in health, by returning to the good old ways of our forefathers, to rise with the sun, and retire to rest " when the bell rings for nine o'clock."

The observations of medical men, whose inquiries have been directed to this point, have decided that from six to eight hours is the amount of sleep demanded by persons in health. Some constitutions require as much as eight, and others no more than six hours of repose. But eight hours is the maximum for all persons in ordinary health, with ordinary occupations. In cases of extra physical exertions, or the debility of disease, or a decayed constitution, more than this is required. Let eight hours, then, be regarded as the ordinary period required for sleep by an industrious people like the Americans.

It thus appears that the laws of our political condition, the laws of the natural world, and the constitution of our bodies, alike demand that we rise with the light of day to prosecute our employments, and that we retire in time for the requisite amount of sleep.

In regard to the effects of protracting the time spent in repose, many extensive and satisfactory investigations have been made. It has been shown that, during sleep, the body perspires most freely, while yet neither food nor exercise are ministering to its wants. Of course, if we continue our slumbers beyond the time required to restore the body to its usual vigor, there is an unperceived undermining of the constitution, by this protracted and debilitating exhalation. This process, in a course of years, renders the body delicate and less able to withstand disease, and in the result shortens life. Sir John Sinclair, who has written a large work on the Causes of Longevity, states, as one result of his extensive investigations, that he has never yet heard or read of a single case of great longevity where the individual was not an early riser. He says that he has found cases in which the individual has violated some one of all the other laws of health, and yet lived to great age; but never a single instance in which any constitution has withstood that undermining consequent on protracting the hours of repose beyond the demands of the system.

Another reason for early rising is, that it is indispensable to a systematic and well-regulated family. At whatever hour the parents retire, children and domestics, wearied by play or labor, must retire early. Children usually awake with the dawn of light, and commence their play, while domestics usually prefer the freshness of morning for their labors. If, then, the parents rise at a late hour, they either induce a habit of protracting sleep in their children and domestics, or else the family are up, and at their pursuits, while their supervisors are in bed.

Any woman who asserts that her children and domestics, in the first hours of day, when their spirits are freshest, will be as well regulated without her presence as with it, confesses that which surely is little for her credit. It is believed that any candid woman, whatever may be her excuse for late rising, will concede that if she could rise early it would be for the advantage of her family. A late breakfast puts back the work, through the whole day, for every member of a family; and if the parents thus occasion the loss of an hour or two to each individual who, but for their delay in the morning, would be usefully employed, they alone are responsible for all this waste of time.

But the practice of early rising has a relation to the general interests of the social community, as well as to that of each distinct family. All that great portion of the community who are employed in business and labor find it needful to rise early; and all their hours of meals, and their appointments for business or pleasure, must be accommodated to these arrangements. Now, if a small portion of the community establish very different hours, it makes a kind of jostling in all the concerns and interests of society. The various appointments for the public, such as meetings, schools, and business hours, must be accommodated to the mass, and not to individuals. The few, then, who establish domestic habits at variance with the majority, are either constantly interrupted in their own arrangements, or else are interfering with the rights and interests of others. This is exemplified in the case of schools. In families where late rising is practiced, either hurry, irregularity, and neglect are engendered in the family, or else the interests of the school, and thus of the community, are sacrificed. In this, and many other matters, it can be shown that the well-being of the bulk of the people is, to a greater or less extent, impaired by this self-indulgent practice. Let any teacher select the unpunctual scholars—a class who most seriously interfere with the interests of the school—and let men of business select those who cause them most waste of time and vexation, by unpunctuality; and it will be found that they are generally among the late risers, and rarely among those who rise early. Thus, late rising not only injures the person and family which indulge in it, but interferes with the rights and convenience of the community; while early rising imparts corresponding benefits of health, promptitude, vigor of action, economy of time, and general effectiveness both to the individuals who practice it and to the families and community of which they are a part.

XV.

DOMESTIC MANNERS.

GOOD MANNERS are the expressions of benevolence in personal intercourse, by which we endeavor to promote the comfort and enjoyment of others, and to avoid all that gives needless uneasiness. It is the exterior exhibition of the di vine precept, which requires us to do to others as we would that they should do to us. It is saying, by our deportment, to all around, that we consider their feelings, tastes, and conveniences, as equal in value to our own.

Good manners lead us to avoid all practices which offend the taste of others; all unnecessary violations of the conventional rules of propriety; all rude and disrespectful language and deportment; and all remarks which would tend to wound the feelings of others.

There is a serious defect in the manners of the American people, especially among the descendants of the Puritan settlers of New-England, which can never be efficiently remedied, except in the domestic circle, and during early life. It is a deficiency in the free expression of kindly feelings and sympathetic emotions, and a want of courtesy in deportment. The causes which have led to this result may easily be traced.

The forefathers of this nation, to a wide extent, were men who were driven from their native land by laws and customs which they believed to be opposed both to civil and religious freedom. The sufferings they were called to endure, the subduing of those gentler feelings which bind us to country, kindred, and home; and the constant subordination of the passions to stern principle, induced characters of great firmness and self-control. They gave up the comforts and refinements of a civilized country, and came as pilgrims to a hard soil, a cold clime, and a heathen shore. They were continually forced to encounter danger, privations, sickness, loneliness, and death; and all these their religion taught them to meet with calmness, fortitude, and submission. And thus it became the custom and habit of the whole mass, to repress rather than to encourage the expression of feeling.

Persons who are called to constant and protracted suffering and privation are forced to subdue and conceal emotion; for the free expression of it would double their own suffering, and increase the sufferings of others. Those, only, who are free from care and anxiety, and whose minds are mainly occupied by cheerful emotions, are at full liberty to unvail their feelings.

It was under such stern and rigorous discipline that the first children in New-England were reared; and the manners and habits of parents are usually, to a great extent, transmitted to children. Thus it comes to pass, that the descendants of the Puritans, now scattered over every part of the nation, are predisposed to conceal the gentler emotions, while their manners are calm, decided, and cold, rather than free and impulsive. Of course, there are very many exceptions to these predominating characteristics.

Other causes to which we may attribute a general want of courtesy in manners are certain incidental results of our domestic institutions. Our ancestors and their descendants have constantly been combating the aristocratic principle which would exalt one class of men at the expense of another. They have had to contend with this principle, not only in civil but in social life. Almost every American, in his own person as well as in behalf of his class, has had to assume and defend the main principle of democracy—that every man's feelings and interests are equal in value to those of every other man. But, in doing this, there has been some want of clear discrimination. Because claims based on distinctions of mere birth, fortune, or position, were found to be injurious, many have gone to the extreme of inferring that all distinctions, involving subordinations, are useless. Such would wrongfully regard children as equals to parents, pupils to teachers, domestics to their employers, and subjects to magistrates—and that, too, in all respects.

The fact that certain grades of superiority and subordination are needful, both for individual and public benefit, has not been clearly discerned; and there has been a gradual tendency to an extreme of the opposite view which has sensibly affected our manners. All the proprieties and courtesies which depend on the recognition of the relative duties of superior and subordinate have been warred upon; and thus we see, to an increasing extent, disrespectful treatment of parents, by children; of teachers, by pupils; of employers, by domestics; and of the aged, by the young. In all classes and circles, there is a gradual decay in courtesy of address.

In cases, too, where kindness is rendered, it is often accompanied with a cold, unsympathizing manner, which greatly lessens its value; while kindness or politeness is received in a similar style of coolness, as if it were but the payment of a just due.

It is owing to these causes that the American people, especially the descendants of the Puritans, do not do themselves justice. For, while those who are near enough to learn their real character and feelings can discern the most generous impulses, and the most kindly sympathies, they are often so vailed behind a composed and indifferent demeanor, as to be almost entirely concealed from strangers.

These defects in our national manners it especially falls to the care of mothers, and all who have charge of the young, to rectify; and if they seriously undertake the matter, and wisely adapt means to ends, these defects will be remedied. With reference to this object, the following ideas are suggested.

The law of Christianity and of democracy, which teaches that all men are born equal in rights, and that their interests and feelings should be regarded as of equal value, seems to be adopted in aristocratic circles, with exclusive reference to the class in which the individual moves. The courtly gentleman addresses all of his own class with politeness and respect; and in all his actions, seems to allow that the feelings and convenience of these others are to be regarded the same as his own. But his demeanor to those of inferior station is not based on the same rule.

Among those who make up aristocratic circles, such as are above them are deemed of superior, and such as are below of inferior, value. Thus, if a young, ignorant, and vicious coxcomb happens to have been born a lord, the aged, the virtuous, the learned, and the well-bred of another class must give his convenience the precedence, and must address him in terms of respect. So sometimes, when a man of "noble birth" is thrown among the lower classes, he demeans himself in a style which, to persons of his own class, would be deemed the height of assumption and rudeness.

Now, the principles of democracy require that the same courtesy which we accord to our own circle shall be extended to every class and condition; and that distinctions of superiority and subordination shall depend, not on accidents of birth, fortune, or occupation, but solely on those mutual relations which the good of all classes equally require. The distinctions demanded in a democratic state are simply those which result from relations that are common to every class, and are for the benefit of all.

It is for the benefit of every class that children be subordinate to parents, pupils to teachers, the employed to their employers, and subjects to magistrates. In addition to this, it is for the general well-being that the comfort or convenience of the delicate and feeble should be preferred to that of the strong and healthy, who would suffer less by any deprivation; that precedence should be given to their elders by the young; and that reverence should be given to the hoary head.

The rules of good-breeding, in a democratic state, must be founded on these principles. It is indeed assumed that the value of the happiness of each individual is the same as that of every other; but as there must be occasions where there are advantages which all can not enjoy, there must be general rules for regulating a selection. Otherwise, there would be constant scrambling among those of equal claims, and brute force must be the final resort; in which case, the strongest would have the best of every thing. The democratic rule, then, is, that superiors in age, station, or office have precedence of subordinates; age and feebleness, of youth and strength; and the feebler sex, of more vigorous man.*

There is, also, a style of deportment and address which is appropriate to these different relations. It is suitable for a superior to secure compliance with his wishes from those subordinate to him by commands; but a subordinate must secure compliance with his wishes from a superior by requests. (Although the kind and considerate manner to subordinates will always be found the most effective as well as the pleasantest, by those in superior station.) It is suitable for a parent, teacher, or employer to admonish for neglect of duty; but not for an inferior to adopt such a course toward a superior. It is suitable for a superior to take precedence of a subordinate, without any remark; but not for an inferior, without previously asking leave, or offering

---

* The universal practice of this nation, in thus giving precedence to woman has been severely commented on by foreigners, and by some who would transfer all the business of the other sex to women, and then have them treated like men. But we hope this evidence of our superior civilization and Christianity may increase rather than diminish.

an apology. It is proper for a superior to use language and manners of freedom and familiarity, which would be improper from a subordinate to a superior.

The want of due regard to these proprieties occasions a great defect in American manners. It is very common to hear children talk to their parents in a style proper only between companions and equals; so, also, the young address their elders; those employed, their employers; and domestics, the members of the family and their visitors, in a style which is inappropriate to their relative positions. But courteous address is required not merely toward superiors; every person desires to be thus treated, and therefore the law of benevolence demands such demeanor toward all whom we meet in the social intercourse of life. "Be ye courteous," is the direction of the apostle in reference to our treatment of *all*.

Good manners can be successfully cultivated only in early life and in the domestic circle. There is nothing which depends so much upon *habit* as the constantly recurring proprieties of good breeding; and if a child grows up without forming such habits, it is very rarely the case that they can be formed at a later period. The feeling that it is of little consequence how we behave at home if we conduct ourselves properly abroad, is a very fallacious one. Persons who are careless and ill-bred at home may imagine that they can assume good manners abroad; but they mistake. Fixed habits of tone, manner, language, and movements can not be suddenly altered; and those who are ill-bred at home, even when they try to hide their bad habits, are sure to violate many of the obvious rules of propriety, and yet be unconscious of it.

And there is nothing which would so effectually remove prejudice against our democratic institutions as the general cultivation of good-breeding in the domestic circle. Good manners are the exterior of benevolence, the minute and constant exhibitions of "peace and good-will;" and the nation, as well as the individual, which most excels in the external demonstration, as well as the internal principle, will be most respected and beloved.

It is only the training of the family state according to its true end and aim that is to secure to woman her true position and rights. When the family is instituted by marriage, it is man who is the head and chief magistrate by the force of his physical power and requirement of the chief responsibility; not less is he so according to the Christian law, by which, when differences arise, the husband has the deciding control, and the wife is to obey. "Where love is, there is no law;" but where love is not, the only dignified and peaceful course is for the wife, however much his superior, to "submit, as to God and not to man."

But this power of nature and of religion, given to man as the controlling head, involves the distinctive duty of the family state, *self-sacrificing love*. The husband is to "honor" the wife, to love her as himself, and thus account her wishes and happiness as of equal value with his own. But more than this, he is to love her "as Christ loved the Church;" that is, he is to "suffer" for her, if need be, in order to support and elevate and ennoble her.

The father then is to set the example of self-sacrificing love and devotion; and the mother, of Christian obedience when it is required. Every boy is to be trained for his future domestic position by labor and sacrifices for his mother and sisters. It is the brother who is to do the hardest and most disagreeable work, to face the storms and perform the most laborious drudgeries. In the family circle, too, he is to give his mother and sister precedence in all the conveniences and comforts of home life.

It is only those nations where the teachings and example of Christ have had most influence that man has ever assumed his obligations of self-sacrificing benevolence in the family. And even in Christian communities, the duty of wives to obey their husbands has been more strenuously urged than the obligations of the husband to love his wife " as Christ loved the Church."

Here it is needful to notice that the distinctive duty of obedience to man does not rest on women who do not enter the relations of married life. A woman who inherits property, or who earns her own livelihood, can institute the family state, adopt orphan children and employ suitable helpers in training them; and then to her will appertain the authority and rights that belong to man as the head of a family. And when every woman is trained to some self-supporting business, she will not be tempted to enter the family state as a subordinate, except by that love for which there is no need of law.

These general principles being stated, some details in regard to domestic manners will be enumerated.

In the first place, there should be required in the family a strict attention to the rules of precedence, and those modes of address appropriate to the various relations to be sustained. Children should always be required to offer their superiors, in age or station, the precedence in all comforts and conveniences, and always address them in a respectful tone and manner. The custom of adding, " Sir," or " Ma'am," to " Yes," or " No," is valuable, as a perpetual indication of a respectful recognition of superiority. It is now going out of fashion, even among the most well bred people; probably from a want of consideration of its importance. Every remnant of courtesy of address, in our customs, should be carefully cherished, by all who feel a value for the proprieties of good breeding.

If parents allow their children to talk to them, and to the grown persons in the family, in the same style in which they address each other, it will be in vain to hope for the courtesy of manner and tone which good breeding demands in the general intercourse of society. In a large family, where the elder children are grown up, and the younger are small, it is important to require the latter to treat the elder in some sense as superiors. There are none so ready as young children to assume airs of equality; and if they are allowed to treat one class of superiors in age and character disrespectfully, they will soon use the privilege universally. This is the reason why the youngest children of a family are most apt to be pert, forward, and unmannerly.

Another point to be aimed at is, to require children always to acknowledge every act of kindness and attention, either by words or manner. If they are so trained as always to make grateful acknowledgments, when receiving favors, one of the objectionable features in American manners will be avoided.

Again, children should be required to ask leave, whenever they wish to gratify curiosity, or use an article which belongs to another. And if cases occur, when they can not comply with the rules of good-breeding, as, for instance, when they must step between a person and the fire, or take the chair of an older person, they should be taught either to ask leave, or to offer an apology.

There is another point of good-breeding, which can not, in all cases, be understood and applied by children in its widest extent. It is that which requires us to avoid all remarks which tend to embarrass, vex, mortify, or in any way wound the feelings of another. To notice personal defects; to allude to others' faults, or the faults of their friends; to speak disparagingly of the sect or party to which a person belongs; to be inattentive when addressed in conversation; to contradict flatly; to speak in contemptuous tones of opinions expressed by another; all these are violations of the rules of good-breeding, which children should be taught to regard. Under this head comes the practice of whispering and staring about, when a teacher, or lecturer, or clergyman is addressing a class or audience. Such inattention is practically saying that what the person is uttering is not worth attending to; and persons of real good-breeding always avoid it. Loud talking and laughing in a large assembly, even when no exercises are going on; yawning and gaping in company; and not looking in the face a person who is addressing you, are deemed marks of ill-breeding.

Another branch of good manners relates to the duties of hospitality. Politeness requires us to welcome visitors with cordiality; to offer them the best accommodations; to address conversation to them; and to express, by tone and manner, kindness and respect. Offering the hand to all visitors at one's own house is a courteous and hospitable custom; and a cordial shake of the hand, when friends meet, would abate much of the coldness of manner ascribed to Americans.

Another point of good breeding refers to the conventional rules of propriety and good taste. Of these, the first class relates to the avoidance of all disgusting or offensive personal habits: such as fingering the hair; obtrusively using a toothpick, or carrying one in the mouth after the needful use of it; cleaning the nails in presence of others; picking the nose; spitting on carpets; snuffing instead of using a handkerchief, or using the article in an offensive manner; lifting up the boots or shoes, as some men do, to tend them on the knee, or to finger them: all these tricks, either at home or in society, children should be taught to avoid.

Another topic, under this head, may be called *table manners*. To persons of good-breeding, nothing is more annoying than violations of the conventional proprieties of the table. Reaching over another person's plate; standing up, to reach distant articles, instead of asking to have them passed; using one's own knife and spoon for butter, salt, or sugar, when it is the custom of the family to provide separate utensils for the purpose; setting cups with the tea dripping from them, on the table-cloth, instead of the mats or small plates furnished; using the table-cloth instead of the napkins; eating fast, and in a noisy manner; putting large pieces in the mouth; looking and eating as if very hungry, or as if anxious to get at certain dishes; sitting at too great a distance from the table, and dropping food; laying the knife and fork on the table-cloth, instead of on the edge of the plate; picking the teeth at table: all these particulars children should be taught to avoid.

It is always desirable, too, to train children, when at table with grown persons, to be silent, except when addressed by others; or else their chattering will interrupt the conversation and comfort of their elders. They should always be required, too, to wait in silence, till all the older persons are helped.

When children are alone with their parents, it is desirable to lead them to converse and to take this as an opportunity to form proper conversational habits. But it should be a fixed rule that, when strangers are present, the children are to listen in silence and only reply when addressed. Unless this is secured, visitors will often be condemned to listen to puerile chattering, with small chance of the proper attention due to guests and superiors in age and station.

Children should be trained, in preparing themselves for the table or for appearance among the family, not only to put their hair, face, and hands in neat order, but also their nails, and to habitually attend to this latter whenever they wash their hands.

There are some very disagreeable tricks which many children practice even in families counted well-bred. Such, for example, are drumming with the fingers on some piece of furniture, or humming a tune while others are talking, or interrupting conversation by pertinacious questions, or whistling in the house instead of out-doors, or speaking several at once and in loud voices to gain attention. All these are violations of good-breeding, which children should be trained to avoid, lest they should not only annoy as children, but practice the same kind of ill manners when mature. In all assemblies for public debate, a chairman or moderator is appointed whose business it is to see that only one person speaks at a time, that no one interrupts a person when speaking, that no needless noises are made, and that all indecorums are avoided. Such an officer is sometimes greatly needed in family circles.

Children should be encouraged freely to use lungs and limbs out-doors, or in hours for sport in the house. But at other times, in the domestic circle, gentle tones and manners should be cultivated. The words *gentleman* and *gentlewoman* came originally from the fact that the uncultivated and ignorant classes used coarse and loud tones, and rough words and movements; while only the refined circles habitually used gentle tones and gentle manners. For the same reason, those born in the higher circles were called "of gentle blood." Thus it came that a coarse and loud voice, and rough, ungentle manners, are regarded as vulgar and plebeian.

All these things should be taught to children, gradually, and with great patience and gentleness. Some parents, with whom good manners are a great object, are in danger of making their children perpetually uncomfortable, by suddenly surrounding them with so many rules that they must inevitably violate some one or other a great part of the time. It is much better to begin with a few rules, and be steady and persevering with these, till a habit is formed, and then take a few more, thus making the process easy and gradual. Otherwise, the temper of children will be injured; or, hopeless of fulfilling so many requisitions, they will become reckless and indifferent to all.

If a few brief, well-considered, and sensible rules of good manners could be suspended in every school-room, and the children all required to commit them to memory, it probably would do more to remedy the defects of American manners and to advance universal good-breeding than any other mode that could be so easily adopted.

But, in reference to those who have enjoyed advantages

for the cultivation of good manners, and who duly estimate its importance, one caution is necessary. Those who never have had such habits formed in youth are under disadvantages which no benevolence of temper can altogether remedy. They may often violate the tastes and feelings of others, not from a want of proper regard for them, but from ignorance of custom, or want of habit, or abstraction of mind, or from other causes which demand forbearance and sympathy, rather than displeasure. An ability to bear patiently with defects in manners, and to make candid and considerate allowance for a want of advantages, or for peculiarities in mental habits, is one mark of the benevolence of real good-breeding.

The advocates of monarchical and aristocratic institutions have always had great plausibility given to their views, by the seeming tendencies of our institutions to insubordination and bad manners. And it has been too indiscriminately conceded, by the defenders of the latter, that such are these tendencies, and that the offensive points in American manners are the necessary result of democratic principles.

But it is believed that both facts and reasoning are in opposition to this opinion. The following extract from the work of De Tocqueville, the great political philosopher of France, exhibits the opinion of an impartial observer, when comparing American manners with those of the English, who are confessedly the most aristocratic of all people.

He previously remarks on the tendency of aristocracy to make men more sympathizing with persons of their own peculiar class, and less so toward those of lower degree: and he then contrasts American manners with the English, claiming that the Americans are much the more affable, mild, and social. "In America, where the privileges of birth never existed and where riches confer no peculiar rights on their possessors, men acquainted with each other are very ready to frequent the same places, and find neither peril nor disadvantage in the free interchange of their thoughts.

If they meet by accident, they neither seek nor avoid intercourse; their manner is therefore natural, frank, and open." "If their demeanor is often cold and serious, it is never haughty or constrained." But an "aristocratic pride is still extremely great among the English; and as the limits of aristocracy are still ill-defined, every body lives in constant dread, lest advantage should be taken of his familiarity. Unable to judge, at once, of the social position of those he meets, an Englishman prudently avoids all contact with him. Men are afraid, lest some slight service rendered should draw them into an unsuitable acquaintance; they dread civilities, and they avoid the obtrusive gratitude of a stranger, as much as his hatred."

Thus, *facts* seem to show that when the most aristocratic nation in the world is compared, as to manners, with the most democratic, the judgment of strangers is in favor of the latter. And if good manners are the outward exhibition of the democratic principle of impartial benevolence and equal rights, surely the nation which adopts this rule, both in social and civil life, is the most likely to secure the desirable exterior. The aristocrat, by his principles, extends the exterior of impartial benevolence to his own class only; the democratic principle requires it to be extended *to all.*

There is reason, therefore, to hope and expect more refined and polished manners in America than in any other land; while all the developments of taste and refinement, such as poetry, music, painting, sculpture, and architecture, it may be expected, will come to as high a state of perfection here as in any other nation.

If this country increases in virtue and intelligence, as it may, there is no end to the wealth which will pour in as the result of our resources of climate, soil, and navigation, and the skill, industry, energy, and enterprise of our countrymen. This wealth, if used as intelligence and virtue dictate, will furnish the means for a superior education to all classes, and every facility for the refinement of taste, intellect, and feeling.

Moreover, in this country, labor is ceasing to be the badge of a lower class; so that already it is disreputable for a man to be " a lazy gentleman." And this feeling must increase, till there is such an equalization of labor as will afford all the time needful for every class to improve the many advantages offered to them. Already through the munificence of some of our citizens, there are literary and scientific advantages offered to all classes, rarely enjoyed elsewhere. In most of our large cities and towns, the advantages of education, now offered to the poorest classes, often without charge, surpass what, some years ago, most wealthy men could purchase for any price. And it is believed that a time will come when the poorest boy in America can secure advantages, which will equal what the heir of the proudest peerage can now command.

The records of the courts of France and Germany, (as detailed by the Duchess of Orleans,) in and succeeding the brilliant reign of Louis the Fourteenth—a period which was deemed the acme of elegance and refinement—exhibit a grossness, a vulgarity, and a coarseness, not to be found among the very lowest of our respectable poor. And the biography of the English Beau Nash, who attempted to reform the manners of the gentry, in the times of Queen Anne, exhibits violations of the rules of decency among the aristocracy, which the commonest yeoman of this land would feel disgraced in perpetrating.

This shows that our lowest classes, at this period, are more refined than were the highest in aristocratic lands, a hundred years ago; and another century may show the lowest classes, in wealth, in this country, attaining as high a polish as adorns those who now are leaders of good manners in the courts of kings.

XVI.

THERE is nothing which has a more abiding influence on the happiness of a family than the preservation of equable and cheerful temper and tones in the housekeeper. A woman who is habitually gentle, sympathizing, forbearing, and cheerful, carries an atmosphere about her which imparts a soothing and sustaining influence, and renders it easier for all to do right, under her administration, than in any other situation.

The writer has known families where the mother's presence seemed the sunshine of the circle around her; imparting a cheering and vivifying power, scarcely realized till it was withdrawn. Every one, without thinking of it, or knowing why it was so, experienced a peaceful and invigorating influence as soon as he entered the sphere illumined by her smile, and sustained by her cheering kindness and sympathy. On the contrary, many a good housekeeper, (good in every respect but this,) by wearing a countenance of anxiety and dissatisfaction, and by indulging in the frequent use of sharp and reprehensive tones, more than destroys all the comfort which otherwise would result from her system, neatness, and economy.

There is a secret, social sympathy which every mind, to a greater or less degree, experiences with the feelings of those around, as they are manifested by the countenance and voice. A sorrowful, a discontented, or an angry countenance produces a silent, sympathetic influence, imparting a sombre shade to the mind, while tones of anger or complaint still more effectually jar the spirits.

No person can maintain a quiet and cheerful frame of mind while tones of discontent and displeasure are sounding on the ear. We may gradually accustom ourselves to the evil till it is partially diminished; but it always is an evil which greatly interferes with the enjoyment of the family state. There are sometimes cases where the entrance of the mistress of a family seems to awaken a slight apprehension in every mind around, as if each felt in danger of a reproof, for something either perpetrated or neglected. A woman who should go around her house with a small stinging snapper, which she habitually applied to those whom she met, would be encountered with feelings very much like those which are experienced by the inmates of a family where the mistress often uses her countenance and voice to inflict similar penalties for duties neglected.

Yet there are many allowances to be made for housekeepers, who sometimes imperceptibly and unconsciously fall into such habits. A woman who attempts to carry out any plans of system, order, and economy, and who has her feelings and habits conformed to certain rules, is constantly liable to have her plans crossed, and her taste violated, by the inexperience or inattention of those about her. And no housekeeper, whatever may be her habits, can escape the frequent recurrence of negligence or mistake, which interferes with her plans.

It is probable that there is no class of persons in the world who have such incessant trials of temper, and temptations to be fretful, as American housekeepers. For a housekeeper's business is not, like that of the other sex, limited to a particular department, for which previous preparation is made. It consists of ten thousand little disconnected items, which can never be so systematically arranged that there is no daily jostling somewhere. And in the best-regulated families, it is not unfrequently the case that some act of forgetfulness or carelessness, from some member, will disarrange the business of the whole day, so that every hour will bring renewed occasion for annoyance. And the more strongly a woman realizes the value of time, and the importance of system and order, the more will she be tempted to irritability and complaint.

The following considerations may aid in preparing a woman to meet such daily crosses with even a cheerful temper and tones.

In the first place, a woman who has charge of a large household should regard her duties as dignified, important, and difficult. The mind is so made as to be elevated and cheered by a sense of far-reaching influence and usefulness. A woman who feels that she is a cipher, and that it makes little difference how she performs her duties, has far less to sustain and invigorate her, than one who truly estimates the importance of her station. A man who feels that the destinies of a nation are turning on the judgment and skill with which he plans and executes, has a pressure of motive and an elevation of feeling which are great safeguards against all that is low, trivial, and degrading.

So, an American mother and housekeeper who rightly estimates the long train of influence which will pass down to thousands, whose destinies, from generation to generation, will be modified by those decisions of her will which regulate the temper, principles, and habits of her family, must be elevated above petty temptations which would otherwise assail her.

Again, a housekeeper should feel that she really has great difficulties to meet and overcome. A person who wrongly thinks there is little danger, can never maintain so faithful a guard as one who rightly estimates the temptations which beset her. Nor can one who thinks that they are trifling difficulties which she has to encounter, and trivial temptations to which she must yield, so much enjoy the just reward of conscious virtue and self-control as one who takes an opposite view of the subject.

A third method is, for a woman deliberately to calculate

on having her best-arranged plans interfered with very often; and to be in such a state of preparation that the evil will not come unawares. So complicated are the pursuits and so diverse the habits of the various members of a family, that it is almost impossible for every one to avoid interfering with the plans and taste of a housekeeper, in some one point or another. It is, therefore, most wise for a woman to keep the loins of her mind ever girt, to meet such collisions with a cheerful and quiet spirit.

Another important rule is, to form all plans and arrangements in consistency with the means at command, and the character of those around. A woman who has a heedless husband, and young children, and incompetent domestics, ought not to make such plans as one may properly form who will not, in so many directions, meet embarrassment. She must aim at just as much as she can probably attain, and no more; and thus she will usually escape much temptation, and much of the irritation of disappointment.

The fifth, and a very important consideration, is, that system, economy, and neatness are valuable, only so far as they tend to promote the comfort and well-being of those affected. Some women seem to act under the impression that these advantages *must* be secured, at all events, even if the comfort of the family be the sacrifice. True, it is very important that children grow up in habits of system, neatness, and order; and it is very desirable that the mother give them every incentive, both by precept and example; but it is still more important that they grow up with amiable tempers, that they learn to meet the crosses of life with patience and cheerfulness; and nothing has a greater influence to secure this than a mother's example. Whenever, therefore, a woman can not accomplish her plans of neatness and order without injury to her own temper or to the temper of others, she ought to modify and reduce them until she can.

The sixth method relates to the government of the tones

of voice. In many cases, when a woman's domestic arrangements are suddenly and seriously crossed, it is impossible not to feel some irritation. But it *is* always possible to refrain from angry tones. A woman can resolve that, whatever happens, she will not speak till she can do it in a calm and gentle manner. *Perfect silence* is a safe resort, when such control can not be attained as enables a person to speak calmly ; and this determination, persevered in, will eventually be crowned with success.

Many persons seem to imagine that tones of anger are needful, in order to secure prompt obedience. But observation has convinced the writer that they are *never* necessary ; that *in all cases*, reproof, administered in calm tones, would be better. A case will be given in illustration.

A young girl had been repeatedly charged to avoid a certain arrangement in cooking. On one day, when company was invited to dine, the direction was forgotten, and the consequence was an accident, which disarranged every thing, seriously injured the principal dish, and delayed dinner for an hour. The mistress of the family entered the kitchen just as it occurred, and at a glance, saw the extent of the mischief. For a moment, her eyes flashed, and her cheeks glowed ; but she held her peace. After a minute or so, she gave directions in a calm voice, as to the best mode of retrieving the evil, and then left, without a word said to the offender.

After the company left, she sent for the girl, alone, and in a calm and kind manner pointed out the aggravations of the case, and described the trouble which had been caused to her husband, her visitors, and herself. She then portrayed the future evils which would result from such habits of neglect and inattention, and the modes of attempting to overcome them ; and then offered a reward for the future, if, in a given time, she succeeded in improving in this respect. Not a tone of anger was uttered ; and yet the severest scolding of a practiced Xantippe could not have secured such contrition, and determination to reform, as were gained by this method.

But similar negligence is often visited by a continuous stream of complaint and reproof, which, in most cases, is met either by sullen silence or impertinent retort, while anger prevents any contrition or any resolution of future amendment.

It is very certain, that some ladies do carry forward a most efficient government, both of children and domestics, without employing tones of anger; and therefore they are not indispensable, nor on any account desirable.

Though some ladies of intelligence and refinement do fall unconsciously into such a practice, it is certainly very unlady-like, and in very bad taste, to *scold ;* and the further a woman departs from all approach to it, the more perfectly she sustains her character as a lady.

Another method of securing equanimity, amid the trials of domestic life is, to cultivate a habit of making allowances for the difficulties, ignorance, or temptations of those who violate rule or neglect duty. It is vain, and most unreasonable, to expect the consideration and care of a mature mind in childhood and youth; or that persons of such limited advantages as most domestics have enjoyed should practice proper self-control and possess proper habits and principles.

Every parent and every employer needs daily to cultivate the spirit expressed in the divine prayer, " Forgive us our trespasses, as we forgive those who trespass against us." The same allowances and forbearance which we supplicate from our Heavenly Father, and desire from our fellow-men in reference to our own deficiencies, we should constantly aim to extend to all who cross our feelings and interfere with our plans.

The last and most important mode of securing a placid and cheerful temper and tones is, by a constant belief in the influence of a superintending Providence. All persons are too much in the habit of regarding the more important events of life exclusively as under the control of Perfect Wisdom. But the fall of a sparrow, or the loss of a hair, they do not feel to be equally the result of his directing agency. In consequence of this, Christian persons who aim at perfect and cheerful submission to heavy afflictions, and who succeed to the edification of all about them, are sometimes sadly deficient under petty crosses. If a beloved child be laid in the grave, even if its death resulted from the carelessness of a domestic or of a physician, the eye is turned from the subordinate agent to the Supreme Guardian of all; and to him they bow, without murmur or complaint. But if a pudding be burnt, or a room badly swept, or an errand forgotten, then vexation and complaint are allowed, just as if these events were not appointed by Perfect Wisdom as much as the sorer chastisement.

A woman, therefore, needs to cultivate the *habitual* feeling that all the events of her nursery and kitchen are brought about by the permission of our Heavenly Father, and that fretfulness or complaint in regard to these is, in fact, complaining at the appointments of God, and is really as sinful as unsubmissive murmurs amid the sorer chastisements of his hand. And a woman who cultivates this habit of referring all the minor trials of life to the wise and benevolent agency of a heavenly Parent, and daily seeks his sympathy and aid to enable her to meet them with a quiet and cheerful spirit, will soon find it the perennial spring of abiding peace and content.

The power of religion to impart dignity and importance to the ordinary and seemingly petty details of domestic life, greatly depends upon the degree of faith in the reality of a life to come, and of its eternal results. A woman who is training a family simply with reference to this life may find exalted motives as she looks forward to unborn generations whose temporal prosperity and happiness are depending upon her fidelity and skill. But one who truly and firmly believes that this life is but the beginning of an eternal career to every immortal inmate of her home, and that the formation of tastes, habits, and character, under her care, will bring forth fruits of good or ill, not only through earthly generations, but through everlasting ages; such a woman secures a calm and exalted principle of action, which no earthly motives can impart.

XVII.

ANY discussion of the equality of the sexes, as to intellectual capacity, seems frivolous and useless, both because it can never be decided, and because there would be no possible advantage in the decision. But one topic, which is often drawn into this discussion, is of far more consequence; and that is, the relative importance and difficulty of the duties a woman is called to perform.

It is generally assumed, and almost as generally conceded, that a housekeeper's business and cares are contracted and trivial; and that the proper discharge of her duties demands far less expansion of mind and vigor of intellect than the pursuits of the other sex. This idea has prevailed because women, as a mass, have never been educated with reference to their most important duties; while that portion of their employments which is of least value has been regarded as the chief, if not the sole, concern of a woman. The covering of the body, the convenience of residences, and the gratification of the appetite, have been too much regarded as the chief objects on which her intellectual powers are to be exercised.

But as society gradually shakes off the remnants of barbarism and the intellectual and moral interests of man rise, in estimation, above the merely sensual, a truer estimate is formed of woman's duties, and of the measure of intellect requisite for the proper discharge of them. Let any man of sense and discernment become the member of a large household, in which a well-educated and pious woman is endeavoring systematically to discharge her multiform duties; let him fully comprehend all her cares, difficulties, and perplexities; and it is probable he would coincide in the opinion that no statesman, at the head of a nation's affairs, had more frequent calls for wisdom, firmness, tact, discrimination, prudence, and versatility of talent, than such a woman.

She has a husband, to whose peculiar tastes and habits she must accommodate herself; she has children whose health she must guard, whose physical constitutions she must study and develop, whose temper and habits she must regulate, whose principles she must form, whose pursuits she must guide. She has constantly changing domestics, with all varieties of temper and habits, whom she must govern, instruct, and direct; she is required to regulate the finances of the domestic state, and constantly to adapt expenditures to the means and to the relative claims of each department. She has the direction of the kitchen, where ignorance, forgetfulness, and awkwardness are to be so regulated that the various operations shall each start at the right time, and all be in completeness at the same given hour. She has the claims of society to meet, visits to receive and return, and the duties of hospitality to sustain. She has the poor to relieve; benevolent societies to aid; the schools of her children to inquire and decide about; the care of the sick and the aged; the nursing of infancy; and the endless miscellany of odd items, constantly recurring in a large family.

Surely, it is a pernicious and mistaken idea, that the duties which tax a woman's mind are petty, trivial, or unworthy of the highest grade of intellect and moral worth. Instead of allowing this feeling, every woman should imbibe, from early youth, the impression that she is in training for the discharge of the most important, the most difficult, and the most sacred and interesting duties that can possibly employ the highest intellect. She ought to feel that her station and responsibilities in the great drama of life are second to none, either as viewed by her Maker, or in the estimation of all minds whose judgment is most worthy of respect.

She who is the mother and housekeeper in a large family is the sovereign of an empire, demanding more varied cares, and involving more difficult duties, than are really exacted of her who wears a crown and professedly regulates the interests of the greatest nation on earth.

There is no one thing more necessary to a housekeeper in performing her varied duties, than *a habit of system and order;* and yet, the peculiarly desultory nature of women's pursuits, and the embarrassments resulting from the state of domestic service in this country, render it very difficult to form such a habit. But it is sometimes the case that women who could and would carry forward a systematic plan of domestic economy do not attempt it, simply from a want of knowledge of the various modes of introducing it. It is with reference to such, that various modes of securing system and order, which the writer has seen adopted, will be pointed out.

A wise economy is nowhere more conspicuous, than in a systematic *apportionment of time* to different pursuits. There are duties of a religious, intellectual, social, and domestic nature, each having different relative claims on attention. Unless a person has some general plan of apportioning these claims, some will intrench on others, and some, it is probable, will be entirely excluded. Thus, some find religious, social, and domestic duties so numerous, that no time is given to intellectual improvement. Others find either social, or benevolent, or religious interests excluded by the extent and variety of other engagements.

It is wise, therefore, for all persons to devise a systematic plan, which they will at least keep in view, and aim to accomplish; and by which a proper proportion of time shall be secured for all the duties of life.

In forming such a plan, every woman must accommodate herself to the peculiarities of her situation. If she has a large family and a small income, she must devote far more time to the simple duty of providing food and raiment than would be right were she in affluence, and with a small family. It is impossible, therefore, to draw out any general plan, which all can adopt. But there are some *general principles*, which ought to be the guiding rules, when a woman arranges her domestic employments. These principles are to be based on Christianity, which teaches us to "seek first the kingdom of God," and to deem food, raiment, and the conveniences of life, as of secondary account. Every woman, then, ought to start with the assumption, that the moral and religious interests of her family are of more consequence than any worldly concern, and that, whatever else may be sacrificed, these shall be the leading object, in all her arrangements, in respect to time, money, and attention.

It is also one of the plainest requisitions of Christianity, that we devote some of our time and efforts to the comfort and improvement of others. There is no duty so constantly enforced, both in the Old and New Testament, as that of charity, in dispensing to those who are destitute of the blessings we enjoy. In selecting objects of charity, the same rule applies to others as to ourselves; their moral and religious interests are of the highest moment, and for them, as well as for ourselves, we are to "seek first the kingdom of God."

Another general principle is, that our intellectual and social interests are to be preferred to the mere gratification of taste or appetite. A portion of time, therefore, must be devoted to the cultivation of the intellect and the social affections.

Another is, that the mere gratification of appetite is to be placed last in our estimate; so that, when a question arises as to which shall be sacrificed, some intellectual, moral, or social advantage, or some gratification of sense, we should invariably sacrifice the last.

As health is indispensable to the discharge of every duty, nothing which sacrifices that blessing is to be allowed in order to gain any other advantage or enjoyment. There are emergencies, when it is right to risk health and life, to save ourselves and others from greater evils; but these are exceptions, which do not militate against the general rule. Many persons imagine that, if they violate the laws of health, in order to attend to religious or domestic duties, they are guiltless before God. But such greatly mistake. We directly violate the law, "Thou shalt not kill," when we do what tends to risk or shorten our own life. The life and happiness of all his creatures are dear to our Creator; and he is as much displeased when we injure our own interests, as when we injure those of others. The idea, therefore, that we are excusable if we harm no one but ourselves, is false and pernicious. These, then, are some general principles, to guide a woman in systematizing her duties and pursuits.

The Creator of all things is a Being of perfect system and order; and, to aid us in our duty in this respect, he has divided our time, by a regularly returning day of rest from worldly business. In following this example, the intervening six days may be subdivided to secure similar benefits. In doing this, a certain portion of time must be given to procure the means of livelihood, and for preparing food, raiment,.and dwellings. To these objects, some must devote more, and others less, attention. The remainder of time not necessarily thus employed, might be divided somewhat in this manner: The leisure of two afternoons and evenings could be devoted to religious and benevolent objects, such as religious meetings, charitable associations, school visiting, and attention to the sick and poor. The leisure of two other days might be devoted to intellectual improvement, and the pursuits of taste. The leisure of another day might be devoted to social enjoyments, ir making or receiving visits; and that of another, to mis cellaneous domestic pursuits, not included in the othei particulars.

It is probable that few persons could carry out such ar arrangement very strictly; but every one can make a sys tematic apportionment of time, and at least *aim* at accom plishing it; and they can also compare with such a gen eral outline, the time which they actually devote to these different objects, for the purpose of modifying any mis taken proportions.

Without attempting any such systematic employment of time, and carrying it out, so far as they can control circumstances, most women are rather driven along by the daily occurrences of life; so that, instead of being the intelligent regulators of their own time, they are the mere sport of circumstances. There is nothing which so distinctly marks the difference between weak and strong minds as the question, whether they control circumstances or circumstances control them.

It is very much to be feared, that the apportionment of time actually made by most women exactly inverts the order required by reason and Christianity. Thus, the furnishing a needless variety of food, the conveniences of dwellings, and the adornments of dress, often take a larger portion of time than is given to any other object. Next after this, comes intellectual improvement; and, last of all, benevolence and religion.

It may be urged, that it is indispensable for most persons to give more time to earn a livelihood, and to prepare food, raiment, and dwellings, than to any other object. But it may be asked, how much of the time, devoted to these objects, is employed in preparing varieties of food not necessary, but rather injurious, and how much is spent for those parts of dress and furniture not indispensable, and merely ornamental? Let a woman subtract from her domestic employments all the time given to pursuits which are of no use, except as they gratify a taste for ornament, or minister increased varieties to tempt the appetite, and she will find that much which she calls "domestic duty," and which prevents her attention to intellectual, benevolent, and religious objects, should be called by a very different name.

No woman has a right to give up attention to the higher interests of herself and others, for the ornaments of person or the gratification of the palate. To a certain extent, these lower objects are lawful and desirable; but when they intrude on nobler interests, they become selfish and degrading. Every woman, then, when employing her hands in ornamenting her person, her children, or her house, ought to calculate whether she has devoted *as much* time to the really more important wants of herself and others. If she has not, she may know that she is doing wrong, and that her system for apportioning her time and pursuits should be altered.

Some persons endeavor to systematize their pursuits by apportioning them to particular hours of each day. For example, a certain period before breakfast, is given to devotional duties; after breakfast, certain hours are devoted to exercise and domestic employments; other hours, to sewing, or reading, or visiting; and others, to benevolent duties. But in most cases, it is more difficult to systematize the hours of each day, than it is to secure some regular division of the week.

In regard to the minutiæ of family work, the writer has known the following methods to be adopted. Monday, with some of the best housekeepers, is devoted to preparing for the labors of the week. Any extra cooking, the purchasing of articles to be used during the week, the assorting of clothes for the wash, and mending such as would otherwise be injured—these, and similar items, belong to this day. Tuesday is devoted to washing, and Wednesday to ironing. On Thursday, the ironing is finished off, the clothes are folded and put away, and all articles which need mending are put in the mending-basket, and attended to. Friday is devoted to sweeping and house-cleaning. On Saturday, and especially the last Saturday of every month, every department is put in order ; the casters and table furniture are regulated, the pantry and cellar inspected, the trunks, drawers, and closets arranged, and every thing about the house put in order for Sunday. By this regular recurrence of a particular time for inspecting every thing, nothing is forgotten till ruined by neglect.

Another mode of systematizing relates to providing proper supplies of conveniences, and proper places in which to keep them. Thus, some ladies keep a large closet, in which are placed the tubs, pails, dippers, soap-dishes, starch, blueing, clothes-lines, clothes-pins, and every other article used in washing ; and in the same, or another place, is kept every convenience for ironing. In the sewing department, a trunk, with suitable partitions, is provided, in which are placed, each in its proper place, white thread of all sizes, colored thread, yarns for mending, colored and black sewing-silks and twist, tapes and bobbins of all sizes, white and colored welting-cords, silk braids and cords, needles of all sizes, papers of pins, remnants of linen and colored cambric, a supply of all kinds of buttons used in the family, black and white hooks and eyes, a yard measure, and all the patterns used in cutting and fitting. These are done up in separate parcels, and labeled. In another trunk, or in a piece-bag, such as has been previously described, are kept all pieces used in mending, arranged in order. A trunk, like the first mentioned, will save many steps, and often much time and perplexity ; while by purchasing articles thus by the quantity, they come much cheaper than if bought in little portions as they are wanted. Such a trunk should be kept locked, and a smaller supply for current use retained in a work-basket.

A full supply of all conveniences in the kitchen and cellar, and a place appointed for each article, very much facilitate domestic labor. For want of this, much vexation and loss of time is occasioned while seeking vessels in use, or in cleansing those employed by different persons for various purposes. It would be far better for a lady to give up some expensive article in the parlor, and apply the money thus saved for kitchen conveniences, than to have a stinted supply where the most labor is to be performed. If our countrywomen would devote more to comfort and convenience, and less to show, it would be a great improvement. Expensive mirrors and pier-tables in the parlor, and an unpainted, gloomy, ill-furnished kitchen, not unfrequently are found under the same roof.

Another important item in systematic economy is, the apportioning of *regular* employment to the various members of a family. If a housekeeper can secure the coöperation of *all* her family, she will find that "many hands make light work." There is no greater mistake than in bringing up children to feel that they must be taken care of, and waited on by others, without any corresponding obligations on their part. The extent to which young children can be made useful in a family would seem surprising to those who have never seen a *systematic* and *regular* plan for utilizing their services. The writer has been in a family where a little girl, of eight or nine years of age, washed and dressed herself and young brother, and made their small beds, before breakfast; set and cleared all the tables for meals, with a little help from a grown person in moving tables and spreading cloths; while all the dusting of parlors and chambers was also neatly performed by her. A brother of ten years old brought in and piled all the wood used in the kitchen and parlor, brushed the boots and shoes, went on errands, and took all the care of the poultry. They were children whose parents could afford to hire servants to do this, but who chose to have their children grow up healthy and industrious, while proper instruction, system, and encouragement made these services rather a pleasure than otherwise, to the children.

Some parents pay their children for such services ; but this is hazardous, as tending to make them feel that they are not bound to be helpful without pay, and also as tending to produce a hoarding, money-making spirit. But where children have no hoarding propensities, and need to acquire a sense of the value of property, it may be well to let them earn money for some extra services rather as a favor. When this is done, they should be taught to spend it for others, as well as for themselves ; and in this way, a generous and liberal spirit will be cultivated.

There are some mothers who take pains to teach their boys most of the domestic arts which their sisters learn. The writer has seen boys mending their own garments and aiding their mother or sisters in the kitchen, with great skill and adroitness ; and, at an early age, they usually very much relish joining in such occupations. The sons of such mothers, in their college life, or in roaming about the world, or in nursing a sick wife or infant, find occasion to bless the forethought and kindness which prepared them for such emergencies. Few things are in worse taste than for a man needlessly to busy himself in women's work ; and yet a man never appears in a more interesting attitude than when, by skill in such matters, he can save a mother or wife from care and suffering. The more a boy is taught to use his hands, in every variety of domestic employment, the more his faculties, both of mind and body, are developed ; for mechanical pursuits exercise the intellect as well as the hands. The early training of New-England boys, in which they turn their hand to almost every thing, is one great reason of the quick perceptions, versatility of mind, and mechanical skill, for which that portion of our countrymen is distinguished.

It is equally important that young girls should be taught to do some species of handicraft that generally is done by men, and especially with reference to the frequent emigration to new territories where well-trained mechanics are scarce. To hang wall-paper, repair locks, glaze windows, and mend various household articles, requires a skill in the use of tools which every young girl should acquire. If she never has any occasion to apply this knowledge and skill by her own hands, she will often find it needful in directing and superintending incompetent workmen.

The writer has known one mode of systematizing the aid of the older children in a family, which, in some cases of very large families, it may be well to imitate. In the case referred to, when the oldest daughter was eight or nine years old, an infant sister was given to her, as her special charge. She tended it, made and mended its clothes, taught it to read, and was its nurse and guardian, through all its childhood. Another infant was given to the next daughter, and thus the children were all paired in this interesting relation. In addition to the relief thus afforded to the mother, the elder children were in this way qualified for their future domestic relations, and both older and younger bound to each other by peculiar ties of tenderness and gratitude.

In offering these examples of various modes of systematizing, one suggestion may be worthy of attention. It is not unfrequently the case, that ladies, who find themselves cumbered with oppressive cares, after reading remarks on the benefits of system, immediately commence the task of arranging their pursuits, with great vigor and hope. They divide the day into regular periods, and give each hour its duty; they systematize their work, and endeavor to bring every thing into a regular routine. But, in a short time, they find themselves baffled, discouraged, and disheartened, and finally relapse into their former desultory ways, in a sort of resigned despair.

The difficulty, in such cases, is, that they attempt too much at a time. There is nothing which so much depends upon *habit*, as a systematic mode of performing duty; and where no such habit has been formed, it is impossible for a novice to start, at once, into a universal mode of systematizing, which none but an adept could carry through. The only way for such persons is to begin with a little at a time. Let them select some three or four things, and resolutely attempt to conquer at these points. In time, a habit will be formed, of doing a few things at regular periods, and in a systematic way. Then it will be easy to add a few more ; and thus, by a gradual process, the object can be secured, which it would be vain to attempt by a more summary course.

Early rising is almost an indispensable condition to success, in such an effort ; but where a woman lacks either the health or the energy to secure a period for devotional duties before breakfast, let her select that hour of the day in which she will be least liable to interruption, and let her then seek strength and wisdom from the only true Source. At this time, let her take a pen, and make a list of all the things which she considers as duties. Then, let a calculation be made, whether there be time enough, in the day or the week, for all these duties. If there be not, let the least important be stricken from the list, as not being duties, and therefore to be omitted. In doing this, let a woman remember that, though "what we shall eat, and what we shall drink, and wherewithal we shall be clothed," are matters requiring due attention, they are very apt to obtain a wrong relative importance, while intellectual, social, and moral interests receive too little regard.

In this country, eating, dressing, and household furniture and ornaments, take far too large a place in the estimate of relative importance ; and it is probable that most women could modify their views and practice, so as to come nearer to the Saviour's requirements. No woman has a right to put a stitch of ornament on any article of dress or furniture, or to provide one superfluity in food, until she is sure she can secure time for all her social, intellectual, benevolent, and religious duties.   If a woman will take the trouble to make such a calculation as this, she will usually find that she has time enough to perform all her duties easily and well.

It is impossible for a conscientious woman to secure that peaceful mind and cheerful enjoyment of life which all should seek, who is constantly finding her duties jarring with each other, and much remaining undone, which she feels that she ought to do.   In consequence of this, there will be a secret uneasiness, which will throw a shade over the whole current of life, never to be removed, till she so efficiently defines and regulates her duties that she can fulfill them all.

And here the writer would urge upon young ladies the importance of forming habits of system, while unembarrassed with those multiplied cares which will make the task so much more difficult and hopeless.   Every young lady can systematize her pursuits, to a certain extent.   She can have a particular day for mending her wardrobe, and for arranging her trunks, closets, and drawers.   She can keep her work-basket, her desk at school, and all her other conveniences, in their proper places, and in regular order. She can have regular periods for reading, walking, visiting, study, and domestic pursuits.   And by following this method in youth, she will form a taste for regularity and a habit of system, which will prove a blessing to her through life.

XVIII.

GIVING IN CHARITY.

It is probable that there is no point of duty whereon conscientious persons differ more in opinion, or where they find it more difficult to form discriminating and decided views, than on the matter of charity. That we are bound to give some of our time, money, and efforts, to relieve the destitute, all allow. But, as to how much we are to give, and on whom our charities shall be bestowed, many a reflecting mind has been at a loss. Yet it seems very desirable that, in reference to a duty so constantly and so strenuously urged by the Supreme Ruler, we should be able so to fix metes and bounds, as to keep a conscience void of offense, and to free the mind from disquieting fears of deficiency.

The writer has found no other topic of investigation so beset with difficulty, and so absolutely without the range of definite rules which can apply to all, in all circumstances. But on this, as on previous topics, there seem to be *general principles,* by the aid of which any candid mind, sincerely desirous of obeying the commands of Christ, however much self-denial may be involved, can arrive at definite conclusions as to its own individual obligations : so that when these are fulfilled, the mind may be at peace.

But for a mind that is worldly, living mainly to seek its own pleasures instead of living to please God, no principles can be so fixed as not to leave a ready escape from all obligation. Such minds, either by indolence (and consequent ignorance) or by sophistry, will convince themselves that a life of engrossing self-indulgence, with perhaps the gift of a few dollars and a few hours of time, may suffice to fulfill the requisitions of the Eternal Judge.

For such minds, no reasonings will avail, till the heart is so changed that to learn the will and follow the example of Jesus Christ become the leading objects of interest and effort. It is to aid those who profess to possess this temper of mind that the following suggestions are offered.

The first consideration which gives definiteness to this subject is a correct view of the object for which we are placed in this world. A great many, even of professed Christians, seem to be acting on the supposition that the object of life is to secure as much as possible of all the various enjoyments placed within reach. Not so teaches reason or revelation. From these we learn that, though the happiness of his creatures is the end for which God created and sustains them, yet this happiness depends not on the various modes of gratification put within our reach, but mainly on *character*. A man may possess all the resources for enjoyment which this world can afford, and yet feel that " all is vanity and vexation of spirit," and that he is supremely wretched. Another may be in want of all things, and yet possess that living spring of benevolence, faith, and hope, which will make an Eden of the darkest prison.

In order to be perfectly happy, man must attain that character which Christ exhibited; and the nearer he approaches it, the more will happiness reign in his breast.

But what was the grand peculiarity of the character of Christ? It was *self-denying benevolence.* He came not to " seek his own;" He " went about doing good," and this was his " meat and drink ;" that is, it was this which sustained the health and life of his mind, as food and drink sustain the health and life of the body. Now, the mind of man is so made that it can gradually be transformed into the same likeness. A selfish being, who, for a whole life, has been nourishing habits of indolent self-indulgence, can by taking Christ as his example, by communion with him, and by daily striving to imitate his character and conduct, form such a temper of mind that "doing good" will become the chief and highest source of enjoyment. And this heavenly principle will grow stronger and stronger, until self-denial loses the more painful part of its character ; and then, *living to make happiness* will be so delightful and absorbing a pursuit, that all exertions, regarded as the means to this end, will be like the joyous efforts of men when they strive for a prize or a crown, with the full hope of success.

In this view of the subject, efforts and self-denial for the good of others are to be regarded not merely as duties enjoined for the benefit of others, but as the moral training indispensable to the formation of that character on which depends our own happiness. This view exhibits the full meaning of the Saviour's declaration, " How hardly shall they that have riches enter into the kingdom of God !" He had before taught that the kingdom of heaven consisted not in such enjoyments as the worldly seek, but in the temper of self-denying benevolence, like his own ; and as the rich have far greater temptations to indolent self-indulgence, they are far less likely to acquire this temper than those who, by limited means, are inured to some degree of self-denial.

But on this point, one important distinction needs to be made ; and that is, between the self-denial which has no other aim than mere self-mortification, and that which is exercised to secure greater good to ourselves and others. The first is the foundation of monasticism, penances, and all other forms of asceticism ; the latter, only, is that which Christianity requires.

A second consideration, which may give definiteness to this subject, is, that the formation of a perfect character involves, not the extermination of any principles of our nature, but rather the regulating of them, according to the rules of reason and religion; so that the lower propensities shall always be kept subordinate to nobler principles. Thus we are not to aim at destroying our appetites, or at needlessly denying them, but rather so to regulate them that they shall best secure the objects for which they were implanted. We are not to annihilate the love of praise and admiration ; but so to control it that the favor of God shall be regarded more than the estimation of men. We are not to extirpate the principle of curiosity, which leads us to acquire knowledge ; but so to direct it, that all our acquisitions shall be useful and not frivolous or injurious. And thus with all the principles of the mind : God has implanted no desires in our constitution which are evil and pernicious. On the contrary, all our constitutional propensities, either of mind or body, he designed we should gratify, whenever no evils would thence result, either to ourselves or others. Such passions as envy, selfish ambition, contemptuous pride, revenge, and hatred, are to be exterminated; for they are either excesses or excrescences, not created by God, but rather the result of our own neglect to form habits of benevolence and self-control.

In deciding the rules of our conduct, therefore, we are ever to bear in mind that the development of the nobler principles, and the subjugation of inferior propensities to them, is to be the main object of effort both for ourselves and for others. And in conformity with this, in all our plans we are to place religious and moral interests as first in estimation, our social and intellectual interests next, and our physical gratifications as subordinate to all.

A third consideration is that, though the means for sustaining life and health are to be regarded as necessaries, without which no other duties can be performed, yet a very large portion of the time spent by most persons in easy circumstances for food, raiment, and dwellings, is for mere *superfluities ;* which are right when they do not involve the sacrifice of higher interests, and wrong when they do. Life and health can be sustained in the humblest dwellings, with the plainest dress, and the simplest food; and, after taking from our means what is necessary for life and health, the remainder is to be so divided, that the larger portion shall be given to supply the moral and intellectual wants of ourselves and others, together with the physical requirements of the destitute, and the smaller share to procure those additional gratifications of taste and appetite which are desirable but not indispensable. Mankind, thus far, have never made this apportionment of their means; although, just as fast as they have risen from a savage state, mere physical wants have been made, to an increasing extent, subordinate to higher objects.

Another very important consideration is that, in urging the duty of charity and the prior claims of moral and religious objects, no rule of duty should be maintained which it would not be right and wise for *all* to follow. And we are to test the wisdom of any general rule by inquiring what would be the result if all mankind should practice according to it. In view of this, we are enabled to judge of the correctness of those who maintain that, to be consistent, men believing in the perils of all those of our race who are not brought under the influence of the Christian system should give up not merely the elegancies but all the superfluities of life, and devote the whole of their means not indispensable to life and health to the propagation of Christianity.

But if this is the duty of any, it is the duty of all; and we are to inquire what would be the result, if all conscientious persons gave up the use of all superfluities. Suppose that two millions of the people of the United States were conscientious persons, and relinquished the use of every thing not absolutely necessary to life and health. Besides reducing the education of the people in all the higher walks of intellectual, social, and even moral development, to very narrow limits, it would instantly throw out of employment one half of the whole community. The writers, book-makers, manufacturers, mechanics, merchants, agriculturists, and all the agencies they employ, would be beggared, and one half of those not reduced to poverty would be obliged to spend all their extra means in simply supplying necessaries to the other half. The use of superfluities, therefore, to a certain extent, is as indispensable to promote industry, virtue, and religion, as any direct giving of money or time; and it is owing entirely to a want of reflection and of comprehensive views, that any men ever make so great a mistake as is here exhibited.

Instead, then, of urging a rule of duty which is at once irrational and impracticable, there is another course, which commends itself to the understandings of all. For whatever may be the practice of intelligent men, they universally concede the principle, that our physical gratifications should always be made subordinate to social, intellectual, and moral advantages. And all that is required for the advancement of our whole race to the most perfect state of society is, simply, that men should act in agreement with this principle. And if only a very small portion of the most intelligent of our race should act according to this rule, under the control of Christian benevolence, the immense supplies furnished for the general good would be far beyond what any would imagine who had never made any calculations on the subject. In this nation alone, suppose the one million and more of professed followers of Christ should give a larger portion of their means for the social, intellectual, and moral wants of mankind, than for the superfluities that minister to their own taste, convenience, and appetite; it would be enough to furnish all the schools, colleges, Bibles, ministers, and missionaries, that the whole world could demand; or, at least, it would be far more than properly qualified agents to administer it could employ.

But it may be objected that, though this view in the

abstract looks plausible and rational, not one in a thousand can practically adopt it. How few keep any account, at all, of their current expenses! How impossible it is to determine, exactly, what are necessaries and what are superfluities! And in regard to women, how few have the control of an income, so as not to be bound by the wishes of a parent or a husband!

In reference to these difficulties, the first remark is, that we are never under obligations to do what is entirely out of our power; so that those persons who can not regulate their expenses or their charities are under no sort of obligation to attempt it. The second remark is that, when a rule of duty is discovered, if we can not fully attain to it, we are bound to *aim* at it, and to fulfill it just so far as we can. We have no right to throw it aside because we shall find some difficult cases when we come to apply it. The third remark is, that no person can tell how much can be done, till a faithful trial has been made. If a woman has never kept any accounts, nor attempted to regulate her expenditures by the right rule, nor used her influence with those that control her plans, to secure this object, she has no right to say how much she can or can not do, till after a fair trial has been made.

In attempting such a trial, the following method can be taken. Let a woman keep an account of all she spends, for herself and her family, for a year, arranging the items under three general heads. Under the first, put all articles of food, raiment, rent, wages, and all conveniences. Under the second, place all sums paid in securing an education, and books, and other intellectual advantages. Under the third head, place all that is spent for benevolence and religion. At the end of the year, the first and largest account will show the mixed items of necessaries and superfluities, which can be arranged so as to gain some sort of idea how much has been spent for superfluities and how much for necessaries. Then, by comparing what is spent for superfluities, with what is spent for intellectual and moral advantages, data will be gained for judging of the past and regulating the future.

Does a woman say she can not do this? let her think whether the offer of a thousand dollars, as a reward for attempting it one year, would not make her undertake to do it; and if so, let her decide, in her own mind, which is most valuable, a clear conscience, and the approbation of God, in this effort to do his will, or one thousand dollars. And let her do it, with this warning of the Saviour before her eyes—"No man can serve two masters." "Ye can not serve God and Mammon."

Is it objected, How can we decide between superfluities and necessities, in this list? It is replied, that we are not required to judge exactly, in all cases. Our duty is, to use the means in our power to assist us in forming a correct judgment; to seek the divine aid in freeing our minds from indolence and selfishness; and then to judge, as well as we can, in our endeavors rightly to apportion and regulate our expenses. Many persons seem to feel that they are bound to do better than they know how. But God is not so hard a master; and after we have used all proper means to learn the right way, if we then follow it according to our ability, we do wrong to feel misgivings, or to blame ourselves, if results come out differently from what seems desirable.

The results of our actions, alone, can never prove us deserving of blame. For men are often so placed that, owing to lack of intellect or means, it is impossible for them to decide correctly. To use all the means of knowledge within our reach, and then to judge, with a candid and conscientious spirit, is all that God requires; and when we have done this, and the event seems to come out wrong, we should never wish that we had decided otherwise. For this would be the same as wishing that we had not followed the dictates of judgment and conscience. As this is a world designed for discipline and trial, untoward events are never to be construed as indications of the obliquity of our past decisions.

But it is probable that a great portion of the women of this nation can not secure any such systematic mode of regulating their expenses. To such, the writer would propose one inquiry : Can not you calculate how much *time* and *money* you spend for what is merely ornamental, and not necessary, for yourself, your children, and your house ? Can not you compare this with the time and money you spend for intellectual and benevolent purposes ? and will not this show the need of some change ? In making this examination, is not this brief rule, deducible from the principles before laid down, the one which should regulate you ? Every person does right in spending some portion of time and means in securing the conveniences and adornments of taste ; but the amount should never exceed what is spent in securing our own moral and intellectual improvement, nor what is spent in benevolent efforts to supply the physical and moral wants of our fellow-men.

In making an examination on this subject, it is sometimes the case that a woman will count among the *necessaries* of life all the various modes of adorning the person or house, practiced in the circle in which she moves ; and, after enumerating the many *duties* which demand attention, counting these as a part, she will come to the conclusion that she has no time, and but little money, to devote to personal improvement or to benevolent enterprises. This surely is not in agreement with the requirements of the Saviour, who calls on us to seek for others, as well as ourselves, *first of all*, " the kingdom of God, and his righteousness."

In order to act in accordance with the rule here presented, it is true that many would be obliged to give up the idea of conforming to the notions and customs of those with whom they associate, and compelled to adopt the maxim, "Be not conformed to this world." In many cases, it would involve an entire change in the style of living. And the writer has the happiness of knowing more cases than one, where persons who have come to similar views on this subject, have given up large and expensive establishments, disposed of their carriages, dismissed a portion of their domestics, and modified all their expenditures, that they might keep a pure conscience, and regulate their charities more according to the requirements of Christianity. And there are persons, well known in the religious world, who save themselves all labor of minute calculation, by devoting so large a portion of their time and means to benevolent objects, that they find no difficulty in knowing that they give more for religious, benevolent, and intellectual purposes than for superfluities.

In deciding what particular objects shall receive our benefactions, there are also general principles to guide us. The first is that presented by our Saviour, when, after urging the great law of benevolence, he was asked, "And who is my neighbor?" His reply, in the parable of "the Good Samaritan," teaches us that any human being whose wants are brought to our knowledge is our neighbor. The wounded man in that parable was not only a stranger, but he belonged to a foreign nation, peculiarly hated; and he had no claim, except that his wants were brought to the knowledge of the wayfaring man. From this we learn that the destitute of all nations become our neighbors, as soon as their wants are brought to our knowledge.

Another general principle is this, that those who are most in need must be relieved in preference to those who are less destitute. On this principle it is, that we think the followers of Christ should give more to supply those who are suffering for want of the bread of eternal life, than for those who are deprived of physical enjoyments. And another reason for this preference is the fact that many who give in charity have made such imperfect advances in civilization and Christianity that the intellectual and moral wants of our race make but a feeble impression on the mind. Relate a pitiful tale of a family reduced to live for weeks on potatoes only, and many a mind would awake to deep sympathy and stretch forth the hand of charity. But describe cases where the immortal mind is pining in stupidity and ignorance, or racked with the fever of baleful passions, and how small the number so elevated in sentiment and so enlarged in their views as to appreciate and sympathize in these far greater misfortunes! The intellectual and moral wants of our fellow-men, therefore, should claim the first place in general Christian attention, both because they are most important, and because they are most neglected; while it should not be forgotten, in giving personal attention to the wants of the poor, that the relief of immediate physical distress, is often the easiest way of touching the moral sensibilities of the destitute.

Another consideration to be borne in mind is that, in this country, there is much less real need of charity in supplying physical necessities than is generally supposed by those who have not learned the more excellent way. This land is so abundant in supplies, and labor is in such demand, that every healthy person can earn a comfortable support. And if all the poor were instantly made virtuous, it is probable that there would be few physical wants which could not readily be supplied by the immediate friends of each sufferer. The sick, the aged, and the orphan would be the only objects of charity. In this view of the case, the primary effort in relieving the poor should be to furnish them the means of earning their own support, and to supply them with those moral influences which are most effectual in securing virtue and industry.

Another point to be attended to is the importance of maintaining a system of *associated* charities. There is no point in which the economy of charity has more improved than in the present mode of combining many small contributions, for sustaining enlarged and systematic plans of charity. If all the half-dollars which are now contributed to aid in organized systems of charity were returned to the donors, to be applied by the agency and discretion of each, thousands and thousands of the treasures, now employed to promote the moral and intellectual wants of mankind, would become entirely useless. In a democracy like ours, where few are very rich and the majority are in comfortable circumstances, this collecting and dispensing of drops and rills is the mode by which, in imitation of nature, the dews and showers are to distill on parched and desert lands. And every person, while earning a pittance to unite with many more, may be cheered with the consciousness of sustaining a grand system of operations which must have the most decided influence in raising all mankind to that perfect state of society which Christianity is designed to bring about.

Another consideration relates to the indiscriminate bestowal of charity. Persons who have taken pains to inform themselves, and who devote their whole time to dispensing charities, unite in declaring that this is one of the most fruitful sources of indolence, vice, and poverty. From several of these the writer has learned that, by their own personal investigations, they have ascertained that there are large establishments of idle and wicked persons in most of our cities, who associate together to support themselves by every species of imposition. They hire large houses, and live in constant rioting on the means thus obtained. Among them are women who have or who hire the use of infant children ; others, who are blind, or maimed, or deformed, or who can adroitly feign such infirmities ; and, by these means of exciting pity, and by artful tales of woe, they collect alms, both in city and country, to spend in all manner of gross and guilty indulgences. Meantime many persons, finding themselves often duped by impostors, refuse to give at all ; and thus many benefactions are withdrawn, which

a wise economy in charity would have secured.   For this
and other reasons, it is wise and merciful to adopt the general rule, never to give alms till we have had some opportunity of knowing how they will be spent.   There are exceptions to this, as to every general rule, which a person
of discretion can determine.   But the practice so common
among benevolent persons, of giving at least a trifle to all
who ask, lest perchance they may turn away some who are
really sufferers, is one which causes more sin and misery
than it cures.

The writer has never known any system for dispensing
charity so successful as the one by which a town or city is
divided into districts ; and each district is committed to the
care of two ladies, whose duty it is, to call on each family
and leave a book for a child, or do some other deed of neigh-
borly kindness, and make that the occasion for entering into
conversation, and learning the situation of all residents in
the district.   By this method, the ignorant, the vicious, and
the poor are discovered, and their physical, intellectual, and
moral wants are investigated.   In some places where the
writer has known this mode pursued, each person retained
the same district, year after year, so that every poor family in
the place was under the watch and care of some intelligent
and benevolent lady, who used all her influence to secure a
proper education for the children, to furnish them with suitable reading, to encourage habits of industry and economy,
and to secure regular attendance on public religious instruction.   Thus, the rich and the poor were brought in
contact, in a way advantageous to both parties ; and if such
a system could be universally adopted, more would be done
for the prevention of poverty and vice than all the wealth
of the nation could avail for their relief.   But this plan can
not be successfully carried out, in this manner, unless there
is a large proportion of intelligent, benevolent, and self-
denying persons, who unite in a systematic plan.

But there is one species of " charity " which needs especial consideration. It is that spirit of kindly love which induces us to refrain from judging of the means and the relative charities of other persons. There have been such indistinct notions, and so many different standards of duty, on this subject, that it is rare for two persons to think exactly alike, in regard to the rule of duty. Each person is bound to inquire and judge for himself, as to his own duty or deficiencies; but as both the resources and the amount of the actual charities of others are beyond our ken, it is as indecorous as it is uncharitable to sit in judgment on their lecisions.

XIX.

THE value of time, and our obligation to spend every hour for some useful end, are what few minds properly realize. And those who have the highest sense of their obligations in this respect, sometimes greatly misjudge in their estimate of what are useful and proper modes of employing time. This arises from limited views of the importance of some pursuits, which they would deem frivolous and useless, but which are in reality necessary to preserve the health of body and mind and those social affections which it is very important to cherish.

Christianity teaches that, for all the time afforded us, we must give account to God; and that we have no right to waste a single hour. But time which is spent in rest or amusement is often as usefully employed as if it were devoted to labor or devotion. In employing our time, we are to make suitable allowance for sleep, for preparing and taking food, for securing the means of a livelihood, for intellectual improvement, for exercise and amusement, for social enjoyments, and for benevolent and religious duties. And it is the *right apportionment* of time, to these various duties, which constitutes its true economy.

In deciding respecting the rectitude of our pursuits, we are bound to aim at some practical good, as the ultimate object. With every duty of this life, our benevolent Creator has connected some species of enjoyment, to draw us to perform it. Thus, the palate is gratified, by performing the duty of nourishing our bodies; the principle of curiosity is gratified in pursuing useful knowledge; the desire of approbation is gratified, when we perform general social duties; and every other duty has an alluring enjoyment connected with it. But the great mistake of mankind has consisted in seeking the pleasures connected with these duties, as the sole aim, without reference to the main end that should be held in view, and to which the enjoyment should be made subservient. Thus, men gratify the palate, without reference to the question whether the body is properly nourished: and follow after knowledge, without inquiring whether it ministers to good or evil; and seek amusement without reference to results.

In gratifying the implanted desires of our nature, we are bound so to restrain ourselves, by reason and conscience, as always to seek the main objects of existence—the highest good of ourselves and others; and never to sacrifice this for the mere gratification of our desires. We are to gratify appetite, just so far as is consistent with health and usefulness; and the desire for knowledge, just so far as will enable us to do most good by our influence and efforts; and no farther. We are to seek social intercourse, to that extent which will best promote domestic enjoyment and kindly feelings among neighbors and friends; and we are to pursue exercise and amusement, only so far as will best sustain the vigor of body and mind.

The laws of the Supreme Ruler, when he became the civil as well as the religious Head of the Jewish theocracy, furnish an example which it would be well for all attentively to consider, when forming plans for the apportionment of time and property. To properly estimate this example, it must be borne in mind, that the main object of God was, to set an example of the temporal rewards that follow obedience to the laws of the Creator, and at the same time to prepare religious teachers to extend the true religion to the whole race of man.

Before Christ came, the Jews were not required to go forth to other nations as teachers of religion, nor were the Jewish nation led to obedience by motives of a life to come. To them God was revealed, both as a father and a civil ruler, and obedience to laws relating solely to this life was all that was required. So low were they in the scale of civilization and mental development, that a system which confined them to one spot, as an agricultural people, and prevented their growing very rich, or having extensive commerce with other nations, was indispensable to prevent their relapsing into the low idolatries and vices of the nations around them, while temporal rewards and penalties were more effective than those of a life to come.

The proportion of time and property, which every Jew was required to devote to intellectual, benevolent, and religious purposes, was as follows :

In regard to property, they were required to give one tenth of all their yearly income to support the Levites, the priests, and the religious service. Next, they were required to give the first-fruits of all their corn, wine, oil, and fruits, and the first-born of all their cattle, for the Lord's treasury, to be employed for the priests, the widow, the fatherless, and the stranger. The first-born, also, of their children, were the Lord's, and were to be redeemed by a specified sum, paid into the sacred treasury. Besides this, they were required to bring a free-will offering to God, every time they went up to the three great yearly festivals. In addition to this, regular yearly sacrifices of cattle and fowls were required of each family, and occasional sacrifices for certain sins or ceremonial impurities. In reaping their fields, they were required to leave unreaped, for the poor, the corners ; not to glean their fields, oliveyards, or vineyards ; and, if a sheaf was left by mistake, they were not to return for it but leave it for the poor.

One twelfth of the people were set apart, having no landed property, to be priests and teachers; and the other tribes were required to support them liberally.

In regard to the time taken from secular pursuits, for the support of education and religion, an equally liberal amount was demanded. In the first place, one seventh part of their time was taken for the weekly sabbath, when no kind of work was to be done. Then the whole nation were required to meet at the appointed place three times a year, which, including their journeys and stay there, occupied eight weeks, or another seventh part of their time. Then the sabbatical year, when no agricultural labor was to be done, took another seventh of their time from their regular pursuits, as they were an agricultural people. This was the amount of time and property demanded by God, simply to sustain education, religion, and morality within the bounds of one nation.

It was promised to this nation and fulfilled by constant miraculous interpositions, that in this life, obedience to God's laws should secure health, peace, prosperity, and long life; while for disobedience was threatened war, pestilence, famine, and all temporal evils. These promises were constantly verified, and in the day of Solomon, when this nation was most obedient, the whole world was moved with wonder at its wealth and prosperity. But up to this time, no attempt was made by God to govern the Israelites by the rewards and penalties of the world to come.

But "when the fullness of time had come," and the race of man was prepared to receive higher responsibilities, Jesus Christ came and "brought life and immortality to light" with a clearness never before revealed. At the same time was revealed the fatherhood of God, not to the Jews alone, but to the whole human race, and the consequent brotherhood of man; and these revelations in many respects changed the whole standard of duty and obligation.

Christ came as "God manifest in the flesh," to set an example of self-sacrificing love, in rescuing the whole family of man from the dangers of the unseen world, and also to teach and train his disciples through all time to follow his example. And those who conform the most consistently to his teachings and example will aim at a standard of labor and self-denial far beyond that demanded of the Jews.

It is not always that men understand the economy of Providence, in that unequal distribution of property which, even under the most perfect form of government, will always exist. Many, looking at the present state of things, imagine that the rich, if they acted in strict conformity to the law of benevolence, would share all their property with their suffering fellow-men. But such do not take into account the inspired declaration that "a man's life consisteth not in the abundance of the things which he possesseth," or, in other words, life is made valuable, not by great possessions, but by such a character as prepares a man to enjoy what he holds. God perceives that human character can be most improved by that kind of discipline which exists when there is something valuable to be gained by industrious efforts. This stimulus to industry could never exist in a community where all are just alike, as it does in a state of society where every man sees possessed by others enjoyments which he desires and may secure by effort and industry. So, in a community where all are alike as to property, there would be no chance to gain that noblest of all attainments, a habit of self-denying benevolence which toils for the good of others, and takes from one's own store to increase the enjoyments of another.

Instead, then, of the stagnation, both of industry and of benevolence, which would follow the universal and equable distribution of property, some men, by superior advantages of birth, or intellect, or patronage, come into possession of a great amount of capital. With these means they are enabled, by study, reading, and travel, to secure expansion of mind and just views of the relative advantages

of moral, intellectual, and physical enjoyments. At the
same time, Christianity imposes obligations corresponding
with the increase of advantages and means. The rich are
not at liberty to spend their treasures chiefly for themselves.
Their wealth is given, by God, to be employed for the best
good of mankind ; and their intellectual advantages are designed, primarily, to enable them to judge correctly in employing their means most wisely for the general good.

Now, suppose a man of wealth inherits ten thousand
acres of real estate ; it is not his duty to divide it among
his poor neighbors and tenants. If he took this course,
it is probable that most of them would spend all in thriftless waste and indolence, or in mere physical enjoyments.
Instead, then, of thus putting his capital out of his hands,
he is bound to retain and so to employ it as to raise his
family and his neighbors to such a state of virtue and intelligence that they can secure far more, by their own efforts and industry, than he, by dividing his capital, could
bestow upon them.

In this view of the subject, it is manifest that the unequal
distribution of property is no evil. The great difficulty is,
that so large a portion of those who hold much capital, instead of using their various advantages for the greatest
good of those around them, employ them for mere selfish
indulgences ; thus inflicting as much mischief on themselves
as results to others from their culpable neglect. A great
portion of the rich seem to be acting on the principle
that the more God bestows on them the less are they under
obligation to practice any self-denial in fulfilling his benevolent plan of raising our race to intelligence and virtue.

But there are cheering examples of the contrary spirit
and prejudice, some of which will be here recorded to influence and encourage others.

A lady of great wealth, high position, and elegant
culture, in one of our large cities, hired and furnished a
house adjacent to her own, and, securing the aid of another

benevolent and cultivated woman, took twelve orphan girls, of different ages, and educated them under their joint care. Not only time and money were given, but love and labor, just as if these were their own children; and as fast as one was provided for, another was taken.

In another city, a young lady with property of her own hired a house and made it a home for homeless and unprotected women, who paid board when they could earn it, and found a refuge when out of employment.

In another city, the wife of one of its richest merchants, living in princely style, took two young girls from the certain road to ruin among the vicious poor. She boarded them with a respectable farmer, and sent them to school, and every week went out, not only to supervise them, but to aid in training them to habits of neatness, industry, and obedience, just as if they were her own children. Next, she hired a large house near the most degraded part of the city, furnished it neatly and with all suitable conveniences to work, and then rented to those among the most degraded whom she could bring to conform to a few simple rules of decency, industry, and benevolence—one of these rules being that they should pay her the rent every Saturday night. To this motley gathering she became chief counselor and friend, quieted their brawls, taught them to aid each other in trouble or sickness, and strove to introduce among them that law of patient love and kindness, illustrated by her own example. The young girls in this tenement she assembled every Saturday at her own house—taught them to sing, heard them recite their Sunday-school lessons, to be sure these were properly learned; taught them to make and mend their own clothing, trimmed their bonnets, and took charge of their Sunday dress, that it might always be in order. Of course, such benevolence drew a stream of ignorance and misery to her door; and so successful was her labor that she hired a second house, and managed it on the same plan. One hot day in August, a friend found her combing the head of a poor, ungainly, foreign girl. She had persuaded a friend to take her from compassion, and she was returned because her head was in such in a state. Finding no one else to do it, the lady herself bravely met the difficulty, and persevered in this daily ministry till the evil was remedied, and the poor girl thus secured a comfortable home and wages.

A young lady of wealth and position, with great musical culture and taste, found among the poor two young girls with fine voices and great musical talent. Gaining her parents' consent, the young lady took one of them home, trained her in music, and saw that her school education was secured, so that when expensive masters and instruments were needed the girl herself earned the money required, as a governess in a family of wealthy friends. Then she aided the sister; and, as the result, one of them is married happily to a man of great wealth, and the other is receiving a large income as a popular musical artist.

Another young girl, educated as a fine musician by her wealthy parents, at the age of sixteen was afflicted with weak eyes and a heart complaint. She strove to solace herself by benevolent ministries. By teaching music to children of wealthy friends she earned the means to relieve and instruct the suffering, ignorant, and poor.

These examples may suffice to show that, even among the most wealthy, abundant modes of self-denying benevolence may be found where there is a heart to seek them.

There is no direction in which a true Christian economy of time and money is more conspicuous than in the style of living adopted in the family state.

Those who build stately mansions, and lay out extensive grounds, and multiply the elegancies of life, to be enjoyed by themselves and a select few, " have their reward" in the enjoyments that end in this life. But those who with equal means adopt a style that enables them largely to devote time and wealth to the elevation and improvement of their fellow-men, are laying up never-failing treasures in heaven.

XX.

THERE is such an intimate connection between the body and mind that the health of one can not be preserved without a proper care of the other. And it is from a neglect of this principle, that some of the most exemplary and conscientious persons in the world suffer a thousand mental agonies from a diseased state of body, while others ruin the health of the body by neglecting the proper care of the mind.

When the mind is excited by earnest intellectual effort, or by strong passions, the blood rushes to the head and the brain is excited. Sir Astley Cooper records that, in examining the brain of a young man who had lost a portion of his skull, whenever " he was agitated by some opposition to his wishes," " the blood was sent with increased force to his brain," and the pulsations " became frequent and violent." The same effect was produced by any intellectual effort; and the flushed countenance which attends earnest study or strong emotions of interest of any kind, is an external indication of the suffused state of the brain from such causes.

In exhibiting the causes which injure the health of the mind, we shall find them to be partly physical, partly intellectual, and partly moral.

The first cause of mental disease and suffering is not unfrequently in the want of a proper supply of duly oxygenized blood. It has been shown that the blood, in passing through the lungs, is purified by the oxygen of the air combining with the superabundant hydrogen and carbon of the venous blood, thus forming carbonic acid and water, which are expired into the atmosphere. Every pair of lungs is constantly withdrawing from the surrounding atmosphere its heathful principle, and returning one which is injurious to human life.

When, by confinement and this process, the air is deprived of its appropriate supply of oxygen, the purification of the blood is interrupted, and it passes without being properly prepared into the brain, producing languor, restlessness, and inability to exercise the intellect and feelings. Whenever, therefore, persons sleep in a close apartment, or remain for a length of time in a crowded or ill-ventilated room, a most pernicious influence is exerted on the brain, and, through this, on the mind. A person who is often exposed to such influences can never enjoy that elasticity and vigor of mind which is one of the chief indications of its health. This is the reason why all rooms for religious meetings, and all school-rooms and sleeping apartments should be so contrived as to secure a constant supply of fresh air from without. The minister who preaches in a crowded and ill-ventilated apartment loses much of his power to feel and to speak, while the audience are equally reduced in their capability of attending. The teacher who confines children in a close apartment diminishes their ability to study, or to attend to instructions. And the person who habitually sleeps in a close room impairs mental energy in a similar degree. It is not unfrequently the case that depression of spirits and stupor of intellect are occasioned solely by inattention to this subject.

Another cause of mental disease is the excessive exercise of the intellect or feelings. If the eye is taxed beyond its strength by protracted use, its blood-vessels become gorged, and the bloodshot appearance warns of the excess and the need of rest. The brain is affected in a similar manner by excessive use, though the suffering and inflamed organ can not make its appeal to the eye. But there are some indications which ought never to be misunderstood or disregarded. In cases of pupils at school or at college, a diseased state, from over-action, is often manifested by increased clearness of mind, and temporary ease and vigor of mental action. In one instance, known to the writer, a most exemplary and industrious pupil, anxious to improve every hour and ignorant or unmindful of the laws of health, first manifested the diseased state of her brain and mind by demands for more studies, and a sudden and earnest activity in planning modes of improvement for herself and others. When warned of her danger, she protested that she never was better in her life; that she took regular exercise in the open air, went to bed in season, slept soundly, and felt perfectly well; that her mind was never before so bright and clear, and study never so easy and delightful. And at this time, she was on the verge of derangement, from which she was saved only by an entire cessation of all intellectual efforts.

A similar case occurred, under the eye of the writer, from over-excited feelings. It was during a time of unusual religious interest in the community, and the mental disease was first manifested by the pupil bringing her hymn-book or Bible to the class-room, and making it her constant resort, in every interval of school duty. It finally became impossible to convince her that it was her duty to attend to any thing else; her conscience became morbidly sensitive, her perceptions indistinct, her deductions unreasonable; and nothing but entire change of scene and exercise, and occupation of her mind by amusement, saved her. When the health of the brain was restored, she found that she could attend to the "one thing needful," not only without interruption of duty or injury to health, but rather so as to promote both. Clergymen and teachers need most carefully to notice and guard against the dangers here alluded to.

Any such attention to religion as prevents the performance of daily duties and needful relaxation is dangerous, and tends to produce such a state of the brain as makes it impossible to feel or judge correctly. And when any morbid and unreasonable pertinacity appears, much exercise and engagement in other interesting pursuits should be urged, as the only mode of securing the religious benefits aimed at. And whenever any mind is oppressed with care, anxiety, or sorrow, the amount of active exercise in the fresh air should be greatly increased, that the action of the muscles may withdraw the blood which, in such seasons, is constantly tending too much to the brain.

There has been a most appalling amount of suffering, derangement, disease, and death, occasioned by a want of attention to this subject, in teachers and parents. Uncommon precocity in children is usually the result of an unhealthy state of the brain; and in such cases medical men would now direct that the wonderful child should be deprived of all books and study, and turned to play out in the fresh air. Instead of this, parents frequently add fuel to the fever of the brain, by supplying constant mental stimulus, until the victim finds refuge in idiocy or an early grave. Where such fatal results do not occur, the brain in many cases is so weakened that the prodigy of infancy sinks below the medium of intellectual powers in after-life.

In our colleges, too, many of the most promising minds sink to an early grave, or drag out a miserable existence, from this same cause. And it is an evil as yet little alleviated by the increase of physiological knowledge. Every college and professional school, and every seminary for young ladies, needs a medical man or woman, not only to lecture on physiology and the laws of health, but empowered by official capacity to investigate the case of every pupil, and, by authority, to enforce such a course of study, exercise and repose, as the physical system requires.

The writer has found by experience that in a large institution there is one class of pupils who need to be restrained by penalties from late hours and excessive study, as much as another class need stimulus to industry.

Under the head of excessive mental action, must be placed the indulgence of the imagination in novel-reading and " castle-building." This kind of stimulus, unless counterbalanced by physical exercise, not only wastes time and energies, but undermines the vigor of the nervous system. The imagination was designed by our wise Creator as a charm and stimulus to animate to benevolent activity; and its perverted exercise seldom fails to bring a penalty.

Another cause of mental disease is the want of the appropriate exercise of the various faculties of the mind. On this point, Dr. Combe remarks : " We have seen that, by disuse, muscles become emaciated, bone softens, blood-vessels are obliterated, and nerves lose their characteristic structure. The brain is no exception to this general rule. The tone of it is also impaired by permanent inactivity, and it becomes less fit to manifest the mental powers with readiness and energy." It is " the withdrawal of the stimulus necessary for its healthy exercise which renders solitary confinement so severe a punishment, even to the most daring minds. It is a lower degree of the same cause which renders continuous seclusion from society so injurious to both mental and bodily health."

" Inactivity of intellect and of feeling is a very frequent predisposing cause of every form of nervous disease. For demonstrative evidence of this position, we have only to look at the numerous victims to be found among persons who have no call to exertion in gaining the means of subsistence, and no objects of interest on which to exercise their mental faculties, and who consequently sink into a state of mental. sloth and nervous weakness." " If we look abroad upon society, we shall find innumerable examples of mental and nervous debility from this cause. When a person of some mental capacity is confined for a long time to an unvarying round of employment which affords neither scope nor stimulus for one half of the faculties, and, from want of education or society, has no external resources; the mental powers, for want of exercise, become blunted, and the perceptions slow and dull." "The intellect and feelings, not being provided with interests external to themselves, must either become inactive and weak, or work upon themselves and become diseased."

"The most frequent victims of this kind of predisposition are females of the middle and higher ranks, especially those of a nervous constitution and good natural abilities; but who, from an ill-directed education, possess nothing more solid than mere accomplishments, and have no materials for thought," and no "occupation to excite interest or demand attention." "The liability of such persons to melancholy, hysteria, hypochondriasis, and other varieties of mental distress, really depends on a state of irritability of the brain, induced by imperfect exercise."

These remarks of a medical man illustrate the principles before indicated; namely, that the demand of Christianity, that we live to promote the general happiness, and not merely for selfish indulgence, has for its aim not only the general good, but the highest happiness of the individual of whom it is required in offering abundant exercise for all the noblest faculties.

A person possessed of wealth, who has nothing more noble to engage attention than seeking personal enjoyment, subjects the mental powers and moral feelings to a degree of inactivity utterly at war with health and mind. And the greater the capacities, the greater are the sufferings which result from this cause. Any one who has read the misanthropic wailings of Lord Byron has seen the necessary result of great and noble powers bereft of their appropriate exercise, and, in consequence, becoming sources of the keenest suffering.

It is this view of the subject which has often awakened feelings of sorrow and anxiety in the mind of the writer, while aiding in the development and education of superior feminine minds, in the wealthier circles. Not because there are not noble objects for interest and effort, abundant, and within reach of such minds; but because long-established custom has made it seem so quixotic to the majority, even of the professed followers of Christ, for a woman of wealth to practice any great self-denial, that few have independence of mind and Christian principle sufficient to overcome such an influence. The more a mind has its powers developed, the more does it aspire and pine after some object worthy of its energies and affections; and they are commonplace and phlegmatic characters who are most free from such deep-seated wants. Many a young woman, of fine genius and elevated sentiment, finds a charm in Lord Byron's writings, because they present a glowing picture of what, to a certain extent, must be felt by every well-developed mind which has no nobler object in life than the pursuit of self-gratification.

If young ladies of wealth could pursue their education under the full conviction that the increase of their powers and advantages increased their obligations to use all for the good of society, and with some plan of benevolent enterprise in view, what new motives of interest would be added to their daily pursuits! And what blessed results would follow to our beloved country, if all well-educated women carried out the principles of Christianity, in the exercise of their developed powers!

The benevolent activities called forth in our late dreadful war illustrate the blessed influence on character and happiness in having a noble object for which to labor and suffer. In illustration of this, may be mentioned the experience of one of the noble women who, in a sickly climate and fervid season, devoted herself to the ministries of a military hospital. Separated from an adored husband, deprived of wonted comforts and luxuries, and toiling in humble and unwonted labors, she yet recalls this as one of the happiest periods of her life. And it was not the mere exercise of benevolence and piety in ministering comfort and relieving suffering. It was, still more, the elevated enjoyment which only an enlarged and cultivated mind can attain, in the inspirations of grand and far-reaching results purchased by such sacrifice and suffering. It was in aiding to save her well-loved country from impending ruin, and to preserve to coming generations the blessings of true liberty and self-government, that toils and suffering became triumphant joys.

Every Christian woman who " walks by faith and not by sight," who looks forward to the results of self-sacrificing labor for the ignorant and sinful as they will enlarge and expand through everlasting ages, may rise to the same elevated sphere of experience and happiness.

On the contrary, the more highly cultivated the mind devoted to mere selfish enjoyment, the more are the sources of true happiness closed and the soul left to helpless emptiness and unrest.

The indications of a diseased mind, owing to the want of the proper exercise of its powers, are apathy, discontent, a restless longing for excitement, a craving for unattainable good, a diseased and morbid action of the imagination, dissatisfaction with the world, and factitious interest in trifles which the mind feels to be unworthy of its powers. Such minds sometimes seek alleviation in exciting amusements ; others resort to the grosser enjoyments of sense. Oppressed with the extremes of languor, or over-excitement, or apathy, the body fails under the wearing process, and adds new causes of suffering to the mind. Such, the compassionate Saviour calls to his service, in the appropriate terms, " Come unto me, all ye that labor and are heavy laden, and I will give you rest. Take my yoke upon you, and learn of me," " and ye shall find rest unto your souls."

XXI.

The topic of this chapter may well be prefaced by an extract from Herbert Spencer on the treatment of offspring. He first supposes that some future philosophic speculator, examining the course of education of the present period, should find nothing relating to the training of children, and that his natural inference would be that our schools were all for monastic orders, who have no charge of infancy and childhood. He then remarks, "Is it not an astonishing fact that, though on the treatment of offspring depend their lives or deaths and their moral welfare or ruin, yet not one word of instruction on the treatment of offspring is ever given to those who will hereafter be parents? Is it not monstrous that the fate of a new generation should be left to the chances of unreasoning custom, or impulse, or fancy, joined with the suggestions of ignorant nurses and the prejudiced counsel of grandmothers?

"If a merchant should commence business without any knowledge of arithmetic or book-keeping, we should exclaim at his folly and look for disastrous consequences. Or if, without studying anatomy, a man set up as a surgeon, we should wonder at his audacity and pity his patients. But that parents should commence the difficult work of rearing children without giving any attention to the principles, physical, moral, or intellectual, which ought to guide them, excites neither surprise at the actors nor pity for the victims."

"To tens of thousands that are killed add hundreds of

thousands that survive with feeble constitutions, and millions not so strong as they should be; and you will have some idea of the curse inflicted on their offspring, by parents ignorant of the laws of life. Do but consider for a moment that the regimen to which children are subject is hourly telling upon them to their life-long injury or benefit, and that there are twenty ways of going wrong to one way of going right, and you will get some idea of the enormous mischief that is almost everywhere inflicted by the thoughtless, hap-hazard system in common use."

" When sons and daughters grow up sickly and feeble, parents commonly regard the event as a visitation of Providence. They assume that these evils come without cause, or that the cause is supernatural. Nothing of the kind. In some cases causes are inherited, but in most cases foolish management is the cause. Very generally parents themselves are responsible for this pain, this debility, this depression, this misery. They have undertaken to control the lives of their offspring, and with cruel carelessness have neglected to learn those vital processes which they are daily affecting by their commands and prohibitions. In utter ignorance of the simplest physiological laws, they have been, year by year, undermining the constitutions of their children, and so have inflicted disease and premature death, not only on them but also on their descendants.

" Equally great are the ignorance and consequent injury, when we turn from the physical to the moral training. Consider the young, untaught mother and her nursery legislation. A short time ago she was at school, where her memory was crammed with words and names and dates, and her reflective faculties scarcely in the slightest degree exercised—where not one idea was given her respecting the methods of dealing with the opening mind of childhood, and where her discipline did not in the least fit her for thinking out methods of her own. The intervening years have been spent in practicing music, fancy work, novel-reading and party-going, no thought having been given to the grave responsibilities of maternity, and scarcely any of that solid intellectual culture obtained which would fit her for such responsibilities; and now see her with an unfolding human character committed to her charge, see her profoundly ignorant of the phenomena with which she has to deal, undertaking to do that which can be done but imperfectly even with the aid of the profoundest knowledge !"

In view of such considerations, every young lady ought to learn how to take proper care of an infant ; for, even if she is never to become the responsible guardian of a nursery, she will often be in situations where she can render benevolent aid to others, in this most fatiguing and anxious duty.

The writer has known instances in which young ladies, who had been trained by their mothers properly to perform this duty, were in some cases the means of saving the lives of infants, and in others, of relieving sick mothers from intolerable care and anguish by their benevolent aid.

On this point, Dr. Combe remarks, " All women are not destined, in the course of nature, to become mothers ; but how very small is the number of those who are unconnected, by family ties, friendship, or sympathy, with the children of others ! How very few are there, who, at some time or other of their lives, would not find their usefulness and happiness increased, by the possession of a kind of knowledge intimately allied to their best feelings and affections ! And how important is it, to the mother herself, that her efforts should be seconded by intelligent, instead of ignorant assistants !"

In order to be prepared for such benevolent ministries, every young lady should improve the opportunity, whenever it is afforded her, for learning how to wash, dress, and tend a young infant; and whenever she meets with such a work as Dr. Combe's, on the management of infants, she ought to read it, and *remember* its contents.

It was the design of the author to fill this chapter chiefly with extracts from various medical writers, giving some of the most important directions on this subject; but finding these extracts too prolix for a work of this kind, she has condensed them into a shorter compass. Some are quoted verbatim, and some are abridged, from the most approved writers on this subject.

"Nearly one half of the deaths, occurring during the first two years of existence, are ascribable to mismanagement, and to errors in diet. At birth, the stomach is feeble, and as yet unaccustomed to food; its cravings are consequently easily satisfied, and frequently renewed." "At that early age, there ought to be no fixed time for giving nourishment. The stomach can not be thus satisfied." "The active call of the infant is a sign, which needs never be mistaken."

"But care must be taken to determine between the crying of pain or uneasiness, and the call for food; and the practice of giving an infant food, to stop its cries, is often the means of increasing its sufferings. After a child has satisfied its hunger, from two to four hours should intervene before another supply is given."

"At birth, the stomach and bowels, never having been used, contain a quantity of mucous secretion, which requires to be removed. To effect this, Nature has rendered the first portions of the mother's milk purposely watery and laxative. Nurses, however, distrusting Nature, often hasten to administer some active purgative; and the consequence often is, irritation in the stomach and bowels, not easily subdued." It is only where the child is deprived of its mother's milk, as the first food, that some gentle laxative should be given.

"It is a common mistake, to suppose that because a woman is nursing, she ought to live very fully, and to add an allowance of wine, porter, or other fermented liquor, to her usual diet. The only result of this plan is, to cause an unnatural fullness in the system, which places the nurse on the brink of disease, and retards rather than increases the food of the infant. More will be gained by the observance of the ordinary laws of health, than by any foolish deviation, founded on ignorance."

There is no point on which medical men so emphatically lift the voice of warning as in reference to administering medicines to infants. It is so difficult to discover what is the matter with an infant, its frame is so delicate and so susceptible, and slight causes have such a powerful influence, that it requires the utmost skill and judgment to ascertain what would be proper medicines, and the proper quantity to be given.

Says Dr. Combe, " That there are cases in which active means must be promptly used to save the child, is perfectly true. But it is not less certain that these are cases of which no mother or nurse ought to attempt the treatment. As a general rule, where the child is well managed, medicine, of any kind, is very rarely required; and if disease were more generally regarded in its true light, not as something thrust into the system, which requires to be expelled by force, but as an aberration from a natural mode of action, produced by some external cause, we should be in less haste to attack it by medicine, and more watchful in its prevention. Accordingly, where a constant demand for medicine exists in a nursery, the mother may rest assured that there is something essentially wrong in the treatment of her children."

" Much havoc is made among infants, by the abuse of calomel and other medicines, which procure momentary relief but end by producing incurable disease ; and it has often excited my astonishment, to see how recklessly remedies of this kind are had recourse to, on the most trifling occasions, by mothers and nurses, who would be horrified if they knew the nature of the power they are wielding, and the extent of injury they are inflicting."

Instead, then, of depending on medicine for the preservation of the health and life of an infant, the following precautions and preventives should be adopted.

" Take particular care of the *food* of an infant. If it is nourished by the mother, her own diet should be simple, nourishing, and temperate. If the child be brought up ' by hand,' the milk of a new-milch cow, mixed with one third water, and sweetened a little with *white* sugar, should be the only food given, until the teeth come. This is more suitable than any preparations of flour or arrowroot, the nourishment of which is too highly concentrated. Never give a child *bread, cake,* or *meat,* before the teeth appear. If the food appear to distress the child after eating, first ascertain if the milk be really from a new-milch cow, as it may otherwise be too old. Learn, also, whether the cow lives on proper food. Cows that are fed on *still-slops,* as is often the case in cities, furnish milk which is very unhealthful."

Be sure and keep a good supply of pure and fresh air in the nursery. On this point, Dr. Bell remarks, respecting rooms constructed without fireplaces and without doors or windows to let in pure air from without, " The sufferings of children of feeble constitutions are increased beyond measure, by such lodgings as these. An action, brought by the commonwealth, ought to lie against those persons who build houses for sale or rent, in which rooms are so constructed as not to allow of free ventilation ; and a writ of lunacy taken out against those who, with the common-sense experience which all have on this head, should spend any portion of their time, still more, should sleep, in rooms thus nearly air-tight."

After it is a month or two old, take an infant out to walk, or ride, in a little wagon, every fair and warm day ;

but be very careful that its feet, and every part of its body, are kept warm ; and be sure that its eyes are well protected from the light. Weak eyes, and sometimes blindness, are caused by neglecting this precaution. Keep the head of an infant cool, never allowing too warm bonnets, nor permitting it to sink into soft pillows when asleep. Keeping an infant's head too warm very much increases nervous irritability ; and this is the reason why medical men forbid the use of caps for infants. But the head of an infant should, especially while sleeping, be protected from draughts of air, and from getting cold.

Be very careful of the skin of an infant, as nothing tends so effectually to prevent disease. For this end, it should be washed all over every morning, and then gentle friction should be applied with the hand, to the back, stomach, bowels, and limbs. The head should be thoroughly washed every day, and then brushed with a soft hair-brush, or combed with a fine comb. If, by neglect, dirt accumulates under the hair, apply with the finger the yolk of an egg, and then the fine comb will remove it all, without any trouble.

Dress the infant so that it will be always warm, but not so as to cause perspiration. Be sure and keep its feet *always* warm ; and for this often warm them at a fire, and use long dresses. Keep the neck and arms covered. For this purpose, wrappers, open in front, made high in the neck, with long sleeves, to put on over the frock, are now very fashionable.

It is better for both mother and child, that it should not sleep on the mother's arm at night, unless the weather be extremely cold. This practice keeps the child too warm, and leads it to seek food too frequently. A child should ordinarily take nourishment but twice in the night. A crib beside the mother, with plenty of warm and light covering, is best for the child ; but the mother must be sure that it is always kept warm.

Never cover a child's head, so that it will inhale the air of its own lungs. In very warm weather, especially in cities, great pains should be taken to find fresh and cool air by rides and sailing. Walks in a public square in the cool of the morning, and frequent excursions in ferry or steamboats, would often save a long bill for medical attendance. In hot nights, the windows should be kept open, and the infant laid on a mattress, or on folded blankets. A bit of straw matting, laid over a feather bed and covered with the under sheet, makes a very cool bed for an infant.

Cool bathing, in hot weather, is very useful; but the water should be very little cooler than the skin of the child. When the constitution is delicate, the water should be slightly warmed. Simply sponging the body freely in a tub, answers the same purpose as a regular bath. In very warm weather, this should be done two or three times a day, always waiting two or three hours after food has been given.

"When the stomach is peculiarily irritable, (from teething,) it is of paramount necessity to withhold all the nostrums which have been so falsly lauded as 'sovereign cures for *cholera infantum.*' The true restoratives for a child threatened with disease are cool air, cool bathing, and cool drinks of simple water, in addition to *proper* food, at stated intervals."

In many cases, change of air from sea to mountain, or the reverse, has an immediate healthful influence and is superior to every other treatment. Do not take the advice of mothers who tell of this, that, and the other thing, which have proved excellent remedies in their experience. Children have different constitutions, and there are multitudes of different causes for their sickness; and what might cure one child, might kill another, which *appeared* to have the same complaint. A mother should go on the general rule of giving an infant very little medicine, and then only by the direction of a discreet and experienced physician. And there are cases, when, according to the views of the most distinguished and competent practitioners, physicians themselves are much too free in using medicines, instead of adopting preventive measures.

Do not allow a child to form such habits that it will not be quiet unless tended and amused. A healthy child should be accustomed to lie or sit in its cradle much of the time; but it should occasionally be taken up and tossed, or carried about for exercise and amusement. An infant should be encouraged to *creep*, as an exercise very strengthening and useful. If the mother fears the soiling of its nice dresses, she can keep a long slip or apron which will entirely cover the dress, and can be removed when the child is taken in the arms. A child should not be allowed, when quite young, to bear its weight on its feet very long at a time, as this tends to weaken and distort the limbs.

Many mothers, with a little painstaking, succeed in putting their infants into their cradle while awake, at regular hours for sleep; and induce regularity in other habits, which saves much trouble. During this training process a child may cry, at first, a great deal; but for a healthy child, this use of the lungs does no harm and tends rather to strengthen than to injure them, unless it becomes exceedingly violent. A child who is trained to lie or sit and amuse itself, is happier than one who is carried and tended a great deal, and thus rendered restless and uneasy when not so indulged.

The most critical period in the life of an infant is that of dentition or teething, especially at the early stages. An adult has thirty-two teeth, but young children have only twenty, which gradually loosen and are followed by the permanent teeth. When the child has ten teeth on each jaw, all that are added are the permanent set, which should be carefully preserved; this caution is needful, as sometimes decay in the first double teeth of the second set are supposed to be of the transient set, and are so neglected, or are removed instead of being preserved by plugging. When the first teeth rise so as to press against the gums, there is always more or less inflammation, causing nervous fretfulness, and the impulse to put every thing into the mouth. Usually there is disturbed sleep, a slight fever, and greater flow of saliva; this is often relieved by letting the child have ice to bite, tied in a rag.

Sometimes the disorder of the mouth extends to the whole system. In difficult teething, one symptom is the jerking back of the head when taking the breath, as if in pain, owing to the extreme soreness of the gums. This is, in extreme cases, attended with increased saliva and a gummy secretion in the corners of the eyes, itching of the nose, redness of cheeks, rash, convulsive twitching of lips and the muscles generally, fever, constipation, and sometimes by a diarrhea, which last is favorable if slight; difficulty of breathing, dilation of the pupils of the eyes, restless motion and moaning; and finally, if not relieved, convulsions and death. The most effective relief is gained by lancing the gums. Every woman, and especially every mother, should know the time and order in which the infant teeth come, and, when any of the above symptoms appear, should examine the mouth, and if a gum is swollen and inflamed, should either have a physician lance it, or if this can not be done, should perform the operation herself. A sharp pen-knife and steady hand making incision to touch the rising tooth will cause no more pain than a simple scratch of the gum, and usually will give speedy relief.

The temporary teeth should not be removed until the new ones appear, as it injures the jaw and coming teeth; but as soon as a new tooth is seen pressing upward, the temporary tooth should be removed, or the new tooth will come out of its proper place. If there is not room where the new tooth appears, the next temporary tooth must be taken out. Great mischief has been done by removing the first teeth before the second appear, thus making a contraction of the jaw.

Most trouble with the teeth of young children comes from neglect to use the brush to remove the tartar that accumulates near the gum, causing disease and decay. This disease is sometimes called *scurvy*, and is shown by an accumulation around the teeth and by inflamed gums that bleed easily. Removal of the tartar by a dentist and cleaning the teeth after every meal with a brush will usually cure this evil, which causes loosening of the teeth and a bad breath.

Much injury is often done to teeth by using improper tooth-powder. Powdered chalk sifted through muslin is approved by all dentists, and should be used once every day. The tooth-brush should be used after every meal, and floss silk pressed between the teeth to remove food lodged there. This method will usually save the teeth from decay till old age.

When an infant seems ill during the period of dentition, the following directions from an experienced physician may be of service. It is now an accepted principle of all the medical world that fevers are to be reduced by cold applications; but an infant demands careful and judicious treatment in this direction; some have extremely sensitive nerves, and cold is painful. For such, tepid sponging should be used near a fire, and the coldness increased gradually. The sensations of the child should be the guide. Usually, but not always, children that are healthy will learn by degrees to prefer cold water, and then it may safely be used.

When an infant becomes feverish, wrapping its body in a towel wrung out in warm or tepid water, and then keeping it warm in a woolen blanket, is a very safe and soothing remedy.

In case of constipation this preparation of food is useful:

One table-spoonful of unbolted flour wet with cold water. Add one pint of hot water, and boil twenty minutes. Add when taken up, one pint of milk. If the stomach seems delicate and irritable, strain out the bran, but in most cases retain it.

In case of diarrhea, walk with the child in arms a great deal in the open air, and give it rice-water to drink.

The warmth and vital influences of the nurse are very important, and make this mode of exercise both more soothing and more efficacious, especially in the open air, the infant being warmly clad.

In case of feverishness from teething or from any other cause, wrap the infant in a towel wrung out in tepid water and then wrap it in a woolen blanket. The water may be cooler according as the child is older and stronger. The evaporation of the water draws off the heat, while the moisture soothes the nerves, and usually the child will fall into a quiet sleep. As soon as it becomes restless, change the wet towel and proceed as before.

The leading physicians of Europe and of this country, in all cases of fevers, use water to reduce them, by this and other modes of application. This method is more soothing than any other, and is as effective for adults as for infants.

Some of the most distinguished physicians of New-York who have examined this chapter give their full approval of the advice given. If there is still distrust as to this mode of using water to reduce fevers, it will be advantageous to read an address on the use of cold applications in fevers, delivered by Dr. William Neftel, before the New-York Academy of Medicine, published in the *New-York Medical Record* for November, 1868 : this can be obtained by inclosing twenty cents to the editor, with the post-office address of the applicant.

XXII.

In regard to the physical education of children, Dr. Clarke, Physician in Ordinary to the Queen of England, expresses views on one point, in which most physicians would coincide. He says, " There is no greater error in the management of children, than that of giving them animal diet very early. By persevering in the use of an over-stimulating diet the digestive organs become irritated, and the various secretions immediately connected with digestion, and necessary to it, are diminished, especially the *biliary secretion*. Children so fed become very liable to attacks of fever, and inflammation, affecting particularly the mucous membranes; and measles and other diseases incident to childhood, are generally severe in their attacks."

The result of the treatment of the inmates of the Orphan Asylum, at Albany, is one which all who have the care of young children should deeply ponder. During the first six years of the existence of this institution, its average number of children was eighty. For the first three years, their diet was meat once a day, fine bread, rice, Indian puddings, vegetables, fruit, and milk. Considerable attention was given to clothing, fresh air, and exercise; and they were bathed once in three weeks. During these three years, from four to six children, and sometimes more, were continually on the sick-list; one or two assistant nurses were necessary; a physician was called two or three times a week; and, in this time, there were between thirty and forty deaths. At the end of this period, the management was changed, in these respects : daily ablutions of the whole body were practiced; bread of unbolted flour was substituted for that of fine wheat; and all animal food was banished. More attention also was paid to clothing, bedding, fresh air, and exercise.

The result was, that the nursery was vacated; the nurse and physician were no longer needed; and, for two years, not a single case of sickness or death occurred. The third year also, there were no deaths, except those of two idiots and one other child, all of whom were new inmates, who had not been subjected to this treatment. The teachers of the children also testified there was a manifest increase of intellectual vigor and activity, while there was much less irritability of temper.

Let parents, nurses, and teachers reflect on the above statement, and bear in mind that stupidity of intellect, and irritability of temper, as well as ill-health, are often caused by the mismanagement of the nursery in regard to the physical training of children.

There is probably no practice more deleterious, than that of allowing children to eat at short intervals, through the day. As the stomach is thus kept constantly at work, with no time for repose, its functions are deranged, and a weak or disordered stomach is the frequent result. Children should be required to keep cakes, nuts, and other good things, which should be sparingly given, till just before a meal, and then they will form a part of their regular supply. This is better than to wait till after their hunger is satisfied by food, when they will eat the niceties merely to gratify the palate, and thus overload the stomach and interrupt digestion.

In regard to the intellectual training of young children, some modification in the common practice is necessary, with reference to their physical well-being. More care is needful, in providing *well-ventilated* school-rooms, and in securing more time for sports in the open air, during school hours. It is very important to most mothers that their young children should be removed from their care during certain school hours; and it is very useful for quite young children, to be subjected to the discipline of a school, and to intercourse with other children of their own age. And, with a suitable teacher, it is no matter how early children are sent to school, provided their health is not endangered by impure air, too much confinement, and too great mental stimulus, which is the chief danger of the present age.

In regard to the formation of the moral character, it has been too much the case that the discipline of the nursery has consisted of disconnected efforts to make children either do, or refrain from doing, certain particular acts. Do this, and be rewarded; do that, and be punished; is the ordinary routine of family government.

But children can be very early taught that their happiness, both now and hereafter, depends on the formation of *habits* of submission, self-denial, and benevolence. And all the discipline of the nursery can be conducted by parents, not only with this general aim in their own minds, but also with the same object daily set before the minds of the children. Whenever their wishes are crossed, or their wills subdued, they can be taught that all this is done, not merely to please the parent, or to secure some good to themselves or to others; but as a part of that merciful training which is designed to form such a character, and such habits, that they can hereafter find their chief happiness in giving up their will to God, and in living to do good to others, instead of living merely to please themselves.

It can be pointed out to them, that they must always submit their will to the will of God, or else be continually miserable. It can be shown how, in the nursery, and in the school, and through all future days, a child must practice the giving up of his will and wishes, when they interfere with the rights and comfort of others; and how important it is, early to learn to do this, so that it will, by habit, become easy and agreeable. It can be shown how children who are indulged in all their wishes, and who are never accustomed to any self-denial, always find it hard to refrain from what injures themselves and others. It can be shown, also, how important it is for every person to form such habits of benevolence toward others that self-denial in doing good will become easy.

Parents have learned, by experience, that children can be constrained by authority and penalties to exercise self-denial, for *their own* good, till a habit is formed which makes the duty comparatively easy. For example, well trained children can be accustomed to deny themselves tempting articles of food, which are injurious, until the practice ceases to be painful and difficult. Whereas, an indulged child would be thrown into fits of anger or discontent, when its wishes were crossed by restraints of this kind.

But it has not been so readily discerned, that the same method is needful in order to form a habit of self-denial in doing good to others. It has been supposed that while children must be forced, by *authority*, to be self-denying and prudent in regard to their own happiness, it may properly be left to their own discretion, whether they will practice any self-denial in doing good to others. But the more difficult a duty is, the greater is the need of parental authority in forming a habit which will make that duty easy.

In order to secure this, some parents turn their earliest efforts to this object. They require the young child always to offer to others a part of every thing which it receives; always to comply with all reasonable requests of others for service; and often to practice little acts of self-denial, in order to secure some enjoyment for others. If one child receives a present of some nicety, he is required to share it with all his brothers and sisters. If one asks his brother to help him in some study or sport, and is met with a denial, the parent requires the unwilling child to act benevolently, and give up some of his time to increase his brother's enjoyment. Of course, in such an effort as this, discretion must be used as to the frequency and extent of the exercise of authority, to induce a habit of benevolence. But where parents deliberately aim at such an object, and wisely conduct their instructions and discipline to secure it, very much will be accomplished.

In regard to forming habits of obedience, there have been two extremes, both of which need to be shunned. One is, a stern and unsympathizing maintenance of parental authority, demanding perfect and constant obedience, without any attempt to convince a child of the propriety and benevolence of the requisitions, and without any manifestation of sympathy and tenderness for the pain and difficulties which are to be met. Under such discipline, children grow up to fear their parents, rather than to love and trust them ; while some of the most valuable principles of character are chilled, or forever blasted.

In shunning this danger, other parents pass to the opposite extreme. They put themselves too much on the footing of equals with their children, as if little were due to superiority of relation, age, and experience. Nothing is exacted, without the implied concession that the child is to be a judge of the propriety of the requisition ; and reason and persuasion are employed, where simple command and obedience would be far better. This system produces a most pernicious influence. Children soon perceive the position thus allowed them, and take every advantage of it. They soon learn to dispute parental requirements, acquire habits of forwardness and conceit, assume disrespectful manners and address, maintain their views with pertinacity, and yield to authority with ill-humor and resentment, as if their rights were infringed upon.

The medium course is for the parent to take the attitude of a superior in age, knowledge, and relation, who has a perfect *right* to control every action of the child, and that, too, without giving any reason for the requisitions. "Obey *because your parent commands*," is always a proper and sufficient reason : though not always the best to give.

But care should be taken to convince the child that the parent is conducting a course of discipline, designed to make him happy; and in forming habits of implicit obedience, self-denial, and benevolence, the child should have the reasons for most requisitions kindly stated; never, however, on the demand of it from the child, as a right, but as an act of kindness from the parent.

It is impossible to govern children properly, especially those of strong and sensitive feelings, without a constant effort to appreciate the value which they attach to their enjoyments and pursuits. A lady of great strength of mind and sensibility once told the writer that one of the most acute periods of suffering in her whole life was occasioned by the burning up of some milkweed-silk, by her mother. The child had found, for the first time, some of this shining and beautiful substance; was filled with delight at her discovery; was arranging it in parcels; planning its future use, and her pleasure in showing it to her companions— when her mother, finding it strewed over the carpet, hastily swept it into the fire, and that, too, with so indifferent an air, that the child fled away, almost distracted with grief and disappointment. The mother little realized the pain she had inflicted, but the child felt the unkindness so severely that for several days her mother was an object almost of aversion. While, therefore, the parent needs to carry on a steady course, which will oblige the child always to give up its will, whenever its own good or the greater claims of others require it, this should be constantly connected with the expression of a tender sympathy for the trials and disappointments thus inflicted.

Those, again, who will join with children and help them in their sports, will learn by this mode to understand the feelings and interests of childhood; while at the same time, they secure a degree of confidence and affection which can not be gained so easily in any other way. And it is to be regretted that parents so often relinquish this most powerful mode of influence to domestics and playmates, who often use it in the most pernicious manner. In joining in such sports, older persons should never yield entirely the attitude of superiors, or allow disrespectful manners or address. And respectful deportment is never more cheerfully accorded, than in seasons when young hearts are pleased and made grateful by having their tastes and enjoyments so efficiently promoted.

Next to the want of all government, the two most fruitful sources of evil to children are, *unsteadiness* in government and *over-government*. Most of the cases in which the children of sensible and conscientious parents turn out badly, result from one or the other of these causes. In cases of unsteady government, either one parent is very strict, severe and unbending, and the other excessively indulgent, or else the parents are sometimes very strict and decided, and at other times allow disobedience to go unpunished. In such cases, children, never knowing exactly when they can escape with impunity, are constantly tempted to make the trial.

The bad effects of this can be better appreciated by reference to one important principle of the mind. It is found to be universally true, that, when any object of desire is put entirely beyond the reach of hope or expectation, the mind very soon ceases to long for it, and turns to other objects of pursuit. But so long as the mind is hoping for some good, and making efforts to obtain it, any opposition excites irritable feelings. Let the object be put entirely beyond all hope, and this irritation soon ceases.

In consequence of this principle, those children who are under the care of persons of steady and decided government know that whenever a thing is forbidden or denied, it is out of the reach of hope; the desire, therefore, soon ceases, and they turn to other objects. But the children of undecided, or of over-indulgent parents, never enjoy this preserving aid When a thing is denied, they never know but either coaxing may win it, or disobedience secure it without any penalty, and so they are kept in that state of hope and anxiety which produces irritation and tempts to insubordination. The children of very indulgent parents, and of those who are undecided and unsteady in government, are very apt to become fretful, irritable, and fractious.

Another class of persons, in shunning this evil, go to the other extreme, and are very strict and pertinacious in regard to every requisition. With them, fault-finding and penalties abound, until the children are either hardened into indifference of feeling, and obtuseness of conscience, or else become excessively irritable or misanthropic.

It demands great wisdom, patience, and self-control, to escape these two extremes. In aiming at this, there are parents who have found the following maxims of very great value:

First: Avoid, as much as possible, the multiplication of rules and absolute commands. Instead of this, take the attitude of advisers. "My child, this is improper, I wish you would remember not to do it." This mode of address answers for all the little acts of heedlessness, awkwardness, or ill-manners so frequently occurring with children. There are cases, when direct and distinct commands are needful; and in such cases, a penalty for disobedience should be as steady and sure as the laws of nature. Where such steadiness and certainty of penalty attend disobedience, children no more think of disobeying than they do of putting their fingers into a burning candle.

The next maxim is, Govern by rewards more than by penalties. Such faults as willful disobedience, lying, dishonesty, and indecent or profane language, should be punished with severe penalties, after a child has been fully instructed in the evil of such practices. But all the constant ly recurring faults of the nursery, such as ill-humor, quarreling, carelessness, and ill-manners, may, in a great many cases, be regulated by gentle and kind remonstrances, and by the offer of some reward for persevering efforts to form a good habit. It is very injurious and degrading to any mind to be kept under the constant fear of penalties. *Love* and *hope* are the principles that should be mainly relied on, in forming the habits of childhood.

Another maxim, and perhaps the most difficult, is, Do not govern by the aid of severe and angry tones. A single example will be given to illustrate this maxim. A child is disposed to talk and amuse itself at table. The mother requests it to be silent, except when needing to ask for food, or when spoken to by its older friends. It constantly forgets. The mother, instead of rebuking in an impatient tone, says, "My child, you must remember not to talk. I will remind you of it four times more, and after that, whenever you forget, you must leave the table and wait till we are done." If the mother is steady in her government, it is not probable that she will have to apply this slight penalty more than once or twice. This method is far more effectual than the use of sharp and severe tones, to secure attention and recollection, and often answers the purpose as well as offering some reward.

The writer has been in some families where the most efficient and steady government has been sustained without the use of a cross or angry tone ; and in others, where a far less efficient discipline was kept up, by frequent severe rebukes and angry remonstrances. In the first case, the children followed the example set them, and seldom used severe tones to each other ; in the latter, the method employed by the parents was imitated by the children, and cross words and angry tones resounded from morning till night, in every portion of the household.

Another important maxim is, Try to keep children in a happy state of mind. Every one knows, by experience, that it is easier to do right and submit to rule when cheerful and happy, than when irritated. This is peculiarly true of children; and a wise mother, when she finds her child fretful and impatient, and thus constantly doing wrong, will often remedy the whole difficulty, by telling some amusing story, or by getting the child engaged in some amusing sport. This strongly shows the importance of learning to govern children without the employment of angry tones, which always produce irritation.

Children of active, heedless temperament, or those who are odd, awkward, or unsuitable in their remarks and deportment, are often essentially injured by a want of patience and self-control in those who govern them. Such children often possess a morbid sensibility which they strive to conceal, or a desire of love and approbation, which preys like a famine on the soul. And yet, they become objects of ridicule and rebuke to almost every member of the family, until their sensibilities are tortured into obtuseness or misanthropy. Such children, above all others, need tenderness and sympathy. A thousand instances of mistake or forgetfulness should be passed over in silence, while opportunities for commendation and encouragement should be diligently sought.

In regard to the formation of habits of self-denial in childhood, it is astonishing to see how parents who are very sensible often seem to regard this matter. . Instead of inuring their children to this duty in early life, so that by habit it may be made easy in after-days, they seem to be studiously seeking to cut them off from every chance to secure such a preparation. Every wish of the child is studiously gratified; and, where a necessity exists of crossing its wishes, some compensating pleasure is offered, in return. Such parents often maintain that nothing shall be put on their table, which their children may not join them in eating. But where, so easily and surely as at the daily meal, can that habit of self-denial be formed, which is so needful

in governing the appetites, and which children must acquire, or be ruined ?   The food which is proper for grown
persons, is often unsuitable for children ; and this is a sufficient reason for accustoming them to see others partake
of delicacies, which they must not share.   Requiring children to wait till others are helped, and to refrain from conversation at table, except when addressed by their elders,
is another mode of forming habits of self-denial and self-
control.   Requiring them to help others first, and to offer
the best to others, has a similar influence.

In forming the moral habits of children, it is wise to take
into account the peculiar temptations to which they are to
be exposed.   The people of this nation are eminently a
trafficking people ; and the present standard of honesty, as
to trade and debts, is very low, and every year seems sinking still lower.   It is, therefore, preëminently important,
that children should be trained to strict *honesty*, both in
word and deed.   It is not merely teaching children to avoid
absolute lying, which is needed : *all kinds of deceit* should
be guarded against ; and all kinds of little dishonest practices be strenuously opposed.   A child should be brought
up with the determined principle, never to *run in debt*, but
to be content to live in a humbler way, in order to secure that true independence, which should be the noblest
distinction of an American citizen.

There is no more important duty devolving upon a
mother, than the cultivation of habits of modesty and propriety in young children.   All indecorous words or deportment should be carefully restrained ; and delicacy and reserve studiously cherished.   It is a common notion, that it
is important to secure these virtues to one sex, more than
to the other ; and, by a strange inconsistency, the sex most
exposed to danger is the one selected as least needing care.
Yet a wise mother will be especially careful that her sons
are trained to modesty and purity of mind.

Yet few mothers are sufficiently aware of the dreadful

penalties which often result from indulged impurity of thought. If children, in *future* life, can be preserved from licentious associates, it is supposed that their safety is secured. But the records of our insane retreats, and the pages of medical writers, teach that even in solitude, and without being aware of the sin or the danger, children may inflict evils on themselves, which not unfrequently terminate in disease, delirium, and death.

There is no necessity for explanations on this point any farther than this ; that certain parts of the body are not to be touched except for purposes of cleanliness, and that the most dreadful suffering comes from disobeying these commands. So in regard to practices and sins of which a young child will sometimes inquire, the wise parent will say, that this is what children can not understand, and about which they must not talk or ask questions. And they should be told that it is always a bad sign, when children talk on matters which parents call vulgar and indecent, and that the company of such children should be avoided. Disclosing details of wrong-doing to young and curious children, often leads to the very evils feared. But parents and teachers, in this age of danger, should be well informed and watchful ; for it is not unfrequently the case, that servants and school-mates will teach young children practices, which exhaust the nervous system and bring on paralysis, mania, and death.

And finally, in regard to the early religious training of children, the examples of the Creator in the early training of our race may safely be imitated. That " He is, and is a rewarder"—that he is everywhere present—that he is a tender Father in heaven, who is grieved when any of his children do wrong, yet ever ready to forgive those who are striving to please him by well-doing, these are the most effective motives to save the young from the paths of danger and sin. The rewards and penalties of the life to come are better adapted to maturer age, than to the imperfect and often false and fearful conceptions of the childish mind.

XXIII.

WHENEVER the laws of body and mind are properly understood, it will be allowed that every person needs some kind of recreation ; and that, by seeking it, the body is strengthened, the mind is invigorated, and all our duties are more cheerfully and successfully performed.

Children, whose bodies are rapidly growing and whose nervous system is tender and excitable, need much more amusement than persons of mature age.   Persons, also, who are oppressed with great responsibilities and duties, or who are taxed by great intellectual or moral excitement, need recreations which physically exercise and draw off the mind from absorbing interests.   Unfortunately, such persons are those who least resort to amusements, while the idle, gay, and thoughtless seek those which are not needed, and for which useful occupation would be a most beneficial substitute.

As the only legitimate object of amusement is to prepare mind and body for the proper discharge of duty, the protracting of such as interfere with regular employments, or induce excessive fatigue, or weary the mind, or invade the proper hours for repose, must be sinful.

In deciding what should be selected, and what avoided, the following are guiding principles.   In the first place, no amusements which inflict needless pain should ever be allowed.   All tricks which cause fright or vexation, and all sports which involve suffering to animals, should be utterly forbidden.   Hunting and fishing, for mere sport, can never be justified. If a man can convince his children that he follows these pursuits to gain food or health, and not for amusement, his example may not be very injurious. But when children see grown persons kill and frighten animals, for sport, habits of cruelty, rather than feelings of tenderness and benevolence, are cultivated.

In the next place, we should seek no recreations which endanger life, or interfere with important duties. As the legitimate object of amusements is to promote health and prepare for some serious duties, selecting those which have a directly opposite tendency, can not be justified. Of course, if a person feels that the previous day's diversion has shortened the hours of needful repose, or induced a lassitude of mind or body, instead of invigorating them, it is certain that an evil has been done which should never be repeated.

Another rule which has been extensively adopted in the religious world is, to avoid those amusements which experience has shown to be so exciting, and connected with so many temptations, as to be pernicious in tendency, both to the individual and to the community. It is on this ground, that horse-racing and circus-riding have been excluded. Not because there is any thing positively wrong in having men and horses run and perform feats of agility, or in persons looking on for the diversion: but because experience has shown so many evils connected with these recreations, that they should be relinquished. So with theatres. The enacting of characters and the amusement thus afforded in themselves may be harmless; and possibly, in certain cases, might be useful: but experience has shown so many evils to result from this source, that it has been deemed wrong to patronize it. So, also, with those exciting games of chance which are employed in gambling.

Under the same head comes dancing, in the estimation of the great majority of the religious world. Still, there are many intelligent, excellent, and conscientious persons who hold a contrary opinion. Such maintain that it is an innocent and healthful amusement, tending to promote ease of manners, cheerfulness, social affection, and health of mind and body ; that evils are involved only in its excess ; that like food, study, or religious excitement, it is only wrong when not properly regulated; and that, if serious and intelligent people would strive to regulate, rather than banish, this amusement, much more good would be secured.

On the other side, it is objected, not that dancing is a sin, in itself considered, for it was once a part of sacred worship; not that it would be objectionable, if it were properly regulated; not that it does not tend, when used in a proper manner, to health of body and mind, to grace of manners, and to social enjoyment : all these things are conceded.   But it is objected to, on the same ground as horse-racing and theatrical entertainments ; that we are to look at amusements as they are, and not as they might be. Horse-races might be so managed as not to involve cruelty, gambling, drunkenness, and other vices.   And so might theatres.   And if serious and intelligent persons undertook to patronize these, in order to regulate them, perhaps they would be somewhat raised from the depths to which they have sunk.   But such persons believe that, with the weak sense of moral obligation existing in the mass of society, and the imperfect ideas mankind have of the proper use of amusements, and the little self-control which men or women or children practice, these will not, in fact, be thus regulated.

And they believe dancing to be liable to the same objections.   As this recreation is actually conducted, it does not tend to produce health of body or mind, but directly the contrary.   If young and old went out to dance together in open air, as the French peasants do, it would be a very different sort of amusement from that which often is witnessed in a room furnished with many lights and filled with guests, both expending the healthful part of the atmosphere, where the young collect, in their tightest dresses, to protract for several hours a kind of physical exertion which is not habitual to them.   During this process, the blood is made to circulate more swiftly than usual, in circumstances where it is less perfectly oxygenized than health requires ; the pores of the skin are excited by heat and exercise ; the stomach is loaded with indigestible articles, and the quiet, needful to digestion, withheld ; the diversion is protracted beyond the usual hour for repose ; and then, when the skin is made the most highly susceptible to damps and miasms, the company pass from a warm room to the cold night-air.   It is probable that no single amusement can be pointed out combining so many injurious particulars as this, which is so often defended as a healthful one.   Even if parents, who train their children to dance, can keep them from public balls, (which is seldom the case,) dancing, as ordinarily conducted in private parlors, in most cases is subject to nearly all the same mischievous influences.

The spirit of Christ is that of self-denying benevolence ; and his great aim, by his teachings and example, was to train his followers to avoid all that should lead to sin, especially in regard to the weaker ones of his family.   Yet he made wine at a wedding, attended a social feast on the Sabbath,* reproved excess of strictness in Sabbath-keeping generally, and forbade no safe and innocent enjoyment. In following his example, the rulers of the family, then, will introduce the most highly exciting amusements only in circumstances where there are such strong principles and habits of self-control that the enjoyment will not involve sin in the actor or needless temptation to the weak.

The course pursued by our Puritan ancestors, in the period succeeding their first perils amid sickness and savages, is an example that may safely be practiced at the present day.   The young of both sexes were educated in the higher branches, in country academies, and very often the closing exercises

* Luke xiv.   In reading this passage, please notice what kind of guests are to be invited to the feast that Jesus Christ recommends.

were theatricals, in which the pupils were performers and their pastors, elders, and parents, the audience. So, at social gatherings, the dance was introduced before minister and wife, with smiling approval. The roaring fires and broad chimneys provided pure air, and the nine o'clock bell ended the festivities that gave new vigor and zest to life, while the dawn of the next day's light saw all at their posts of duty, with heartier strength and blither spirits.

No indecent or unhealthful costumes offended the eye, no half-naked dancers of dubious morality were sustained in a life of dangerous excitement, by the money of Christian people, for the mere amusement of their night hours. No shivering drivers were deprived of comfort and sleep, to carry home the midnight followers of fashion; nor was the quiet and comfort of servants in hundreds of dwellings invaded for the mere amusement of their superiors in education and advantages. The command "we that are strong, ought to bear the infirmities of the weak, and not to please ourselves," was in those days not reversed. Had the drama and the dance continued to be regulated by the rules of temperance, health, and Christian benevolence, as in the days of our forefathers, they would not have been so generally banished from the religious world. And the question is now being discussed, whether they can be so regulated at the present time as not to violate the laws, either of health or benevolence.*

In regard to home amusements, card-playing is now indulged in, in many conscientious families from which it formerly was excluded, and for these reasons: it is claimed that this is a quiet home amusement, which unites pleas-

---

* Fanny Kemble Butler remarked to the present writer that she regarded theatres wrong, chiefly because of the injury involved to the actors. Can a Christian mother contribute money to support young women in a profession from which she would protect her own daughter, as from degradation and that, too, simply for the amusement of herself and family? Would this be following the self-sacrificing benevolence of Christ and his apostles?

antly the aged with the young ; that it is not now employed in respectable society for gambling, as it formerly was; that to some young minds it is a peculiarly fascinating game, and should be first practiced under the parental care, till the excitement of novelty is past, thus rendering the danger to children less, when going into the world; and, finally, that habits of self-control in exciting circumstances may and should be thus cultivated in the safety of home. Many parents who have taken this course with their sons in early life, believe that it has proved rather a course of safety than of danger. Still, as there is great diversity of opinion, among persons of equal worth and intelligence, a mutual spirit of candor and courtesy should be practiced. The sneer at bigotry and narrowness of views, on one side, and the uncharitable implication of want of piety, or sense, on the other, are equally ill-bred and unchristian. Truth on this subject is best promoted, not by ill-natured crimination and rebuke, but by calm reason, generous candor, forbearance, and kindness.

There is another species of amusement, which a large portion of the religious world formerly put under the same condemnation as the preceding. This is novel-reading. The confusion and difference of opinion on this subject have arisen from a want of clear and definite distinctions. Now, as it is impossible to define what are novels and what are not, so as to include one class of fictitious writings and exclude every other, it is impossible to lay down any rule respecting them. The discussion, in fact, turns on the use of those works of imagination which belong to the class of fictitious narratives. That this species of reading is not only lawful but necessary and useful, is settled by divine examples, in the parables and allegories of Scripture. Of course, the question must be, what kind of fabulous writings must be avoided, and what allowed.

In deciding this, no specific rules can be given; but it must be a matter to be regulated by the nature and circumstances of each case. No works of fiction which tend to throw the allurements of taste and genius around vice and crime should ever be tolerated; and all that tend to give false views of life and duty should also be banished. Of those which are written for mere amusement, presenting scenes and events that are interesting and exciting and having no bad moral influence, much must depend on the character and circumstances of the reader. Some minds are torpid and phlegmatic, and need to have the imagination stimulated: such would be benefited by this kind of reading. Others have quick and active imaginations, and would be as much injured by excess. Some persons are often so engaged in absorbing interests, that any thing innocent, which will for a short time draw off the mind, is of the nature of a medicine; and, in such cases, this kind of reading is useful.

There is need, also, that some men should keep a supervision of the current literature of the day, as guardians, to warn others of danger. For this purpose, it is more suitable for editors, clergymen, and teachers to read indiscriminately, than for any other class of persons; for they are the guardians of the public weal in matters of literature, and should be prepared to advise parents and young persons of the evils in one direction and the good in another. In doing this, however, they are bound to go on the same principles which regulate physicians, when they visit infected districts—using every precaution to prevent injury to themselves; having as little to do with pernicious exposures, as a benevolent regard to others will allow; and faithfully employing all the knowledge and opportunities thus gained for warning and preserving others. There is much danger, in taking this course, that men will seek the excitement of the imagination for the mere pleasure it affords, under the plea of preparing to serve the public, when this is neither the aim nor the result.

In regard to the use of such works by the young, as a

general rule, they ought not to be allowed to any except those of a dull and phlegmatic temperament, until the solid parts of education are secured and a taste for more elevated reading is acquired. If these stimulating condiments in literature be freely used in youth, all relish for more solid reading will in a majority of cases be destroyed. If parents succeed in securing habits of cheerful and implicit obedience, it will be very easy to regulate this matter, by prohibiting the reading of any story-book, until the consent of the parent is obtained.

The most successful mode of forming a taste for suitable reading, is for parents to select interesting works of history and travels, with maps and pictures suited to the age and attainments of the young, and spend an hour or two each day or evening, in aiming to make truth as interesting as fiction. Whoever has once tried this method will find that the uninjured mind of childhood is better satisfied with what they know is true, when wisely presented, than with the most exciting novels, which they know are false.

Perhaps there has been some just ground of objection to the course often pursued by parents in neglecting to provide suitable and agreeable substitutes for the amusements denied. But there is a great abundance of safe, healthful, and delightful recreations, which all parents may secure for their children. Some of these will here be pointed out.

One of the most useful and important, is the cultivation of flowers and fruits. This, especially for the daughters of a family, is greatly promotive of health and amusement. It is with the hope that many young ladies, whose habits are now so formed that they can never be induced to a course of active domestic exercise so long as their parents are able to hire domestic service, may yet be led to an employment which will tend to secure health and vigor of constitution, that much space will be given in the second volume of this work, to directions for the cultivation of fruits and flowers.

It would be a most desirable improvement, if all schools for young women could be furnished with suitable grounds and instruments for the cultivation of fruits and flowers, and every inducement offered to engage the pupils in this pursuit. No father, who wishes to have his daughters grow up to be healthful women, can take a surer method to secure this end. Let him set apart a portion of his ground for fruits and flowers, and see that the soil is well prepared and dug over, and all the rest may be committed to the care of the children. These would need to be provided with a light hoe and rake, a dibble or garden trowel, a watering-pot, and means and opportunities for securing seeds, roots, bulbs, buds, and grafts, all which might be done at a trifling expense. Then, with proper encouragement and by the aid of a few intelligible and practical directions, every man who has even half an acre could secure a small Eden around his premises.

In pursuing this amusement children can also be led to acquire many useful habits. Early rising would, in many cases, be thus secured ; and if they were required to keep their walks and borders free from weeds and rubbish, habits of order and neatness would be induced. Benevolent and social feelings could also be cultivated, by influencing children to share their fruits and flowers with friends and neighbors, as well as to distribute roots and seeds to those who have not the means of procuring them. A woman or a child, by giving seeds or slips or roots to a washerwoman, or a farmer's boy, thus inciting them to love and cultivate fruits and flowers, awakens a new and refining source of enjoyment in minds which have few resources more elevated than mere physical enjoyments. Our Saviour directs us in making feasts, to call, not the rich who can recompense again, but the poor who can make no returns. So children should be taught to dispense their little treasures not alone to companions and friends, who will probably return similar favors ; but to those who have no means of making any return. If the rich, who acquire a love for the enjoyments of taste and have the means to gratify it, would aim to extend among the poor the cheap and simple enjoyment of fruits and flowers, our country would soon literally "blossom as the rose."

If the ladies of a neighborhood would unite small contributions, and send a list of flower-seeds and roots to some respectable and honest florist, who would not be likely to turn them off with trash, they could divide these among themselves and their poor neighbors, so as to secure an abundant variety at a very small expense. A bag of flower-seeds, which can be obtained at wholesale for four cents, would abundantly supply a whole neighborhood; and by the gathering of seeds in the autumn, could be perpetuated.

Another very elevating and delightful recreation for the young is found in *music*. Here the writer would protest against the practice common in many families, of having the daughters learn to play on the piano whether they have a taste and an ear for music, or not. A young lady who does not sing well, and has no great fondness for music, does nothing but waste time, money, and patience in learning to play on the piano. But all children can be taught to sing in early childhood, if the scientific mode of teaching music in schools could be more widely introduced, as it is in Prussia, Germany, and Switzerland. Then young children could read and sing music as easily as they can read language; and might take any tune, dividing themselves into bands, and sing off at sight the endless variety of music which is prepared. And if parents of wealth would take pains to have teachers qualified for the purpose, who should teach all the young children in the community, much would be done for the happiness and elevation of the rising generation. This is an element of education which we are glad to know is, year by year, more extensively and carefully cultivated; and it is not only a means of culture, but also an amusement, which children relish in the highest degree; and which they can enjoy at home, in the fields, and in visits abroad.

Another domestic amusement is the collecting of shells, plants, and specimens in geology and mineralogy, for the formation of cabinets. If intelligent parents would procure the simpler works which have been prepared for the young, and study them with their children, a taste for such recreations would soon be developed. The writer has seen young boys, of eight and ten years of age, gathering and cleaning shells from rivers, and collecting plants and mineralogical specimens, with a delight bordering on ecstasy; and there are few, if any, who by proper influences would not find this a source of ceaseless delight and improvement.

Another resource for family diversion is to be found in the various games played by children, and in which the joining of older members of the family is always a great advantage to both parties, especially those in the open air.

All medical men unite in declaring that nothing is more beneficial to health than hearty laughter; and surely our benevolent Creator would not have provided risibles, and made it a source of health and enjoyment to use them, if it were a sin so to do. There has been a tendency to asceticism, on this subject, which needs to be removed. Such commands as forbid *foolish* laughing and jesting, "*which are not convenient*," and which forbid all idle words and vain conversation, can not apply to any thing except what is foolish, vain, and useless. But jokes, laughter, and sports, when used in such a degree as tends only to promote health and happiness, are neither vain, foolish, nor " not convenient." It is the excess of these things, and not the moderate use of them, which Scripture forbids. The prevailing temper of the mind should be serious, yet cheerful; and there are times when relaxation and laughter are not only proper but necessary and right for all. There is nothing better for this end than that parents and older persons should join in the sports of childhood. Mature minds can always make such diversions more entertaining to children, and can exert a healthful moral influence over their minds; and at the same time can gain exercise and amusement for themselves. How lamentable that so many fathers, who could be thus useful and happy with their children, throw away such opportunities, and wear out soul and body in the pursuit of gain or fame!

Another resource for children is the exercise of mechanical skill. Fathers, by providing tools for their boys, and showing them how to make wheelbarrows, carts, sleds, and various other articles, contribute both to the physical, moral, and social improvement of their children. And in regard to little daughters, much more can be done in this way than many would imagine. The writer, blessed with the example of a most ingenious and industrious mother, had not only learned before the age of twelve to make dolls, of various sorts and sizes, but to cut and fit and sew every article that belongs to a doll's wardrobe. This, which was done by the child for mere amusement, secured such a facility in mechanical pursuits, that, ever afterward, the cutting and fitting of any article of dress, for either sex, was accomplished with entire ease.

When a little girl begins to sew, her mother can promise her a small bed and pillow, as soon as she has sewed a patch quilt for them; and then a bedstead, as soon as she has sewed the sheets and cases for pillows; and then a large doll to dress, as soon as she has made the under-garments; and thus go on till the whole contents of the baby-house are earned by the needle and skill of its little owner. Thus the task of learning to sew will become a pleasure; and every new toy will be earned by useful exertion. A little girl can be taught, by the aid of patterns prepared for the purpose, to cut and fit all articles necessary for her doll. She can also be provided with a little wash-tub and irons.

and thus keep in proper order a complete miniature domestic establishment.

Besides these recreations, there are the enjoyments secured in walking, riding, visiting, and many other employments which need not be recounted. Children, if trained to be healthful and industrious, will never fail to discover resources of amusement; while their guardians should lend their aid to guide and restrain them from excess.

There is need of a very great change of opinion and practice in this nation in regard to the subject of social and domestic duties. Many sensible and conscientious men spend all their time abroad in business; except perhaps an hour or so at night, when they are so fatigued as to be unfitted for any social or intellectual enjoyment. And some of the most conscientious men in the country will add to their professional business public or benevolent enterprises, which demand time, effort, and money; and then excuse themselves for neglecting all care of their children, and efforts for their own intellectual improvement, or for the improvement of their families, by the plea that they have no time for it.

All this arises from the want of correct notions of the binding obligation of our social and domestic duties. The main object of life is not to secure the various gratifications of appetite or taste, but to form such a character, for ourselves and others, as will secure the greatest amount of present and future happiness. It is of far more consequence, then, that parents should be intelligent, social, affectionate, and agreeable at home and to their friends, than that they should earn money enough to live in a large house and have handsome furniture. It is far more needful for children that a father should attend to the formation of their character and habits, and aid in developing their social, intellectual, and moral nature, than it is that he should earn money to furnish them with handsome clothes and a variety of tempting food.

It will be wise for those parents who find little time to attend to their children, or to seek amusement and enjoyment in the domestic and social circle, because their time is so much occupied with public cares or benevolent objects, to inquire whether their first duty is not to train up their own families to be useful members of society. A man who neglects the mind and morals of his children, to take care of the public, is in great danger of coming under a similar condemnation to that of him who, neglecting to provide for his own household, has " denied the faith, and is worse than an infidel."

There are husbands and fathers who conscientiously subtract time from their business to spend at home, in reading with their wives and children, and in domestic amusements which at once refresh and improve. The children of such parents will grow up with a love of home and kindred which will be the greatest safeguard against future temptations, as well as the purest source of earthly enjoyment.

There are families, also, who make it a definite object to keep up family attachments, after the children are scattered abroad; and, in some cases, secure the means for doing this by saving money which would otherwise have been spent for superfluities of food or dress. Some families have adopted, for this end, a practice which, if widely imitated, would be productive of much enjoyment. The method is this: On the first day of each month, some member of the family, at each extreme point of dispersion, takes a folio sheet, and fills a part of a page. This is sealed and mailed to the next family, who read it, add another contribution, and then mail it to the next. Thus the family circular, once a month, goes from each extreme to all the members of a widely-dispersed family, and each member becomes a sharer in the joys, sorrows, plans, and pursuits of all the rest. At the same time, frequent family meetings are sought; and the expense thus incurred is cheerfully met by retrenchments in other directions. The sacrifice of some unnecessary physical indulgence will often purchase many social and domestic enjoyments, a thousand times more elevating and delightful than the retrenched luxury.

There is no social duty which the Supreme Law-giver more strenuously urges than hospitality and kindness to strangers, who are classed with the widow and the fatherless as the special objects of Divine tenderness. There are some reasons why this duty peculiarly demands attention from the American people.

Reverses of fortune, in this land, are so frequent and un-expected, and the habits of the people are so migratory, that there are very many in every part of the country who, having seen all their temporal plans and hopes crushed, are now pining among strangers, bereft of wonted comforts, without friends, and without the sympathy and society so needful to wounded spirits. Such, too frequently, sojourn long and lonely, with no comforter but Him who "knoweth the heart of a stranger."

Whenever, therefore, new-comers enter a community, inquiry should immediately be made as to whether they have friends or associates, to render sympathy and kind attentions; and, when there is any need for it, the ministries of kind neighborliness should immediately be offered. And it should be remembered that the first days of a stranger's sojourn are the most dreary, and that civility and kindness are doubled in value by being offered at an early period.

In social gatherings the claims of the stranger are too apt to be forgotten; especially in cases where there are no peculiar attractions of personal appearance, or talents, or high standing. Such a one should be treated with attention, *because* he is a stranger; and when communities learn to act more from principle, and less from selfish impulse, on this subject, the sacred claims of the stranger will be less frequently forgotten.

The most agreeable hospitality to visitors who become

inmates of a family, is that which puts them entirely at ease. This can never be the case where the guest perceives that the order of family arrangement is essentially altered, and that time, comfort, and convenience are sacrificed for his accommodation.

Offering the best to visitors, showing a polite regard to every wish expressed, and giving precedence to them, in all matters of comfort and convenience, can be easily combined with the easy freedom which makes the stranger feel at home; and this is the perfection of hospitable entertainment.

XXIV.

ONE of the most interesting and instructive illustrations of the design of our Creator, in the institution of the family state, is the preservation of the aged after their faculties decay and usefulness in ordinary modes seems to be ended. By most persons this period of infirmities and uselessness is anticipated with apprehension, especially in the case of those who have lived an active, useful life, giving largely of service to others, and dependent for most resources of enjoyment on their own energies.

To lose the resources of sight or hearing, to become feeble in body, so as to depend on the ministries of others, and finally to gradually decay in mental force and intelligence, to many seems far worse than death. Multitudes have prayed to be taken from this life when their usefulness is thus ended.

But a true view of the design of the family state, and of the ministry of the aged and helpless in carrying out this design, would greatly lessen such apprehensions, and might be made a source of pure and elevated enjoyment.

The Christian virtues of patience with the unreasonable, of self-denying labor for the weak, and of sympathy with the afflicted, are dependent, to a great degree, on cultivation and habit, and these can be gained only in circumstances demanding the daily exercise of these graces. In this aspect, continued life in the aged and infirm should be regarded as a blessing and privilege to a family, especially to the young, and the cultivation of the graces that are demanded by that relation should be made a definite and interesting part of their education. A few of the methods to be attempted for this end will be suggested.

In the first place, the object for which the aged are preserved in life, when in many cases they would rejoice to depart, should be definitely kept in recollection, and a sense of gratitude and obligation be cultivated. They should be looked up to and treated as ministers sustained by our Heavenly Father in a painful experience, expressly for the good of those around them. This appreciation of their ministry and usefulness will greatly lessen their trials and impart consolation. If in hours of weariness and infirmity they wonder why they are kept in a useless and helpless state to burden others around, they should be assured that they are not useless ; and this not only by word, but, better still, by the manifestation of those virtues which such opportunities alone can secure.

Another mode of cheering the aged is to engage them in the domestic games and sports which unite the old and the young in amusement. Many a weary hour may thus be enlivened for the benefit of all concerned. And here will often occur opportunities of self-denying benevolence in relinquishing personal pursuits and gratification thus to promote the enjoyment of the infirm and dependent. Reading aloud is often a great source of enjoyment to those who by age are deprived of reading for themselves. So the effort to gather news of the neighborhood and impart it, is another mode of relieving those deprived of social gatherings.

There is no period in life when those courtesies of good breeding which recognize the relations of superior and inferior should be more carefully cherished than when there is need of showing them toward those of advancing age. To those who have controlled a household, and still more to those who in public life have been honored and admired, the decay of mental powers is peculiarly trying, and every effort should be made to lessen the trial by courteous attention to their opinions, and by avoiding all attempts to con trovert them, or to make evident any weakness or fallacy in their conversation.

In regard to the decay of bodily or mental faculties, much more can be done to prevent or retard them than is gen-rally supposed, and some methods for this end which have been gained by observation or experience will be pre-sented.

As the exercise of all our faculties tends to increase their power, unless it be carried to excess, it is very important that the aged should be provided with useful employment, suited to their strength and capacity. Nothing hastens de-cay so fast as to remove the *stimulus* of useful activity. It should become a study with those who have the care of the aged to interest them in some useful pursuit, and to con-vince them that they are in some measure actively con-tributing to the general welfare. In the country and in families where the larger part of the domestic labor is done without servants, it is very easy to keep up an interest in domestic industrial employments. The tending of a small garden in summer—the preparation of fuel and food, the mending of household utensils—these and many other occu-pations of the hands will keep alive activity and interest, in a man; while for women there are still more varied resources. There is nothing that so soon hastens decay and lends acerbity to age as giving up all business and responsibility, and every mode possible should be devised to prevent this result.

As age advances, all the bodily functions move more slowly, and consequently the generation of animal heat, by the union of oxygen and carbon in the capillaries, is in smaller proportion than in the midday of life. For this reason some practices, safe for the vigorous, must be relin-quished by the aged; and one of these is the use of the cold bath. It has often been the case that rheumatism has been caused by neglect of this caution. More than or dinary care should be taken to preserve animal heat in the aged, especially in the hands and the feet.

In many families will be found an aged brother, or sister, or other relative who has no home, and no claim to a refuge in the family circle but that of kindred. Sometimes they are poor and homeless, for want of a faculty for self-supporting business; and sometimes they have peculiarities of person or disposition which render their society undesirable. These are cases where the pitying tenderness of the Saviour should be remembered, and for his sake patient kindness and tender care be given, and he will graciously accept it as an offering of love and duty to himself. "Inasmuch as ye have done it to the least of these my brethren, ye have done it to me."

It is sometimes the case that even parents in old age have had occasion to say with the forsaken King Lear, "How sharper than a serpent's tooth it is to have a thankless child!" It is right training in early life alone that will save from this.

In the opening of China and the probable influx of its people, there is one cause for congratulation to a nation that is failing in the virtue of reverence. The Chinese are distinguished above all other nations for their respect for the aged, and especially for their reverence for aged parents and conformity to their authority, even to the last. This virtue is cultivated to a degree that is remarkable, and has produced singular and favorable results on the national character, which it is hoped may be imparted to the land to which they are flocking in such multitudes. For with all their peculiarities of pagan philosophy and their oriental eccentricities of custom and practical life, they are everywhere renowned for their uniform and elegant courtesy—a most commendable virtue, and one arising from habitual deference to the aged more than from any other source.

XXV.

THE CARE OF SERVANTS.

ALTHOUGH in earlier ages the highest born, wealthiest, and proudest ladies were skilled in the simple labors of the household, the advance of society toward luxury has changed all that in lands of aristocracy and classes, and at the present time America is the only country where there is a class of women who may be described as *ladies* who do their own work. By a lady we mean a woman of education, cultivation, and refinement, of liberal tastes and ideas, who, without any very material additions or changes, would be recognized as a lady in any circle of the Old World or the New.

The existence of such a class is a fact peculiar to American society, a plain result of the new principles involved in the doctrine of universal equality.

When the colonists first came to this country, of however mixed ingredients their ranks might have been composed, and however imbued with the spirit of feudal and aristocratic ideas, the discipline of the wilderness soon brought them to a democratic level; the gentleman felled the wood for his log-cabin side by side with the plowman, and thews and sinews rose in the market. "A man was deemed honorable in proportion as he lifted his hand upon the high trees of the forest." So in the interior domestic circle. Mistress and maid, living in a log-cabin together, became companions, and sometimes the maid, as the one well-trained in domestic labor, took precedence of the mistress. It also became natural and unavoidable that children should begin to work as early as they were capable of it.

The result was a generation of intelligent people brought up to labor from necessity, but devoting to the problem of labor the acuteness of a disciplined brain. The mistress, outdone in sinews and muscles by her maid, kept her superiority by skill and contrivance. If she could not lift a pail of water, she could invent methods which made lifting the pail unnecessary,—if she could not take a hundred steps without weariness, she could make twenty answer the purpose of a hundred.

Slavery, it is true, was to some extent introduced into New-England, but it never suited the genius of the people, never struck deep root or spread so as to choke the good seed of self-helpfulness. Many were opposed to it from conscientious principle—many from far-sighted thrift, and from a love of thoroughness and well-doing which despised the rude, unskilled work of barbarians. People, having once felt the thorough neatness and beauty of execution which came of free, educated, and thoughtful labor, could not tolerate the clumsiness of slavery.

Thus it came to pass that for many years the rural population of New-England, as a general rule, did their own work, both out-doors and in. If there were a black man or black woman or bound girl, they were emphatically only the *helps*, following humbly the steps of master and mistress, and used by them as instruments of lightening certain portions of their toil. The master and mistress, with their children, were the head workers.

Great merriment has been excited in the old country because, years ago, the first English travelers found that the class of persons by them denominated servants, were in America denominated *help*, or helpers. But the term was the very best exponent of the state of society. There were few servants, in the European sense of the word; there was a society of educated workers, where all were practically equal, and where, if there was a deficiency in one family and an excess in another, a *helper*, not a servant in the European sense, was hired. Mrs. Brown, who has several sons and no daughters, enters into agreement with Mrs. Jones, who has several daughters and no sons. She borrows a daughter, and pays her good wages to help in her domestic toil, and sends a son to help the labors of Mr. Jones. These two young people go into the families in which they are to be employed in all respects as equals and companions, and so the work of the community is equalized. Hence arose, and for many years continued, a state of society more nearly solving than any other ever did the problem of combining the highest culture of the mind with the highest culture of the muscles and the physical faculties.

Then were to be seen families of daughters, handsome, strong women, rising each day to their in-door work with cheerful alertness—one to sweep the room, another to make the fire, while a third prepared the breakfast for the father and brothers who were going out to manly labor : and they chatted meanwhile of books, studies, embroidery ; discussed the last new poem, or some historical topic started by graver reading, or perhaps a rural ball that was to come off next week. They spun with the book tied to the distaff; they wove ; they did all manner of fine needle-work ; they made lace, painted flowers, and, in short, in the boundless consciousness of activity, invention, and perfect health, set themselves to any work they had ever read or thought of. A bride in those days was married with sheets and table-cloths of her own weaving, with counterpanes and toilet-covers wrought in divers embroidery by her own and her sisters' hands. The amount of fancy-work done in our days by girls who have nothing else to do, will not equal what was done by these who performed, besides, among them, the whole work of the family.

In those former days most women were in good health,

debility and disease being the exception. Then, too, was seen the economy of daylight and its pleasures. They were used to early rising, and would not lie in bed, if they could. Long years of practice made them familiar with the shortest, neatest, most expeditious method of doing every household office, so that really for the greater part of the time in the house there seemed, to a looker-on, to be nothing to do. They rose in the morning and dispatched husband, father, and brothers to the farm or wood-lot; went sociably about, chatting with each other, skimmed the milk, made the butter, and turned the cheeses. The forenoon was long; ten to one, all the so-called morning work over, they had leisure for an hour's sewing or reading before it was time to start the dinner preparations. By two o'clock the house-work was done, and they had the long afternoon for books, needle-work, or drawing—for perhaps there was one with a gift at her pencil. Perhaps one read aloud while others sewed, and managed in that way to keep up a great deal of reading.

It is said that women who have been accustomed to doing their own work become hard mistresses. They are certainly more sure of the ground they stand on—they are less open to imposition—they can speak and act in their own houses more as those "having authority," and therefore are less afraid to exact what is justly their due, and less willing to endure impertinence and unfaithfulness. Their general error lies in expecting that any servant ever will do as well for them as they will do for themselves, and that an un-trained, undisciplined human being ever *can* do house-work, or any other work, with the neatness and perfection that a person of trained intelligence can.

It has been remarked in our armies that the men of cul-tivation, though bred in delicate and refined spheres, can bear up under the hardships of camp-life better and longer than rough laborers. The reason is, that an educated mind knows how to use and save its body, to work it and spare it, as an uneducated mind can not; and so the college-bred youth brings himself safely through fatigues which kill the unreflective laborer.

Cultivated, intelligent women, who are brought up to do the work of their own families, are labor-saving institutions. They make the head save the wear of the muscles. By forethought, contrivance, system, and arrangement they lessen the amount to be done, and do it with less expense of time and strength than others. The old New-England motto, *Get your work done up in the forenoon*, applied to an amount of work which would keep a common Irish servant toiling from daylight to sunset.

A lady living in one of our obscure New-England towns, where there were no servants to be hired, at last, by sending to a distant city, succeeded in procuring a raw Irish maid-of-all-work, a creature of immense bone and muscle, but of heavy, unawakened brain. In one fortnight she established such a reign of Chaos and old Night in the kitchen and through the house that her mistress, a delicate woman, encumbered with the care of young children, began seriously to think that she made more work each day than she performed, and dismissed her. What was now to be done? Fortunately, the daughter of a neighboring farmer was going to be married in six months, and wanted a little ready money for her *trousseau*. The lady was informed that Miss So-and-so would come to her, not as a servant, but as hired "help." She was fain to accept any help with gladness.

Forthwith came into the family-circle a tall, well-dressed young person, grave, unobtrusive, self-respecting, yet not in the least presuming, who sat at the family table and observed all its decorums with the modest self-possession of a lady. The new-comer took a survey of the labors of a family of ten members, including four or five young children, and, looking, seemed at once to throw them into system; matured her plans, arranged her hours of washing, ironing, baking, and cleaning; rose early, moved deftly; and in a single day the slatternly and littered kitchen assumed that neat, orderly appearance that so often strikes one in New-England farm-houses. The work seemed to be all gone. Every thing was nicely washed, brightened, put in place, and staid in place; the floors, when cleaned, remained clean; the work was always done, and not doing; and every afternoon the young lady sat neatly dressed in her own apartment, either quietly writing letters to her betrothed, or sewing on her bridal outfit. Such is the result of employing those who have been brought up to do their own work. That tall, fine-looking girl, for aught we know, may yet be mistress of a fine house on Fifth Avenue; and if she is, she will, we fear, prove rather an exacting mistress to Irish Bridget; but she will never be threatened by her cook and chambermaid, after the first one or two have tried the experiment.

Those remarkable women of old were made by circumstances. There were, comparatively speaking, no servants to be had, and so children were trained to habits of industry and mechanical adroitness from the cradle, and every household process was reduced to the very minimum of labor. Every step required in a process was counted, every movement calculated; and she who took ten steps, when one would do, lost her reputation for "faculty." Certainly such an early drill was of use in developing the health and the bodily powers, as well as in giving precision to the practical mental faculties. All household economies were arranged with equal niceness in those thoughtful minds. A trained housekeeper knew just how many sticks of hickory of a certain size were required to heat her oven, and how many of each different kind of wood. She knew by a sort of intuition just what kinds of food would yield the most palatable nutriment with the least outlay of accessories in cooking. She knew to a minute the time when each article must go into and be withdrawn from her oven; and if she could only lie in her chamber and direct, she could guide an intelligent child through the processes with mathematical certainty.

It is impossible, however, that any thing but early training and long experience can produce these results, and it is earnestly to be wished that the grandmothers of New-England had written down their experiences for our children; they would have been a mine of maxims and traditions better than any other " traditions of the elders " which we know of.

In this country, our democratic institutions have removed the superincumbent pressure which in the Old World confines the servants to a regular orbit. They come here feeling that this is somehow a land of liberty, and with very dim and confused notions of what liberty is. They are very extensively the raw, untrained Irish peasantry, and the wonder is, that, with all the unreasoning heats and prejudices of the Celtic blood, all the necessary ignorance and rawness, there should be the measure of comfort and success there is in our domestic arrangements.

But, as long as things are so, there will be constant changes and interruptions in every domestic establishment, and constantly recurring interregnums when the mistress must put her own hand to the work, whether the hand be a trained or an untrained one. As matters now are, the young housekeeper takes life at the hardest. She has very little strength,—no experience to teach her how to save her strength. She knows nothing experimentally of the simplest processes necessary to keep her family comfortably fed and clothed; and she has a way of looking at all these things which makes them particularly hard and distasteful to her. She does not escape being obliged to do house-work at intervals, but she does it in a weak, blundering, confused way, that makes it twice as hard and disagreeable as it need be.

Now, if every young woman learned to do house-work,

and cultivated her practical faculties in early life, she would, in the first place, be much more likely to keep her servants, and, in the second place, if she lost them temporarily, would avoid all that wear and tear of the nervous system which comes from constant ill-success in those departments on which family health and temper mainly depend. This is one of the peculiarities of our American life, which require a peculiar training. Why not face it sensibly?

Our land is now full of motorpathic institutions to which women are sent at a great expense to have hired operators stretch and exercise their inactive muscles. They lie for hours to have their feet twigged, their arms flexed, and all the different muscles of the body worked for them, because they are so flaccid and torpid that the powers of life do not go on. Would it not be quite as cheerful, and a less expensive process, if young girls from early life developed the muscles in sweeping, dusting, starching, ironing, and all the multiplied domestic processes which our grandmothers knew of? A woman who did all these, and diversified the intervals with spinning on the great and little wheel, did not need the gymnastics of Dio Lewis or of the Swedish Movement Cure, which really are a necessity now. Does it not seem poor economy to pay servants for letting our muscles grow feeble, and then to pay operators to exercise them for us? I will venture to say that our grandmothers in a week went over every movement that any gymnast has invented, and went over them to some productive purpose too.

The first business of a housekeeper in America is that of a teacher. She can have a good table only by having practical knowledge, and tact in imparting it. If she understands her business practically and experimentally, her eye detects at once the weak spot; it requires only a little tact, some patience, some clearness in giving directions, and all comes right.

If we carry a watch to a watchmaker, and undertake to show him how to regulate the machinery, he laughs and goes on his own way; but if a brother-machinist makes suggestions, he listens respectfully. So, when a woman who knows nothing of woman's work undertakes to instruct one who knows more than she does, she makes no impression; but a woman who has been trained experimentally, and shows she understands the matter thoroughly, is listened to with respect.

Let a woman make her own bread for one month, and, simple as the process seems, it will take as long as that to get a thorough knowledge of all the possibilities in the case; but after that, she will be able to command good bread by the aid of all sorts of servants; in other words, will be a thoroughly prepared teacher.

Although bread-making seems a simple process, it yet requires delicate care and watchfulness. There are fifty ways to spoil good bread; there are a hundred little things to be considered and allowed for, that require accurate observation and experience. The same process that will raise good bread in cold weather will make sour bread in the heat of summer; different qualities of flour require variations in treatment, as also different sorts and conditions of yeast; and when all is done, the baking presents another series of possibilities which require exact attention.

A well-trained mind, accustomed to reflect, analyze, and generalize, has an advantage over uncultured minds even of double experience. Poor as your cook is, she now knows more of her business than you do. After a very brief period of attention and experiment, you will not only know more than she does, but you will convince her that you do, which is quite as much to the purpose.

In the same manner, lessons must be given on the washing of silver and the making of beds. Good servants do not often come to us; they must be *made* by patience and training; and if a girl has a good disposition and a reasonable degree of handiness, and the housekeeper understands her profession, a good servant may be made out of an indifferent one. Some of the best girls have been those who came directly from the ship, with no preparation but docility and some natural quickness. The hardest cases to be managed are not of those who have been taught nothing, but of those who have been taught wrongly—who come self-opinionated, with ways which are distasteful, and contrary to the genius of one's housekeeping. Such require that their mistress shall understand at least so much of the actual conduct of affairs as to prove to the servant that there are better ways than those in which she has been trained.

So much has been said of the higher sphere of woman, and so much has been done to find some better work for her that, insensibly, almost every body begins to feel that it is rather degrading for a woman in good society to be much tied down to family affairs ; especially since in these Woman's Rights Conventions there is so much dissatisfaction expressed at those who would confine her ideas to the kitchen and nursery.

Yet these Woman's Rights Conventions are a protest against many former absurd, unreasonable ideas—the mere physical and culinary idea of womanhood as connected only with puddings and shirt-buttons, the unjust and unequal burdens which the laws of harsher ages had cast upon the sex. Many of the women connected with these movements are as superior in every thing properly womanly as they are in exceptional talent and culture. There is no manner of doubt that the sphere of woman is properly to be enlarged. Every woman has rights as a human being which belong to no sex, and ought to be as freely conceded to her as if she were a man,—and first and foremost, the great right of doing any thing which God and nature evidently have fitted her to excel in. If she be made a natural orator, like Miss Dickinson, or an astronomer, like Mrs.

Somerville, or a singer, like Grisi, let not the technical rules of womanhood be thrown in the way of her free use of her powers.

Still, *per contra*, there has been a great deal of crude, disagreeable talk in these conventions, and too great tendency of the age to make the education of woman anti-domestic. It seems as if the world never could advance, except like ships under a head-wind, tacking and going too far, now in this direction, and now in the opposite. Our common-school system now rejects sewing from the education of girls, which very properly used to occupy many hours daily in school a generation ago. The daughters of laborers and artisans are put through algebra, geometry, trigonometry, and the higher mathematics, to the entire neglect of that learning which belongs distinctively to woman. A girl often can not keep pace with her class, if she gives any time to domestic matters; and accordingly she is excused from them all during the whole term of her education. The boy of a family, at an early age, is put to a trade, or the labors of a farm; the father becomes impatient of his support, and requires of him to take care for himself. Hence an interrupted education—learning coming by snatches in the winter months or in the intervals of work.

As the result, the young women in some of our country towns are, in mental culture, much in advance of the males of the same household; but with this comes a physical delicacy, the result of an exclusive use of the brain and a neglect of the muscular system, with great inefficiency in practical domestic duties. The race of strong, hardy, cheerful girls, that used to grow up in country places, and made the bright, neat, New-England kitchens of old times—the girls that could wash, iron, brew, bake, harness a horse and drive him, no less than braid straw, embroider, draw, paint, and read innumerable books—this race of women, pride of olden time, is daily lessening; and in their stead come the fragile, easily-fatigued, languid girls of a modern age, drilled in book-learning, ignorant of common things. The great danger of all this, and of the evils that come from it, is, that society, by and by, will turn as blindly against female intellectual culture as it now advocates it, and having worked disproportionately one way, will work disproportionately in the opposite direction.

Domestic service is the great problem of life here in America; the happiness of families, their thrift, well-being, and comfort, are more affected by this than by any one thing else. The modern girls, as they have been brought up, can not perform the labor of their own families as in those simpler, old-fashioned days; and what is worse, they have no practical skill with which to instruct servants, who come to us, as a class, raw and untrained. In the present state of prices, the board of a domestic costs double her wages, and the waste she makes is a more serious matter still.

Many of the domestic evils in America originate in the fact that, while society here is professedly based on new principles which ought to make social life in every respect different from the life of the Old World, yet these principles have never been so thought out and applied as to give consistency and harmony to our daily relations. America starts with a political organization based on a declaration of the primitive freedom and equality of all men. Every human being, according to this principle, stands on the same natural level with every other, and has the same chance to rise according to the degree of power or capacity given by the Creator. All our civil institutions are designed to preserve this equality, as far as possible, from generation to generation: there is no entailed property, there are no hereditary titles, no monopolies, no privileged classes—all are to be as free to rise and fall as the waves of the sea.

The condition of domestic service, however, still retains about it something of the influences from feudal times, and from the near presence of slavery in neighboring States.

All English literature of the world describes domestic service in the old feudal spirit and with the old feudal language, which regarded the master as belonging to a privileged class and the servant to an inferior one. There is not a play, not a poem, not a novel, not a history, that does not present this view. The master's rights, like the rights of kings, were supposed to rest in his being born in a superior rank. The good servant was one who, from childhood, had learned " to order himself lowly and reverently to all his betters." When New-England brought to these shores the theory of democracy, she brought, in the persons of the first pilgrims, the habits of thought and of action formed in aristocratic communities. Winthrop's Journal, and all the 'old records of the earlier colonists, show households where masters and mistresses stood on the " right divine" of the privileged classes, howsoever they might have risen up against authorities themselves.

The first consequence of this state of things was a universal rejection of domestic service in all classes of American-born society. For a generation or two there was, indeed, a sort of interchange of family strength,—sons and daughters engaging in the service of neighboring families, in default of a sufficient working-force of their own, but always on conditions of strict equality. The assistant was to share the table, the family sitting-room, and every honor and attention that might be claimed by son or daughter. When families increased in refinement and education so as to make these conditions of close intimacy with more uncultured neighbors disagreeable, they had to choose between such intimacies and the performance of their own domestic toil. No wages could induce a son or daughter of New England to take the condition of a servant on terms which they thought applicable to that of a slave. The slightest hint of a separate table was resented as an insult; not to enter the front door, and not to sit in the front parlor on state occasions, was bitterly commented on as a personal indignity.

The well-taught, self-respecting daughters of farmers, the class most valuable in domestic service, gradually retired from it. They preferred any other employment, however laborious. Beyond all doubt, the labors of a well-regulated family are more healthy, more cheerful, more interesting, because less monotonous, than the mechanical toils of a factory; yet the girls of New-England, with one consent, preferred the factory, and left the whole business of domestic service to a foreign population; and they did it mainly because they would not take positions in families as an inferior laboring-class by the side of others of their own age who assumed as their prerogative to live without labor.

"I can't let you have one of my daughters," said an energetic matron to her neighbor from the city, who was seeking for a servant in her summer vacation; "if you hadn't daughters of your own, may be I would; but my girls are not going to work so that your girls may live in idleness."

It was vain to offer money. "We don't need your money, ma'am; we can support ourselves in other ways; my girls can braid straw, and bind shoes, but they are not going to be slaves to any body."

In the Irish and German servants who took the place of Americans in families, there was, to begin with, the tradition of education in favor of a higher class; but even the foreign population became more or less infected with the spirit of democracy. They came to this country with vague notions of freedom and equality, and in ignorant and uncultivated people such ideas are often more unreasonable for being vague. They did not, indeed, claim a seat at the table and in the parlor, but they repudiated many of those habits of respect and courtesy which belonged to their former condition, and asserted their own will and way in the round, unvarnished phrase which they supposed to be their right as republican citizens. Life became a sort of domestic wrangle and struggle between the employers, who secretly confessed their weakness, but endeavored openly to assume the air and bearing of authority, and the employed, who knew their power and insisted on their privileges.

From this cause domestic service in America has had less of mutual kindliness than in old countries. Its terms have been so ill-understood and defined that both parties have assumed the defensive; and a common topic of conversation in American female society has often been the general servile war which in one form or another was going on in their different families—a war as interminable as would be a struggle between aristocracy and common people, undefined by any bill of rights or constitution, and therefore opening fields for endless disputes.

In England, the class who go to service *are* a class, and service is a profession; the distance between them and their employers is so marked and defined, and all the customs and requirements of the position are so perfectly understood, that the master or mistress has no fear of being compromised by condescension, and no need of the external voice or air of authority. The higher up in the social scale one goes, the more courteous seems to become the intercourse of master and servant; the more perfect and real the power, the more is it veiled in outward expression—commands are phrased as requests, and gentleness of voice and manner covers an authority which no one would think of offending without trembling.

But in America all is undefined. In the first place, there is no class who mean to make domestic service a profession to live and die in. It is universally an expedient, a stepping-stone to something higher; your best servants always have some thing else in view as soon as they have laid by a little money; some form of independence which shall give them a home of their own is constantly in mind. Families look forward to the buying of landed homesteads, and the scattered brothers and sisters work awhile in domestic service to gain the common fund for the purpose; your seamstress intends to become a dressmaker, and take in work at her own house; your cook is pondering a marriage with the baker, which shall transfer her toils from your cooking-stove to her own.

Young women are eagerly rushing into every other employment, till feminine trades and callings are all overstocked. We are continually harrowed with tales of the sufferings of distressed needle-women, of the exactions and extortions practiced on the frail sex in the many branches of labor and trade at which they try their hands; and yet women will encounter all these chances of ruin and starvation rather than make up their minds to permanent domestic service.

Now, what is the matter with domestic service? One would think, on the face of it, that a calling which gives a settled home, a comfortable room, rent-free, with fire and lights, good board and lodging, and steady, well-paid wages, would certainly offer more attractions than the making of shirts for tenpence, with all the risks of providing one's own sustenance and shelter.

Is it not mainly from the want of a definite idea of the true position of a servant under our democratic institutions that domestic service is so shunned and avoided in America, and that it is the very last thing which an intelligent young woman will look to for a living? It is more the want of personal respect toward those in that position than the labor incident to it which repels our people from it. Many would be willing to perform these labors, but they are not willing to place themselves in a situation where their self-respect is hourly wounded by the implication of a degree of inferiority, *which does not follow any kind of labor or service in this country but that of the family.*

There exists in the minds of employers an unsuspected spirit of superiority, which is stimulated into an active form by the resistance which democracy inspires in the working-class. Many families think of servants only as a necessary evil, their wages as exactions, and all that is allowed them as so much taken from the family; and they seek in every way to get from them as much and to give them as little as possible. Their rooms are the neglected, ill-furnished, incommodious ones—and the kitchen is the most cheerless and comfortless place in the house.

Other families, more good-natured and liberal, provide their domestics with more suitable accommodations, and are more indulgent; but there is still a latent spirit of something like contempt for the position. That they treat their servants with so much consideration seems to them a merit entitling them to the most prostrate gratitude; and they are constantly disappointed and shocked at that want of sense of inferiority on the part of these people which leads them to appropriate pleasant rooms, good furniture, and good living as mere matters of common justice.

It seems to be a constant surprise to some employers that servants should insist on having the same human wants as themselves. Ladies who yawn in their elegantly furnished parlors, among books and pictures, if they have not company, parties, or opera to diversify the evening, seem astonished and half indignant that cook and chambermaid are more disposed to go out for an evening gossip than to sit on hard chairs in the kitchen where they have been toiling all day. The pretty chambermaid's anxieties about her dress, the minutes she spends at her small and not very clear mirror, are sneeringly noticed by those whose toilet-cares take up serious hours; and the question has never apparently occurred to them why a serving-maid should not want to look pretty as well as her mistress. She is a woman as well as they, with all a woman's wants and weaknesses; and her dress is as much to her as theirs to them.

A vast deal of trouble among servants arises from impertinent interferences and petty tyrannical exactions on the part of employers. Now, the authority of the master and mistress of a house in regard to their domestics extends simply to the things they have contracted to do and the hours during which they have contracted to serve; otherwise than this, they have no more right to interfere with them in the disposal of their time than with any mechanic whom they employ. They have, indeed, a right to regulate the hours of their own household, and servants can choose between conformity to these hours and the loss of their situation; but, within reasonable limits, their right to come and go at their own discretion, in their own time, should be unquestioned.

If employers are troubled by the fondness of their servants for dancing, evening company, and late hours, the proper mode of proceeding is to make these matters a subject of distinct contract in hiring. The more strictly and perfectly the business matters of the first engagement of domestics are conducted, the more likelihood there is of mutual quiet and satisfaction in the relation. It is quite competent to every housekeeper to say what practices are or are not consistent with the rules of her family, and what will be inconsistent with the service for which she agrees to pay. It is much better to regulate such affairs by cool contract in the outset than by warm altercations and protracted domestic battles.

As to the terms of social intercourse, it seems somehow to be settled in the minds of many employers that their servants owe them and their family more respect than they and the family owe to the servants. But do they? What is the relation of servant to employer in a democratic country? Precisely that of a person who for money performs any kind of service for you. The carpenter comes into your house to put up a set o shelves—the cook comes into your kitchen to cook your dinner. You never think that the carpenter owes you any more respect than you owe to him because he is in your house doing your behests; he is your fellow-citizen, you treat him with respect, you expect to be treated with respect by him. You have a claim on him that he shall do your work according to your directions—no more.

Now, I apprehend that there is a very common notion as to the position and rights of servants which is quite different from this. Is it not a common feeling that a servant is one who may be treated with a degree of freedom by every member of the family which he or she may not return? Do not people feel at liberty to question servants about their private affairs, to comment on their dress and appearance, in a manner which they would feel to be an impertinence, if reciprocated? Do they not feel at liberty to express dissatisfaction with their performances in rude and unceremonious terms, to reprove them in the presence of company, while yet they require that the dissatisfaction of servants shall be expressed only in terms of respect? A woman would not feel herself at liberty to talk to her milliner or her dress-maker in language as devoid of consideration as she will employ toward her cook or chambermaid. And yet both are rendering her a service which she pays for in money, and one is no more made her inferior thereby than the other. Both have an equal right to be treated with courtesy. The master and mistress of a house have a right to require courteous treatment from all whom their roof shelters; but they have no more right to exact it of servants than of every guest and every child, and they themselves owe it as much to servants as to guests.

In order that servants may be treated with respect and courtesy, it is not necessary, as in simpler patriarchal days, that they sit at the family-table. Your carpenter or plumber does not feel hurt that you do not ask him to dine with you, nor your milliner and mantua-maker that you do not exchange ceremonious calls and invite them to your parties. It is well understood that your relations with them are of a mere business character. They never take it as an assumption of superiority on your part that you do not admit them

to relations of private intimacy.   There may be the most
perfect respect and esteem and even friendship between
them and you, notwithstanding.   So it may be in the case
of servants.   It is easy to make any person understand that
there are quite other reasons than the assumption of personal superiority for not wishing to admit servants to the family
privacy.   It was not, in fact, to sit in the parlor or at the
table, in themselves considered, that was the thing aimed at
by New-England girls ; these were valued only as signs that
they were deemed worthy of respect and consideration, and,
where freely conceded, were often in point of fact declined.

Let servants feel, in their treatment by their employers
and in the atmosphere of the family, that their position is
held to be a respectable one ; let them feel, in the mistress
of the family, the charm of unvarying consideration and
good manners; let their work-rooms be made convenient
and comfortable, and their private apartments bear some
reasonable comparison in point of agreeableness to those of
other members of the family, and domestic service will be
more frequently sought by a superior and self-respecting
class.   There are families in which such a state of things
prevails ; and such families, amid the many causes which
unite to make the tenure of service uncertain, have generally been able to keep good permanent servants.

There is an extreme into which kindly disposed people
often run with regard to servants which may be mentioned here.   They make pets of them.   They give extrava-
gant wages and indiscreet indulgences, and, through indolence and easiness of temper, tolerate neglect of duty.
Many of the complaints of the ingratitude of servants
come from those who have spoiled them in this way ; while
many of the longest and most harmonious domestic unions
have sprung from a simple, quiet course of Christian justice
and benevolence, a recognition of servants as fellow-beings
and fellow-Christians, and a doing to them as we would in
like circumstances that they should do to us.

The mistresses of American families, whether they like

it or not, have the duties of missionaries imposed upon them by that class from which our supply of domestic servants is drawn. They may as well accept the position cheerfully, and, as one raw, untrained hand after another passes through their family, and is instructed by them in the mysteries of good house-keeping, comfort themselves with the reflection that they are doing something to form good wives and mothers for the republic.

The complaints made of Irish girls are numerous and loud; the failings of green Erin, alas! are but too open and manifest; yet, in arrest of judgment, let us move this consideration: let us imagine our own daughters between the ages of sixteen and twenty-four, untaught and inexperienced in domestic affairs as they commonly are, shipped to a foreign shore to seek service in families. It may be questioned whether, as a whole, they would do much better. The girls that fill our families and do our house-work are often of the age of our own daughters, standing for themselves, without mothers to guide them, in a foreign country, not only bravely supporting themselves, but sending home in every ship remittances to impoverished friends left behind. If our daughters did as much for us, should we not be proud of their energy and heroism?

When we go into the houses of our country, we find a majority of well-kept, well-ordered, and even elegant establishments, where the only hands employed are those of the daughters of Erin. True, American women have been their instructors, and many a weary hour of care have they had in the discharge of this office; but the result on the whole is beautiful and good, and the end of it, doubtless, will be peace.

Instead, then, of complaining that we can not have our own peculiar advantages and those of other nations too, or imagining how much better off we should be if things were different from what they are, it is much wiser and more Christianlike to strive cheerfully to conform to actual circumstances; and, after remedying all that we can control, patiently to submit to what is beyond our power. If domestics are found to be incompetent, unstable, and unconformed to their station, it is Perfect Wisdom which appoints these trials to teach us patience, fortitude, and self-control; and if the discipline is met in a proper spirit, it will prove a blessing rather than an evil.

But to judge correctly in regard to some of the evils involved in the state of domestic service in this country, we should endeavor to conceive ourselves placed in the situation of those of whom complaint is made, that we may not expect from them any more than it would seem right should be exacted from us in similar circumstances.

It is sometimes urged against domestics that they exact exorbitant wages. But what is the rule of rectitude on this subject? Is it not the universal law of labor and of trade that an article is to be valued according to its scarcity and the demand? When wheat is scarce, the farmer raises his price; and when a mechanic offers services difficult to be obtained, he makes a corresponding increase of price. And why is it not right for domestics to act according to a rule allowed to be correct in reference to all other trades and professions? It is a fact, that really good domestic service must continue to increase in value just in proportion as this country waxes rich and prosperous; thus making the proportion of those who wish to hire labor relatively greater, and the number of those willing to go to service less.

Money enables the rich to gain many advantages which those of more limited circumstances can not secure. One of these is, securing good servants by offering high wages; and this, as the scarcity of this class increases, will serve constantly to raise the price of service. It is right for domestics to charge the market value, and this value is always decided by the scarcity of the article and the amount of demand. Right views of this subject will sometimes serve to diminish hard feelings toward those who would otherwise be wrongfully regarded as unreasonable and exacting.

Another complaint against servants is that of instability and discontent, leading to perpetual change. But in reference to this, let a mother or daughter conceive of their own circumstances as so changed that the daughter must go out to service. Suppose a place is engaged, and it is then found that she must sleep in a comfortless garret; and that, when a new domestic comes, perhaps a coarse and dirty foreigner, she must share her bed with her. Another place is offered, where she can have a comfortable room and an agreeable room-mate; in such a case, would not both mother and daughter think it right to change ?

Or suppose, on trial, it was found that the lady of the house was fretful or exacting and hard to please, or that her children were so ungoverned as to be perpetual vexations ; or that the work was so heavy that no time was allowed for relaxation and the care of a wardrobe ; and another place offers where these evils can be escaped ; would not mother and daughter here think it right to change ? And is it not right for domestics, as well as their employers, to seek places where they can be most comfortable ?

In some cases, this instability and love of change would be remedied, if employers would take more pains to make a residence with them agreeable, and to attach servants to the family by feelings of gratitude and affection. There are ladies, even where well-qualified domestics are most rare, who seldom find any trouble in keeping good and steady ones. And the reason is, that their servants know they can not better their condition by any change within reach. It is not merely by giving them comfortable rooms, and good food, and presents, and privileges, that the attachment of domestic servants is secured ; it is by the manifestation of a friendly and benevolent interest in their comfort and improvement. This is exhibited in bearing patiently with their faults ; in kindly teaching them how to improve ; in showing them how to make and take proper care of their clothes; in guarding their health; in teaching them to read if necessary, and supplying them with proper books; and in short, by endeavoring, so far as may be, to supply the place of parents. It is seldom that such a course would fail to secure steady service, and such affection and grati- tude that even higher wages would be ineffectual to tempt them away. There would probably be some cases of un- grateful returns; but there is no doubt that the course in- dicated, if generally pursued, would very much lessen the evil in question.

When servants are forward and bold in manners and dis- respectful in address, they may be considerately taught that those who are among the best-bred and genteel have cour- teous and respectful manners and language to all they meet: while many who have wealth, are regarded as vulgar, be- cause they exhibit rude and disrespectful manners. The very term *gentle man* indicates the refinement and delicacy of address which distinguishes the high-bred from the coarse and vulgar.

In regard to appropriate dress, in most cases it is difficult for an employer to interfere, *directly*, with comments or ad- vice. The most successful mode is to offer some service in mending or making a wardrobe, and when a confidence in the kindness of feeling is thus gained, remarks and sugges- tions will generally be properly received, and new views of propriety and economy can be imparted. In some cases it may be well for an employer who, from appearances, antici- pates difficulty of this kind, in making the preliminary con- tract or agreement to state that she wishes to have the room, person, and dress of her servants kept neat and in order, and that she expects to remind them of their duty, in this particular, if it is neglected. Domestic servants are very apt to neglect the care of their own chambers and clothing; and such habits have a most pernicious influence on their well-being and on that of their children in future domestic life. An employer, then, is bound to exercise a parental care over them, in these respects.

There is one great mistake, not unfrequently made, in the management both of domestics and of children, and that is, in supposing that the way to cure defects is by finding fault as each failing occurs. But instead of this being true, in many cases the directly opposite course is the best; while, in all instances, much good judgment is required in order to decide when to notice faults and when to let them pass unnoticed. There are some minds very sensitive, easily discouraged, and infirm of purpose. Such persons, when they have formed habits of negligence, haste, and awkwardness, often need expressions of sympathy and encouragement rather than reproof. They have usually been found fault with so much that they have become either hardened or desponding; and it is often the case, that a few words of commendation will awaken fresh efforts and renewed hope. In al most every case, words of kindness, confidence, and encouragement should be mingled with the needful admonitions or reproof.

It is a good rule, in reference to this point, to *forewarn* instead of finding fault. Thus, when a thing has been done wrong, let it pass unnoticed, till it is to be done again; and then, a simple request to have it done in the right way will secure quite as much, and probably more, willing effort, than a reproof administered for neglect. Some persons seem to take it for granted that young and inexperienced minds are bound to have all the forethought and discretion of mature persons; and freely express wonder and disgust when mishaps occur for want of these traits. But it would be far better to save from mistake or forgetfulness by previous caution and care on the part of those who have gained experience and forethought; and thus many occasions of complaint and ill-humor will be avoided.

Those who fill the places of heads of families are not very apt to think how painful it is to be chided for neglect of duty or for faults of character. If they would sometimes imagine themselves in the place of those whom they control, with some person daily administering reproof to them, in the same *tone and style* as they employ to those who are under them, it might serve as a useful check to their chidings. It is often the case, that persons who are most strict and exacting and least able to make allowances and receive palliations, are themselves peculiarly sensitive to any thing which implies that they are in fault. By such, the spirit implied in the Divine petition, " Forgive us our trespasses as we forgive those who trespass against us," needs especially to be cherished.

One other consideration is very important. There is no duty more binding on Christians than that of patience and meekness under provocations and disappointment. Now, the tendency of every sensitive mind, when thwarted in its wishes, is to complain and find fault, and that often in tones of fretfulness or anger. But there are few servants who have not heard enough of the Bible to know that angry or fretful fault-finding from the mistress of a family, when her work is not done to suit her, is not in agreement with the precepts of Christ. They notice and feel the inconsistency; and every woman, when she gives way to feelings of anger and impatience at the faults of those around her, lowers herself in their respect, while her own conscience, unless very much blinded, can not but suffer a wound.

In speaking of the office of the American mistress as being a missionary one, we are far from recommending any controversial interference with the religious faith of our servants. It is far better to incite them to be good Christians in their own way than to run the risk of shaking their faith in all religion by pointing out to them what seem to us the errors of that in which they have been educated. The general purity of life and propriety of demeanor of so many thousands of undefended young girls cast yearly upon our shores, with no home but their church, and no shield but their religion, are a sufficient proof that this religion exerts an influence over them not to be lightly trifled with.

But there is a real unity even in opposite Christian forms; and the Roman Catholic servant and the Protestant mistress, if alike possessed by the spirit of Christ, and striving to conform to the Golden Rule, can not help being one in heart, though one go to mass and the other to meeting.

Finally, the bitter baptism through which we have passed, the life-blood dearer than our own which has drenched distant fields, should remind us of the preciousness of distinctive American ideas. They who would seek in their foolish pride to establish the pomp of liveried servants in America are doing that which is simply absurd. A servant can never in our country be the mere appendage to another man, to be marked like a sheep with the color of his owner; he must be a fellow-citizen, with an established position of his own, free to make contracts, free to come and go, and having in his sphere titles to consideration and respect just as definite as those of any trade or profession whatever.

Moreover, we can not in this country maintain to any great extent large retinues of servants. Even with ample fortunes, they are forbidden by the general character of society here, which makes them cumbrous and difficult to manage. Every mistress of a family knows that her cares increase with every additional servant. Two keep the peace with each other and their employer; three begin a possible discord, which possibility increases with four, and becomes certain with five or six. Trained housekeepers, such as regulate the complicated establishments of the old world, form a class that are not, and from the nature of the case never will be, found in any great numbers in this country. All such women, as a general thing, are keeping, and prefer to keep, houses of their own.

A moderate style of housekeeping, small, compact, and simple domestic establishments, must necessarily be the general order of life in America. So many openings of profit are to be found in this country, that domestic service necessarily wants the permanence which forms so agreeable a feature of it in the old world.

This being the case, it should be an object in America to exclude from the labors of the family all that can, with greater advantage, be executed out of it by combined labor.

Formerly, in New-England, soap and candles were to be made in each separate family; now, comparatively few take this toil upon them. We buy soap of the soap-maker, and candles of the candle-factor. This principle might be extended much further. In France, no family makes its own bread, and better bread can not be eaten than can be bought at the appropriate shops. No family does its own washing; the family's linen is all sent to women who, making this their sole profession, get it up with a care and nicety which can seldom be equaled in any family.

How would it simplify the burdens of the American housekeeper to have washing and ironing day expunged from her calendar! How much more neatly and compactly could the whole domestic system be arranged! If all the money that each separate family spends on the outfit and accommodations for washing and ironing, on fuel, soap, starch, and the other requirements, were united in a fund to create a laundry for every dozen families, one or two good women could do in first rate style what now is very indifferently done by the disturbance and disarrangement of all other domestic processes in these families. Whoever sets neighborhood-laundries on foot will do much to solve the American housekeeper's hardest problem.

Again, American women must not try with three servants to carry on life in the style which in the old world requires sixteen; they must thoroughly understand, and be prepared *to teach*, every branch of housekeeping; they must study to make domestic service desirable, by treating their servants in a way to lead them to respect themselves and to feel themselves respected; and there will gradually be evolved from the present confusion a solution of the domestic problem which shall be adapted to the life of a new and growing world.

XXVI.

IT is interesting to notice in the histories of our Lord the prominent place given to the care of the sick. When he first sent out the apostles, it was to heal the sick as well as to preach. Again, when he sent out the seventy, their first command was to "heal the sick," and next to say, "the kingdom of God has come nigh unto you." The body was to be healed first, in order to attend to the kingdom of God, even when it was "brought nigh."

Jesus Christ spent more time and labor in the cure of men's bodies than in preaching, even if we subtract those labors with his earthly father by which family homes were provided. When he ascended to the heavens, his last recorded words to his followers, as given by Mark, were, that his disciples should "lay hands on the sick," that they might recover. Still more directly is the duty of care for the sick exhibited in the solemn allegorical description of the last day. It was those who visited the sick that were the blessed; it was those who did not visit the sick who were told to "depart." Thus are we abundantly taught that one of the most sacred duties of the Christian family is the training of its inmates to care and kind attention to the sick.

Every woman who has the care of young children, or of a large family, is frequently called upon to advise what shall be done for some one who is indisposed; and often, in circumstances where she must trust solely to her own judgment. In such cases, some err by neglecting to do any thing at all, till the patient is quite sick; but a still greater number err from excessive and injurious dosing.

The two great causes of the ordinary slight attacks of illness in a family, are, sudden chills, which close the pores of the skin, and thus affect the throat, lungs, or bowels; and the excessive or improper use of food. In most cases of illness from the first cause, bathing the feet, and some aperient drink to induce perspiration, are suitable remedies.

In case of illness from improper food, or excess in eating, *fasting* for one or two meals, to give the system time and chance to relieve itself, is the safest remedy. Sometimes, a gentle cathartic of castor-oil may be needful; but it is best first to try fasting. A safe relief from injurious articles in the stomach is an emetic of warm water; but to be effective, several tumblerfuls must be given in quick succession, and till the stomach can receive no more.

The following extract from a discourse of Dr. Burne, before the London Medical Society, contains important information: " In civilized life, the causes which are most generally and continually operating in the production of diseases are, affections of the mind, improper diet, and retention of the intestinal excretions. The undue retention of excrementitious matter allows of the absorption of its more liquid parts, which is a cause of great impurity to the blood, and the excretions, thus rendered hard and knotty, act more or less as extraneous substances, and, by their irritation, produce a determination of blood to the intestines and to the neighboring viscera, which ultimately ends in inflammation. It also has a great effect on the whole system; causes a determination of blood to the head, which oppresses the brain and dejects the mind; deranges the functions of the stomach; causes flatulency; and produces a general state of discomfort."

Dr. Combe remarks on this subject: " In the natural

and healthy state, under a proper system of diet, and with sufficient exercise, the bowels are relieved regularly, once every day." *Habit* " is powerful in modifying the result, and in sustaining healthy action when once fairly establish ed. Hence the obvious advantage of observing as much regularity in relieving the system, as in taking our meals." It is often the case that soliciting nature at a regular period, once a ,day, will remedy constipation without medicine, and induce a regular and healthy state of the bowels. " When, however, as most frequently happens, the constipation arises from the absence of all assistance from the abdominal and respiratory muscles, the first step to be taken is, again to solicit their aid; first, by removing all impediments to free respiration, such as stays, waistbands, and belts; secondly, by resorting to such active exercise as shall call the muscles into full and regular action ; * and lastly, by proportioning the quantity of food to the wants of the system, and the condition of the digestive organs.

" If we employ these means, systematically and perseveringly, we shall rarely fail in at last restoring the healthy action of the bowels, with little aid from medicine. But if we neglect these modes, we may go on for years, adding pill to pill, and dose to dose, without ever attaining the end at which we aim."

" There is no point in which a woman needs more know-

---

* The most effective mode of exercising the abdominal and respiratory muscles, in order to remedy constipation, is by a continuous alternate contraction of the muscles of the abdomen and diaphragm. By contracting the muscles of the abdomen, the intestines are pressed inward and upward, and then the muscles of the diaphragm above contract and press them downward and outward. Thus the blood is drawn to the torpid parts to stimulate to the healthful action, while the agitation moves their contents downward. An invalid can thus exercise the abdominal muscles in bed. The proper time is just after a meal. This exercise, continued ten minutes a day, including short intervals of rest, and persevered in for a week or two, will cure most ordinary cases of constipation, provided proper food is taken. Coarse bread and fruit are needed for this purpose in most cases.

ledge and discretion than in administering remedies for what seem slight attacks, which are not supposed to re- quire the attention of a physician. It is little realized that purgative drugs are unnatural modes of stimulating the internal organs, tending to exhaust them of their secre- tions, and to debilitate and disturb the animal economy. For this reason, they should be used as little as possible; and fasting, and perspiration, and the other methods pointed out, should always be first resorted to."

When medicine must be given, it should be borne in mind that there are various classes of purgatives, which pro- duce very diverse effects. Some, like salts, operate to thin the blood, and reduce the system; others are stimulating; and others have a peculiar operation on certain organs. Of course, great discrimination and knowledge are needed, in order to select the kind which is suitable to the particu- lar disease, or to the particular constitution of the invalid. This shows the folly of using the many kinds of pills, and other quack medicines, where no knowledge can be had of their composition. Pills which are good for one kind of disease, might operate as poison in another state of the system.

It is very common in cases of colds, which affect the lungs or throat, to continue to try one dose after another for relief. It will be well to bear in mind at such times, that all which goes into the stomach must be first absorbed into the blood before it can reach the diseased part; and that there is some danger of injuring the stomach, or other parts of the system, by such a variety of doses, many of which, it is probable, will be directly contradictory in their nature, and thus neutralize any supposed benefit they might separately impart.

When a cold affects the head and eyes, and also impedes breathing through the nose, great relief is gained by a wet napkin spread over the upper part of the face, cover- ing the nose except an opening for breath. This is to be covered by folds of flannel fastened over the napkin with a handkerchief. So also a wet towel over the throat and whole chest, covered with folds of flannel, often relieves oppressed lungs.

Ordinarily, a cold can be arrested on its first symptoms by coverings in bed and a bottle of hot water, securing free perspiration. Often, at its first appearance, it can be stopped by a spoonful or two of whisky, or any alcoholic liquor, in hot water, taken on going to bed. Warm covering to induce perspiration will assist the process. These simple remedies are safest. Perspiration should always be followed by a towel-bath.

It is very unwise to tempt the appetite of a person who is indisposed. The cessation of appetite is the warning of nature that the system is in such a state that food can not be digested. When food is to be given to one who has no desire for it, beef-tea is the best in most cases.

The following suggestions may be found useful in regard to nursing the sick. As nothing contributes more to the restoration of health than pure air, it should be a primary object to keep a sick-room well ventilated. At least twice in the twenty-four hours, the patient should be well covered, and fresh air freely admitted from out of doors. After this, if need be, the room should be restored to a proper temperature, by the aid of an open fire. Bedding and clothing should also be well aired, and frequently changed; as the exhalations from the body, in sickness, are peculiarly deleterious. Frequent ablutions of the whole body, if possible, are very useful; and for these, warm water may be employed, when cold water is disagreeable.

A sick-room should always be kept very neat and in perfect order; and all haste, noise, and bustle should be avoided. In order to secure neatness, order, and quiet, in case of long illness, the following arrangement should be made. Keep a large box for fuel, which will need to be filled only twice in twenty-four hours. Provide also and keep in the room or an adjacent closet, a small tea-kettle, a saucepan, a pail of water for drinks and ablutions, a pitcher, a covered porringer, two pint bowls, two tumblers, two cups and saucers, two wine-glasses, two large and two small spoons; also a dish in which to wash these articles; a good supply of towels and a broom. Keep a slop-bucket near by to receive the wash of the room. Procuring all these articles at once, will save much noise and confusion.

Whenever medicine or food is given, spread a clean towel over the person or bed-clothing, and get a clean handkerchief, as nothing is more annoying to a weak stomach than the stickiness and soiling produced by medicine and food.

Keep the fire-place neat, and always wash all articles and put them in order as soon as they are out of use. A sick person has nothing to do but look about the room; and when every thing is neat and in order, a feeling of comfort is induced, while disorder, filth, and neglect are constant objects of annoyance which, if not complained of, are yet felt.

One very important particular in the case of those who are delicate in constitution, as well as in the case of the sick, is the preservation of warmth, especially in the hands and the feet. The *equal* circulation of the blood is an important element for good health, and this is impossible when the extremities are habitually or frequently cold. It is owing to this fact that the coldness caused by wetting the feet is so injurious. In cases where disease or a weak constitution causes a feeble or imperfect circulation, great pains should be taken to dress the feet and hands warmly, especially around the wrists and ankles, where the blood-vessels are nearest to the surface and thus most exposed to cold. Warm elastic wristlets and anklets would save many a feeble person from increasing decay or disease.

When the circulation is feeble from debility or disease, the union of carbon and oxygen in the capillaries is slower than in health, and therefore care should be taken to preserve the heat thus generated by warm clothing and protection from cold draughts. In nervous debility, it is peculiarly important to preserve the animal heat, for its excessive loss especially affects weak nerves. Many an invalid is carelessly and habitually suffering cold feet, who would recover health by proper care to preserve animal heat, especially in the extremities.

The following are useful directions for dressing a blister. Spread thinly, on a linen cloth, an ointment composed of one third of beeswax to two thirds of tallow; lay this upon a linen cloth folded many times. With a sharp pair of scissors make an aperture in the lower part of the blister-bag, with a little hole above to give it vent. Break the raised skin as little as possible. Lay on the cloth spread as directed. The blister at first should be dressed as often as three times in a day, and the dressing renewed each time. Hot fomentations in most cases will be as good as a blister, less painful, and safer.

Always prepare food for the sick in the neatest and most careful manner. It is in sickness that the senses of smell and taste are most susceptible of annoyance; and often, little mistakes or negligences in preparing food will take away all appetite.

Food for the sick should be cooked on coals, that no smoke may have access to it; and great care must be taken to prevent, by stirring, any adherence to the bottom of the cooking vessel, as this always gives a disagreeable taste.

Keeping clean handkerchiefs and towels at hand, cooling the pillows, sponging the hands with water, (with care to dry them thoroughly,) swabbing the mouth with a clean linen rag on the end of a stick, are modes of increasing the comfort of the sick. Always throw a shawl over a sick person when raised up.

Be careful to understand a physician's directions, and *to obey them implicitly.* If it be supposed that any other person knows better about the case than the physician, dismiss the physician, and employ that person in his stead.

It is always best to consult the physician as to where medicines shall be purchased, and to show the articles to him before using them, as great impositions are practiced in selling old, useless, and adulterated drugs. Always put labels on vials of medicine, and keep them out of the reach of children.

Be careful to label all powders, and particularly all *white powders*, as many poisonous medicines in this form are easily mistaken for others which are harmless.

In nursing the sick, always speak gently and cheeringly; and, while you express sympathy for their pain and trials, stimulate them to bear all with fortitude, and with resignation to the Heavenly Father who "doth not willingly afflict," and "who causeth all things to work together for good to them that love him." Offer to read the Bible or other devotional books, whenever it is suitable, and will not be deemed obtrusive.

Miss Ann Preston, one of the most refined as well as talented and learned female physicians, in a published article, gives valuable instruction as to the training of nurses. She claims that every woman should be trained for this office, and that some who have special traits that fit them for it should make it their daily professional business. She remarks that the indispensable qualities in a good nurse are common sense, conscientiousness, and sympathetic benevolence: and thus continues :

" God himself made and commissioned one set of nurses; and in doing this and adapting them to utter helplessness and weakness, what did he do ? He made them to love the dependence and to see something to admire in the very perversities of their charge. He made them to humor the caprices and regard both reasonable and unreasonable complainings. He made them to bend tenderly over the disturbed and irritated, and fold them to quiet assurance in arms made soft with love; in a word, he made *mothers!* And, other things being equal, whoever has most maternal tenderness and warm sympathy with the sufferer is the best nurse." And it is those most nearly endowed by nature with these traits who should be select- ed to be trained for the sacred office of nurse to the sick, while, in all the moral training of womanhood, this ideal should be the aim.

Again, Miss Preston wisely suggests that " persons may be conscientious and benevolent and possess good judg- ment in many respects, and yet be miserable nurses of the sick for want of training and right knowledge.

" *Knowledge,* the assurance that one knows what to do, always gives *presence of mind*—and presence of mind is important not only in a sick-room but in every home. Who has not known consternation in a family when some one has fainted, or been burned, or cut, while none were present who knew how to stop the flowing blood, or revive the fainting, or apply the saving application to the burn? And yet knowledge and efficiency in such cases would save many a life, and be a most fitting and desirable accom- plishment in every woman."

" We are slow to learn the mighty influence of common agencies, and the greatness of little things, in their bear- ing upon life and health. The woman who believes it takes no strength to bear a little noise or some disagreea- b e announcements, and loses patience with the weak, ner- vous invalid who is agonized with creaking doors or shoes, or loud, shrill voices, or rustling papers, or sharp, fidgety motions, or the whispering so common in sick-rooms and often so acutely distressing to the sufferer, will soon cor- rect such misapprehensions by herself experiencing a ner- vous fever."

Here the writer would put in a plea for the increasing multitudes of nervous sufferers not confined to a sick- room, and yet exposed to all the varied sources of pain incident to an exhausted nervous system, which often cause more intolerable and also more wearing pain than other kinds of suffering.

" An exceeding acuteness of the senses is the result of many forms of nervous disease.   A heavy breath, an urwashed hand, a noise that would not have been noticed in health, a crooked table-cover or bed-spread may disturb or oppress ; and more than one invalid has spoken in my hearing of the sickening effect produced by the nurse tasting her food, or blowing in her drinks to make them cool.   One woman, and a sensible woman too, told me her nurse had turned a large cushion upon her bureau with the back part in front.   She determined not to be disturbed nor to speak of such a trifle, but after struggling *three hours* in vain to banish the annoyance, she was forced to ask to have the cushion placed right."

In this place should be mentioned the suffering caused to persons of reduced nervous power not only by the smoke of tobacco, but by the fetid effluvium of it from the breath and clothing of persons who smoke.   Many such are sickened in society and in car-traveling, and to a degree little imagined by those who gain a dangerous pleasure at the frequent expense of the feeble and suffering.

Miss Preston again remarks, " It is often exceedingly important to the very weak, who can take but very little nutriment, to have that little whenever they want it.   I have known invalids sustain great injury and suffering ; when exhausted for want of food, they have had to wait and wait, feeling as if every minute was an hour, while some well-fed nurse delayed its coming.   Said a lady, ' It makes me hungry now to think of the meals she brought me upon that little waiter when I was sick, such brown thin toast, such good broiled beef, such fragrant tea, and every thing looking so exquisitely nice !   If at any time I did not think of any thing I wanted, nor ask for food, she did not annoy me with questions, but brought some little delicacy at the proper time, and when it came, I could take it.'

"If there is one purpose of a personal kind for which it is especially desirable to lay up means, it is for being well nursed in sickness; yet in the present state of society, this is absolutely impossible, even to the wealthy, because of the scarcity of competent nurses. Families worn down with the long and extreme illness of a member require relief from one whose feelings will be less taxed, and who can better endure the labor.

"But alas! how often is it impossible, for love or money, to obtain one capable of taking the burden from the exhausted sister or mother or daughter, and how often in consequence they have died prematurely or struggled through weary years with a broken constitution. Appeal to those who have made the trial, and you will find that very seldom have they been able to have those who by nature or by training were competent for their duties. Ignorant, unscrupulous, inattentive—how often they disturb and injure the patient! A physician told me that one of his patients had died because the nurse, contrary to orders, had at a critical period washed her with cold water. I have known one who, by stealth, quieted a fretful child with laudanum, and of others who exhausted the sick by incessant talking. One lady said that when, to escape this distressing garrulity, she closed her eyes, the nurse exclaimed aloud, 'Why, she is going to sleep while I am talking to her.'

"A few only of the sensible, quiet, and loving women, whose presence everywhere is a blessing, have qualified themselves and followed nursing as a business. Heaven bless that few! What a sense of relief have I seen pervade a family when such a one has been procured; and what a treasure seemed found!

"There is very commonly an extreme susceptibility in the sick to the *moral atmosphere* about them. They feel the healthful influence of the presence of a true-hearted attendant and repose in it, though they may not be able to define the cause; while dissimulation, falsehood, recklessness, coarseness, jar terribly and injuriously on their heightened sensibilities. 'Are the Sisters of Charity really better nurses than most other women?' I asked an intelligent lady who had seen much of our military hospitals. 'Yes, they are,' was her reply. 'Why should it be so?' 'I think it is because with them it is a work of self-abnegation, and of duty to God, and they are so quiet and self-forgetful in its exercise that they do it better, while many other women show such self-consciousness and are so fussy!'"

Is there any reason why every Protestant woman should not be trained for this self-denying office as *a duty owed to God?*

We can not better close this chapter than by one more quotation from the same intelligent and attractive writer: "The good nurse is an artist. O the pillowy, soothing softness of her touch, the neatness of her simple, unrustling dress, the music of her assured yet gentle voice and tread, the sense of security and rest inspired by her kind and hopeful face, the promptness and attention to every want, the repose that like an atmosphere encircles her, the evidence of heavenly goodness, and love that she diffuses!" Is not such an art as this worth much to attain?

In training children to the Christian life, one very important opportunity occurs whenever sickness appears in the family or neighborhood. The repression of disturbing noises, the speaking in tones of gentleness and sympathy, the small offices of service or nursing in which children can aid, should be inculcated as ministering to the Lord and Elder Brother of man, who has said, "Inasmuch as ye have done it unto one of the least of these my brethren, ye have done it to me."

One of the blessed opportunities for such ministries is given to children in the cultivation of flowers. The entrance into a sick-room of a smiling, healthful child, bringing an offering of flowers raised by its own labor, is like an angel of comfort and love, " and alike it blesseth him who gives and him who takes."

A time is coming when the visitation of the sick, as a part of the Christian life, will hold a higher consideration than is now generally accorded, especially in the cases of uninteresting sufferers who have nothing to attract kind attentions, except that they are suffering children of our Father in heaven, and " one of the least" of the brethren of Jesus Christ.

XXVII.

CHILDREN should be taught the following modes of saving life, health and limbs in cases of sudden emergency, before a medical adviser can be summoned.

In case of a common cut, bind the lips of the wound together with a rag, and put on nothing else. If it is large, lay narrow strips of sticking-plaster obliquely across the wound. In some cases it is needful to draw a needle and thread through the lips of the wound, and tie the two sides together.

If an artery be cut, it must be tied as quickly as possible, or the person will soon bleed to death. The blood from an artery is a brighter red than that from the veins, and spirts out in jets at each beat of the heart. Take hold of the end of the artery and tie it or hold it tight till a surgeon comes. In this case, and in all cases of bad wounds that bleed much, tie a tight bandage near and above the wound, inserting a stick into the bandage and twisting as tight as can be borne, to stop the immediate effusion of blood.

Bathe bad bruises in hot water. Arnica water hastens a cure, but is injurious and weakening to the parts when used too long and too freely.

A sprain is relieved from the first pains by hot fomentations, or the application of very hot bandages, but entire rest is the chief permanent remedy. The more the limb is used, especially at first, the longer the time required for the small broken fibres to knit together. The sprained leg should be kept in a horizontal position. When a leg is broken, tie it to the other leg, to keep it still till a surgeon comes. Tie a broken arm to a piece of thin wood, to keep it still till set.

In the case of bad burns that take off the skin, creosote water is the best remedy. If this is not at hand, wood-soot (not coal) pounded, sifted, and mixed with lard is nearly as good, as such soot contains creosote. When a dressing is put on, do not remove it till a skin is formed under it. If nothing else is at hand for a bad burn, sprinkle flour over the place where the skin is off and then let it remain, protected by a bandage. The chief aim is to keep the part without skin from the air.

In case of drowning, the aim should be to clear the throat, mouth and nostrils, and then produce the natural action of the lungs in breathing as soon as possible, at the same time removing wet clothes and applying warmth and friction to the skin, especially the hands and feet, to start the circulation. The best mode of cleansing the throat and mouth of choking water is to lay the person on the face, and raise the head a little, clearing the mouth and nostrils with the finger, and then apply hartshorn or camphor to the nose. This is safer and surer than a common mode of lifting the body by the feet, or rolling on a barrel to empty out the water.

To start the action of the lungs, first lay the person on the face and press the back along the spine to expel all air from the lungs. Then turn the body nearly, but not quite over on to the back, thus opening the chest so that the air will rush in if the mouth is kept open. Then turn the body to the face again and expel the air, and then again nearly over on to the back; and so continue for a long time. Friction, dry and warm clothing, and warm applications should be used in connection with this process. This is a much better mode than using bellows, which sometimes will close the opening to the windpipe. The above is the mode recommended by Dr. Marshall Hall, and is approved by the best medical authorities.

Certain articles are often kept in the house for cooking or medical purposes, and sometimes by mistake are taken in quantities that are poisonous.

Soda, saleratus, potash, or any other alkali can be rendered harmless in the stomach by vinegar, tomato-juice, or any other acid. If sulphuric or oxalic acid are taken, pounded chalk in water is the best antidote. If those are not at hand, strong soapsuds have been found effective. Large quantities of tepid water should be drank after these antidotes are taken, so as to produce vomiting.

Lime or *baryta* and its compounds demand a solution of glauber salts or of sulphuric acid.

Iodine or *Iodide of Potassium* demands large draughts of wheat flour or starch in water, and then vinegar and water. The stomach should then be emptied by vomiting with as much tepid water as the stomach can hold.

Prussic acid, a violent poison, is sometimes taken by children in eating the pits of stone fruits or bitter almonds which contain it. The antidote is to empty the stomach by an emetic, and give water of ammonia or chloric water. Affusions of cold water all over the body, followed by warm hand friction, is often a remedy alone, but the above should be added if at command. *Antimony* and its compounds demand drinks of oak bark, or gall nuts, or very strong green tea.

Arsenic demands oil or melted fat, with magnesia or lime water in large quantities, till vomiting occurs.

Corrosive Sublimate, (often used to kill vermin,) and any other form of mercury, requires milk or whites of eggs in large quantities. The whites of twelve eggs in two quarts of water, given in the largest possible draughts every three minutes till free vomiting occurs, is a good remedy. Flour and water will answer, though not so surely as the above. Warm water will help, if nothing else is in reach. The same remedy answers when any form of copper, or tin, or zinc poison is taken, and also for creosote.

Lead and its compounds require a dilution of Epsom or Glauber salts, or some strong, acid drink, as lemon or tomatoes.

Nitrate of Silver demands salt water drank till vomiting occurs.

Phosphorus (sometimes taken by children from matches) needs magnesia and copious drinks of gum Arabic, or gum water of any sort.

Alcohol, in dangerous quantities, demands vomiting with warm water.

When one is violently sick from excessive use of *tobacco*, vomiting is a relief, if it arise spontaneously. After that, or in case it does not occur, the juice of a lemon and perfect rest, in a horizontal position on the back, will relieve the nausea and faintness, generally soothing the foolish and over-wrought patient into a sleep.

Opium demands a quick emetic. The best is a heaping table-spoonful of powdered mustard, in a tumblerful of warm water; or powdered alum in half-ounce doses and strong coffee alternately in warm water. Give acid drinks after vomiting. If vomiting is not elicited thus, a stomach pump is demanded. Dash cold water on the head, apply friction, and use all means to keep the person awake and in motion.

Strychnia demands also quick emetics.

The stomach should be emptied always after taking any of these antidotes, by a warm water emetic.

In case of bleeding at the lungs, or stomach, or throat, give a tea-spoonful of dry salt, and repeat it often. For bleeding at the nose, put ice, or pour cold water on the back of the neck, keeping the head elevated.

If a person be struck with lightning, throw pailfuls of cold water on the head and body, and apply mustard poultices on the stomach, with friction of the whole body and inflation of the lungs, as in the case of drowning. The same mode is to be used when persons are stupified by fumes of coal, or bad air.

In thunderstorms, shut the doors and windows. The safest part of a room is its centre; and where there is a feather-bed in the apartment, that will be found the most secure resting-place.

A lightning-rod if it be well pointed, and run deep into the earth, is a certain protection to a circle around it, whose diameter equals the height of the rod above the highest chimney. But it protects *no farther* than this extent.

In case of fire, wrap about you a blanket, a shawl, a piece of carpet, or any other woolen cloth, to serve as protection. Never read in bed, lest you fall asleep, and the bed be set on fire. If your clothes get on fire, never run, but lie down, and roll about till you can reach a bed or carpet to wrap yourself in, and thus put out the fire. Keep young children in woolen dresses, to save them from the risk of fire.

XXVIII.

SEWING, CUTTING, AND MENDING.

EVERY young girl should be taught to do the following kinds of stitch with propriety : Over-stitch, hemming, running, felling, stitching, back-stitch and run, buttonhole-stitch, chain-stitch, whipping, darning, gathering, and cross-stitch.

In doing over-stitch, the edges should always be first fitted, either with pins or basting, to prevent puckering. In turning wide hems, a paper measure should be used, to make them even. Tucks, also, should be regulated by a paper measure. A fell should be turned, before the edges are put together, and the seam should be over-sewed before felling. All biased or goring seams should be felled. For stitching, draw a thread, and take up two or three threads at a stitch.

In cutting buttonholes, it is best to have a pair of scissors, made for the purpose, which cut very neatly. For broadcloth, a chisel and board are better. The best stitch is made by putting in the needle, and then turning the thread round it near the eye. This is better than to draw the needle through, and then take up a loop. A stay thread should first be put across each side of the buttonhole, and also a bar at each end before working it. In working the buttonhole, keep the stay thread as far from the edge as possible. A small bar should be worked at each end.

Whipping is done better by sewing *over*, and not under. The roll should be as fine as possible, the stitches short, the thread strong, and in sewing, every gather should be taken up.

The rule for *gathering* in shirts is, to draw a thread, and then take up two threads and skip four. In *darning*, after the perpendicular threads are run, the crossing threads should interlace exactly, taking one thread and leaving one, like woven threads. It is better to run a fine thread around a hole and draw it together, and then darn across it.

The neatest sewers always fit and baste their work before sewing; and they say they always save time in the end by so doing, as they never have to pick out work on account of mistakes.

It is wise to sew closely and tightly all new garments which will never be altered in shape; but some are more nice than wise, in sewing frocks and old garments in the same style. However, this is the least common extreme. It is much more frequently the case that articles which ought to be strongly and neatly made are sewed so that a nice sewer would rather pick out the threads and sew over again than to be annoyed with the sight of grinning stitches, and vexed with constant rips.

If the thread kinks in sewing, break it off and begin at the other end. In using spool-cotton, thread the needle with the end which comes off first, and not the end where you break it off. This often prevents kinks.

Work-baskets.—It is very important to neatness, comfort, and success in sewing, that a lady's work-basket should be properly fitted up. The following articles are needful to the mistress of a family : a large basket to hold work; having in it fastened a smaller basket or box, containing a needle-book in which are needles of every size, both blunts and sharps, with a larger number of those sizes most used; also small and large darning-needles, for woolen, cotton, and silk; two tape needles, large and small; nice scissors for fine work, button-hole scissors; an emery bag; two balls of white and yellow wax; and two thimbles, in case one should be mislaid. When a person is troubled with damp fingers, a lump of soft chalk in a paper is useful to rub on the ends of the fingers.

Besides this box, keep in the basket common scissors; small shears; a bag containing tapes of all colors and sizes, done up in rolls; bags, one containing spools of white and another of colored cotton thread, and another for silks wound on spools or papers; a box or bag for nice buttons, and another for more common ones; a bag containing silk braid, welting cords, and galloon binding. Small rolls of pieces of white and brown linen and cotton are also often needed. A brick pin-cushion is a great convenience in sewing, and better than screw cushions. It is made by covering half a brick with cloth, putting a cushion on the top, and covering it tastefully. It is very useful to hold pins and needles while sewing, and to fasten long seams when basting and sewing.

To make a Frock.—The best way for a novice is to get a dress fitted (not sewed) at the best mantua-maker's. Then take out a sleeve, rip it to pieces, and cut out a paper pattern. Then take out half of the waist, (it must have a seam in front,) and cut out a pattern of the back and fore-body, both lining and outer part. In cutting the patterns, iron the pieces smooth, let the paper be stiff, and with a pin prick holes in the paper, to show the gore in front and the depths of the seams. With a pen and ink, draw lines from each pin-hole to preserve this mark. Then baste the parts together again, in doing which the unbasted half will serve as a pattern. When this is done, a lady of common ingenuity can cut and fit a dress by these patterns. If the waist of a dress be too tight, the seam under the arm must be let out; and in cutting a dress an allowance should be made for letting it out if needful, at this seam.

The linings for the waists of dresses should be stiffened with cotton or linen. In cutting bias-pieces for trimming, they will not set well unless they are exact. In cutting them, use a long rule, and a lead pencil or piece of chalk. Welting-cords should be covered with bias-pieces ; and it saves time, in many cases, to baste on the welting-cord at the same time that you cover it. The best way to put on hooks and eyes is to sew them on double broad tape, and sew this on the frock lining. They can be moved easily, and do not show where they are sewed on.

In putting on linings of skirts at the bottom, be careful to have it a very little fuller than the dress, or it will shrink and look badly. All thin silks look much better with lining, and last much longer, as do aprons also. In putting a lining to a dress, baste it on each separate breadth, and sew it at the seams, and it looks much better than to have it fastened only at the bottom. Make notches in selvedge, to prevent it from drawing up the breadth. Dresses which are to be washed should not be lined.

Figured silks do not generally wear well if the figure be large and satin-like. Black and plain-colored silks can be tested by procuring samples, and making creases in them ; fold the creases in a bunch, and rub them against a rough surface of moreen or carpeting. Those which are poor will soon wear off at the creases.

Plaids look becoming for tall women, as they shorten the appearance of the figure. Stripes look becoming on a large person, as they reduce the apparent size. Pale persons should not wear blue or green, and brunettes should not wear light delicate colors, except shades of buff, fawn, or straw color. Pearl white is not good for any complexion. Dead white and black look becoming on almost all persons. It is best to try colors by candle-light for evening dresses, as some colors which look very handsome in the daylight are very homely when seen by candle-light. Never be in haste to be first. in a fashion, and never go to the extremes.

Linen and Cotton.—In buying linen, seek for that which

has a round close thread and is perfectly white ; for if it be not white at first, it will never afterward become so. Much that is called linen at the shops is half cotton, and does not wear so well as cotton alone. Cheap linens are usually of this kind. It is difficult to discover which are all linen ; but the best way is to find a lot presumed to be good, take a sample, wash it, and ravel it. If this be good, the rest of the same lot will probably be so. If you can not do this, draw a thread each way, and if both appear equally strong it is probably all linen. Linen and cotton must be put in clean water, and boiled, to get out the starch, and then ironed.

A "long piece " of linen, a yard wide, will, with care and calculation, make eight shirts. In cutting it, take a shirt of the right size as a guide in fitting and basting. Bosom-pieces and false collars must be cut and fitted by patterns which suit the person for whom the articles are designed. Gentlemen's night-shirts are made like other shirts, except that they are longer, and do not have bosoms and cuffs for starching.

In cutting chemises, if the cotton or linen is a yard wide, cut off small half-gores at the top of the breadths and set them on the bottom. Use a long rule and a pencil in cutting gores. In cutting cotton which is quite wide, a seam can be saved by cutting out two at once, in this manner : cut off three breadths, and with a long rule and a pencil, mark and cut off the gores ; thus from one breadth cut off two gores the whole length, each gore one fourth of the breadth at the bottom, and tapering off to a point at the top. The other two breadths are to have a gore cut off from each, which is one fourth wide at the top and two fourths at bottom. Arrange these pieces right and they will make two chemises, one having four seams and the other three. This is a much easier way of cutting than sewing the three breadths together in bag fashion, as is often done. The biased or goring seams must always be felled.   The sleeves and neck can be cut according to the taste of the wearer, by another chemise for a pattern.   There should be a lining around the arm-holes and stays at all corners.   Six yards of yard width will make two chemises.

Long night-gowns are best cut a little goring.   It requires five yards for a long night-gown, and two and a half for a short one.   Linen night caps wear longer than cotton ones, and do not like them turn yellow.   They should be ruffled with linen, as cotton borders will not last so long as the cap.   A double-quilted wrapper is a great comfort, in case of sickness.   It may be made of two old dresses.   It should not be cut full, but rather like a gentleman's study-gown, having no gathers or plaits, but large enough to slip off and on with ease.   A double-gown of calico is also very useful.   Most articles of dress, for grown persons or children, require patterns.

Old silk dresses quilted for skirts are very serviceable. White flannel is soiled so easily and shrinks so much in washing that it is a good plan to color it.   Cotton flannel is also good for common skirts.   In making up flannel, back-stitch and run the seams and then cross-stitch them open.   Nice flannel for infants can be ornamented with very little expense of time, by turning up the hem on the right side, and making a little vine at the edge with saddler's silk. The stitch of the vine is a modification of button-hole stitch.

Mending.   Silk dresses will last much longer, by ripping out the sleeves when thin, and changing the arms and also the breadths of the skirt.   Tumbled black silk, which is old and rusty, should be dipped in water, then be drained for a few minutes, without squeezing or pressing, and then ironed.   Coffee or cold tea is better than water.   Sheets when worn thin in the middle should be ripped, and the other edges sewed together.   Window-curtains last much longer if lined, as the sun fades and rots them.

Broadcloth should be cut with reference to the way the

nap runs. When pantaloons are thin, it is best to newly
seat them, cutting the piece inserted in a curve, as corners
are difficult to fit. Hose can be cut down when the feet
are worn. Take an old stocking and cut it up for a pattern. Make the heel short. In sewing, turn each edge
and run it down, and then sew over the edges. This is
better than to stitch and then cross-stitch. "Run" thin
places in stockings, and it will save darning a hole. If
shoes are worn through on the sides, in the upper-leather,
slip pieces of broadcloth under, and sew them around the
holes.

Bedding. The best beds are thick hair mattresses,
which for persons in health are good for winter as well as
summer use. Mattresses may also be made of husks, dried
and drawn into shreds; also of alternate layers of cotton
and moss. The most profitable sheeting is the Russian,
which will last three times as long as any other. It is
never perfectly white. Unbleached cotton is good for winter. It is poor economy to make narrow and short sheets,
as children and domestics will always slip them off, and
soil the bed-tick and bolster. They should be three yards
long, and two and a half wide, so that they can be tucked
in all around. All bed-linen should be marked and num-
bered, so that a bed can always be made properly, and all
missing articles be known.

XXIX.

A SHALLOW fireplace saves wood and gives out more heat than a deeper one. A false back of brick may be put up in a deep fireplace. Hooks for holding up the shovel and tongs, a hearth-brush and bellows, and brass knobs to hang them on, should be furnished to every fireplace. An iron bar across the andirons aids in keeping the fire safe and in good order. Steel furniture is neater, handsomer, and more easily kept in order than that made of brass.

Use green wood for logs, and mix green and dry wood for the fire ; and then the wood-pile will last much longer. Walnut, maple, hickory, and oak wood are best ; chestnut or hemlock is bad, because it snaps. Do not buy a load in which there are many crooked sticks. Learn how to measure and calculate the solid contents of a load, so as not to be cheated. A cord of wood should be equivalent to a pile eight feet long, four feet wide and four feet high ; that is, it contains $(8\times4\times4=128)$ one hundred and twenty-eight cubic or solid feet. A city " load " is usually one third of a cord. Have all your wood split and piled under cover for winter. Have the green wood logs in one pile, dry wood in another, oven-wood in another, kindlings and chips in another, and a supply of charcoal to use for broiling and ironing in another place. Have a brick bin for ashes, and never allow them to be put in wood. When quitting fires at night, never leave a burning stick across the andirons, nor on its end, without quenching it. See that no fire adheres to the broom or brush, remove all arti-

cles from the fire, and have two pails filled with water in
the kitchen where they will not freeze.

Rooms heated by stoves should always have some opening for the admission of fresh air, or they will be injurious
to health. The dryness of the air, which they occasion,
should be remedied by placing a vessel filled with water
on the stove, otherwise, the lungs or eyes will be injured.
A large number of plants in a room prevents this dryness
of the air. Where stove-pipes pass through fire-boards, the
hole in the wood should be much larger than the pipe, so
that there may be no danger of the wood taking fire. The
unsightly opening thus occasioned should be covered with
tin. When pipes are carried through floors or partitions,
they should always pass either through earthen crocks,
or what are known as tin stove-pipe thimbles, which may
be found in any stove store or tinsmith's. Lengthening a
pipe will increase its draught.

For those who use *anthracite coal*, that which is broken
or screened is best for grates, and the nut-coal for small
stoves. Three tons are sufficient in the Middle States, and
four tons in the Northern, to keep one fire through the
winter. That which is bright, hard, and clean is best;
and that which is soft, porous, and covered with damp dust
is poor. It will be well to provide two barrels of charcoal
for kindling to every ton of anthracite coal. Grates for
bituminous coal should have a flue nearly as deep as the
grate; and the bars should be round and not close together. The better draught there is, the less coal-dust is made.
Every grate should be furnished with a poker, shovel,
tongs, blower, coal-scuttle, and holder for the blower. The
latter may be made of woolen, covered with old silk, and
hung near the fire.

Coal-stoves should be carefully put up, as cracks in the
pipe, especially in sleeping rooms, are dangerous.

LIGHTS.

Professor Phin, of the *Manufacturer and Builder*, has kindly given us some late information on this important topic, which will be found valuable.

In choosing the source of our light, the great points to be considered are, first, the influence on the eyes, and secondly, economy. It is poor economy to use a bad light. Modern houses in cities, and even in large villages, are furnished with gas; where gas is not used, sperm-oil, kerosene or coal-oil, and candles are employed. Gas is the cheapest, (or ought to be;) and if properly used, is as good as any. Good sperm-oil burned in an Argand lamp—that is, a lamp with a circular wick, like the astral lamp and others—is perhaps the best; but it is expensive and attended with many inconveniences. Good kerosene oil gives a light which leaves little to be desired. Candles are used only on rare occasions, though many families prefer to manufacture into candles the waste grease that accumulates in the household. The economy of any source of light will depend so much upon local circumstances that no absolute directions can be given.

The effect produced by light on the eyes depends upon the following points : First, *Steadiness.* Nothing is more injurious to the eyes than a flickering, unsteady flame. Hence, all flames used for light-giving purposes ought to be surrounded with glass chimneys or small shades. No naked flame can ever be steady. Second, *Color.* This depends greatly upon the temperature of the flame. A hot flame gives a bright, white light; a flame which has not a high temperature gives a dull, yellow light, which is very injurious to the eyes. In the naked gas-jet a large portion of the flame burns at a low temperature, and the same is the case with the flame of the kerosene lamp when the height of the chimney is not properly proportioned to the amount of oil consumed; a high wick needs a high chimney. In the case of a well-trimmed Ar gand oil-lamp, or an Argand burner for gas, the flame is in general most intensely hot, and the light is of a clear white character.

The third point which demands attention is the *amount of heat* transmitted from the flame to the eyes. It often happens that people, in order to economize light, bring the lamp quite close to the face. This is a very bad habit. The heat is more injurious than the light. Better burn a larger flame, and keep it at a greater distance.

It is also well that various sized lamps should be provided to serve the varying necessities of the household in regard to quantity of light. One of the very best forms of lamp is that known as the " student's reading-lamp," which is, in the burner, an Argand. Provide small lamps with handles for carrying about, and broad-bottomed lamps for the kitchen, as these are not easily upset. Hand and kitchen lamps are best made of metal, unless they are to be used by very careful persons.

Sperm-oil, lard, tallow, etc., have been superseded to such an extent by kerosene that it is scarcely worth while to give any special directions in regard to them. In the choice of kerosene, attention should be paid to two points : its *safety* and its *light-giving qualities*. Kerosene is not a simple fluid, like water ; but is a mixture of several liquids, all of which boil at different temperatures. Good kerosene oil should be purified from all that portion which boils or evaporates at a low temperature ; for it is the production of this vapor, and its mixture with atmospheric air, that gives rise to those terrible explosions which sometimes occur when a light is brought near a can of poor oil. To test the oil in this respect, pour a little into an iron spoon, and heat it over a lamp until it is moderately warm to the touch. If the oil produces vapor which can be set on fire by means of a flame held a short distance above the surface of the liquid, it is bad. Good oil poured into a teacup or on the floor does not easily take fire when a light is brought in contact with it. Poor oil will instantly ignite under the same circumstances, and hence, the breaking of a lamp filled with poor oil is always attended by great peril of a conflagration. Not only the safety but also the light-giving qualities of kerosene are greatly enhanced by the removal of these volatile and dangerous oils. Hence, while good kerosene should be clear in color and free from all matters which can gum up the wick and thus interfere with free circulation and combustion, it should also be perfectly safe. It ought to be kept in a cool, dark place, and carefully excluded from the air.

The care of lamps requires so much attention and discretion, that many ladies choose to do this work themselves, rather than trust it with domestics. To do it properly, provide the following things: an old waiter to hold all the articles used; a lamp-filler, with a spout, small at the end, and turned up to prevent oil from dripping; proper wicks, and a basket or box to hold them; a lamp-trimmer made for the purpose, or a pair of *sharp* scissors; a small soap-cup and soap; some washing soda in a broad-mouthed bottle; and several soft cloths to wash the articles and towels to wipe them. If every thing, after being used, is cleansed from oil and then kept neatly, it will not be so unpleasant a task as it usually is, to take care of lamps.

The inside of lamps and oil-cans should be cleansed with soda dissolved in water. Be careful to drain them well, and not to let any gilding or bronze be injured by the soda coming in contact with it. Put one table-spoonful of soda to one quart of water. Take the lamp to pieces and clean it as often as necessary. Wipe the chimney at least once a day, and wash it whenever mere wiping fails to cleanse it. Some persons, owing to the dirty state of their chimneys, lose half the light which is produced. Keep dry fingers in trimming lamps. Renew the wicks before they get too short. They should never be allowed to burn shorter than an inch and a half.

In regard to *shades*, which are always well to use, on lamps or gas, those made of glass or porcelain are now so cheap that we can recommend them as the best without any reservation. Plain shades, making the light soft and even, do not injure the eyes. Lamps should be lighted with a strip of folded or rolled paper, of which a quantity should be kept on the mantelpiece. Weak eyes should always be especially shaded from the lights. Small screens, made for the purpose, should be kept at hand. A person with weak eyes can use them safely much longer when they are protected from the glare of the light. Fill the entry-lamp every day, and cleanse and fill night-lanterns twice a week, if used often. A good night-lamp is made with a small one-wicked lamp and a roll of tin to set over it. Have some holes made in the bottom of this cover, and it can then be used to heat articles. Very cheap floating tapers can be bought to burn in a teacup of oil through the night.

TO MAKE CANDLES.

The nicest candles are those run in moulds. For this purpose, melt together one quarter of a pound of white wax, one quarter of an ounce of camphor, two ounces of alum, and ten ounces of suet or mutton-tallow. Soak the wicks in lime-water and saltpetre, and when dry, fix them in the moulds and pour in the melted tallow. Let them remain one night to cool; then warm them a little to loosen them, draw them out, and when they are hard, put them in a box in a dry and cool place.

To make dipped candles, cut the wicks of the right length, double them over rods, and twist them. They should first be dipped in lime-water or vinegar, and dried. Melt the tallow in a large kettle, filling it to the top with hot water, when the tallow is melted. Put in wax and powdered alum, to harden them. Keep the tallow hot over a portable furnace, and fill the kettle with hot water as fast as the tallow is used up. Lay two long strips of narrow board on which to hang the rods; and set flat pans under, on the floor, to catch the grease. Take several rods at once, and wet the wicks in the tallow; straighten and smooth them when cool. Then dip them as fast as they cool, until they become of the proper size. Plunge them obliquely and not perpendicularly; and when the bottoms are too large, hold them in the hot grease till a part melts off Let them remain one night to cool; then cut off the bottoms, and keep them in a dry, cool place. Cheap lights are made, by dipping rushes in tallow; the rushes being first stripped of nearly the whole of the hard outer covering and the pith alone being retained with just enough of the tough bark to keep it stiff.

XXX.

THE CARE OF ROOMS.

It would be impossible in a work dealing, as this does, with general principles of house-keeping, to elaborate in full the multitudinous details which arise for attention and intelligent care. These will be more largely treated of in the book soon to be published for the present writer, (the senior authoress of this volume.) Yet, in the different departments of family labor, there are certain leading matters concerning which a few hints may be found useful in aiding the reader to carry into operation the instructions and ideas of the earlier chapters of this book, and in promoting the general comfort and convenience of families.

And first, asking the reader to bear in mind that these suggestions are chiefly applicable to country homes, not within easy reach of all the conveniences which go under the name of "modern improvements," we will say a few words on the care of *Parlors*.

In hanging pictures, put them so that the lower part shall be opposite the eye. Cleanse the glass of pictures with whiting, as water endangers the pictures. Gilt frames can be much better preserved by putting on a coat of copal varnish, which with proper brushes, can be bought of carriage or cabinet-makers. When dry, it can be washed with fair water. Wash the brush in spirits of turpentine.

Curtains, ottomans, and sofas covered with worsted, can be cleansed with wheat bran, rubbed on with flannel. Shades of linen or cotton, on rollers and pulleys, are always useful to shut out the sun from curtains and carpets. Paper curtains, pasted on old cotton, are good for chambers. Put them on rollers, having cords nailed to them, so that when the curtain falls, the cord will be wound up. Then, by pulling the cord, the curtain will be rolled up.

Varnished furniture should be rubbed only with silk, except occasionally, when a little sweet-oil should be rubbed over, and wiped off carefully. For unvarnished furniture, use bees-wax, a little softened with sweet-oil; rub it in with a hard brush, and polish with woolen and silk rags. Some persons rub in linseed-oil; others mix bees-wax with a little spirits of turpentine and rosin, making it so that it can be put on with a sponge, and wiped off with a soft rag. Others keep in a bottle the following mixture: two ounces of spirits of turpentine, four table-spoonfuls of sweet-oil, and one quart of milk. This is applied with a sponge, and wiped off with a linen rag.

Hearths and jambs, of brick, look best painted over with black lead, mixed with soft-soap. Wash the bricks which are nearest the fire with redding and milk, using a painter's brush. A sheet of zinc, covering the whole hearth, is cheap, saves work, and looks very well. A tinman can fit it properly.

Stone hearths should be rubbed with a paste of powdered stone, (to be procured of the stone-cutters,) and then brushed with a stiff brush. Kitchen hearths, of stone, are improved by rubbing in lamp-oil.

Stains can be removed from marble, by oxalic acid and water, or oil of vitriol and water, left on a few minutes, and then rubbed dry. Gray marble is improved by linseed-oil. Grease can be taken from marble, by ox-gall and potter's clay wet with soapsuds, (a gill of each.) It is better to add, also, a gill of spirits of turpentine. It improves the looks of marble, to cover it with this mixture, leaving it two days, and then rubbing it off.

Unless a parlor is in constant use, it is best to sweep it only once a week, and at other times use a whisk-broom and dust-pan. When a parlor with handsome furniture is to be swept, cover the sofas, centre table, piano, books, and mantelpiece with old cottons kept for the purpose. Remove the rugs and shake them, and clean the jambs, hearth, and fire-furniture. Then sweep the room, moving every article. Dust the furniture with a dust-brush and a piece of old silk. A painter's brush should be kept, to remove dust from ledges and crevices. The dust-cloths should be often shaken and washed, or else they will soil the walls and furniture when they are used. Dust ornaments and fine books with feather brushes, used for no other purpose.

Chambers and Bedrooms are of course a portion of the house to be sedulously and scrupulously attended to, if either health or comfort are aimed at in the family. And first, every mistress of a family should see, not only that all sleeping-rooms in her house *can be* well ventilated at night, but that they actually are so. Where there is no provision made for the introduction of pure air, in the construction of the house, and in the bedroom itself no open fire-place to allow the easy exit of foul air, a door should be left open into an entry or room where fresh air is admitted; or else a small opening should be made in a window, taking care not to allow a draught of air to cross the bed. The debility of childhood, the lassitude of domestics, and the ill-health of families, are often caused by neglecting to provide a supply of pure air.

It is not deemed necessary to add much to the earlier chapters treating of bedroom conveniences; but one subject is of marked importance, as being characteristic of good or poor housekeeping—that is, the *making of beds.*

Few servants will make a bed properly, without much attention from the mistress of the family; and every young woman who expects to have a household of her own to manage should be able to do it well herself, and to instruct others in doing it. The following directions should be given to those who do this work:

Open the windows, and lay off the bed-covering on two chairs, at the foot of the bed. If it be a feather-bed, after it is well aired, shake the feathers from each corner to the middle; then take up the middle, shake it well, and turn the bed over. Then push the feathers in place, making the head higher than the foot, and the sides even, and as high as the middle part. A mattress, whether used on top of a feather-bed or by itself, should in like manner be well aired and turned. Then put on the bolster and the under sheet, so that the wrong side of the sheet shall go next the bed, and the *marking* always come at the head, tucking in all around. Then put on the pillows, evenly, so that the open ends shall come to the sides of the bed, and spread on the upper sheet so that the wrong side shall be next the blankets, and the marked end always at the head. This arrangement of sheets is to prevent the part where the feet lie from being reversed, so as to come to the face; and also to prevent the parts soiled by the body from coming to the bedtick and blankets. Put on the other covering, except the outer one, tucking in all around, and then turn over the upper sheet at the head, so as to show a part of the pillows. When the pillow-cases are clean and smooth, they look best outside of the cover, but not otherwise. Then draw the hand along the side of the pillows, to make an even indentation, and then smooth and shape the whole outside. A nice housekeeper always notices the manner in which a bed is made; and in some parts of the country, it is rare to see this work properly performed.

The writer would here urge every mistress of a family, who keeps more than one domestic servant, to provide them with single beds, that they might not be obliged to sleep with all the changing domestics, who come and go so often. Where the room is too small for two beds, a narrow truckle-bed kept under another during the day will answer. Domestics should be furnished with washing conveniences in their chambers, and be encouraged to keep their persons and rooms neat and in order.

The care of the Kitchen, Cellar, and Store-room is necessarily the foundation of all proper housekeeping.

If parents wish their daughters to grow up with good domestic habits, they should have, as one means of securing this result, a neat and cheerful kitchen. A kitchen should always, if possible, be entirely above-ground, and well lighted. It should have a large sink, with a drain running under-ground, so that all the premises may be kept sweet and clean. If flowers and shrubs be cultivated around the doors and windows, and the yard near them be kept well turfed, it will add very much to their agreeable appearance. The walls should often be cleaned and whitewashed, to promote a neat look and pure air. The floor of a kitchen should be painted, or, what is better, covered with an oilcloth. To procure a kitchen oilcloth as cheaply as possible, buy cheap tow cloth, and fit it to the size and shape of the kitchen. Then have it stretched, and nailed to the south side of the barn, and, with a brush, cover it with a coat of thin rye paste. When this is dry, put on a coat of yellow paint, and let it dry for a fortnight. It is safest to first try the paint, and see if it dries well, as some paint never will dry. Then put on a second coat, and at the end of another fortnight, a third coat. Then let it hang two months, and it will last, uninjured, for many years. The longer the paint is left to dry, the better. If varnished, it will last much longer.

A sink should be scalded out every day, and occasionally with hot lye. On nails, over the sink, should be hung three good dish-cloths, hemmed, and furnished with loops; one for dishes not greasy, one for greasy dishes, and one for washing greasy pots and kettles. These should be put in the wash every week. The lady who insists upon this will not be annoyed by having her dishes washed with dark, musty and greasy rags, as is too frequently the case.

Under the sink should be kept a slop-pail; and, on a shelf by it, a soap-dish and two water-pails. A large boiler of warm soft water should always be kept over the fire, well covered, and a hearth-broom and bellows be hung near the fire. A clock is a very important article in the kitchen, in order to secure regularity at meals.

WASHING DISHES.

No item of domestic labor is so frequently done in a negligent manner, by domestics, as this. A full supply of conveniences will do much toward the remedy of this evil. A swab, made of strips of linen tied to a stick, is useful to wash nice dishes, especially small, deep articles. Two or three towels, and three dish-cloths should be used. Two large tin tubs, painted on the outside, should be provided; one for washing, and one for rinsing; also, a large old waiter, on which to drain the dishes. A soap-dish, with hard soap, and a fork, with which to use it, a slop-pail, and two pails for water, should also be furnished. The following rules for washing dishes will aid in promoting the desired care and neatness:

1. Scrape the dishes, putting away any food which may remain on them, and which it may be proper to save for future use. Put grease into the grease-pot, and whatever else may be on the plates into the slop-pail. Save tea-leaves for sweeping. Set all the dishes, when scraped, in regular piles, the smallest at the top.

2. Put the nicest articles in the wash-dish, and wash them in hot suds with the swab or nicest dish-cloth. Wipe all metal articles as soon as they are washed. Put all the rest into the rinsing-dish, which should be filled with hot water. When they are taken out, lay them to drain on the waiter. Then rinse the dish-cloth, and hang it up wipe the articles washed, and put them in their places.

3. Pour in more hot water, wash the greasy dishes with the dish-cloth made for them, rinse them, and set them to drain. Wipe them, and set them away. Wash the knives and forks, *being careful that the handles are never put in water;* wipe them, and then lay them in a knife-dish, to be scoured.

4. Take a fresh supply of clean suds, in which wash the milk-pans, buckets, and tins. Then rinse and hang up this dish-cloth, and take the other, with which, wash the roaster, gridiron, pots, and kettles. Then wash and rinse the dish-cloth, and hang it up. Empty the slop-bucket, and scald it. Dry metal teapots and tins before the fire. Then put the fire-place in order, and sweep and dust the kitchen.

Some persons keep a deep and narrow vessel, in which to wash knives with a swab, so that a careless servant *can not* lay them in the water while washing them. This article can be carried into the eating-room, to receive the knives and forks when they are taken from the table.

KITCHEN FURNITURE.

Crockery.—Brown earthen pans are said to be best for milk and for cooking. Tin pans are lighter, and more convenient, but are too cold for many purposes. Tall earthen jars, with covers, are good to hold butter, salt, lard, etc. Acids should never be put into the red earthen ware, as there is a poisonous ingredient in the glazing which the acid takes off. Stone ware is better and stronger, and safer every way than any other kind.

Iron Ware.—Many kitchens are very imperfectly supplied with the requisite conveniences for cooking. When a person has sufficient means, the following articles are all desirable: A nest of iron pots, of different sizes, (they should be slowly heated when new,) a long iron fork, to take out articles from boiling water; an iron hook, with a handle, to lift pots from the crane; a large and small gridiron, with grooved bars, and a trench to catch the grease; a Dutch oven, called also a bake-pan; two skillets, of different sizes, and a spider, or flat skillet, for frying; a griddle, a waffle-iron, tin and iron bake and bread pans; two ladles, of different sizes; a skimmer; iron skewers; a toasting-iron; two teakettles, one small and one large one; two brass kettles, of different sizes, for soap-boiling, etc. Iron kettles, lined with porcelain, are better for preserves. The German are the best. Too hot a fire will crack them, but with care in this respect, they will last for many years.

Portable charcoal furnaces, of iron or clay, are very useful in summer, in washing, ironing, and stewing, or making preserves. If used in the house, a strong draught must be made, to prevent the deleterious effects of the charcoal. A box and mill, for spice, pepper, and coffee, are needful to those who use these articles. Strong knives and forks, a sharp carving-knife, an iron cleaver and board, a fine saw, steelyards, chopping-tray and knife, an apple-parer, steel for sharpening knives, sugar-nippers, a dozen iron spoons, also a large iron one with a long handle, six or eight flat-irons, one of them very small, two iron-stands, a ruffle-iron, a crimping-iron, are also desirable.

Tin Ware.—Bread-pans; large and small patty-pans; cake-pans, with a centre tube to insure their baking well; pie-dishes, (of block-tin;) a covered butter-kettle; covered kettles to hold berries; two sauce-pans; a large oil-can; (with a cock;) a lamp-filler; a lantern; broad bottomed candlesticks for the kitchen; a candle-box; a funnel; a reflector for baking warm cakes; an oven or tin-kitchen; an apple-corer; an apple-roaster; an egg-boiler; two sugar-scoops, and flour and meal-scoop; a set of mugs; three dippers; a pint, quart, and gallon measure; a set of scales and weights; three or four pails, painted on the outside; a slop-bucket with a tight cover, painted on the outside; a milk-strainer; a gravy-strainer; a colander; a dredging-box; a pepper-box; a large and small grater; a cheese-box; also a large box for cake, and a still larger one for bread, with tight covers. Bread, cake, and cheese, shut up in this way, will not grow dry as in the open air.

Wooden Ware.—A nest of tubs; a set of pails and bowls; a large and small sieve; a beetle for mashing potatoes; a spade or stick for stirring butter and sugar; a bread-board, for moulding bread and making pie-crust; a coffee-stick; a clothes-stick; a mush-stick; a meat-beetle, to pound tough meat; an egg-beater; a ladle, for working butter; a bread-trough, (for a large family;) flour-buckets, with lids, to hold sifted flour and Indian meal; salt-boxes; sugar-boxes; starch and indigo-boxes; spice-boxes; a bosom-board; a skirt-board; a large ironing-board; two or three clothes-frames; and six dozen clothes-pins.

Basket Ware.—Baskets of all sizes, for eggs, fruit, marketing, clothes, etc.; also chip-baskets. When often used, they should be washed in hot suds.

Other Articles.—Every kitchen needs a box containing balls of brown thread and twine, a large and small darning needle, rolls of waste paper and old linen and cotton, and a supply of common holders. There should also be another box, containing a hammer, carpet-tacks, and nails of all sizes, a carpet-claw, screws and a screw-driver, pincers, gimlets of several sizes, a bed-screw, a small saw, two chisels, (one to use for button-holes in broadcloth,) two awls and two files.

In a drawer or cupboard should be placed cotton table-cloths for kitchen use; nice crash towels for tumblers, marked T T; coarser towels for dishes marked T; six large roller-towels; a dozen hand-towels, marked H T; and a dozen hemmed dish-cloths with loops. Also two thick linen pudding or dumpling-cloths, a jelly-bag made of white flannel, to strain jelly, a starch-strainer, and a bag for boiling clothes.

In a closet should be kept, arranged in order, the following articles : the dust-pan, dust-brush, and dusting-cloths, old flannel and cotton for scouring and rubbing, large sponges for washing windows and looking-glasses, a long brush for cobwebs, and another for washing the outside of windows, whisk-brooms, common brooms, a coat-broom or brush, a whitewash-brush, a stove-brush, shoe-brushes and blacking, articles for cleaning tin and silver, leather for cleaning metals, bottles containing stain-mixtures and other articles used in cleansing.

CARE OF THE CELLAR.

A cellar should often be whitewashed, to keep it sweet. It should have a drain to keep it perfectly dry, as standing water in a cellar is a sure cause of disease in a family. It is very dangerous to leave decayed vegetables in a cellar. Many a fever has been caused by the poisonous miasm thus generated. The following articles are desirable in a cellar: a safe, or movable closet, with sides of wire or perforated tin, in which cold meats, cream, and other articles should be kept; (if ants be troublesome, set the legs in tin cups of water;) a refrigerator, or a large wooden-box, on feet, with a lining of tin or zinc, and a space between the tin and wood filled with powdered charcoal, having at the bottom a place for ice, a drain to carry off the water, and also movable shelves and partitions. In this, articles are kept cool. It should be cleaned once a week. Filtering jars to purify water should also be kept in the cellar. Fish and cabbages in a cellar are apt to scent a house, and give a bad taste to other articles.

STOREROOM.

Every house needs a storeroom, in which to keep tea, coffee, sugar, rice, candles, etc. It should be furnished with jars, having labels, a large spoon, a fork, sugar and flour-scoops, a towel, and a dish-cloth.

MODES OF DESTROYING INSECTS AND VERMIN.

Bed-bugs should be kept away, by filling every chink in the bedstead with putty, and if it be old, painting it over. Of all the mixtures for killing them, *corrosive sublimate and alcohol* is the surest. This is a strong poison.

Cockroaches may be destroyed by pouring boiling water into their haunts, or setting a mixture of arsenic mixed with Indian meal and molasses where they are found. Chloride of lime and sweetened water will also poison them.

Fleas.—If a dog be infested with these insects, put him in a tub of warm soapsuds, and they will rise to the surface. Take them off, and burn them. Strong perfumes about the person diminish their attacks. When caught between the fingers, plunge them in water, or they will escape.

Crickets.—Scalding, and sprinkling Scotch snuff about the haunts of these insects, are remedies for the annoyance caused by them.

Flies can be killed in great quantities, by placing about the house vessels filled with sweetened water and *cobalt*. Six cents' worth of cobalt is enough for a pint of water. It is very poisonous.

Mosquitoes.—Close nets around a bed are the only sure protection at night against these insects. Spirits of hartshorn is the best antidote for their bite. Salt and water is good.

Red or Black Ants may be driven away by scalding their haunts, and putting Scotch snuff wherever they go for food. Set the legs of closets and safes in pans of water, and they can not get at them.

Moths.—Airing clothes does not destroy moths, but laying them in a hot sun does. If articles be tightly sewed up in linen when laid away, and fine tobacco put about them, it is a sure protection. This should be done in April.

Rats and Mice.—A good cat is the best remedy for these annoyances. Equal quantities of hemlock (or *cicuta*) and old cheese will poison them; but this renders the house liable to the inconvenience of a bad smell. This evil, however, may be lessened, by placing a dish containing oil of vitriol poured on saltpetre where the smell is most annoying. Chloride of lime and water is also good.

In using any of the above-mentioned poisons, great care should be taken to guard against their getting into any article of food or any utensil or vessel used for cooking or keeping food, or where children can get at them.

XXXI.

FIRST, let us say a few words on the *Preparation of Soil.* If the garden soil be clayey and adhesive, put on a covering of sand, three inches thick, and the same depth of well-rotted manure. Spade it in as deep as possible, and mix it well. If the soil be sandy and loose, spade in clay and ashes. Ashes are good for all kinds of soil, as they loosen those which are close, hold moisture in those which are sandy, and destroy insects. The best kind of soil is that which will hold water the longest without becoming hard when dry.

To prepare Soil for Pot-plants, take one fourth part of common soil, one fourth part of well-decayed manure, and one half of vegetable mould, from the woods or from a chip-yard. Break up the manure fine, and sift it through a lime-screen, (or coarse wire sieve.) These materials must be thoroughly mixed. When the common soil which is used is adhesive, and indeed in most other cases, it is necessary to add sand, the proportion of which must depend on the nature of the soil.

To Prepare a Hot-Bed, dig a pit six feet long, five feet wide, and thirty inches deep. Make a frame of the same size, with the back two feet high, the front fifteen inches, and the sides sloped from the back to the front. Make two sashes, each three feet by five, with the panes of glass lapping like shingles instead of having cross-bars. Set the frame over the pit, which should then be filled with fresh horse-dung, which has not lain long nor been sodden by water

Tread it down hard; then put into the frame light and very rich soil, six or eight inches deep, and cover it with the sashes for two or three days. Then stir the soil, and sow the seeds in shallow drills, placing sticks by them, to mark the different kinds. Keep the frame covered with the glass whenever it is cold enough to chill the plants; but at all other times admit fresh air, which is indispensable to their health. When the sun is quite warm, raise the glasses enough to admit air, and cover them with matting or blankets, or else the sun may kill the young plants. Water the bed at evening with water which has stood all day, or, if it be fresh drawn, add a little warm water. If there be too much heat in the bed, so as to scorch or wither the plants, lift the sashes, water freely, shade by day; make deep holes with stakes, and fill them up when the heat is reduced. In very cold nights, cover the sashes and frame with straw-mats.

For Planting Flower Seeds.—Break up the soil, till it is very soft, and free from lumps. Rub that nearest the surface between the hands, to make it fine. Make a circular drill a foot in diameter. Seeds are to be planted either deeper or nearer the surface, according to their size. For seeds as large as sweet peas, the drill should be half an inch deep. The smallest seeds must be planted very near the surface, and a very little fine earth be sifted over them. After covering them with soil, beat them down with a trowel, so as to make the earth as compact as it is after a heavy shower. Set up a stick in the middle of the circle, with the name of the plant heavily written upon it with a dark lead pencil. This remains more permanent if white-lead be first rubbed over the surface. Never plant when the soil is very wet. In very dry times, water the seeds at night. Never use very cold water. When the seeds are small, many should be planted together, that they may assist each other in breaking the soil. When the plants are an inch high, thin them out, leaving only one or two, if the plant be a large one, like the balsam; five or six, when it is of a medium size; and eighteen or twenty of the smaller size. Transplanting, unless the plant be lifted with a ball of earth, retards the growth about a fortnight. It is best to plant at two different times, lest the first planting should fail, owing to wet or cold weather.

To plant Garden-Seeds, make the beds from one to three yards wide; lay across them a board a foot wide, and with a stick, make a furrow on each side of it, one inch deep. Scatter the seeds in this furrow, and cover them. Then lay the board over them, and step on it, to press down the earth. When the plants are an inch high, thin them out, leaving spaces proportioned to their sizes. Seeds of similar species, such as melons and squashes, should not be planted very near to each other, as this causes them to degenerate. The same kinds of vegetables should not be planted in the same place for two years in succession. The longer the rows are, the easier is the after culture.

Transplanting should be done at evening, or which is better, just before a shower. Take a round stick sharpened at the point, and make openings to receive the plants. Set them a very little deeper than they were before, and press the soil firmly round them. Then water them, and cover them for three or four days, taking care that sufficient air be admitted. If the plant can be removed without disturbing the soil around the root, it will not be at all retarded by transplanting. Never remove leaves and branches, unless a part of the roots be lost.

To Re-pot House-Plants, renew the soil every year, soon after the time of blossoming. Prepare soil as previously directed. Loosen the earth from the pot by passing a knife around the sides. Turn the plant upside down, and remove the pot. Then remove all the matted fibres at the bottom, and all the earth, except that which adheres to the roots. From woody plants, like roses, shake off all the earth.　Take the new pot, and put a piece of broken earthen-ware over the hole at the bottom, and then, holding the plant in the proper position, shake in the earth around it.　Then pour in water to settle the earth, and heap on fresh soil, till the pot is even full.　Small pots are considered better than large ones, as the roots are not so likely to rot, from excess of moisture.

In the Laying out of Yards and Gardens, there is room for much judgment and taste.　In planting trees in a yard, they should be arranged in groups, and never planted in straight lines, nor sprinkled about as solitary trees.　The object of this arrangement is to imitate Nature, and secure some spots of dense shade and some of clear turf.　In yards which are covered with turf, beds can be cut out of it, and raised for flowers.　A trench should be made around, to prevent the grass from running on them.　These beds can be made in the shape of crescents, ovals, or other fanciful forms.

In laying out beds in gardens and yards, a very pretty bordering can be made, by planting them with common flax-seed, in a line about three inches from the edge.　This can be trimmed with shears, when it grows too high.

For Transplanting Trees, the autumn is the best time. Take as much of the root as possible, especially the little fibres, which should never become dry.　If kept long before they are set out, put wet moss around them and water them.　Dig holes larger than the extent of the roots; let one person hold the tree in its former position, and another place the roots carefully as they were before, cutting off any broken or wounded root.　*Be careful not to let the tree be more than an inch deeper than it was before.*　Let the soil be soft and well manured; shake the tree as the soil is shaken in, that it may mix well among the small fibres.　Do not tread the earth down, while filling the hole; but, when it is full, raise a slight mound of say four inches deep around the stem to hold water, and fill it.　Never cut off leaves nor branches, unless some of the roots are lost. Tie the trees to a stake, and they will be more likely to live. Water them often.

The Care of House-Plants is a matter of daily attention, and well repays all labor expended upon it. The soil of house-plants should be renewed every year as previously directed. In winter, they should be kept as dry as they can be without wilting. Many house-plants are injured by giving them too much water, when they have little light and fresh air. This makes them grow spindling. The more fresh air, warmth and light they have, the more water is needed. They ought not to be kept very warm in winter, nor exposed to great changes of atmosphere. Forty degrees is a proper temperature for plants in winter, when they have little sun and air. When plants have become spindling, cut off their heads entirely, and cover the pot in the earth, where it has the morning sun only. A new and flourishing head will spring out. Few house-plants can bear the sun at noon. When insects infest plants, set them in a closet or under a barrel, and burn tobacco under them. The smoke kills any insect enveloped in it. When plants are frozen, cold water and a gradual restoration of warmth are the best remedies. Never use very cold water for plants at any season.

XXXII

THIS is an occupation requiring much attention and constant care. Bulbous roots are propagated by offsets; some growing on the top, others around the sides. Many plants are propagated by cutting off twigs, and setting them in earth, so that two or three eyes are covered. To do this, select a side shoot, ten inches long, two inches of it being of the preceding year's growth, and the rest the growth of the season when it is set. Do this when the sap is running, and put a piece of crockery at the bottom of the shoot, when it is buried. One eye, at least, must be under the soil. Water it and shade it in hot weather.

Plants are also propagated by layers. To do this, take a shoot which comes up near the root, bend it down so as to bring several eyes under the soil, leaving the top above-ground. If the shoot be cut half through, in a slanting direction, at one of these eyes, before burying it, the result is more certain. Roses, honeysuckles, and many other shrubs are readily propagated thus. They will generally take root by being simply buried; but cutting them as here directed is the best method. Layers are more certain than cuttings.

Budding and Grafting, for all woody plants, are favorite methods of propagation. In all such plants, there is an outer and inner bark, the latter containing the sap vessels, in which the nourishment of the tree ascends. The success of grafting or inoculating consists in so placing the bud or graft that the sap vessels of the inner bark shall exactly join those of the plant into which they are grafted, so that the sap may pass from one into the other.

The following are directions for *budding*, which may be performed at any time from July to September:

Select a smooth place on the stock into which you are to insert the bud. Make a horizontal cut across the rind through to the firm wood; and from the middle of this, make a slit downward perpendicularly, an inch or more long, through to the wood. Raise the bark of the stock on each side of the perpendicular cut, for the admission of the bud, as is shown in the annexed engraving, (Fig. 64.) Then take a shoot of this year's growth, and slice from it a bud, taking an inch below and an inch above it,

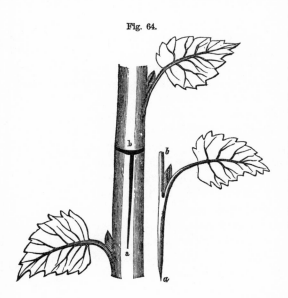

Fig. 64.

and some portion of the wood under it. Then, carefully slip off the woody part under the bud. Examine whether the eye or germ of the bud be perfect. If a little hole appear in that part, the bud has lost its root, and another must be selected. Insert the bud, so that *a*, of the bud, shall pass to a, of the stock; then *b*, of the bud, must be cut off, to match the cut b, in the stock, and fitted exactly to it, as it is this alone which insures success. Bind the parts with fresh bass or woolen yarn, beginning a little below the bottom of the perpendicular slit, and winding it closely around every part, except just over the eye of the bud, until you arrive above the horizontal cut. Do not bind it too tightly, but just sufficient to exclude air, sun, and wet. This is to be removed after the bud is firmly fixed, and begins to grow.

Seed-fruit can be budded into any other seed-fruit, and stone-fruit into any other stone-fruit; but stone and seed-fruits can not be thus mingled.

Rose-bushes can have a variety of kinds budded into the same stock. Hardy roots are the best stocks. The branch above the bud must be cut off the next March or April after the bud is put in. Apples and pears are more easily propagated by ingrafting than by budding.

Ingrafting is a similar process to budding, with this advantage, that it can be performed on large trees, whereas budding can be applied only on small ones. The two common kinds of ingrafting are whip-grafting and split-grafting. The first kind is for young trees, and the other for large ones.

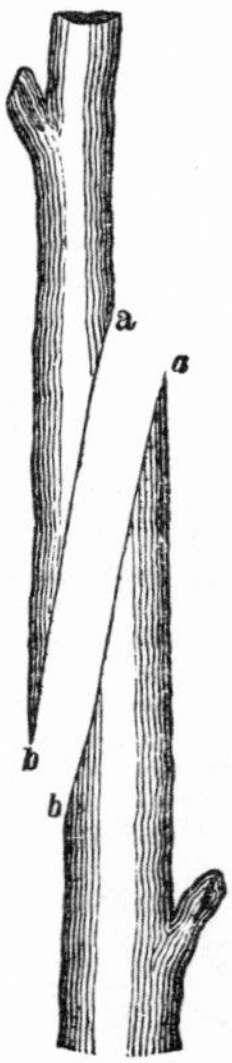

The time for ingrafting is from May to October. The cuttings must be taken from horizontal shoots, between Christmas and March, and kept in a damp cellar. In performing the operation, cut off in a sloping direction (as seen in Fig. 65) the tree or limb to be grafted. Then cut off in a corresponding slant the slip to be grafted on. Then put them together, so that the inner bark of each shall match exactly on one side, and tie them firmly together with yellow yarn. It is not essential that both be of equal size; if the bark of each meet together exactly

Fig. 65.

on *one* side, it answers the purpose. But the two must not differ much in size. The slope should be an inch and a half, or more, in length. After they are tied together, the place should be covered with a salve or composition of bees-wax and rosin. A mixture of clay and cow-dung will answer the same purpose. This last must be tied on with a cloth. Grafting is more convenient than budding, as grafts can be sent from a great distance; whereas buds must be taken in July or August, from a shoot of the present year's growth, and can not be sent to any great distance.

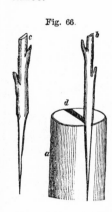

Fig. 66.

This engraving (Fig. 66) exhibits the mode called stock-grafting; *a* being the limb of a large tree, which is sawed off and split, and is to be held open by a small wedge till the grafts are put in. A graft inserted in the limb is shown at *b*, and at *c* is one not inserted, but designed to be put in at *d*, as two grafts can be put into a large stock. In inserting the graft, be careful to make the edge of the inner bark of the graft meet exactly the edge of the inner bark of the stock; for on this success depends. After the grafts are put in, the wedge must be withdrawn, and the whole of the stock be covered with the thick salve or composition before mentioned, reaching from where the grafts are inserted to the bottom of the slit. Be careful not to knock or move the grafts after they are put in.

Pruning is an operation of constant exercise, for keeping plants and trees in good condition. The following rules are from a distinguished horticulturist : Prune off all dead wood, and all the little twigs on the main limbs. Retrench branches, so as to give light and ventilation to the interior of the tree. Cut out the straight and perpendicular shoots, which give little or no fruit; while those which are most nearly horizontal, and somewhat curving, give fruit abundantly and of good quality, and should be sustained. Superfluous and ill-placed buds may be rubbed off at any time; and no buds pushing out after midsummer should be spared. In choosing between shoots to be retained, preserve the lowest placed, and on lateral shoots, those which are nearest the origin. When branches cross each other so as to rub, remove one or the other. Remove all suckers from the roots of trees or shrubs. Prune after the sap is in full circulation, (except in the case of grapes,) as the wounds then heal best. Some think it best to prune before the sap begins to run. Pruning-shears, and a pruning-pole, with a chisel at the end, can be procured of those who deal in agricultural utensils.

Thinning is also an important but very delicate operation. As it is the office of the leaves to absorb nourishment from the atmosphere, they should never be removed, except to mature the wood or fruit. In doing this, remove such leaves as shade the fruit, as soon as it is ready to ripen. To do it earlier impairs the growth. Do it gradually at two different times. Thinning the fruit is important, as tending to increase its size and flavor, and also to promote the longevity of the tree. If the fruit be thickly set, take off one half at the time of setting. Revise in June, and then in July, taking off all that may be spared. One *very large* apple to every square foot is a rule that may be a sort of guide in other cases. According to this, two hundred large apples would be allowed to a tree whose extent is fifteen feet by twelve. If any person think this thinning excessive, let him try two similar trees, and thin one as directed and leave the other unthinned. It will be found that the thinned tree will produce an equal weight, and fruit of much finer flavor.

XXXIII.

THE CULTIVATION OF FRUIT.

By a little attention to this matter, a lady with the help of her children can obtain a rich abundance of all kinds of fruit. The writer has resided in families where little boys of eight, ten, and twelve years old amused themselves, under the direction of their mother, in planting walnuts, chestnuts, and hazelnuts, for future time; as well as in planting and inoculating young fruit-trees of all descriptions. A mother who will take pains to inspire a love for such pursuits in her children, and who will aid and superintend them, will save them from many temptations, and at a trifling expense secure to them and herself a rich reward in the choicest fruits. The information given in this work on this subject may be relied on as sanctioned by the most experienced nursery-men.

The soil for a nursery should be rich, well dug, dressed with well-decayed manure, free from weeds, and protected from cold winds. Fruit-seeds should be planted in the autumn, an inch and a half or two inches deep, in ridges four or five feet apart, pressing the earth firmly over the seeds. While growing, they should be thinned out, leaving the best ones a foot and a half apart. The soil should be kept loose, soft, and free from weeds. They should be inoculated or ingrafted when of the size of a pipe stem; and in a year after this may be transplanted to their permanent stand. Peach-trees sometimes bear in two years from budding, and in four years from planting if well kept.

In a year after transplanting, take pains to train the head aright. Straight upright branches produce *gourmands*, or twigs bearing only leaves. The side branches which are angular or curved yield the most fruit. For this reason, the limbs should be trained in curves, and perpendicular twigs should be cut off if there be need of pruning. The last of June is the time for this Grass should never be allowed to grow within four feet of a large tree, and the soil should be kept loose to admit air to the roots. Trees in orchards should be twenty-five feet apart. The soil *under* the top soil has much to do with the health of the trees. If it be what is called *hard-pan*, the trees will deteriorate. Trees need to be manured and to have the soil kept open and free from weeds.

Filberts can be raised in any part of this country.

Figs can be raised in the Middle, Western, and Southern States. For this purpose, in the autumn loosen the roots on one side, and bend the tree down to the earth on the other; then cover it with a mound of straw, earth, and boards, and early in the spring raise it up and cover the roots.

Currants grow well in any but a wet soil. They are propagated by cuttings. The old wood should be thinned in the fall and manure be put on. They can be trained into small trees.

Gooseberries are propagated by layers and cuttings. They are best when kept from suckers and trained like trees. One third of the old wood should be removed every autumn.

Raspberries do best when shaded during a part of the day. They are propagated by layers, slips, and suckers. There is one kind which bears monthly; but the varieties of this and all other fruits are now so numerous that we can easily find those which are adapted to the special circumstances of the case.

Strawberries require a light soil and vegetable manure. They should be transplanted in April or September, and be set eight inches apart, in rows nine inches asunder, and in beds which are two feet wide, with narrow alleys between them. A part of these plants are *non-bearers.* These have large flowers with showy stamens and high black anthers. The *bearers* have short stamens, a great number of pistils, and the flowers are every way less showy. In blossom-time, pull out all the non-bearers. Some think it best to leave one non-bearer to every twelve bearers, and others pull them all out. Many beds never produce any fruit, because all the plants in them are non-bearers. Weeds should be kept from the vines. When the vines are matted with young plants, the best way is to dig over the beds in cross lines, so as to leave some of the plants standing in little squares, while the rest are turned under the soil. This should be done over a second time in the same year.

To Raise Grapes, manure the soil, and keep it soft and free from weeds. A gravelly or sandy soil, and a south exposure are best. Transplant the vines in the early spring, or better in the fall. Prune them the first year so as to have only two main branches, taking off all other shoots as fast as they come. In November, cut off all of these two branches except four eyes. The second year, in the spring, loosen the earth around the roots, and allow only two branches to grow, and every month take off all side shoots. When they are very strong, preserve only a part, and cut off the rest in the fall. In November, cut off all the two main stems except eight eyes. After the second year, no more pruning is needed, except to reduce the side shoots, for the purpose of increasing the fruit. All the pruning of grapes (except nipping side shoots) must be done when the sap is not running, or they will bleed to death. Train them on poles, or lattices, to expose them to the air and sun. Cover tender vines in the autumn. Grapes are propagated by cuttings, layers, and seeds. For cuttings, select in the autumn well-ripened wood of the former year, and take five joints for each. Bury them till April; then soak them for some hours, and set them out *aslant,* so that all the eyes but one shall be covered.

Apples, grapes, and such like fruit can be preserved in their natural state by packing them when dry and solid in dry sand or saw-dust, putting alternate layers of fruit and cotton, saw-dust or sand. Some saw-dust gives a bad flavor to the fruit.

Modes of Preserving Fruit-Trees.—Heaps of ashes or tanner's bark around peach-trees prevent the attack of the worm. The *yellows* is a disease of peach-trees, which is spread by the pollen of the blossom. When a tree begins to turn yellow, take it away with all its roots, before it blossoms again, or it will infect other trees. Planting tansy around the roots of fruit-trees is a sure protection against worms, as it prevents the moth from depositing her egg. Equal quantities of salt and saltpetre, put around the trunk of a peach-tree, half a pound to a tree, improve the size and flavor of the fruit. Apply this about the first of April; and if any trees have worms already in them, put on half the quantity in addition in June. To young trees just set out, apply one ounce in April, and another in June, close to the stem. Sandy soil is best for peaches.

Apple-trees are preserved from insects by a wash of strong lye to the body and limbs, which, if old, should be first scraped. Caterpillars should be removed by cutting down their nests in a damp day. Boring a hole in a tree infested with worms, and filling it with sulphur, will often drive them off immediately.

The *fire-blight* or *brûlure* in pear-trees can be stopped by cutting off all the blighted branches. It is supposed by some to be owing to an excess of sap, which is remedied by diminishing the roots.

The *curculio*, which destroys plums and other stone-fruit, can be checked only by gathering up all the fruit that falls, (which contains their eggs,) and destroying it. The *canker-worm* can be checked by applying a bandage around the body of the tree, and every evening smearing it with fresh tar.

XXXIV.

THE CARE OF DOMESTIC ANIMALS.

One of the most interesting illustrations of the design of our benevolent Creator in establishing the family state is the nature of the domestic animals connected with it. At the very dawn of life, the infant watches with delight the graceful gambols of the kitten, and soon makes it a playmate. Meantime, its out-cries when hurt appeal to kindly sympathy, and its sharp claws to fear; while the child's mother has a constant opportunity to inculcate kindness and care for weak and ignorant creatures. Then the dog becomes the out-door playmate and guardian of early childhood, and he also guards himself by cries of pain, and protects himself by his teeth. At the same time, his faithful loving nature and caresses awaken corresponding tenderness and care; while the parent again has a daily opportunity to inculcate these virtues toward the helpless and dependent. As the child increases in knowledge and reason, the horse, cows, poultry, and other domestic animals come under his notice. These do not ordinarily express their hunger or other sufferings by cries of distress, but depend more on the developed reason and humanity of man. And here the parent is called upon to instruct a child in the nature and wants of each, that he may intelligently provide for their sustenance and for their protection from injury and disease.

To assist in this important duty of home life, which so often falls to the supervision of woman, the following information is prepared through the kindness of one of the editors of a prominent, widely known agricultural paper.

Domestic animals are very apt to catch the spirit and temper of their masters. A surly man will be very likely to have a cross dog and a biting horse. A passionate man will keep all his animals in ·n·ral fear of him, making them snappish, and liable to hurt those of whom they are not afraid.

It is, therefore, most important that all animals should be treated uniformly with kindness. They are all capable of returning affection, and will show it very pleasantly if we manifest affection for them. They also have intuitive perceptions of our emotions which we can not conceal. A sharp, ugly dog will rarely bite a person who has no fear of him. A horse knows the moment a man mounts or takes the reins whether he is afraid or not; and so it is with other animals.

If live stock can not be well fed, they ought not to be kept. One well wintered horse is worth as much as two that drag through on straw, and by browsing the hedge-rows. The same is true of oxen, and emphatically so of cows. The owner of a half-starved dog loses the use of him almost altogether; for, at the very time—the night—when he is most needed as a guard, he must be off scouring the country for food.

Shelter in winter is most important for cows. They should have good tight stables or byres, well ventilated, and so warm that water in a pail will only freeze a little on the top the severest nights. Oxen should have the same stabling, though they bear cold better. Horses in stables will bear almost any degree of cold, if they have all they can eat. Sheep, except young lambs, are well enough sheltered in dry sheds, with one end open. Cattle, sheep, and dogs do not sweat as horses do, they "loll;" that is, water or slabber runs from their ·tongues; hence, they are not liable to take cold as the horse is. Hogs bea·

cold pretty well ; but they eat enough to convince any one that true economy lies in giving them warm sties in winter, for the colder they are the more they eat. Fowls will not lay in cold weather unless they have light and warm quarters.

Cleanliness is indispensable, if one would keep his animals healthy. In their wild state all our domestic animals are very clean, and, at the same time, very healthy. The hog is not naturally a dirty animal, but quite the reverse. He enjoys currying as much as a horse or a cow, and would be as careful of his litter as a cat if he had a fair chance.

Horses ought to be groomed daily ; cows and oxen as often as twice a week; dogs should be washed with soapsuds frequently. Stables should be cleaned out daily. Absorbents of liquid in stables should be removed as often as they become wet. Dry earth is one of the best absorbents, and is especially useful in the fowl-house. Hogs in pens should have straw for their rests or lairs, and it should be often renewed.

Parasitic Vermin.—These are lice, fleas, ticks, the scale insects, and other pests which afflict our live stock. There are many ways of destroying them ; the best and safest is a free use of *carbolic acid soap.* The larger animals, as well as hogs, dogs, and sheep may be washed in strong suds of this soap, without fear, and the application repeated after a week. This generally destroys both the creatures and their eggs. Hen lice are best destroyed by greasing the fowls, and dusting them with flowers of sulphur. Sitting hens must never be greased, but the sulphur may be dusted freely in their nests, and it is well to put it in all hens' nests.

Salt and Water.—All animals except poultry require salt, and all, free supplies of fresh water.

Light.—Stables, or places where any kind of animals are confined, should have plenty of light. Windows are not more important in a house than in a barn. The *sun* should come in freely; and if it shines directly upon the stock, all the better. When beeves and sheep are fattening very rapidly, the exclusion of the light makes them more quiet, and fatten faster; but their state is an unnatural and hardly a healthy one.

Exercise in the open air is important for breeding animals. It is especially necessary for horses of all kinds. Cows need very little and swine none, unless kept for breeding.

Breeding.—Always use thorough-bred males, and improvement is certain.

Horses.—The care which horses require varies with the circumstances in which the owner is placed, and the uses to which they are put. In general, if kept stabled, they should be fed with good upland hay, almost as much as they will eat; and if absent from the stable, and at work most of the day, they should have all they will eat of hay, together with four to eight quarts of oats or an equal weight of other grain or meal. Barley is good for horses, and so is dry corn. Corn-meal put upon cut hay, wet and well-mixed, is good, steady feed, if not in too large quantities. Four quarts a day may be fed unmixed with other grain; but if the horse be hard worked and needs more, mix the meal with wheat bran, or linseed oil-cake meal, or use corn and oats ground together; carrots are especially wholesome. A quart of linseed oil-cake meal, daily, is an excellent occasional addition to a horse's feed, when carrots can not be had. It gives a lustre to his coat, and brings the new coat of hair out in the spring. A stabled horse needs daily exercise, as much as to trot three miles. Where a horse is traveling, it is well to give him six quarts of oats in the morning, four at noon, and six at night.

Thorough grooming is indispensable to the health of horses. Especial care should be taken of the legs and fetlocks, that no dirt remain to cause that distressing disease, *grease* or *scratches*, which results from filthy fetlocks and

standing in dirty stables. When a horse comes in from
work on muddy roads with dirty legs, they should be immediately cleaned, the dirt brushed off, then rubbed with
straw; then, if very dirty, washed clean and rubbed dry
with a piece of sacking. A horse should never stand in a
draught of cold air, if he can not turn and put his back to it.
If sweaty or warm from work, he should be blanketed, if
he is to stand a minute in the winter air. If put at once
into the stable, he should be stripped and rubbed down
with straw actively for five minutes or more, and then
blanketed. The blanket must be removed in an hour, and
the horse given water and feed, if it is the usual time. It
will not hurt him to eat hay when hot, unless he be thoroughly exhausted, when all food should be withheld for a
while.

It is very comforting to a tired horse, when he is too
hot to drink, to sponge out his mouth with cool water. A
horse should never drink when very hot, nor be turned
into a yard to " cool off," even in summer, neither should
he be turned out to pasture before he is quite cool.

Cows.—Gentle but firm treatment will make a cow easy
to milk and to handle in every way. If stabled or yarded,
cows should have access to water at all times, or have it
frequently offered to them. Clover hay is probably the
best steady food for milch cows. Cornstalks cut up, thoroughly soaked with water for half a day, and then sprinkled with corn or oil-cake meal is perhaps unsurpassed
as good winter food for milch cows. The amount of meal
may vary. With plenty of oil-meal, there is little danger
of feeding too much, as that is loosening to the bowels and
a safe nutritious article. Corn-meal alone, in large quantities, is too heating. Roots should, if possible, form part
of the diet of a milch cow, especially before and soon after
calving; feed well before this period, yet not to make the
cow very fat; but it is better to err in that way than to
have her " come in " thin. Take the calf away from the

mother as soon as it stands up, and the separation will worry neither dam nor young. This is always best, unless the calf is to be kept with the cow. The calf will soon learn to drink its food, if two fingers be held in its mouth. Let it have all the first drawn milk for three days as soon as milked; after this, skimmed milk warmed to blood heat. Soon a little fine scalded meal may be mixed with the milk; and it will, at three to five weeks old, nibble hay and grass. It is well also to keep a box containing some dry wheat-bran and fine corn-meal mixed in the calf-pen, so that calves may take as much as they like.

In milking, put the fingers around the teat close to the bag; then firmly close the forefingers of each hand alter-nately, immediately squeezing with the other fingers. The forefingers prevent the milk flowing back into the bag, while the others press it out. Sit with the left knee close to the right hind leg of the cow, the head pressed against her flank, the left hand always ready to ward off a blow from her feet, which the gentlest cow may give al-most without knowing it, if her tender teats be cut by long nails, or if a wart be hurt, or her bag be tender. She must be stripped *dry* every time she is milked, or she will dry up; and if she gives much milk, it pays to milk three times a day, as nearly eight hours apart as possible. Never stop while milking till done, as this will cause the cow to stop giving milk.

To tether a cow, tie her by one hind leg, making the rope fast above the fetlock joint, and protecting the limb with a piece of an old bootleg or similar thing. The knot must be one that will not slip; regular fetters of iron bound with leather are much better.

A cow should go unmilked two months before calving, and her milk should not be used by the family till four days after that time.

Swine.—The filthy state of hog-pens is allowed on account of the amount of manure they will make by working over

all sorts of vegetable matter, spoiled hay, weeds, etc., etc.
This is unhealthy for the family near and also for the animal. The hog is, naturally, a cleanly animal, and if given
a chance he will keep himself very neat and clean.
Breeding sows should have the range of a small pasture,
and be regularly fed. They need fresh water constantly
and often suffer for lack of it when they have liquid swill,
which they do not like to drink. All hogs should have a
warm, dry, well-littered pen to lie in, away from flies and
disturbance of any kind. They are fond of charcoal, and
it is worth while frequently to throw a few handfuls where
they can get at it. It has a very beneficial effect on the
appetite, regulates the tone of the stomach and digestive
organs, and can not do any harm. Pigs ought always to be
well fed and kept growing fast; and when being fattened,
they should be penned always, the herd being sorted so
that all may have an equal chance. It is well to feed
soft corn in the ear; but hard corn should always be
ground and cooked for pigs.

Sheep.—In the winter, sheep need deep, well-littered,
dry sheds, dry yards, and hay, wheat, or oat straw, as much
as they will eat. They should be kept gaining by grain regularly fed to them, and so distributed that each gets its
share. Corn, either whole or ground, or oil-cake meal, or
both, are used for fattening sheep. They will easily surfeit
themselves on any grain except oil-meal, which is very safe
feed for them, and usually economical. Strong sheep will
often drive the weaker ones away, and so get more than
their share of food and make themselves sick. This must
be guarded against, and the flock sorted, keeping the weaker and stronger apart.

Sheep are very useful in clearing land of brush and certain weeds, which they gnaw down and kill. To accomplish this, the land must be overstocked, and it is best not to
keep sheep on short pasturage more than a few weeks at a
time; but if they are returned after a few days, it will serve

as good a purpose as if they were to be kept on all the time. Sheep at pasture must be restrained by good fences, or they will be a great nuisance. Dog-proof hedge fences of Osage orange are to be highly recommended, wherever this plant will grow. Mutton sheep will generally pay better to raise than merinos, but they need more care.

Poultry.—Few objects of labor are more remunerative than poultry, raised on a moderate scale. *Turkeys*, when young, need great care; some animal food, dry, warm quarters, and must be kept out of the wet grass, and kept in when it rains. As soon as fledged, they become very hardy, and, with free range, will almost take care of themselves. *Geese* need water and good grass pasture. *Ducks* do very well without water to swim in, if they have all they need to drink. They will lay a great many eggs if kept shut in a pen until say eight o'clock in the morning. If let out earlier, they wander away, and will hide their nests, and lay only about as many eggs as they can cover. It is best to set duck's eggs under hens, and to keep young ducks shut up in a dry roomy pen for four weeks, at least. *Fowls* need light, warm, dry quarters in winter, plenty of feed, but not too much. They relish animal food, and ought to have some frequently to make them lay. Pork or beef scrap-cake can be bought for two to three cents a pound, and is very good for them. Any kind of grain is good for poultry. Nothing is better than wheat screenings. Early hatched chickens must be kept in a warm, dry, sunny room, with plenty of gravel, and the hen should have no more than eight or nine chickens to brood; though in summer, one hen will take good care of fifteen. Little chickens, turkeys, and ducks need frequent feeding, and must have their water changed often. It is well to grease the body of the hen and the heads of the chicks with lard, in order to prevent their becoming lousy.

Hens set about twenty days, and should be well fed and watered. Cold or damp weather is bad for young fowls, and when they have been chilled, pepper-corns are a good remedy, in addition to the warmth of an inclosed dry place.

The most absorbing part of the " Woman's question " of the present time is the remedy for the varied sufferings of women who are widows or unmarried, and without means of support. As yet, few are aware how many sources of lucrative enterprise and industry lie open to woman in the employments directly connected with the family state. A woman can invest capital in the dairy and qualify herself to superintend a dairy farm as well as a man. And if she has no capital of her own, if well trained for this business, she can find those who have capital ready to furnish—an investment that well managed will become profitable. And, too, the raising of poultry, of hogs, and of sheep are all within the reach of a woman with proper abilities and training for this business. So that if a woman chooses, she can find employment both interesting and profitable in studying the care of domestic animals.

Bees.—But one of the most profitable as well as interesting kinds of business for a woman is the care of bees. In a recent agricultural report, it is stated that one lady bought four hives for ten dollars, and in five years she was offered one thousand five hundred dollars for her stock, and refused it as not enough. In addition to this increase of her capital, in one of these five years she sold twenty-two hives and four hundred and twenty pounds of honey. It is also stated that in five years one man, from six colonies of bees to start with, cleared eight thousand pounds of honey and one hundred and fifty-four colonies of bees.

The raising of bees and their management is so curious and as yet unknown an art in most parts of our country, that any directions or advice will be omitted in this volume, as requiring too much space, and largely set forth and illustrated in the second part. When properly instructed, almost any woman in the city, as easily as in the country, can manage bees, and make more profit than in any other method demanding so little time and labor. But in the modes ordinarily practiced, few can make any great profit in this employment.

It is hoped a time is at hand when every woman will be trained to some employment by which she can secure to herself an independent home and means to support a family, in case she does not marry, or is left a widow, with herself and a family to support.

XXXV

IN some particulars, the Chinese are in advance of our own nation in neatness, economy, and healthful domestic arrangements. In China, not a particle of manure is wasted, and all that with us is sent off in drains and sewers from water-closets and privies, is collected in a neat manner and used for manure. This is one reason that the compact and close packing of inhabitants in their cities is practica ble, and it also accounts for the enormous yields of some of their crops.

The earth-closet is an invention which relieves the most disagreeable item in domestic labor, and prevents the disa-greeable and unhealthful effluvium which is almost inevita-ble in all family residences. The general principle of construction is somewhat like that of a water-closet, except that in place of water is used dried earth. The resulting compost is without disagreeable odor, and is the richest spe-cies of manure. The expense of its construction and use is no greater than that of the common water-closet; indeed, when the outlays for plumber's work, the almost inevitable troubles and disorders of water-pipes in a house, and the constant stream of petty repairs consequent upon careless construction or use of water-works are considered, the earth-closet is in itself much cheaper, besides being an accumu-lator of valuable matter.

To give a clear idea of its principles, mode of fabrication, and use, we can not do better than to take advantage of the permission given by Mr. George E. Waring, Jr., of

Newport, R. I., author of an admirable pamphlet on the subject, published in 1868 by " The Tribune Association" of New-York. Mr. Waring was formerly Agricultural Engineer of the New-York Central Park, and has given much attention to sanitary and agricultural engineering, having published several valuable works bearing in the same general direction. He is now consulting director of " The Earth-Closet Company," Hartford, Ct., which manufactures the apparatus and all things appertaining to it—any part which might be needed to complete a home-built structure. But with generous and no less judicious freedom, they are endeavoring to extend the knowledge of this wholesome and economical process of domestic sanitary engineering as widely as possible, and so allow us to present the following instructions for those who may desire to construct their own apparatus.

In the brief introduction to his pamphlet, Mr. Waring says :

" It is sufficiently understood, by all who have given the least thought to the subject, that the waste of the most vital elements of the soil's fertility, through our present practice of treating human excrement as a thing that is to be hurried into the sea, or buried in underground vaults, or in some other way put out of sight and out of reach, is full of danger to our future prosperity.

" Our bodies have come out of our fertile fields; our prosperity is based on the production and the exchange of the earth's fruits; and all our industry has its foundation in arts and interests connected with, or dependent on, a successful agriculture.

" Liebig asserts that the greatness of the Roman empire was sapped by the *Cloaca Maxima*, through which the entire sewage of Rome was washed into the Tiber. The yearly decrease of productive power in the older grain regions of the West, and the increasing demand for manures in the Atlantic States, sufficiently prove that our own country is no exception to the rule that has established its sway over Europe.

" The large class who will fail to feel the force of the agricultural reasons in favor of the reform which this pamphlet is written to uphold, will realize, more clearly than farmers will, the importance of protecting dwellings against the gravest annoyance, the most fertile source of disease, and the most certain vehicle of contagion."

Nevertheless, Mr. Waring thinks that the agricultural argument is no mean or unimportant one, and says :

" The importance of any plan by which the excrement of our bodies may be returned to our fields is in a measure shown in the following extract from an article that I furnished for the *American Agricultural Annual* for 1868.

" The average population of New-York City—including its temporary visitors—is probably not less than 1,000,000. This population consumes food equivalent to at least 30,-000,000 bushels of corn in a year. Excepting the small proportion that is stored up in the bodies of the growing young, which is fully offset by that contained in the bodies of the dead, the constituents of the food are returned to the air by the lungs and skin, or are voided as excrement. That which goes to the air was originally taken from the air by vegetation, and will be so taken again : here is no waste. The excrement contains all that was furnished by the mineral elements of the soil on which the food was produced.

" This all passes into the sewers, and is washed into the sea. Its loss to the present generation is complete.

. . . " 30,000,000 bushels of corn contain, among other minerals, nearly 7000 tons of phosphoric acid, and this amount is annually lost in the wasted night-soil of New-York City.*

---

* Other mineral constituents of food—important ones, too—are washed away in even greater quantities through the same channels ; but this element is the best for illustration because its effect in manure is the most

" Practically the human excrement of the whole country is nearly all so disposed of as to be lost to the soil. The present population of the United States is not far from 35,000,000. On the basis of the above calculation, their annual food contains 200,000 tons of phosphoric acid, being the amount contained in about 900,000 tons of bones, which, at the price of the best flour of bone, (for manure,) would be worth over $50,000,000. It would be a moderate estimate to say that the other constituents of food are of at least equal value with the other constituents of the bone, and to assume $50,000,000 as the money value of the wasted night-soil of the United States every year.

" In another view, the importance of this waste can not be estimated in money. Money values apply, rather, to the products of labor and to the exchange of these products. The waste of fertilizing matter reaches farther than the destruction or exchange of products : it lessens the ability to produce.

" If mill-streams were failing year by year, and steam were yearly losing force, and the ability of men to labor were yearly growing less, the doom of our prosperity would not be more plainly written, than if this slow but certain impoverishment of our soil were sure to continue.

. . . . " But the good time is coming, when (as now in China and Japan) men must accept the fact that the soil is not a warehouse to be plundered—only a factory to be worked. Then they will save their raw material, instead of wasting it, and, aided by nature's wonderful laws, will weave over and over again the fabric by which we live and prosper. Men will build up as fast as men destroy ; old matters will be reproduced in new forms, and, as the

striking, even so small a dressing as twenty pounds per acre, producing a marked effect on all cereal crops. Ammonia, too,which is so important that it is usual in England to estimate the value of manure in exact proportion to its supply of this element, is largely yielded by human excrement.

decaying forests feed the growing wood, so will all consumed food yield food again."

With the above brief extract, we shall cease using marks of quotation, as the following information and statements are appropriated bodily, either directly or with mere modifications for brevity, from the little pamphlet of Mr. Waring.

The earth-closet is the invention of the Rev. Henry Moule, of Fordington Vicarage, Dorsetshire, England.

It is based on the power of clay, and the decomposed organic matter found in the soil, to absorb and retain all offensive odors and all fertilizing matters; and it consists, essentially, of a mechanical contrivance (attached to the ordinary seat) for measuring out and discharging into the vault or pan below a sufficient quantity of sifted dry earth to entirely cover the solid ordure and to absorb the urine.

The discharge of earth is effected by an ordinary pull-up similar to that used in the water-closet, or (in the self-acting apparatus) by the rising of the seat when the weight of the person is removed.

The vault or pan under the seat is so arranged that the accumulation may be removed at pleasure.

From the moment when the earth is discharged, and the evacuation is covered, all offensive exhalation entirely ceases. Under certain circumstances, there may be, at times, a slight odor as of guano mixed with earth; but this is so trifling and so local, that a commode arranged on this plan may, without the least annoyance, be kept in use in any room.

This statement is made as the result of personal experience. Mr. Waring says:

" I have in constant use in a room in my house an earth-closet commode; and even when the pan is entirely full, with the accumulation of a week's use, visitors examining it invariably say, with some surprise, 'You don't mean that this particular one has been used!' "

HOW TO MAKE AN EARTH-CLOSET.

The principle on which the earth-closet is based is as free to all as is the earth itself, and any person may adopt his own method of applying it. All that is *necessary* is to have a supply of coarsely sifted sun-dried earth with which to cover the bottom of the vessel to be used, and after use to cover the deposit. A small box of earth, and a tin scoop are sufficient to prevent the gravest annoyance of the sick-room. But, of course, for constant use, it is desirable to have a more convenient apparatus—something which requires less care, and is less troublesome in many ways.

To this end, the patent invention of Mr. Moule is applicable. This comprises a tight receptacle under the seat, a reservoir for storing dry earth, and an apparatus to measure out the requisite quantity, and throw it upon the deposit.

Fig. 67.

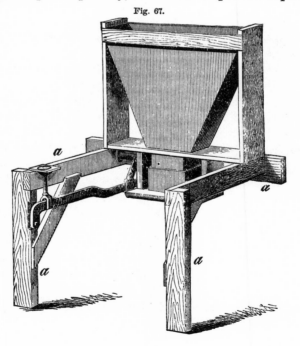

The arrangement of the mechanism is shown in Fig. 67. A hopper-shaped reservoir, made of galvanized iron, is supported by a framework at the back of the seat, which rests on the framework a, a. Connected with the handle at the right-hand side, there is an iron lever, which operates a movable box at the bottom of the reservoir, and causes it to discharge its contents directly under the seat. When the handle is dropped, the box returns to its position, and is immediately filled preparatory to another use.

The hopper-shaped reservoir is supported by two pivots, and has a slight rocking or vibrating motion imparted to it by each lifting of the lever. This prevents the earth from becoming clogged, and insures its regular delivery

THE "PULL-UP" APPARATUS.

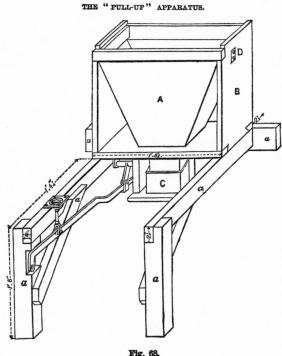

Fig. 68.

The construction is more clearly shown in Fig. 68.

In this figure, A is the vibrating hopper for holding the earth. Its capacity may be increased to any desired extent by building above it a straight-sized box of any height. It is not unusual, in fixed privies, to make this reservoir large enough to hold a supply for several months. As the earth is dry, there is no occasion for the use of any thing better than common pine boards in making this addition to the reservoir.

B is one side of the wooden frame by which the hopper is supported, and it may be made of one inch pine or spruce.

C is a box of lacquered or galvanized iron, without either top or bottom. It moves on two pivots, one of which is shown on its exposed side. In its present position, its upper end opens into the hopper, and its lower end is closed by the stationary board over which it stands. When the handle is pulled up, the lever, which is connected with the box, jerks it rapidly up, so that its back side closes the opening of the reservoir, and its bottom opens to the front. In its movement it discharges its contents of earth forward under the seat. When the handle is dropped, the box returns to its natural position, and is charged again.

D is one of the pivots—a corresponding one being on the other side—by which the hopper is supported, and on which it vibrates.

a, a, a, a, a, a, are the parts of the framework, the dimensions of which in feet and inches are given.

The only essential part not shown is an earthen-ware pan without a bottom, similar to the pan of a water-closet, only not so deep and with a larger opening, which is attached to the under side of the seat, and which in a measure prevents the rising of dust, and conducts the urine to the point at which the most earth falls. This is the least important part of the invention, but it has a certain advantage.

The self-acting apparatus is more complicated, and persons wishing it would do best to apply directly to the Company.

In the circular published by the Earth-Closet Company, the following directions are given :

" An ordinary fixed closet requires the apparatus to be placed at the back of, and in connection with, the usual seat ; the reservoir for containing the earth being placed above it. Under it there should be a chamber or vault about four feet by three wide, and of any convenient depth, with a paved or asphalted bottom, and the sides lined with cement.

COMMODES.

Fig. 69.—Commode, 3 ft. 3 in. high, 1 ft. 11 in. wide, 2 ft. 2 in. deep.

Should there be an existing cesspool, it may be altered to the above dimensions. Into this the deposit and earth fall, and may remain there three, six, or twelve months, and continue perfectly inodorous and innoxious, merely requiring to be occasionally leveled by a rake or hoe. If, however, it should be found impossible or inconvenient to have a vault underneath, a movable trough, of iron or tarred wood, on wheels, may be substituted. In this case, it will be advisable to raise the seat somewhat above the floor, to allow the trough to be of sufficient size.

" By one form of construction, (the ' pull-up,') the pulling up of a handle releases a sufficient quantity of the dry earth, which is thrown into the pit or vault, covering the deposit and completely preventing all smell. By another, (the ' self-acting,') the same effect is produced by the action of the seat. The apparatus may be placed in, and adapted to, almost any existing closet or privy, and so arranged that the supply and removal of earth may be carried on inside or outside as desired."

The following is taken from the company's circular :

" In the commode, the apparatus and earth-reservoir are self-contained, and a movable pail takes the place of the chamber or vault above described. This must be emptied as often as necessary, and the contents may be applied to the garden or field, or be allowed to accumulate in a heap under cover until wanted for use. This accumulation is inodorous, and rapidly becomes dry. The commode can stand in any convenient place in or out of doors. For use in bedrooms, hospital wards, infirmaries, etc., the commode is invaluable. It is entirely free from those faint, depressing odors common to portable water-closets and night-stools, and through its admission one of the greatest miseries of human life, the foul smells of the sick-room, and one of the most frequent means of communicating infection, may be entirely prevented. It is invariably found that, if any failure takes place, it arises from the earth *not being proper-*

ly dry. Too much importance can not be attached to this requirement. The earth-commode will no more act properly without dry earth, than will a water-closet without water.

" These commodes are made in a variety of patterns, from the cottage commode to the more expensive ones in mahogany or oak, and vary in price accordingly. They are made to act either by a handle, as in the ordinary water-closet, or self-acting on rising from the seat. The earth-reservoir is calculated to hold enough for about twenty-five times; and where earth is scarce, or the manure required of extraordinary strength, the product may be dried as many as seven times, and without losing any of its deodorizing properties.

" If care be taken to cast one service of earth into the pail when first placed in the commode, and to have the commonest regard to cleanliness, not the least offensive smell will be perceptible, though the receptacle remain unemptied for weeks. Care must also be taken that no liquid, but that which they are intended to receive, be thrown into the pails."

The pail used in the commode is made of galvanized iron, and is shaped very much like an ordinary coal-hod. It has a cover of the same material, and it may be carried from an upper floor with no more offensiveness than a hodful of common earth.

Fig. 70 represents a cross-section of the commode, and will enable the reader more clearly to understand the construction and operation of the apparatus.

a is the opening in the seat; *b*, the " pan ;" *c*, the pail for receiving the deposit; *d*, the hopper for containing the earth supply; *e*, the box by which the earth is measured, and by which it is thrown into the pail when moved to the position *e'* by the operation of the " pull-up ;" *f*, a door by which the pail is shut in; *g*, the cover of the seat; *h*, the cover of the hopper; *i*, a platform which prevents the escape of earth from *e*.

Fig. 70.

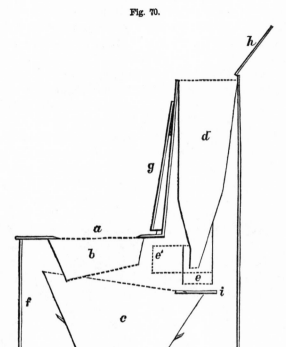

HOW TO USE THE EARTH-CLOSET.

Under this head, the circular issued by the original London company contains the following :

"The first requirement for the proper working of the earth-closet is earth perfectly dry and sifted.

"Earth alone is proved to be the best deodorizer, and far superior to any disinfectants ; but where it is difficult to obtain earth abundantly, sifted ashes, as before stated, may be mixed with it in proportion of two of earth to one of ashes.

"As the first requirement is *dry earth sifted*, and as this is usually thought to be a great difficulty in the way of the adoption of the dry earth system, the following remarks will at once remove such an impression.

" The earth-commode and closet, if used by six persons daily, will require, on an average, about one hundred weight of earth per week. This may be dried for family use in a drawer made to fit under the kitchen range, and which may be filled with earth one morning and left until the next. The drawer should reach to within two inches of the bottom bar of the grate. A frame with a handle, covered with fine wire-netting, forming a kind of shovel, should be placed on this drawer; the finer ashes will fall through, mixing with the earth, whilst the cinders will remain on the top, to be, from time to time, thrown on the fire.

" Of course, the most economical method is to provide in the summer-time a winter store of dry earth, which may be kept in an out-house, shed, or other convenient place, just as we lay in a winter store of coals.

" THINGS TO BE OBSERVED.

" Let one fall of earth be in the pail before using.

" The earth must be dry and sifted.

" Sand must not be used.

" No ' slops ' must be thrown down.

" The handle must be pulled up with a jerk, and let fall sharply."

REPEATED USE OF EARTH.

Concerning the value and use of the product of the earth-closet, the following is copied from the London company's circular. (It will be noticed that reference is made to *the repeated use of the same earth*. When the ordure is completely dried and decomposed, it has not only lost its odor, but it has become, like all decomposed organic matter, an excellent disinfectant, and the fifth or sixth time that the same earth is passed through the closet it is fully as effective in destroying odors as it was when used for the first time, and of course each use adds to its value as manure, until it becomes as strong as Peruvian guano, which is now worth seventy-five dollars per ton. In fact, it may be made so rich that *one hundred pounds will be a good dressing for an acre of land.*)

" If the closet is over a water-tight cesspool or pit, it will require emptying at the end of three or six months. The produce, which will be quite inodorous, should be thrown together in a heap, sheltered from wet, and occasionally turned over. At the end of a few weeks, it will be dry and fit for use.

" If the receptacle be an iron trough or pail, the contents should be thrown together, re-dried, and used over again, four or five times. In a few weeks they will be dry and fit for use ; the value being increased by repeated action. The condition of the manure should be much the same as that of guano, and fit for drilling.

The inventor of the earth-closet, Rev. Mr. Moule, says :

" It was to this point (the power of earth or clay to absorb the products of the decomposition of manure) but particularly to the *repeated action*, and consequently the repeated use of the same earth, that I first directed the attention of the public. I then pointed out: First. That a very small portion of dry and sifted earth (one and a half pints) is sufficient by covering the deposit, to prevent fermentation, (which so soon sets in whenever water is used,) and the consequent generation and emission of noxious gases. Second. That if within a few hours, or even a few days, the mass that would be formed by the repeated layers of deposit, be intimately mixed by a coarse rake or spade, or by a mixer made for the purpose, then, in five or ten minutes, neither to the eye or sense of smell is any thing perceptible but so˙ much earth. . . . When about three cart-loads of sifted earth had thus been used for my family, (which averaged fifteen persons,) and left under a shed, I found that the material first employed was sufficiently dried to be used again. This process of alternate mixing and drying was renewed five times, the earth still retaining its absorbent powers apparently unimpaired. Of the visitors taken to the spot, none could guess the nature of the compost, though in some cases the heap which they visited in the afternoon had been turned over that same morning. . .

" It is only in towns, where the delivery, stowage, and removal of earth is attended with cost and difficulty, that any artificial aid for drying the compost would be desirable. On premises not cramped for space, the atmosphere, especially with a glass roof to the shed, will act sufficiently fast.

" You may by means of it (the earth system) have a privy close to the house and a closet up-stairs, from neither of which shall proceed any offensive smell or any noxious gas. A projection from the back of the cottage, eight feet long and six feet wide, would be amply sufficient for this purpose. The nearer three or four feet down-stairs, would be occupied by the privy, in which, by the seat, would be a receptacle for dry earth. The 'soil' and earth would fall into the further five or four feet, which would form the covered and closed shed for mixing and drying. Up-stairs, the arrangement would be much the same, the deposit being made to fall clear of every wall. Through this closet the removal of noxious and offensive matters in time of sickness, and of slop-buckets, would be immediate and easy ; and if the shed below be kept well supplied with earth, all effluvium would be almost immediately checked. As to the trouble which this will cause, a very little experience will convince the cottager that it is less instead of greater, than the women generally go through at present, while the value of the manure will afford an inducement to exertion.

.   .   .   .

" The truth is, that the machinery is more simple, much less expensive, and far less liable to injury than that of the water-closet. The supply of earth to the house is as easy as that of coals. To the closet it may be supplied more easily than water is supplied by a forcing-pump, and to the commode it can be conveyed just as coal is carried to the chamber. After use, it can be removed in either case by the bucket or box placed under the seat, or from the fixed reservoir, with less offense than that of the ordinary slop-bucket—indeed, (I speak after four years' experience,) with as little offense as is found in the removal of coal-ashes. So that, while servants and others will shrink from novelty and at first imagine difficulties, yet many, to my knowledge, would now vastly prefer the daily removal of the bucket or the soil to either the daily working of a forcing-pump or to being called upon once a year, or once in three years, to assist in emptying a vault or cesspool."

To the above complete and convincingly apt arguments and statements of fact, we do not care to add any thing. All that we desire is to direct public attention to the admirable qualities of this Earth System, and to suggest that, at least for those living in the country away from the many conveniences of city life, great water power, and mechanical assistance, the use of it will conduce largely to the economy of families, the health of neighborhoods, and the increasing fertility and prosperity of the country round about.

XXXVI.

THERE is no department of science, as applied to practical matters, which has so often baffled experimenters as the healthful mode of warming and ventilating houses. The British nation spent over a million on the House of Parliament for this end, and failed. Our own government has spent half a million on the Capitol, with worse failure; and now it is proposed to spend a million more. The reason is, that the old open fireplace has been supplanted by less expensive modes of heating, destructive to health; and science has but just begun experiments to secure a remedy for the evil.

The open fire warms the person, the walls, the floors and the furniture by radiation, and these, together with the fire, warm the air by convection. For the air resting on the heated surfaces is warmed by convection, rises and gives place to cooler particles, causing a constant heating of its particles by movement. Thus in a room with an open fire, the person is warmed in part by radiation from the fire and the surrounding walls and furniture, and in part by the warm air surrounding the body.

In regard to the warmth of air, the thermometer is not an exact index of its temperature. For all bodies are constantly radiating their heat to cooler adjacent surfaces until all come to the same temperature. This being so, the thermometer is radiating its heat to walls and surrounding objects, in addition to what is subtracted by the air that surrounds it, and thus the air is really several degrees warmer than the thermometer indicates. A room at 70°

by the thermometer is usually filled with air five or more degrees warmer than this.

Now, the cold air is denser than warm, and therefore contains more oxygen. Consequently, the cooler the air inspired, the larger the supply of oxygen and of the vitality and vigor which it imparts. Thus, the great problem for economy of health is to warm the person as much as possible by radiated heat, and supply the lungs with cool air. For when we breathe air at from 16° to 20°, we take double the amount of oxygen that we do when we inhale it at 80° to 90°, and consequently can do double the amount of muscle and brain work.

Warming by an open fire is nearest to the natural mode of the Creator, who heats the earth and its furniture by the great central fire of heaven, and sends cool breezes for our lungs. But open fires involve great destruction of fuel and expenditure of money, and in consequence economic methods have been introduced to the great destruction of health and life.

Of these methods, the most popular is that by which radiated heat is banished, and all warmth is gained by introducing heated air. This is the method employed in our national Capitol, where both warming and ventilation are attempted by means of *fans* worked by steam, which force in the heated air. This is an expensive mode, used only for large establishments, and its entire failure at our capitol will probably prevent in future any very extensive use of it.

But the most common mode of warming is by heated air introduced from a furnace. The chief objection to this is the loss of all radiated heat, and the consequent necessity of breathing air which is debilitating both from its heat and also from being usually deprived of the requisite moisture provided by the Creator in all out-door air. Another objection is the fact that it is important to health to preserve an equal circulation of the blood, and the greatest impediment to this is a mode of heating which keeps the head in warmer air than the feet. This is especially deleterious in an age and country where active brains are constantly drawing blood from the extremities to the head. All furnace-heated rooms have coldest air at the feet, and warmest around the head. It is also rarely the case that furnace-heated houses have proper arrangements for carrying off the vitiated air.

There are some recent scientific discoveries that relate to impure air which may properly be introduced here. It is shown by the microscope that *fermentation* is a process which generates extremely minute plants, that gradually increase till the whole mass is pervaded by this vegetation. The microscope also has revealed the fact that, in certain diseases, these microscopic plants are generated in the blood and other fluids of the body, in a mode similar to the ordinary process of fermentation.

And, what is very curious, each of these peculiar diseases generates diverse kinds of plants. Thus in the typhoid fever, the microscope reveals in the fluids of the patient a plant that resembles in form some kinds of sea-weed. In chills and fever, the microscopic plant has another form, and in small-pox still another. A work has recently been published in Europe, in which representations of these various microscopic plants generated in the fluids of the diseased persons are exhibited, enlarged several hundred times by the microscope. All diseases that exhibit these microscopic plants are classed together, and are called *Zymotic*, from a Greek word signifying *to ferment*.

These zymotic diseases sometimes have a *local* origin, as in the case of ague caused by miasma of swamps; and then they are named *endemic*. In other cases, they are caused by persona. contact with the diseased body or its clothing, as the itch or small-pox; or else by effluvia from the sick, as in measles. Such are called *contagious* or *infec-*

tious. In other cases, diseases result from some unknown cause in the atmosphere, and affect numbers of people at the same time, as in influenza or scarlet fever, and these are called *epidemics.*

It is now regarded as probable that most of these diseases are generated by the microscopic plants which float in an impure or miasmatic atmosphere, and are taken into the blood by breathing.

Recent scientific investigations in Great Britain and other countries prove that the *power of resisting* these diseases depends upon the purity of the air which has been *habitually* inspired. The human body gradually accommodates itself to unhealthful circumstances, so that people can live a long time in bad air. But the "reserve power" of the body, that is, the power of resisting disease, is under such circumstances gradually destroyed, and then an epidemic easily sweeps away those thus enfeebled. The plague of London, that destroyed thousands every day, came immediately after a long period of damp, warm days, when there was no wind to carry off the miasma thus generated; while the people, by long breathing of bad air, were all prepared, from having sunk into a low vitality, to fall before the pestilence.

Multitudes of public documents show that the fatality of epidemics is always proportioned to the degree in which impure air has previously been respired. Sickness and death are therefore regulated by the degree in which air is kept pure, especially in case of diseases in which medical treatment is most uncertain, as in cholera and malignant fevers.

Investigations made by governmental authority, and by boards of health in this country and in Great Britain, prove that zymotic diseases ordinarily result from impure air generated by vegetab e or animal decay, and that in almost all cases they can be prevented by keeping the air pure. The decayed animal matter sent off from the skin and lungs in a close, unventilated bedroom is one thing that generates these zymotic diseases. The decay of animal and vegetable matter in cellars, sinks, drains, and marshy districts is another cause; and the decayed vegetable matter thrown up by plowing up of decayed vegetable matter in the rich soil in new countries is another.

In the investigations made in certain parts of Great Britain, it appeared that in districts where the air is pure the deaths average 11 in 1000 each year; while in localities most exposed to impure miasma, the mortality was 45 in every thousand. At this rate, thirty-four persons in every thousand died from poisoned air, who would have preserved health and life by well-ventilated homes in a pure atmosphere. And, out of all who died, the proportion who owed their deaths to foul air was more than three fourths. Similar facts have been obtained by boards of health in our own country.

Mr. Leeds gives statistics showing, that in Philadelphia, by improved modes of ventilation and other sanitary methods, there was a saving of 3237 lives in two years; and a saving of three fourths of a million of dollars, which would pay the whole expense of the public schools. Philadelphia being previously an unusually cleanly and well-ventilated city, what would be the saving of life, health, and wealth were such a city as New-York perfectly cleansed and ventilated?

Here it is proper to state again that conflicting opinions are found in many writers on ventilation in regard to the position of ventilating registers to carry off vitiated air. Most writers state that the impure air is heavier, and falls to the bottom of a room. After consulting scientific men extensively on this point, the writer finds the true result to be as follows: Carbonic acid is heavier than common air, and, unmixed, falls to the floor. But by the principle of *diffusion of gases*, the air thrown from the lungs, though at first it sinks a little, is gradually diffused, and in a heated room, in the majority of cases, it is found more abundantly at the top than at the bottom of the room, though in certain circumstances it is more at the bottom. For this reason, registers to carry off impure air should be placed at both the top and bottom of a room.

In arranging for pure air in dwellings, it is needful to proportion the air admitted and discharged to the number of persons. As a guide to this, we have the following calculation : On an average, every adult vitiates about half a pint of air at each inspiration, and inspires twenty times a minute. This would amount to one hogshead of air vitiated every hour by every grown person. To keep the air pure, this amount should enter and be carried out every hour for each person. If, then, ten persons assemble in a dining-room, ten hogsheads of air should enter and ten be discharged each hour. By the same rule, a gathering of five hundred persons demands the entrance and discharge of five hundred hogsheads of air every hour, and a thousand persons require a thousand hogsheads of air every hour.

In calculating the size of registers and conductors, then, we must have reference to the number of persons who are to abide in a dwelling; while for rooms or halls intended for large gatherings, a far greater allowance must be made.

The most successful mode before the public, both for warming and ventilation, is that of Lewis Leeds, who was employed by government to ventilate the military hospitals and also the treasury building at Washington. This method has been adopted in various school-houses, and also by A. T. Stewart in his hotel for women in New-York City. The Leeds plan embraces the mode of heating both by radiation and convection, very much resembling the open fireplace in operation, and yet securing great economy. It is modeled strictly after the mode adopted by the Creator in warming and ventilating the earth, the home of his great earthly family. It aims to have a passage of pure air through every room, as the breezes pass over the hills, and to have a method of warming chiefly by radiation, as the earth is warmed by the sun. In addition to this, the air is to be provided with moisture, as it is supplied outdoors by exhalations from the earth and its trees and plants.

The mode of accomplishing this is by placing coils of steam, or hot water pipes, under windows, which warm the parlor walls and furniture, partly by radiation, and partly by the air warmed on the heated surfaces of the coils. At the same time, by regulating registers, or by simply opening the lower part of the window, the pure air, guarded from immediate entrance into the room, is admitted directly upon the coils, so that it is partially warmed before it reaches the person: and thus cold drafts are prevented. Then the vitiated air is drawn off through registers both at the top and bottom of the room, opening into a heated exhausting flue, through which the constantly ascending current of warm air carries it off. These heated coils are often used for warming houses without any arrangement for carrying off the vitiated air, when, of course, their peculiar usefulness is gone.

The moisture may be supplied by a broad vessel placed on or close to the heated coils, giving a large surface for evaporation. When rooms are warmed chiefly by radiated heat, the air can be borne much cooler than in rooms warmed by hot-air furnaces, just as a person in the radiating sun can bear much cooler air than in the shade. A time will come when walls and floors will be contrived to radiate heat instead of absorbing it from the occupants of houses, as is generally the case at the present time, and then all can breathe pure and cool air.

We are now prepared to examine more in detail the modes of warming and ventilation employed in the dwellings planned for this work.

In doing this, it should be remembered that the aim is not

to give plans of houses to suit the architectural taste or the domestic convenience of persons who intend to keep several servants, and care little whether they breathe pure or bad air, nor of persons who do not wish to educate their children to manual industry or to habits of close economy.

On the contrary, the aim is, first, to secure a house in which every room shall be perfectly ventilated both day and night, and that too without the watchful care and constant attention and intelligence needful in houses not provided with a proper and successful mode of ventilation.

The next aim is, to arrange the conveniences of domestic labor so as to save time, and also to render such work less repulsive than it is made by common methods, so that children can be trained to love house-work. And lastly, economy of expense in house-building is sought. These things should be borne in mind in examining the plans of this work.

In the Cottage plan, (Chap II. Fig. 1,) the pure air for rooms on the ground floor is to be introduced by a wooden conductor one foot square, running under the floor from the front door to the stove-room; with cross branches to the two large rooms. The pure air passes through this, protected outside by wire netting, and delivered inside through registers in each room, as indicated in Fig. 1.

In case open Franklin stoves are used in the large rooms, the pure air from the conductor should enter behind them, and thus be partially warmed. The vitiated air is carried off at the bottom of the room through the open stoves, and also at the top by a register opening into a conductor to the exhausting warm-air shaft, which, it will be remembered, is the square chimney, containing the iron pipe which receives the kitchen stove-pipe. The stove-room receives pure air from the conductor, and sends off impure air and the smells of cooking by a register opening directly into the exhausting shaft; while its hot air and smoke, passing through the iron pipe, heat the air of the shaft, and produce the exhausting current.   The construction of the exhausting or warm-air shaft is described on page 63.

The large chambers on the second floor (Fig. 12) have pure air conducted from the stove-room through registers that can be closed if the heat or smells of cooking are unpleasant.   The air in the stove-room will always be moist from the water of the stove boiler.

The small chambers have pure air admitted from windows sunk at top half an inch; and the warm, vitiated air is conducted by a register in the ceiling which opens into a conductor to the exhausting warm-air shaft at the centre of the house, as shown in Fig. 17.

The basement or cellar is ventilated by an opening into the exhausting air shaft, to remove impure air, and a small opening over each glazed door to admit pure air.   The doors open out into a "well," or recess, excavated in the earth before the cellar, for the admission of light and air, neatly bricked up and whitewashed.   The doors are to be made entirely of strong, thick glass sashes, and this will give light enough for laundry work; the tubs and ironing-table being placed close to the glazed door.   The floor must be plastered with water-lime, and the walls and ceiling be whitewashed, which will add reflected light to the room.   There will thus be no need of other windows, and the house need not be raised above the ground.   Several cottages have been built thus, so that the ground floors and conservatories are nearly on the same level; and all agree that they are pleasanter than when raised higher.

When a window in any room is sunk at the top, it should have a narrow shelf in front inclined to the opening, so as to keep out the rain.   In small chambers for one person, an inch opening is sufficient, and in larger rooms for two persons, a two-inch opening is needed.   The openings into the exhausting air flue should vary from eight inches to twelve inches square, or more, according to the number of persons who are to sleep in the room.

The time when ventilation is most difficult is the medium weather in spring and fall, when the air, though damp, is similar in temperature outside and in. Then the warm-air flue is indispensable to proper ventilation. This is especially needed in a room used for school or church purposes.

Every room used for large numbers should have its air regulated not only as to its warmth and purity, but also as to its supply of moisture; and for this purpose will be found very convenient the instrument called the Hygrodeik,* which shows at once the temperature and the moisture. A work by Dr. Derby on Anthracite Coal, scientific men say has done much mischief by an *unproved* theory that the discomfort of furnace heat is caused by the passage of carbonic *oxide* through the iron of the furnace heaters, and *not* by want of moisture. God made the air right, and taking out its moisture *must* be wrong.

The preceding remarks illustrate the advantages of the cottage plan in respect to ventilation. The economy of the mode of warming next demands attention. In the first place, it should be noted that the chimney being at the centre of the house, no heat is lost by its radiation through outside walls into open air, as is the case with all fireplaces and grates that have their backs and flues joined to an outside wall.

In this plan, all the radiated heat from the stove serves to warm the walls of adjacent rooms in cold weather; while in the warm season, the non-conducting summer casings of the stove send all the heat not used in cooking either into the exhausting warm-air shaft or into the central cast-iron pipe. In addition to this, the sliding doors of the stove-room (which should be only six feet high, meeting the partition coming from the ceiling) can be opened in cool days, and then the heat from the stove would temper the rooms each side of the kitchen. In hot weather, they could be kept

* It is manufactured by N. M. Lowe, Boston, and sold by him and J. Queen & Co., Philadelphia.

closed except when the stove is used, and then opened only
for a short time. The Franklin stoves in the large room
would give the radiating warmth and cheerful blaze of an
open fire, while radiating heat also from all their surfaces.
In cold weather, the air of the larger chambers could be
tempered by registers admitting warm air from the stove-
room, which would always be sufficiently moistened by
evaporation from the stationary boiler. The conservatories in winter, protected from frost by double sashes, would
contribute agreeable moisture to the larger rooms. In case
the size of a family required more rooms, another story
could be ventilated and warmed by the same mode, with
little additional expense.

We will next notice the economy of time, labor, and
expense secured by this cottage plan. The laundry work
being done in the basement, all the cooking, dish-washing,
etc., can be done in the kitchen and stove-room on the
ground floor. But in case a larger kitchen is needed, the
lounges can be put in the front part of the large room, and
the movable screen placed so as to give a work-room adjacent to the kitchen, and the front side of the same be used
for the eating-room. Where the movable screen is used,
the floor should be oiled wood. A square piece of carpet can
be put in the centre of the front part of the room, to keep
the feet warm when sitting around the table, and small
rugs can be placed before the lounges or other sitting-places,
for the same purpose.

Most cottages are so divided by entries, stairs, closets,
etc., that there can be no large rooms. But in this plan,
by the use of the movable screen, two fine large rooms can
be secured whenever the family work is over, while the
conveniences for work will very much lessen the time
required.

In certain cases, where the closest economy is needful,
two small families can occupy the cottage, by having a
movable screen in both rooms, and using the kitchen in

common, or divide it and have two smaller stoves. Each kitchen will then have a window and as much room as is given to the kitchen in great steamers that provide for several hundred.

Whoever plans a house with a view to economy must arrange rooms around a central chimney, and avoid all projecting appendages. Dormer windows are far more expensive than common ones, and are less pleasant. Every addition projecting from a main building greatly increases expense of building, and still more of warming and ventilating.

It should be introduced, as one school exercise in every female seminary, to plan houses with reference to economy of time, labor, and expense, and also with reference to good architectural taste; and the teacher should be qualified to point out faults and give the instruction needed to prevent such mistakes in practical life. Every girl should be trained to be "a wise woman" that "buildeth her house" aright.

There is but one mode of ventilation yet tried, that will, at all seasons of the year and all hours of the day and night, secure pure air without dangerous draughts, and that is by an exhausting warm-air flue. This is always secured by an open fireplace, so long as its chimney is kept warm by any fire. And in many cases, a fireplace with a flue of a certain dimension and height will secure good ventilation except when the air without and within are at the same temperature.

When no exhausting warm-air flue can be used, the opening of doors and windows is the only resort. Every sleeping-room *without a fireplace that draws smoke well* should have a window raised at the bottom or sunk at the top at least an inch, with an inclined shelf outside or in, to keep out rain, and then it is properly ventilated. Or a door should be kept opened into a hall with an open window. Let the bed-clothing be increased, so as to keep warm in bed, and protect the head also, and then the more air comes into a sleeping-room the better for health.

In reference to the warming of rooms and houses already built, there is no doubt that stoves are the most economical mode, as they radiate heat and also warm by convection. The grand objection to their use is the difficulty of securing proper ventilation. If a room is well warmed by a stove and then a suitable opening made for the entrance of a good supply of out-door air, and by a mode that will prevent dangerous draughts, all is right as to pure air. But in this case, the feet are always on cold floors, surrounded by the coldest air, while the head is in air of much higher temperature.

There is a great difference as to healthfulness and economy in the great variety of stoves with which the market is filled. The competition in this manufacture is so stringent, and so many devices are employed by agents, that there is constant and enormous imposition on the public and an incredible outlay on poor stoves, that soon burn out or break, while they devour fuel beyond calculation. If some benevolent and scientific organization could be formed that would, from disinterested motives, afford some reliable guidance to the public, it probably would save both millions of money and much domestic discomfort.

The stove described in Chapter V. is protected by patents in its chief advantages, but this has not restrained many of the trade from incorporating some of its leading excellencies and claiming to have added superior elements. Others will inform any who inquire for it, that it is out of market, because later stoves have proved superior. Should any who read this work wish to be sure of securing this stove, and also of gaining minute directions for its use, they may apply to the writer, Miss C. E. Beecher, 69 West 38th Street, New-York, inclosing 25 cents.

She will then forward the manufacturers' printed descriptive circulars, and her own advice as to the best selection

from the different sizes, and directions for its use, based on
her own personal experience and that of many friends.
Should any purchases be made through this medium, the
manufacturers have agreed to pay a certain percentage
into the treasury of the Benevolent Association mentioned
at the close of this volume.

There is no more dangerous mode of heating a room
than by a gas-stove. There is inevitably more or less
leakage of the gas which it is unhealthful to breathe.
And proper ventilation is scarcely ever secured by those
who use such stoves. The same fatal elements of imperfect ventilation with its attendant horrors of disease, ex-
travagant wastefulness of material, of fuel, of labor, of
time, and of destruction to the apparatus itself, seem con-
comitants of all ordinary stoves and cooking arrangements
of the present day, unless those who use them are constant
and unremitting in the exercise of intelligent watchfulness,
guarding against these evils. And in view of the almost
inevitable stupidity and carelessness of servants, who generally have charge of such things, and the frequent
thoughtlessness even of intelligent women who manage
their own kitchens, the writer believes she is doing a public service by offering her own experience as a guide to
simpler, cheaper, and more wholesome means of living and
preparing the family food.

XXXVII.

CARE OF THE HOMELESS, THE HELPLESS, AND THE VICIOUS.

In considering the duties of the Christian family in regard to the helpless and vicious classes, some recently developed facts need to be considered. We have stated that the great end for which the family was instituted is the training to virtue and happiness of our whole race, as the children of our Heavenly Father, and this with chief reference to their eternal existence after death. In the teachings of our Lord we find that it is for sinners—for the lost and wandering sheep, that he is most tenderly concerned. It is not those who by careful training and happy temperaments have escaped the dangers of life that God and good angels most anxiously watch. " For there is more joy in heaven over one sinner that repenteth than over ninety and nine that went not astray."

The hardest work of all is to restore a guilty, selfish, hardened spirit to honor, truth, and purity; and this is the divine labor to which the pitying Saviour calls all his true followers; to lift up the fallen, to sustain the weak, to protect the tempted, to bind up the broken-hearted, and especially to rescue the sinful. This is the peculiar privilege of woman in the sacred retreat of a " Christian home." And it is for such self-denying ministries that she is to train all who are under her care and influence, both by her teaching and by her example.

In connection with these distinctive principles of Christ for which the family state was instituted, let the following facts be considered. The Massachusetts Board of State

Charities, consisting of some of the most benevolent and intelligent gentlemen of that State, in pursuance of their official duty visited all the State institutions, and held twenty-five meetings during the year 1867–8. By these visits and consequent discussions they arrived at certain conclusions, which may be briefly condensed as follows.

No state or nation excels Massachusetts in a wise and generous care of the helpless, poor, and vicious. The agents employed for this end are frugal, industrious, intelligent, and benevolent men and women, with high moral principles. The pauper and criminal classes requiring to be cared for by Massachusetts are less in proportion to the whole number of inhabitants than in any other state or nation. Yet, admirable as are these comparative results, there is room for improvement in a most important particular. The report of the Board urges that the present mode of collecting special classes in great establishments, though it may be the best in a choice of evils, is not the best method for the physical, social, and moral improvement of those classes ; as it involves many unfortunate influences (which are stated at large :) and the report suggests that a better way would be to scatter these unfortunates from temporary receiving asylums into families of Christian people all over the State.

It is suggested in view of the above, that collecting fallen women into one large community is not the best way to create a pure moral atmosphere; and that gathering one or two hundred children in one establishment is not so good for them as to give each child a home in some loving Christian family. So of the aged and the sick, the blessings of a quiet home, and the tender, patient nursing of true Christian love, must be sought in a Christian family, not in a great asylum.

In view of these important facts and suggestions, it may be inquired, if the great end and aim of the family state is to train the inmates to self-denying love and labor for the weak, the suffering, and the sinful, how can it be done where there are no young children, no aged persons, no invalids, and no sinful ones for whom such sacrifices are to be made?

Why are orphan children thrown upon the world, why are the aged held in a useless, suffering life, except that they may aid in cultivating tender love and labor for the helpless, and reverence for the hoary head? And yet, how few children are trained thus to regard the orphan, the aged, the helpless, and the vicious around them!

Great houses are built for these destitute ones, and all the labor and self-denial in taking care of them is transferred to paid agents, while thousands of families are thus deprived of all opportunity to cultivate the distinctive virtues of the Christian household.

In this connection, let us look at some facts recently published in the city of New-York. The writer, Rev. W. O. Van Meter, says in his report:

" The following astounding statistics are carefully selected from the Reports of the Police, Board of Health, Citizens' Association, and more than twelve years' personal experience."

He then gives the following description of a section of the city only a few rods from the stores and residences of those who count their wealth by hundreds of thousands and millions, many of them professing to be followers of Christ:

"First, we see old sheds, stable lofts, dilapidated buildings, too worthless to be repaired, lofts over warehouses and shops; cellars, too worthless for business purposes, and too unhealthy for horses or pigs, and therefore occupied by human beings at high rent.—Second, houses erected for tenant purposes. Take one near our Mission, as a fair specimen of the better class of '*model*' tenant houses. It contains one hundred and twenty-six families—is entered at the sides from alleys eight feet wide ; and by reason of another barrack of equal height, the rooms are so darkened, that on a cloudy day it is impossible to sew in them without artificial light. It has not one room that can be thoroughly ventilated.

" The vaults and sewers which are to carry off the filth of one hundred

and twenty-six families have grated openings in the alleys, and door-
ways in the cellars, through which the deadly miasma penetrates and
poisons the air of the house and courts.   The water-closets for the
whole vast establishment are a range of stalls, without doors, and
accessible not only from the building, but even from the street.   Com
fort here is out of the question ; common decency impossible. and the
horrid brutalities of the passenger-ship are day after day repeated, but
on a larger scale.

" In similar dwellings are living five hundred and ten thousand persons, (nearly one half of the inhabitants of the city,) chiefly from the laboring classes, of very moderate means, and also the uncounted thousands of those who do not know to-day what they shall have to live on
to-morrow.   This immense population is found chiefly in an area of less
than four square miles.   The vagrant and neglected children among
them would form a procession in double file eight miles long from the
Battery to Harlem.

" In the Fourth ward, the tenant-house population is crowded at the
rate of two hundred and ninety thousand inhabitants to the square
mile.   Such packing was probably never equaled in any other city.
Were the buildings occupied by these miserable creatures removed, and
the people placed by each other, there would be but one and two ninths
of a square yard for each, and this unparalleled packing is *increasing*.
Two hundred and twenty-four families in the ward live below the sidewalk, many of them *below high-water mark*.   Often in very high tide they
are driven from their cellars or lie in bed until the tide ebbs.   Not one half
of the houses have any drain or connection with the sewer.   The liquid
refuse is emptied on the sidewalk or into the street, giving forth sickening exhalations, and uniting its fetid streams with others from similar
sources.   There are more than four hundred families in this ward whose
homes can nly be reached by wading through a disgusting deposit of
filthy refuse.   'In one tenant-house one hundred and forty-six were
sick with small-pox,typhus fever, scarlatina, measles, marasmus, phthisis
pulmonalis, dysentery, and chronic diarrhea.   In another, containing
three hundred and forty-nine persons, *one in nineteen died* during the
year, and on the day of inspection, which was during the most healthy
season of the year, there were one hundred and fifteen persons sick!
In another (in the Sixth Ward, but near us,) are sixty-five families ;
seventy-seven persons were sick or diseased at the time of inspection,
and one in four *always* sick.   In fifteen of these families twenty-five
children were living, thirty-seven had died.'

" Here are found the lowest class of sailor boarding-houses, dance-
houses, and dens of infamy.   There are *less than two dwelling-houses*

for each rum-hole. Here are the poorest, vilest, most degraded, and
desperate representatives of all nations. In the homes of thousands
here, a ray of sunlight never shines, a flower never blooms, a bird song
is never heard, a breath of pure air never breathed."

A procession of vagrant and neglected children that in
double file would reach eight miles, living in such filth,
vice, and unhealthful pollution; all of them God's children,
all Christ's younger brethren, to save whom he humbled
himself, even to the shameful death of the cross!

Meantime, the city of New-York has millions of wealth
placed in the hands of men and women who profess to be
followers of Jesus Christ, and to have consecrated themselves, their time, and their wealth to his service. And they
daily are passing and repassing within a stone's throw of the
streets where all this misery and sin are accumulated!

So in all our large cities and towns all over the land are
found similar, if not so extensive, collections of vice and
misery. And even where there are not such extremes of
degradation, there are contrasts of condition that should
"give us pause." For example, in the vicinity of our large
towns and cities will be seen spacious mansions inhabited
by professed followers of Jesus Christ, each surrounded by
ornamented grounds. Not far from them will be seen
small tenement-houses, abounding with children, each house
having about as many square yards of land as the large
houses have square acres. In the small tenements, the boys
rise early and go forth with the father to work from eight to
ten hours, with little opportunity for amusement or for
reading or study. In the large houses, the boys sleep till
a late breakfast, then lounge about till school-time, then
spend three hours in school, stimulating brain and nerves.
Then home to a hearty dinner, and then again to school.

So with the girls: in the tenement-houses, they go to
kitchens and shops to work most of the day, with little
chance for mental culture or the refinements of taste. In
the large mansions, the daughters sleep late, do little or no

labor for the family, and spend their time in school, or in light reading, ornamental accomplishments, or amusement.

Thus one class are trained to feel that they are a privileged few for whom others are to work, while they do little or nothing to promote the improvement or enjoyment of their poorer neighbors.

Then, again, labor being confined chiefly to the unrefined and uncultivated, is disgraced and rendered unattractive to the young. One class is overworked, and the body deteriorates from excess. The other class overwork the brain and nerves, and the neglected muscles grow thin, flabby, and weak.

Notice also the style in which they accumulate the elegances of civilization without even an attempt to elevate their destitute neighbors to such culture and enjoyment. Their expensive pictures multiply on their frescoed walls, their elegant books increase in their closed bookcases, their fine pictures and prints remain shut in portfolios, to be only occasionally opened by a privileged few. Their handsome equipages are for the comfortable and prosperous— not for the feeble and poor who have none of their own. All their social amusements are exclusive, and their expensive entertainments are for those only who can return the same to them.

Our Divine Master thus teaches. "When thou makest a feast, call not thy kinsmen or thy rich neighbors, lest they also bid thee again, and a recompense be made thee. But when thou makest a feast, call the poor, for they can not recompense thee; for thou shalt be recompensed at the resurrection of the just." Again, our Lord, after performing the most servile office, taught thus: "If I, your Lord and Master, have washed your feet, ye ought to wash one another's feet."

In all these large towns and cities are women of wealth and leisure, who profess to be followers of Jesus Christ. Some of them, having property in their own right, live in large mansions, with equipage and servants demanding a large outlay. They travel abroad, and gather around themselves the elegant refinements of foreign lands. They give, perhaps, a tenth of their time and income (which is far less than was required of the Jews) for benevolent purposes, and then think and say that they have consecrated themselves and *all* they have to the service of Christ.

If there is any thing plainly taught in the New Testament it is, that the followers of Christ are to be different and distinct from the world around them; "a peculiar people," and subject to opposition and ill-will for their distinctive peculiarities.

Of these peculiarities demanded, *humility* and *meekness* are conspicuous: "Come and learn of me, for I am meek and lowly, and ye shall find rest." Now, the grand aim of the rich, worldly, and ambitious is to be at least equal, or else to rise higher than others, in wealth, honor, and position. This is the great struggle of humanity in all ages, especially in this country, and among all classes, to *rise higher*—to be as rich or richer than others—to be as well dressed—to be more learned, or in more honored positions than others. This was the very thing that made contention among the apostles, even in the company of their Lord, as they walked and "disputed who should be the greatest." "And Jesus sat down and called the twelve, and said unto them, If any man desire to be first, the same *shall be last and servant of all;*" and "he that is least among you shall be great."

At another time, the ambitious mother of two disciples came and asked that her sons might have the *highest* place in his kingdom, and the other disciples were "moved with indignation." Then the Lord taught them that the honor and glory of his kingdom was to be exactly the reverse of this world; and that whoever would be great must be a *minister*, and who would be chief must be a *servant;* even as the Son of Man came not to be ministered to, but to minister.

Again, he rebuked the love of high position and the desire of being counted wise as teachers of others: "Be not ye called Rabbi, neither be ye called Master; but he that is greatest among you shall be your servant, and whosoever exalteth himself shall be abased."

Then, as to the strife after wealth, into which all are now rushing so earnestly, the Lord teaches: "Lay not up for yourselves treasures on earth. Whosoever of you forsaketh not all that he hath can not be my disciple. Sell that ye have, and give alms; provide yourselves with bags that wax not old—a treasure in heaven that faileth not." To the rich young man, asking how to gain eternal life, the reply was, "Sell all thou hast, and give to the poor, and come and follow me." When the poor widow cast in *all her living*, she was approved. When the first Christians were "filled with the Holy Ghost," they sold all their possessions, to be distributed to those that had need, and were approved.

And nowhere do we find any direction or approval of laying up money for self or for children. A man is admonished to provide sustenance and education for his family, but never to lay up money for them; and the history of the children of the rich is a warning that, even in a temporal view, the chances are all against the results of such use of property. We are to spend all to *save the world*. For this we are to labor and sacrifice ease and wealth, and we are to train children to the same self-sacrificing labors. All that is spent for earthly pleasure ends here. Nothing goes into the future world as a good secured but training our own and other immortal minds. Thus only can we lay up treasures in heaven.

There is a crisis at hand in the history of individuals, of the church, and of our nation, which must inaugurate a new enterprise to save "the whole world." There must be something coming in the Christian churches more consistent, more comprehensive, more in keeping with the command of our ascending Lord—" Go ye (*all* my followers) into *all the world*, and preach the gospel to every creature; he that believeth shall be saved, and he that believeth not shall be damned!"

It is in hope and anticipation of such a "revival" of the true, self-denying spirit of Christ and of his earnest followers, that plans have been drawn for simple modes of living, in which both labor and economy may be practiced for benevolent ends, and yet without sacrificing the refinements of high civilization. One method is exhibited in the first chapters, adapted to country residence. In what follows will be presented a plan for a city home, having the same aim.

The chief points are to secure economy of labor and time by the *selection and close packing of conveniences,* and also economy of health by a proper mode of *warming and ventilation.* In this connection will be indicated opportunities and modes that thus may be attained for aiding to save the vicious, comfort the suffering, and instruct the ignorant.

Fig. 71 is the ground plan of a city tenement occupying two lots of twenty-two feet front, in which there can be no side windows; as is the case with most city houses. There are two front and two back-parlors, each twenty feet square, with a bedroom and kitchen appended to each : making four complete sets of living-rooms. A central hall runs from basement to roof, and is lighted by skylights. There is also a ventilating recess running from basement to roof with whitened walls, and windows opening into it secure both light and air to the bedrooms. On one end of this recess is a trash-flue closed with a door in the basement, and opening into each story, which must be kept closed to prevent an upward draught, causing dust and light articles to rise. At the other end is a dumb-waiter, running from cellar to roof, and opening into the hall of each story. Four chimneys are constructed near the centre of the house, one for each suite of rooms, to receive a smoke-pipe of cast-iron or terra cotta, as described previously, with a space around it for warm air; and this serves as the exhausting-shaft to carry off the vitiated air from parlors, kitchens, bedrooms, and water-closets. In each kitchen is a stove such as is described in Chapter IV., its pipe connecting with the central cast-iron or terra cotta pipe. The stove can be inclosed by sliding doors shutting off the heat in warm weather. These kitchen stoves, and a large stove in the basement to warm the central hall, would suffice for all the rooms, except in the coldest months, when a small terra cotta stove, made for this purpose, or even an ordinary iron stove, placed by one window in each of the parlors, would give the additional heat needed: while fresh air could be admitted from the windows behind the stove, and thus be partially warmed.

This exhibits the essential feature and peculiarity of Mr. Leeds's system of ventilation, before described. Fresh air, admitted at the bottom of a slightly raised window, is to enter below a window-seat which projects over the stove; the air being thus warmed before entering the room. The flue of the stove is seen (in the finished corner of Fig. 71, which is a model for the four other suites of rooms on each floor) running along the wall to the *front* chimney, which also receives the corresponding stove-flue from the nearest window in the adjoining parlor: the same arrangement being repeated at the back of the house. Thus, the two front and back chimneys are for the heating and ventilating parlor stoves; the four central chimneys for cooking, heating, and ventilation.

When possible, in a large building, steam generated in the basement heater will be found better than the parlor stove. In this case, the room will be heated by the coil of steam-pipe mentioned before; the slab covering it being the window-seat, or guard, under which the cool fresh air is conducted to be warmed before passing into the room.

Fig. 71.

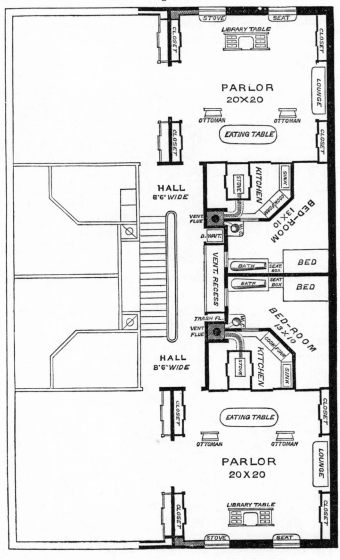

Fig. 72 shows one side of the parlor, giving a series of sliding-doors, behind which are hooks, shelves, and "shelf-boxes," as described earlier in the book.

Fig. 72.

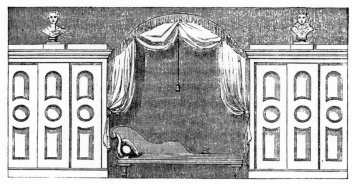

The recess occupied by the sofa stands between these two closets.   In case the room is used for sleeping, the double couch on page 30 might be substituted for the sofa, serving as a lounge by day, and two single beds by night.   The curtain hanging above can be so fastened by rings on a strong semi-circular wire as to be let down while dressing and undressing, as is done in some of our steamboats.

Fig. 73.

Pockets and hooks on the inside of the curtains may be made very useful.

Fig. 73 represents another side of the same room where are two large windows, each having a cushioned seat in its recess, (although one may be occupied by a stove, as described above.) A study-table with drawers on both the front and back sides furnishes large accommodations for many small articles.

Fig. 74 represents a third side of the same room, with sliding doors glazed from top to bottom to give light to the bedroom and kitchen.

Fig. 74.

The fourth side appears on the ground plan (Fig. 71.) The ottomans and a few chairs will complete the needful furniture.

By means of forms, shelves, and shelf-boxes, the kitchen could hold all stores and implements for cooking and setting tables, on the method shown page 34. The eating table is close to the kitchen and sink, so that few steps are required to bring and remove every article. Thus stove, sink, cooking materials, the table and its furniture, are all in close proximity, and yet, when the inmates are seated at table, the sliding-doors will shut out the kitchen, while the bad air and smells of cooking are carried off by the ventilating exhaust-shaft.

The bedroom has a bath-tub and water-closet. The tub need not be more than four feet long, and a half-cover raised by a hinge will, when down, hold wash-bowl and pitcher, when the tub is not in use. Around the bedroom high and wide shelves and shelf-boxes near the ceiling serve to store large articles; and narrower shelves with pegs under them for clothing, protected by a curtain, furnish other conveniences for storage. The trash-flue serves to send off rubbish with but few steps, and the dumb waiter brings up fuel, stores, etc. Each bedroom must be provided with a ventilating register at the top, connecting with the warm foul-air flue in the chimney.

For a family of four persons, one parlor, with its kitchen and bedroom, couches and side closets, would supply all needful accommodations. For a larger family, sliding-doors into the adjacent parlor, its appended kitchen being arrang ed for another bedroom, would accommodate a family of ten persons.

A front and a back entrance may be in the basement, which can be used for family stores, each family having one room. A general laundry with drying closets could be provided in the attic, and lighted from the roof.

Such a building, four stories high, would accommodate sixteen families of four members, or eight larger families, and provide light, warmth, ventilation, and more comforts and conveniences than are usually found in most city houses built for only one family. Here young married persons with frugal and benevolent tastes could commence house-keeping in a style of comfort and good taste rarely excelled in mansions of the rich. The spaces usually occupied by stairs, entries, closets, etc., would on this plan be thrown into fine large airy rooms, with every convenience close at hand.

In one of our large cities is to be found a Christian lady who inherited a handsome establishment with means to sup-port it in the style common to the rich. In the spirit of Christ she " sold all that she had, and gave to the poor," by establishing a *Home for Incurables*, and making her home with them, giving her time and wealth to promoting their temporal comfort and spiritual welfare. Was this doing *more* than her duty—*more* than the example and teachings of Christ require?

Suppose several ladies of similar views and character in one city, having only moderate wealth and leisure, unite to erect such a building as the one described, in a light and healthful part of the city of New-York, and then should take up their residence in it, and from the vast accumulation of misery and sin at hand on every side, should select the orphans, the aged, the sick, and the sinful, and spend time and money for their temporal and spiritual elevation; would they do *more* than the example and teachings of Christ enjoin? Or would their enjoyment, even in this life, be diminished by exchanging a routine chiefly of personal gratification for such self-denying ministries? It was "for *the joy* that was set before Him" through the everlasting ages that our Lord " endured the cross," and it is to the same supernal glories that he invites his followers, and by the same path he trod.

Here it probably will be said that all rich women can not do what is here suggested, owing to multitudinous claims, or to incapacity of mind or body for carrying out such an attempt. It will also be said that there are many other ways for practicing self-denial besides selling our homes and taking a humbler style of living. This is all true. But we are told that there are "greatest" and "least" in that kingdom of heaven where the chief happiness is in living to serve others, and not for self. Those who can not change their expensive style of living, and are obliged to spend most of their thoughts and wealth on self and those who are a part of self, will be among the least and lowest in happiness and honor, while those who take the low places on earth to raise others will be the happiest and most honored in the kingdom of heaven.

There are many residences in our large cities where women claiming to be Christ's followers live in almost solitary grandeur till the warm season, and then shut them up to spend their time at watering-places or country resorts. The property invested in such city establishments, and the income required to keep them up, would secure "Christian homes" to many suffering, neglected, homeless children of Christ, who are living in impure air, with all the debasing influences found in city tenement-houses. Meantime, the owners of this wealth are suffering in mind and body for want of some grand and noble object in life. If such could not personally live in such an establishment as is here described, by self-denying arrangements and combination with others they could provide and superintend one.

Our minds are created in the image of our Father in heaven, and capable of being made happy, as his is, by the outpouring of blessings on others. And when we are invited by our divine Lord to take his yoke and bear his burden, it is for our own highest happiness as well as for the good of others. And whoever truly obeys finds the yoke easy and the burden light, and that they bring rest to the soul. But those who shrink from the true good, to live a life of self-indulgent ease, will surely find that mere earthly enjoyments pall on the taste, that they perish in the using, that they never satisfy the cravings of a soul created for a higher sphere and nobler mission.

The Bible represents that there is an emergency—a great conflict in the world unseen—and that we on earth, who are Christ's people, are to take a part in this conflict and in the "fellowship of his sufferings," to redeem his children from the slavery of sin and eternal death; and there is the same call to labor and sacrifice now as there was when he commanded, "Go into all the world and preach the Gospel to *every* creature."

But is not the larger part of the church—especially those who have wealth—practically living on no higher princi-

ples than the pious Jews and virtuous heathen ? Are they
not living just as if there were no great emergency, no
terrible risks and danger to their fellow-men in the life to
come ? Are they not living just as if all men were safe
after they leave this world, and all we need to aim at is to
make ourselves and others virtuous and happy in this life,
without disturbing anxiety about the life to come? And
is the *training* of most Christian families diverse from that
of pious Jews, in reference to the dangers of our fellow-
men in the future state, and the consequent duty of labor
and sacrifice in order to extend the true religion all over
the earth ?

One mode of avoiding self-denial in style of living is by
the plea that, if all rich Christians gave up the expensive
establishments common to this class and adopted such
economies as are here suggested, it would tend to lower
civilization and take away support from those living by the
fine arts. But while the world is rushing on to such pro-
fuse expenditure, will not all these elegancies and refinements be abundantly supported, and is there as much danger in this direction as there is of avoiding the self-denying
example of Christ and his early followers ? They gave up
all they had, and "were scattered abroad, preaching the
word;" and was there any reason existing then for self-
denying labor that does not exist now ? There are more
idolaters and more sinful men now, in actual numbers,
than there were then; while teaching them the way of
eternal life does not now, as it did then, involve the "loss
of all things " and " deaths often."

Moreover, would not the fine arts, in the end, be better
supported by imparting culture and refined tastes to the
neglected ones? Teaching industry, thrift, and benevolence is far better than scattering alms, which often do
more harm than good; and would not enabling the masses
to enjoy the fine arts and purchase in a moderate style sub-
serve the interests of civilization as truly as for the rich

to accumulate treasures for themselves in the common exclusive style ?

Suppose some Protestant lady of culture and fortune should unite with an associate of congenial taste and benevolence to erect such a building as here described, and then devote her time and wealth to the elevation and salvation of the sinful and neglected, would she sacrifice as much as does a Lady of the Sacred Heart or a Sister of Charity, many of whom have been the daughters of princes and nobles ? They resign to their clergy and superiors not only the control of their wealth but their time, labor, and conscience. In doing this, the Roman Catholic lady is honored and admired as a saint, while taught that she is doing *more* than her duty, and is thus laying up a store of good works to repay for her own past deficiencies, and also to purchase grace and pardon for humbler sinners. If this is really believed, how soothing to a wounded conscience ! And what a strong appeal to generous and Christian feeling ! And the more terrific the pictures of purgatory and hell, the stronger the appeal to these humane and benevolent principles.

But how would it be with the Protestant woman practicing such self-denial ? For example, the lady of wealth and culture, who gave up her property and time to provide a home for incurables—would her pastor say she was doing *more* than her duty ? and if not, would he preach to other rich women who, in other ways, could humble themselves to raise up the poor, the ignorant, and the sinful, that they are doing *less* than their duty ?

Is it not sometimes the case, that both minister and people, by example, at least, seem to teach that, the more riches increase, the less demand there is for economy, labor, and self-denial for the benefit of the destitute and the sinful ?

Protestants are little aware of the strong attractions which are drawing pious and benevolent women toward the Roman Catholic Church. To the poor and neglected in humble life are offered a quiet home, with sympathy and honored work. To the refined and ambitious are offered the best society and high positions of honor and trust. To the sinful are offered pardon for past offenses and a fresh supply of "grace" for all acts of penitence or of benevolence To the anxiously conscientious, perplexed with contentions as to doctrines and duties, are offered an infallible pope and clergy to decide what is truth and duty, and what is the true interpretation of the Bible, while they are taught that the "faith" which saves the soul is implicit belief in the teachings of the Roman Catholic Church. All this enables many, even of the intelligent, to receive the other parts of a system that contradicts both common sense and the Bible.

Meantime, a highly educated priesthood, with no family ties to distract attention, are organizing and employing devoted, self-denying women, all over the land, to perform the distinctive work that Protestant women, if wisely trained and organized by their clergy, could carry out in thousands of scattered Christian homes and villages.

In the Protestant churches, women are educated only to be married; and when not married, there is no position provided which is deemed as honorable as that of a wife. But in the Roman Catholic Church, the unmarried woman who devotes herself to works of Christian benevolence is the most highly honored, and has a place of comfort and respectability provided which is suited to her education and capacity. Thus come great nunneries, with lady superiors to control conscience and labor and wealth.

But a time is coming when the family state is to be honored and ennobled by single women, qualified to sustain it by their own industries; women who will both support and train the children of their Lord and Master in the true style of Protestant independence, controlled by no superior but Jesus Christ. And in the Bible they will find the Father of the faithful, to both Jews and Gentiles, their great exemplar. For nearly one hundred years Abra ham had no child of his own ; but his househo.d, whom he trained to the number of three hundred and eighteen, were children of others. And he was the friend of God, chosen to be father of many nations, because he would " command his household to do justice and judgment and keep the way of the Lord."

The woman who from true love consents to resign her independence and be supported by another, while she bears children and trains them for heaven, has a noble mission ; but the woman who earns her own independence that she may train the neglected children of her Lord and Saviour has a still higher one. And a day is coming when Protestant women will be *trained* for this their highest ministry and profession as they never yet have been.

XXXVIII.

THE spirit of Christian missions to heathen lands and the organizations to carry them forward commenced, in most Protestant lands, within the last century. The writer can remember the time when an annual collection for domestic missions was all the call for such benefactions in a wealthy New-England parish; while such small pittances were customary that the sight of a dollar-bill in the collection, even from the richest men of the church-members, produced a sensation.

In the intervening period since that time, the usual mode of extending the Gospel among the heathen has been for a few of the most self-sacrificing men and women to give up country and home and all the comforts and benefits of a Christian community, and then commence the family state amid such vice and debasement that it was ruinous to children to be trained in its midst. And so the result has been, in multitudes of cases, that children were born only to be sent from parents to be trained by strangers, and the true "Christian family" could not be exhibited in heathen lands. And as a Christian neighborhood, in its strictest sense, consists of a collection of Christian families, such a community has been impossible in most cases among the heathen.

When our Lord ascended, his last command was, "Go ye into all the world, and preach the Gospel to *every* creature." For ages, most Christian people have supposed this command was limited to the apostles. In the present day, it has

Fig. 75.

been extended to include a few men and women who should practice the chief labor and self-sacrifice, while most of the church lived at ease, and supposed they were obeying this command, by giving a small portion of their abundance to support those who performed the chief labor and self-sacrifice.

But a time is coming when Christian churches will understand this command in a much more comprehensive sense; and the " Christian family" and " Christian neighborhood" will be the grand ministry of salvation. In order to assist in making this a practicable anticipation, some additional drawings are given in this chapter. The aim is to illustrate one mode of commencing a Christian neighborhood that is so economical and practical that two or three ladies, with very moderate means, could carry it out.

A small church, a school-house, and a comfortable family dwelling may all be united in one building, and for a very moderate sum, as will be illustrated by the following example.

At the head of the first chapter is a sketch which represents a perspective view of the kind of edifice indicated. On the opposite page (Fig. 75) is an enlarged and more exact view of the front elevation of the same, which is now building in one of the most Southern States, where tropical plants flourish. The three magnificent trees on the drawing heading the first chapter are live-oaks adorned with moss, rising over one hundred feet high and being some thirty or more feet in circumference. Nearly under their shadow is the building to be described.

Fig. 76 is the ground plan, which includes one large room twenty-five feet wide and thirty-five feet long, having a bow window at one end, and a kitchen at the other end. The bow-window has folding-doors, closed during the week, and within is the pulpit for Sunday service. The large room may be divided either by a movable screen or by sliding-doors with a large closet on either side. The doors make a more perfect separation; but the screen affords more room for storing family conveniences, and also secures more perfect ventilation for the whole large room by the exhaust-flue.

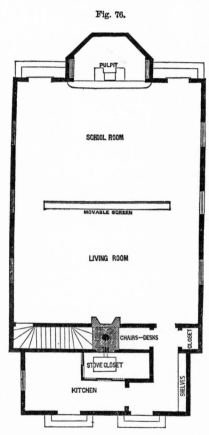

Fig. 76.

Thus, through the week, the school can be in one division, and the other still a sizable room, and the kitchen be used for teaching domestic economy and also for the eating-room. On Sunday, if there is a movable screen, it can be moved back to the fireplace; or otherwise, the sliding-doors may be opened, giving the whole space to the congregation. The chimney is finished off outside as a steeple. It incloses a cast-iron or terra cotta pipe, which receives the stove-pipe of the kitchen and also pipes connecting the two fire-places with the large pipe, and finds exit above the slats of the steeple at the projections. Thus the chimney is made an exhaust-shaft for carrying off vitiated air from all the rooms both above and below, which have openings into it made for the purpose.

Two good-sized chambers are over the large lower story, as shown in Fig. 77. Large closets are each side of these chambers, where are slatted openings to admit pure air ; and under these openings are registers placed to enable pure air to pass through the floor into the large room below. Thus a perfect mode of ventilation is secured for a large number.

On Sunday, the folding-doors of the bow-window are to be opened for the pulpit, the sliding-doors opened, or the screen moved back, and camp - chairs brought from the adjacent closet to seat a congregation of worshipers.

During the week, the family work is to be done in the kitchen, and the room adjacent be used for both a school and an eating-room. Here the aim will be, during the week, to collect the children of the neighborhood, to be taught not only to read, write, and cipher, but to perform in the best manner all the practical duties of the family state. Two ladies residing in this building can make an illustration of the highest kind of "Christian family," by adopting two orphans, keeping in training one or two servants to send out for the benefit of other families, and also providing for an invalid or aged member of Christ's neglected ones. Here also they could employ boys and girls in various kinds of floriculture, horticulture, bee-raising, and other out-door employments, by which an income could be received and young men and women trained to industry and thrift, so as to earn an independent livelihood.

The above attempt has been made where, in a circuit of fifty miles, with a thriving population, not a single church is open for Sunday worship, and not a school to be found except what is provided by faithful Roman Catholic nuns, who, indeed, are found engaged in similar labors all over our country. The cost of such a building, where lumber is $50 a hundred and labor $3 a day, would not much exceed $1200.

Such destitute settlements abound all over the West and South, while, along the Pacific coast, China and Japan are sending their pagan millions to share our favored soil, climate, and government.

Meantime, throughout our older States are multitudes of benevolent, well-educated, Christian women in unhealthful factories, offices, and shops; and many, also, living in refined leisure, who yet are pining for an opportunity to aid in carrying the Gospel to the destitute. Nothing is needed but *funds* that are in the keeping of thousands of Christ's professed disciples, and *organizations* for this end, which are at the command of the Protestant clergy.

Let such a truly "Christian family" be instituted in any destitute settlement, and soon its gardens and fields would cause "the desert to blossom as the rose," and around would soon gather a "Christian neighborhood." The school-house would no longer hold the multiplying worshipers. A central church would soon appear, with its appended accommodations for literary and social gatherings and its appliances for safe and healthful amusements.

The cheering example would soon spread, and ere long colonies from these prosperous and Christian communities would go forth to shine as "lights of the world" in all the now darkened nations. Thus the "Christian family" and "Christian neighborhood" would become the grand ministry, as they were designed to be, in training our whole race for heaven.

This final chapter should not close without a few encouraging words to those who, in view of the many difficult duties urged in these pages, sorrowfully review their past mistakes and deficiencies. None can do this more sincerely than the writer. How many things have been done unwisely even with good motives! How many have been left undone that the light of present knowledge would have secured!

In this painful review, the good old Bible comes as the abundant comforter. The Epistle to the Romans was written especially to meet such regrets and fears. It teaches that all men are sinners, in many cases from ignorance of what is right, and in many from stress of temptation, so that neither Greek nor Jew can boast of his own righteousness. For it is not "by works of righteousness" that we are to be considered and treated as righteous persons, but through a "faith that *works by love;*" that *faith* or *belief* which is not a mere intellectual conviction, but a *controlling purpose* or spiritual principle which *habitually controls* the feelings and conduct. And so long as there is this constant aim and purpose to obey Christ in all things, mistakes in judgment as to what is right and wrong are pitied, "even as a father pitieth his children," when from ignorance they run into harm. And even the most guilty transgressors are freely forgiven when truly repentant and faithfully striving to forsake the error of their ways.

Moreover, this tender and pitiful Saviour is the Almighty One who rules both this and the invisible world, and who "from every evil still educes good." This life is but the infant period of our race, and much that we call evil, in his wise and powerful ruling may be for the highest good of all concerned.

The Blessed Word also cheers us with pictures of a dawn
ing day to which we are approaching, when a voice shall
be heard under the whole heavens, saying, " Alleluia"—
" the kingdoms of this world are become the kingdoms of
our Lord and of his Christ, and he shall reign forever
and ever." And " a great voice out of heaven" will pro-
claim, " Behold, the tabernacle of God is with men, and
he shall dwell with them, and they shall be his people.
And God himself shall be with them, and be their God.
And God shall wipe away all tears from their eyes; and
there shall be no more death, neither sorrow, nor crying;
neither shall there be any more pain; for the former things
are passed away."

The author still can hear the echoes of early life, when
her father's voice read to her listening mother in exulting
tones the poet's version of this millennial consummation,
which was the inspiring vision of his long life-labors—a
consummation to which all their children were consecrated,
and which some of them may possibly live to behold.

> " O scenes surpassing fable, and yet true !
> Scenes of accomplished bliss ! which who can see,
> Though but in distant prospect, and not feel
> His soul refreshed with foretaste of the joy !

> " Rivers of gladness water all the earth,
> And clothe all climes with beauty ; the reproach
> Of barrenness is past.   The fruitful field
> Laughs with abundance ; and the land once lean,
> Or fertile only in its own disgrace,
> Exults to see its thistly curse repealed.

> " Error has no place :
> That creeping pestilence is driven away ;
> The breath of Heaven has chased it.   In the heart
> No passion touches a discordant string,
> But all is harmony and love.   Disease
> Is not : the pure and uncontaminate blood
> Holds its due course, nor fears the frost of age.

One song employs all nations; and all cry,
'Worthy the Lamb, for he was slain for us!'
The dwellers in the vales and on the rocks
Shout to each other; and the mountain-tops
From distant mountains catch the flying joy;
Till, nation after nation taught the strain,
Earth rolls the rapturous hosanna round.

" Behold the measure of the promise filled!
See Salem built, the labor of a God!
Bright as a sun the sacred city shines;
All kingdoms and all princes of the earth
Flock to that light; the glory of all lands
Flows into her; unbounded is her joy,
And endless her increase. Thy rams are there,
Nebaioth, and the flocks of Kedar there;
The looms of Ormus and the mines of Ind,
And Saba's spicy groves pay tribute there.

" Praise is in all her gates: upon her walls,
And in her streets, and in her spacious courts,
Is heard salvation. Eastern Java there
Kneels with the native of the farthest west;
And Æthiopia spreads abroad the hand,
And worships. Her report has traveled forth
Into all lands. From every clime they come
To see thy beauty, and to share thy joy,
O Zion! an assembly such as earth
Saw never, such as Heaven stoops down to see!"*

* Cowper's *Task.*

AN APPEAL

TO AMERICAN WOMEN.

SENIOR AUTHOR OF THIS VOLUME.

———•••———

MY HONORED COUNTRYWOMEN:

IT is now over forty years that I have been seeking to elevate the character and condition of our sex, relying, as to earthly aid, chiefly on your counsel and coöperation. I am sorrowful at results that have followed these and similar efforts, and ask your sympathy and aid.

Let me commence with a brief outline of the past. I commenced as an educator in the city of Hartford, Ct., when only the primary branches and one or two imperfect accomplishments were the ordinary school education, and was among the first pioneers in seeking to introduce some of the higher branches. The staid, conservative citizens queried of what use to women were Latin, Geometry, and Algebra, and wondered at a request for six recitation rooms and a study-hall for a school of nearly a hundred, who had as yet only one room. The appeal was then made to benevolent, intelligent women, and by their influence all that was sought was liberally bestowed.

But the course of study then attempted was scarcely half of what is now pursued in most of our colleges for young women, while there has been added a round and extent of accomplishments then unknown. Yet this moderate amount so stimulated brain and nerves, and so excited competition, that it became needful to enforce a rule, requiring a daily report, that only two hours a day had been devoted to study out of school hours. Even this did not avail to save from injured health both the teacher who projected these improvements and many of her pupils. This example and that of similar institutions spread all over the nation, with constantly increasing demand for more studies, and decreasing value and respect for domestic pursuits and duties.

Ten years of such intellectual excitement exhausted the nervous fountain, and my profession as a school-teacher was ended.

The next attempt was to introduce Domestic Economy as *a science to be studied* in schools for girls. For a while it seemed to succeed; but ere long was crowded out by Political Economy and many other economies, except those most needed to prepare a woman for her difficult and sacred duties.

In the progress of years, it came to pass that the older States teemed with educated women, qualified for no other department of woman's profession but that of a school-teacher, while the newer States abounded in children without schools.

I again appealed to my countrywomen for help, addressing them through the press and also by the assistance of a brother (in assemblies in many chief cities) in order to raise funds to support an agent. The funds were bestowed, and thus the services of Governor Slade were secured, and, mainly by these agencies, nearly one thousand teachers were provided with schools, chiefly in the West.

Meantime, the intellectual taxation in both private and public schools, the want of proper ventilation in both families and schools, the want of domestic exercise which is so valuable to the feminine constitution, the pernicious modes of dress, and the prevailing neglect of the laws of health, resulted in the general decay of health among women. At the same time, the overworking of the brain and nerves, and the "cramming" system of study, resulted in a deficiency of mental development which is very marked. It is now a subject of general observation that young women, at this day, are decidedly inferior in mental power to those of an earlier period, notwithstanding their increased advantages. For the mind, crowded with undigested matter, is debilitated the same as is the body by over-feeding.

Recent scientific investigations give the philosophy of these results. For example, Professor Houghton, of Trinity College, Dublin, gives as one item of protracted experiments in animal chemistry, that two hours of severe study abstracts as much vital strength as is demanded by a whole day of manual labor. The reports of the Massachusetts Board of Education add other facts that, in this connection, should be deeply pondered. For example, in one public school of eighty-five pupils only fifty-four had refreshing sleep; fifty-nine had headaches or constant weariness, and only fifteen were perfectly well. In this school it was found, and similar facts are common in all our public and high schools, that, in addition to six school-hours, thirty-one studied three hours and a half; thirty-five, four hours; and twelve, from four to seven hours. And yet the most learned medical men maintain that the time devoted to brain labor, daily, should not exceed six hours for healthy men, and three hours for growing children.

Alarmed at the dangerous tendencies of female education, I made another appeal to my sex, which resulted in the organization of the American Woman's Education Association, the object being to establish *endowed* professional schools, in connection with literary institutions, in which woman's profession should be honored and taught as are the professions of men, and where woman should be trained for some self-supporting business. From this effort several institutions of a high literary character have come into existence at the West, but the organization and endowment of the professional schools is yet incomplete from many combining impediments, the chief being a want of appreciation of woman's profession, and of the *science* and *training* which its high and sacred duties require. But the reports of the Association will show that never before were such superior intellectual advantages secured to a new country by so economical an outlay.

Let us now look at the dangers which are impending. And first, in regard to the welfare of the family state, the decay of the female constitution and health has involved such terrific sufferings, in addition to former cares and pains of maternity, that multitudes of both sexes so dread the risks of marriage as either to avoid it, or meet them by methods *always* injurious and often criminal. Not only so, multitudes of intelligent and conscientious persons, in private and by the press, unaware of the penalties of violating nature, openly impugn the inspired declaration, "Children are a heritage of the Lord."

Add to these, other influences that are robbing home of its safe and peaceful enjoyments. Of such, the condition of of domestic service is not the least. We abound in domestic helpers from foreign shores, but they are to a large extent thriftless, ignorant, and unscrupulous, while as thriftless and inexperienced housekeepers, from boarding-school life, have no ability to train or to control. Hence come antagonism and ceaseless "worries" in the parlor, nursery, and kitchen, while the husband is wearied with endless complaints of breakage, waste of fuel and food, neglect, dishonesty, and deception, and home is any thing but a harbor of comfort and peace. Thus come clubs to draw men from comfortless homes, and, next, clubs for the deserted women.

Meantime, domestic service—disgraced, on one side, by the stigma of our late slavery, and, on the other, by the influx into our kitchens of the uncleanly and ignorant—is shunned by the self-respecting and well educated, many of whom prefer either a miserable pittance or the career of vice to this fancied degradation. Thus comes the overcrowding in all avenues for woman's work, and the consequent lowering of wages to starvation prices for long protracted toils.

From this come diseases to the operatives, bequeathed often to their offspring. Factory girls must stand ten hours or more, and consequently in a few years debility and disease ensue, so that they never can rear healthy children, while the foreigners who supplant them in kitchen labor are almost the only strong and healthy women to rear large families. The sewing-machine, hailed as a blessing, has proved a curse to the poor; for it takes away profits from needlewomen, while employers testify that women who use this machine for steady work, in two years or less become hopelessly diseased and can rear no children. Thus it is that the controlling political majority of New-England is passing from the educated to the children of ignorant foreigners.

Add to these disastrous influences, the teachings of "free love;" the baneful influence of spiritualism, so called; the fascinations of the *demi-monde;* the poverty of thousands of women who, but for desperate temptations, would be pure—all these malign influences are sapping the foundations of the family state.

Meantime, many intelligent and benevolent persons imagine that the grand remedy for the heavy evils that oppress our sex is to introduce woman to political power and office, to make her a party in primary political meetings, in political caucuses, and in the scramble and fight for political offices ; thus bringing into this dangerous *melée* the distinctive tempting power of her sex. Who can look at this new danger without dismay ?

But it is neither generous nor wise to join in the calumny and ridicule that are directed toward philanthropic and conscientious laborers for the good of our sex, because we fear their methods are not safe. It would be far wiser to show by example a better way.

Let us suppose that our friends have gained the ballot and the powers of office : are there any real beneficent measures for our sex, which they would enforce by law and penalties, that fathers, brothers, and husbands would not grant to a united petition of our sex, or even to a majority of the wise and good ? Would these not confer what the wives, mothers, and sisters deemed best for themselves and the children they are to train, very much sooner than they would give power and office to our sex to enforce these advantages by law ? Would it not be a wiser thing to *ask* for what we need, before trying so circuitous and dangerous a method ? God has given to man the physical power, so that all that woman may gain, either by petitions or by ballot, will be the gift of love or of duty ; and the ballot never will be accorded till benevolent and conscientious men are the majority—a millennial point far beyond our present ken.

The American Woman's Education Association aims at a plan which its members believe, in its full development, will more effectually remedy the " wrongs of woman " than any other urged on public notice. Its general aim has been stated ; its details will appear at another time and place. Its managers include ladies of high character and position from six religious denominations, and also some of the most reliable business men of New-York. Any person wno is desirous to aid by contributions to this object can learn more of the details of the plan by addressing me at No. 69 West Thirty-eighth Street. But it is needful to state that letters from those who seek aid or employment of any sort can not be answered at present, nor for some months to come.

Every woman who wishes to aid in this effort for the safety and elevation of our sex can do so by promoting the sale of this work, and its introduction as a text-book into schools. An edition for the use of schools will be in readiness next fall, which will contain school exercises, and questions that will promote thought and discussion in class-rooms, in reference to various topics included in the science of Domestic Economy. And it is hoped that a previous large sale of the present volume will prepare the public mind to favor the introduction of this branch of study into both public and private schools. Ladies who write for the press, and all those who have influence with editors, can aid by directing general attention to this effort.

All the profits of the authors derived from the edition of this volume prepared for schools, will be paid into the Treasury of the A. W. E. Association, and the amount will be stated in the annual reports.

The complementary volume of this work will follow in a few months, and will consist, to a great extent, of *receipts and directions* in all branches of domestic economy, especially in the department of *healthful and economical cooking.* The most valuable receipts in my *Domestic Receipt-Book,* heretofore published by the Harpers, will be retained, and a very large number added of new ones, which are healthful, economical, and in many cases ornamental. One special aim will be to point out modes of *economizing labor* in preparing food.

Many directions will be given that will save from purchasing poisonous milk, meats, beers, and other medicated drinks. Directions for detecting poisonous ingredients in articles for preserving the hair, and in cosmetics for the complexion, which now are ruining health, eye-sight, and comfort all over the nation, will also be given.

Particular attention will be given to modes of preparing and preserving clothing, at once economical, healthful, and in good taste.

A large portion of the book will be devoted to instruction, in the various ways in which women may *earn an independent livelihood*, especially in employments that can be pursued in sunlight and the open air.

Should any who read this work wish for more minute directions in regard to ventilation of a house already built, or one projected, they can obtain his aid by addressing Lewis Leeds, No. 110 Broadway, New-York City. His associate, Mr. Herman Kreitler, who prepared the architectural plans in this work relating to Mr. Leeds's system, can be addressed at the same place.

CATHARINE E. BEECHER.

NEW-YORK, June 1, 1869.

APPENDIX.

A GLOSSARY

[Many words not contained in this GLOSSARY will be found explained in the body of the work, in the places where they first occur.]

Action brought by the Commonwealth : A prosecution conducted in the name of the public, or by the authority of the State.

Albumen : Nourishing matter stored up between the undeveloped germ and its protecting wrappings in the seed of many plants. It is the flowery part of grain, the oily part of poppy seeds, the fleshy part in cocoa-nuts, etc.

Alcoholic : Made of or containing alcohol, an inflammable liquid which is the basis of ardent spirits.

Alkali, (plural, *alkalies :)* A chemical substance, which has the property of combining with and neutralizing the properties of acids, producing salts by the combination. Alkalies change most of the vegetable blues and purples to green, red to purple, and yellow to brown. *Caustic alkali:* An alkali deprived of all impurities, being thereby rendered more caustic and violent in its operation. This term is usually applied to pure potash. *Fixed alkali :* An alkali that emits no characteristic smell, and can not be volatilized or evaporated without great difficulty. Potash and soda are called the fixed alkalies. Soda is also called a *fossil* or *mineral alkali,* and potash the *vegetable alkali. Volatile alkali :* An elastic, transparent, colorless, and consequently an invisible gas, known by the name of ammonia or ammoniacal gas. The odor of spirits of hartshorn is caused by this gas.

Anglo-American : English-American, relating to Americans descended from English ancestors.

Anther : That part of the stamen of a flower which contains the pollen or farina, a sort of mealy powder or dust, which is necessary to the production of the flower.

Anthracite : One of the most valuable kinds of mineral coal, containing no bitumen. It is very abundant in the United States.

Aperient : Opening.

Archæology : A discourse or treatise on antiquities.

Arrow-root : A white powder, obtained from the fecula or starch of several species of tuberous plants in the East and West-Indies, Bermuda, and other places. That from Bermuda is most highly esteemed. It is used as an article for the table, in the form of puddings, and also as a highly nutritive, easily digested, and agreeable food for invalids. It derives its name from having been originally used by the Indians as a remedy for the poison of their arrows, by mashing and applying it to the wound.

Articulating process : The protuberance or projecting part of a bone, by which it is so joined to another bone as to enable the two to move upon each other

Asceticism : The state of an ascetic or hermit, who flies from society and lives in retirement, or who practices a greater degree of mortification and austerity than others do, or who inflicts extraordinary severities upon himself.

Astral lamp : A lamp, the principle of which was invented by Benjamin Thompson, (a native of Massachusetts, and afterward Count Rumford,) in which the oil is contained in a large horizontal ring, having at the centre a burner which communicates with the ring by tubes. The ring is placed a little below the level of the flame, and from its large surface affords a supply of oil for many hours.

Astute : Shrewd.

Auricles : (From a Latin word, signifying the ear,) the name given to two appendages of the heart, from their fancied resemblance to the ear.

Baglivi, (George :) An eminent physician, who was born at Ragusa, in 1668, and was educated at Naples and Paris. Pope Clement XIV., on the ground of his great merit, appointed him, while a very young man, Professor of Anatomy and Surgery in the College of Sapienza, at Rome. He wrote several works, and did much to promote the cause of medical science. He died A.D. 1706.

Bass, or bass-wood: A large forest-tree of America, sometimes called the lime-tree. The wood is white and soft, and the bark is sometimes used for bandages.

Bell, Sir Charles : A celebrated surgeon, who was born in Edinburgh, in the year 1778. He commenced his career in London, in 1806, as a lecturer on Anatomy and Surgery. In 1830, he received the honors of knighthood, and in 1836 was appointed Professor of Surgery in the College of Edinburgh. He died near Worcester, in England, April 29th, 1842. His writings are very numerous and have been much celebrated. Among the most important of these, to general readers, are his *Illustrations of Paley's Natural Theology,* and his treatise on *The Hand, its Mechanism and Vital Endowments, as evincing Design.*

Bergamot : A fruit which was originally produced by ingrafting a branch of a citron or lemon-tree upon the stock of a peculiar kind of pear, called the bergamot pear.

Biased Cut diagonally from one corner to another of a square or rectangular piece of cloth. *Bias pieces:* Triangular pieces cut as above mentioned.

Bituminous: Containing *bitumen,* which is an inflammable mineral substance, resembling tar or pitch in its properties and uses. Among different bituminous substances, the names *naphtha* and *petroleum* have been given to those which are fluid, *maltha* to that which has the consistence of pitch, and *asphaltum* to that which is solid.

Blight: A disease in plants by which they are blasted or prevented from producing fruit.

Blonde lace: Lace made of silk.

Blood heat: The temperature which the blood is always found to maintain, or ninety-eight degrees of Fahrenheit's thermometer.

Blue vitriol: Sulphate of copper.

Blunts: Needles of a short and thick shape, distinguished from *Sharps,* which are long and slender.

Bocking: A kind of thin carpeting or coarse baize.

Botany: (From a Greek word signifying an herb,) a knowledge of plants; the science which treats of plants.

Brazil wood: The central part or heart of a large tree which grows in Brazil, called the *Cæsalpinia echinata.* It produces very lively and beautiful red tints, but they are not permanent.

Bronze: A metallic composition, consisting of copper and tin.

Brûlure: A French term, denoting a burning or scalding; a blasting of plants.

Brussels, (carpet:) A kind of carpeting, so called from the city of Brussels, in Europe. Its basis is composed of a warp and woof of strong linen threads, with the warp of which are intermixed about five times the quantity of woolen threads of different colors.

Bulb: A root with a round body, like the onion, turnip, or hyacinth.

Bulbous: Having a bulb.

Byron, (George Gordon,) Lord: A celebrated poet, who was born in London, January 22d, 1788, and died in Missolonghi, in Greece, April 18th, 1824.

Calisthenics: From two Greek words—καλος, *kalos,* beauty, and σθενος, *sthenos,* strength, being the union of both.

Camwood: A dyewood, procured from a leguminous (or pod-bearing) tree, growing on the western coast of Africa, and called *Baphianitida.*

Canker-worm: A worm which is very destructive to trees and plants. It springs from an egg deposited by a miller that issues from the ground, and in some years destroys the leaves and fruit of apple and other trees.

Capillary: A minute, hair-like tube.

Carbon: A simple, inflammable body, forming the principal part of wood and coal, and the whole of the diamond.

Carbonic acid: A compound gas, consisting of one part of carbon and two parts of oxygen ; fatal to animal life. It has lately been obtained in a solid form.

Carbonic Oxide: A compound, consisting of one part of carbon and one part of oxygen ; it is fatal to animal life. Burns with a pale, blue flame, forming carbonic acid.

Carmine: A crimson color, the most beautiful of all the reds. It is prepared from a decoction of the powdered cochineal insect, to which alum and other substances are added.

Caseine: One of the great forms of blood-making matter; the cheesy or curd-part of milk ; found in both animal and vegetable kingdoms.

Caster: A small vial or vessel for the table, in which to put vinegar, mustard, pepper, etc. Also, a small wheel on a swivel-joint, on which furniture may be turned in any direction.

Chancellor of the Exchequer: In England, the highest judge of the law ; the principal financial minister of a government, and the one who manages its revenue.

Chateau: A castle, a mansion.

Chemistry: The science which treats of the elementary constituents of bodies.

Chinese belle, deformities of : In China, it is the fashion to compress the feet of female infants, to prevent their growth ; in consequence of which, the feet of all the females of China are distorted, and so small that the individuals can not walk with ease.

Chloride: A compound of chlorine and some other substance. *Chlorine* is a simple substance, formerly called oxymuriatic acid. In its pure state, it is a gas of green color, (hence its name, from a Greek word signifying green.) Like oxygen, it supports the combustion of some inflammable substances. *Chloride of lime* is a compound of chlorine and lime.

Cholera infantum: A bowel-complaint to which infants are subject.

Chyle: A white juice formed from the chyme, and consisting of the finer and more nutritious parts of the food. It is afterward converted into blood.

Chyme: The result of the first process which food undergoes in the stomach previously to its being converted into chyle.

Cicuta: The common American hemlock, an annual plant of four or five feet in height, and found commonly along walls and fences and about old ruins and buildings. It is a virulent poison as well as one of the most important and valuable medicinal vegetables. It is a very different plant from the hemlock-tree or *Pinus Canadensis.*

Clarke, (*Sir Charles Mansfield,*) *Dr.:* A distinguished English physician and surgeon, who was born in London, May 28th, 1782. He was appointed physician to Queen Adelaide, wife of King William IV., in

1830, and in 1831 he was created a baronet. He was the author of several valuable medical works.

Cobalt : A brittle metal, of a reddish-gray color and weak metallic lustre, used in coloring glass. It is not easily melted nor oxidized in the air.

Cochineal : A color procured from the cochineal insect, (or *Coccus cacti,*) which feeds upon the leaves of several species of the plant called cactus, and which is supposed to derive its coloring matter from its food. Its natural color is crimson ; but, by the addition of a preparation of potash, it yields a rich scarlet dye.

Cologne-water : A fragrant perfume, which derives its name from having been originally made in the city of Cologne, which is situated on the river Rhine, in Germany. The best kind is still procured from that city.

Comparative anatomy : The science which has for its object a comparison of the anatomy, structure, and functions of the various organs of animals, plants, etc., with those of the human body.

Confection : A sweetmeat ; a preparation of fruit with sugar ; also a preparation of medicine with honey, syrup, or similar saccharine substance, for the purpose of disguising the unpleasant taste of the medicine.

Cooper, Sir Astley Paston : A celebrated English surgeon, who was born at Brooke, in Norfolk county, England, August 23d, 1768, and commenced the practice of surgery in London, in 1792. He was appointed surgeon to King George IV., in 1827, was created a baronet in 1821, and died February 12th, 1841. He was the author of many valuable works.

Copal : A hard, shining, transparent resin, of a light citron color, brought originally from Spanish-America, and now almost wholly from the East-Indies. It is principally employed in the preparation of *copal varnish.*

Copper, Sulphate of : See *Sulphate of copper.*

Copperas : (Sulphate of iron or green vitriol,) a bright green mineral substance, formed by the decomposition of a peculiar ore of iron called pyrites, which is a sulphuret of iron. It is first in the form of a greenish-white powder or crust, which is dissolved in water, and beautiful green crystals of copperas are obtained by evaporation. It is principally used in dyeing and in making black ink. Its solution, mixed with a decoction of oak bark, produces a black color.

Coronary : Relating to a crown or garland. In anatomy, it is applied to arteries which encompass the heart, in the manner, as it is fancied, of a garland.

Corrosive sublimate : A poisonous substance, composed of chlorine and quicksilver.

Cosmetics : Preparations which some people foolishly think will preserve and beautify the skin.

Cream of tartar : See *Tartar.*

Curculio : A weevil or worm, which affects the fruit of the plum-tree and sometimes that of the apple-tree, causing the unripe fruit to fall to the ground.

Cuvier, Baron : The most eminent naturalist of the present age ; was born A. D. 1769, and died A.D. 1832. He was Professor of Natura History in the College of France, and held various important posts under the French government at different times. His works on Nat ural History are of the greatest value.

Cynosure : The constellation of the Lesser Bear, containing the star near the North Pole, by which sailors steer. It is used, in a figurative sense, as synonymous with *pole-star* or *guide,* or any thing to which the eyes of many are directed.

De Tocqueville : See *Tocqueville.*

Diamond cement : A cement sold in the shops, and used for mending broken glass and similar articles.

Drab : A thick woolen cloth, of a light brown or dun color. The name is sometimes used for the color itself.

Dredging-box : A box with holes in the top, used to sift or scatter flour on meat when roasting.

Drill : (In husbandry,) to sow grain in rows, drills, or channels ; the row of grain so sowed.

Duchess of Orleans : See *Orleans.*

The *East,* and the *Eastern States :* Those of the United States situated in the north-east part of the country, including Maine, New-Hampshire, Massachusetts, Rhode Island, Connecticut, and Vermont.

Elevation, (of a house :) A plan representing the upright view of a house, as a ground-plan shows its appearance on the ground.

Euclid : A celebrated mathematician, who was born in Alexandria, in Egypt, about two hundred and eighty years before Christ. He distinguished himself by his writings on music and geometry. The most celebrated of his works is his *Elements of Geometry,* which is in use at the present day. He established a school at Alexandria, which became so famous that, from his time to the conquest of Alexandria by the Saracens, (A.D. 646,) no mathematician was found who had not studied at Alexandria. Ptolemy, King of Egypt, was one of his pupils ; and it was to a question of this king, whether there was not a shorter way of coming at geometry than by the study of his *Elements,* that Euclid made the celebrated answer, " There is no royal path to geometry."

Equator or *equinoctial line :* An imaginary line passing round the earth, from east to west and directly under the sun, which always shines nearly perpendicularly down upon all countries situated near the equator.

Evolve : To throw off, to discharge.

Exchequer : A court in England in which the Chancellor presides, and where the revenues of and the debts due to the king, are recovered. This court was originally established by King William, (called "the Conqueror,") who died A.D. 1087; and its name is derived from a checkered cloth (French *echiquier,* a chess-board, checker-work) on the table.

Excretion : Something discharged from the body, a separation of animal matters.

Excrementitious : Consisting of matter excreted from the body ; containing excrements.

Fahrenheit, (Gabriel Daniel :) A celebrated natural philosopher, who was born at Dantzig, A.D. 1686. He made great improvements in the thermometer, and his name is sometimes used for that instrument

Farinaceous : Mealy, tasting like meal.

Fell : To turn down on the wrong side the raw edges of a seam after it has been stitched, run, or sewed, and then to hem or sew it to the cloth.

Festivals of the Jews, the three great annual : These were, the Feast of the Passover, that of Pentecost, and that of Tabernacles ; on occasion of which, all the males of the nation were required to visit the temple at Jerusalem, in whatever part of the country they might reside. See Exodus 23 : 14, 17; 34 : 23 ; Leviticus 23 : 4 ; Deuteronomy 16 : 16. The Passover was kept in commemoration of the deliverance of the Israelites from Egypt, and was so named because the night before their departure the destroying angel, who slew all the first-born of the Egyptians, *passed over* the houses of the Israelites without entering them. See Exodus 12. The Feast of Pentecost was so called from a word meaning *the fiftieth,* because it was celebrated on the fiftieth day after the Passover, and was instituted in commemoration of the giving of the Law from Mount Sinai on the fiftieth day from the departure out of Egypt. It is also called the Feast of Weeks, because it was kept seven weeks after the Passover. Seè Exodus 34 : 22 ; Leviticus 23 : 15–21 ; Deuteronomy 16 : 9, 10. The Feast of Tabernacles, or Feast of Tents, was so called because it was celebrated under tents or tabernacles of green boughs, and was designed to commemorate their dwelling in tents during their passage through the wilderness. At this feast they also returned thanks to God for the fruits of the earth after they had been gathered. See Exodus 23 : 16 ; Leviticus 23 : 34–44 ; Deuteronomy 16 : 13 ; and also St. John 7 : 2.

Fire-blight : A disease in the pear and some other fruit-trees, in which they appear burnt as if by fire. It is supposed by some to be caused by an insect, others suppose it to be caused by an over-abundance of sap.

Fluting-iron : An instrument for making flutes, channels, furrows, or hollows in ruffles, etc.

Foundation muslin : A nice kind of buckram, stiff and white, used for the foundation or basis of bonnets, etc.

Free States : A phrase formerly used to distinguish those States in which slavery was not allowed, as distinguished from Slave States, in which slavery did exist.

French chalk : A variety of the mineral called talc, unctuous to the touch, of greenish color, glossy, soft, and easily scratched, and leaving a silvery line when drawn on paper. It is used for marking on cloth, and extracting grease-spots.

Fuller's earth : A species of clay remarkable for its property of absorbing oil, for which reason it is valuable for extracting grease from cloth, etc. It is used by fullers in scouring and cleansing cloth, whence its name.

Fustic : The wood of a tree which grows in the West-Indies called *Morus tinctoria.* It affords a durable but not very brilliant yellow dye, and is also used in producing some greens and drab colors.

Gastric : (From the Greek γαστήρ, *gaster,* the belly,) belonging or relating to the belly, or stomach. *Gastric juice :* The fluid which dissolves the food in the stomach. It is limpid, like water, of a saltish taste, and without odor.

Geology : The science which treats of the formation of the earth.

Gluten : The glue-like, sticky, tenacious substance which gives adhesiveness to dough. The principle of gelly, (now generally written *jelly.*)

Gore : A triangular piece of cloth. *Goring :* Cut in a triangular shape.

Gothic : A peculiar and strongly-marked style of architecture, sometimes called the ecclesiastical style, because it is most frequently used in cathedrals, churches, abbeys, and other religious edifices. Its principle seems to have originated in the imitation of groves and bowers, under which the ancients performed their sacred rites ; its clustered pillars and pointed arches very well representing the trunks of trees and their interlocking branches.

Gourmand or *Gormand :* A glutton, a greedy eater. In agriculture, it is applied to twigs which take up the sap but bear only leaves.

Green vitriol : See *Copperas.*

Griddle : An iron pan, of a peculiarly broad and shallow construction, used for baking cakes.

Ground-plan : The map or plan of the floor of any building, in which the various apartments, windows, doors, fire-places, and other things are represented, like the rivers, towns, mountains, roads, etc., on a map.

Gum Arabic : A vegetable juice which exudes through the bark of the *Acacia, Mimosa nilotica,* and some other similar trees growing in Arabia, Egypt, Senegal, and Central Africa. It is the purest of all gums.

Hardpan : The hard, unbroken layer of earth below the mould or cultivated soil.

Hartshorn, (spirits of:) A volatile alkali, originally prepared from the horns of the stag or hart, but now procured from various other substances.   It is known by the name of ammonia or spirits of ammonia.

Hemlock : see *Cicuta.*

Horticulturist : One skilled in horticulture, or the art of cultivating gardens : horticulture being to the garden what agriculture is to the farm, the application of labor and science to a limited spot, for convenience, for profit, or for ornament—though implying a higher state of cultivation than is common in agriculture.   It includes the cultivation of culinary vegetables and of fruits, and forcing or exotic gardening as far as respects useful products.

Hydrogen : A very light, inflammable gas, of which water is in part composed.   It is used to inflate balloons.

Hypochondriasis : Melancholy, dejection, a disorder of the imagination, in which the person supposes he is afflicted with various diseases.

Hysteria or *hysterics :* A spasmodic, convulsive affection of the nerves, to which women are subject.   It is somewhat similar to hypochondriasis in men.

Ingrain : A kind of carpeting, in which the threads are dyed in the grain or raw material before manufacture.

Ipecac : (An abbreviation of *ipecacuanha,*) an Indian medicinal plant, acting as an emetic.

Isinglass : A fine kind of gelatin or glue, prepared from the swimming-bladders of fishes, used as a cement, and also as an ingredient in food and medicine.   The name is sometimes applied to a transparent mineral substance called mica.

Jams : A side-piece or post.

Kamtschadales : Inhabitants of *Kamtschatka,* a large peninsula situated on the north-eastern coast of Asia, having the North Pacific Ocean on the east.   It is remarkable for its extreme cold, which is heightened by a range of very lofty mountains extending the whole length of the peninsula, several of which are volcanic.   It is very deficient in vegetable productions, but produces a great variety of animals, from which the richest and most valuable furs are procured.   The inhabitants are in general below the common height, but have broad shoulders and large heads.   It is under the dominion of Russia.

Kerosene : Refined *Petroleum,* which see.

Kink : A knotty twist in a thread or rope.

Lambrequin : Originally a kind of pendent scarf or covering attached to a helmet to protect and adorn it.   Hence, a pendent ornamental curtain over a window.

Lapland : A country at the extreme north part of Europe, where it is very cold.   It contains lofty mountains, some of which are covered with perpetual snow and ice.

Latin : The language of the Latins or inhabitants of Latium, the principal country of ancient Italy. After the building of Rome, that city became the capital of the whole country.

Leguminous : Pod-bearing.

Lent : A fast of the Christian Church, (lasting forty days, from Ash-Wednesday to Easter,) in commemoration of our Saviour's miraculous fast of forty days and forty nights in the wilderness. The word Lent means spring, this fast always occurring at that season of the year.

Levite : One of the tribe of Levi, the son of Jacob, which tribe was set apart from the others to minister in the services of the Tabernacle, and the Temple at Jerusalem. The priests were taken from this tribe. See Numbers 1 : 47-53.

Ley : Water which has percolated through ashes, earth, or other substances, dissolving and imbibing a part of their contents. It is generally spelled *lye.*

Linnæus, (Charles :) A native of Sweden, and the most celebrated naturalist of his age. He was born May 13th, 1707, and died January 11th, 1778. His life was devoted to the study of natural history. The science of botany, in particular, is greatly indebted to his labors. His *Amœnitates Academicæ* (Academical Recreations) is a collection of the dissertations of his pupils, edited by himself, a work rich in matters relating to the history and habits of plants. He was the first who arranged Natural History into a regular system, which has been generally called by his name. His proper name was Linné.

Lobe : A division, a distinct part ; generally applied to the two divisions of the lungs.

Loire : The largest river of France, being about five hundred and fifty miles in length. It rises in the mountains of Cevennes, and empties into the Atlantic Ocean about forty miles below the city of Nantes. It divides France into two almost equal parts.

London Medical Society : A distinguished association, formed in 1773. It has published some valuable volumes of its transactions. It has a library of about 40,000 volumes, which is kept in a house presented to the Society, in 1788, by the celebrated Dr. Lettsom, who was one of its first members.

Louis XIV. : A celebrated King of France and Navarre, who was born September 5th, 1638, and died September 1st, 1715. His mother having before had no children, though she had been married twenty-two years, his birth was considered as a particular favor from heaven, and he was called the " Gift of God." He is sometimes styled " Louis the Great," and his reign is celebrated as an era of magnificence and learning, and is notorious as a period of licentiousness. He left behind him monuments of unprecedented splendor and expense, consisting of palaces, gardens, and other like works.

Lumbar : (From the Latin *lumbus,* the loin,) relating or pertaining to the loins.

Lunacy, writ of : A judicial proceeding to ascertain whether a person be a lunatic.

Mademoiselle : The French word for miss, a young girl.

Magnesia : A light and white alkaline earth, which enters into the composition of many rocks, communicating to them a greasy or soapy feeling and a striped texture, with sometimes a greenish color.

Malaria : (Italian, *mal'aria, bad air,*) a noxious vapor or exhalation ; a state of the atmosphere or soil, or both, which, in certain regions and in warm weather, produces fever, sometimes of great violence.

Mammon : Riches, the Syrian god of riches. See Luke 16 : 11–13 ; St. Matthew 6 : 24.

Mexico : A country situated south-west of the United States and extending to the Pacific Ocean.

Miasms : Such particles or atoms as are supposed to arise from distempered, putrefying, or poisonous bodies.

Michilimackinac or *Mackinac :* (Now frequently corrupted into *Mackinaw,* which is the usual pronunciation of the name,) a military post in the State of Michigan, situated upon an island, about nine miles in circuit, in the strait which connects Lakes Michigan and Huron. It is much resorted to by Indians and fur-traders. The highest summit of the island is about three hundred feet above the lakes and commands an extensive view of them.

Midsummer : With us, the time when the sun arrives at his greatest distance from the equator, or about the twenty-first of June, called also the summer solstice, (from the Latin *sol, the sun,* and *sto, to stop or stand still,*) because when the sun reaches this point he seems to stand still for some time, and then appears to retrace his steps. The days are then longer than at any other time.

Migrate : To remove from one place to another ; to change residence.

Mildew : A disease of plants ; a mould, spot, or stain in paper, cloths, etc., caused by moisture.

Militate : To oppose, to operate against.

Millinet : A coarse kind of stiff muslin, formerly used for the foundation or basis of bonnets, etc.

Mineralogy : A science which treats of the inorganic natural substances found upon or in the earth, such as earths, salts, metals, etc., and which are called by the general name of minerals.

Minutiæ : The smallest particulars.

Monasticism : Monastic life ; religiously recluse life in a monastery or house of religious retirement.

Montagu, Lady Mary Wortley : One of the most celebrated among the female literary characters of England. She was daughter of Evelyn, Duke of Kingston, and was born about 1690, at Thoresby, in England

She displayed uncommon abilities at a very early age, and was edu cated by the best masters in the English, Latin, Greek, and French languages. She accompanied her husband (Edward Wortley Montagu) on an embassy to Constantinople, and her correspondence with her friends was published and much admired. She introduced the practice of inoculation for the small-pox into England, which proved of great benefit to millions. She died at the age of seventy-two, A.D. 1762.

Moral Philosophy : The science which treats of the motives and rules of human actions, and of the ends to 'which they ought to be directed.

Moreen : A kind of woolen stuff used for curtains, covers of cushions, bed hangings, etc.

Mortise : A cavity cut into a piece of timber to receive the end of another piece called the *Tenon.*

Mucous : Having the nature of *mucus,* a glutinous, sticky, thready, transparent fluid, of a salt savor, produced by different membranes of the body, and serving to protect the membranes and other internal parts against the action of the air, food, etc. The fluid of the mouth and nose is mucus.

Mucous membrane : That membrane which lines the mouth, nose, intestines, and other open cavities of the body.

Muriatic acid : An acid composed of chlorine and hydrogen, called also, hydrochloric acid and spirit of salt.

Mush-stick : A stick to use in stirring *mush,* which is corn-meal boiled in water.

Nankeen or *Nankin :* A light cotton cloth, originally brought from Nankin, in China, whence its name.

Nash, (*Richard :*) Commonly called *Beau Nash,* or King of Bath, a celebrated leader of the fashions in England. He was born at Swansea, in South-Wales, October 8th, 1674, and died in the city of Bath, (England,) February 3d, 1761.

Natural History : The history of animals, plants, and minerals.

Natural Philosophy : The science which treats of the powers of nature, the properties of natural bodies, and their action one upon another. It is sometimes called *physics.*

New-milch cow : A cow which has recently calved.

Newton, (*Sir Isaac :*) An eminent English philosopher and mathematician, who was born on Christmas day, 1642, and died March 20th, 1727. He was much distinguished for his very important discoveries in Optics and other branches of Natural Philosophy. See the first volume of *Pursuit of Knowledge under Difficulties,* forming the fourteenth volume of *The School Library,* larger series.

Night-Soil : Human excrement, so-called because usually removed from privies by night.

Non-bearers : Plants which bear no flowers nor fruit.

Northern States : Those of the United States situated in the northern and eastern part of the country.

Ordinary : See *Physician in ordinary.*

Oil of Vitriol : (sulphuric acid, or vitriolic acid,) an acid composed of oxygen and sulphur.

Oino-mania : A disease of the brain produced by excessive use of alcoholic stimulants ; derived from two Greek words, *oinos*, wine, and *mania*, madness. The same disease sometimes arises from overuse of tobacco and other stimulants of the nerves.

Orleans, (Elizabeth Charlotte de Bavière,) Duchess of : Second wife of Philippe, the brother of Louis XIV., was born at Heidelberg, May 26th, 1652, and died at the palace of St. Cloud, in Paris, December 8th, 1722. She was author of several works ; among which were *Memoirs and Anecdotes of the Court of Louis XIV.*

Ottoman : A kind of hassock or thick mat for kneeling upon ; so-called from being used by the Ottomans or Turks.

Oxalic acid : a vegetable acid, which exists in sorrel.

Oxide : A compound of a substance with oxygen, though not enough oxygen to produce an acid ; for example, oxide of iron, or rust of metals.

Oxidize : To combine oxygen with a body without producing acidity.

Oxygen : The vital element of air, a simple and very important substance which exists in the atmosphere and supports the breathing of animals and the burning of combustibles. It was called oxygen from two Greek words, signifying to produce acid, from its power of giving acidity to many compounds in which it predominates.

Oxygenized : Combined with oxygen.

Pancreas : A gland within the abdomen just below and behind the stomach, and providing a fluid to assist digestion. In animals, it is called the sweet-bread. *Pancreatic :* Belonging to the pancreas.

Parterre : A level division of ground, a flower-garden.

Pearlash: The common name for impure carbonate of potash, which in a purer form is called *Saleratus.*

Peristaltic : Contracting in successive circles ; worm-like.

Petroleum : Rock oil, an inflammable, bituminous liquid exuding from rocks or from the earth in the neighborhood of the carboniferous or coal-bearing formation.

Phosphorus : One of the elementary substances.

Physician in Ordinary to the Queen : The physician who attends the Queen in ordinary cases of illness.

Pitt, William : A celebrated English statesman, son of the Earl of Chatham. He was born May 28th, 1759, and at the age of twenty-three was made Chancellor of the Exchequer, and soon afterward Prime Minister. He died January 23d, 1806.

Political Economy : The science which treats of the general causes affecting the production, distribution, and consumption of articles of exchangeable value, in reference to their effects upon national wealth and welfare.

Pollen : The fertilizing dust of flowers, produced by the stamens and falling upon the pistils inorder to render a flower capable of producing fruit or seed.

Potter's clay : The clay used in making articles of pottery.

Prairie : A French word, signifying *meadow.* In the United States, it is applied to the remarkable natural meadows or plains which are found in the Western States. In some of these vast and nearly level plains, the traveler may wander for days without meeting with wood or water, and see no object rising above the plane of the horizon. They are very fertile.

Prime Minister : The person appointed by the ruler of a nation to have the chief direction and management of the public affairs.

Process : A protuberance or projecting part of a bone.

Pulmonary : Belonging to or affecting the lungs. *Pulmonary artery :* An artery which passes through the lungs, being divided into several branches, which form a beautiful network over the air-vessels, and finally empty themselves into the left auricle of the heart.

Puritans : A sect which professed to follow the pure word of God in opposition to traditions, human constitutions, and other authorities. In the reign of Queen Elizabeth, part of the Protestants were desirous of introducing a simpler, and, as they considered it, a *purer* form of church government and worship than that established by law, from which circumstance they were called *Puritans.* In process of time, this party increased in numbers and openly broke off from the church, laying aside the English liturgy, and adopting a service-book published at Geneva by the disciples of Calvin. They were treated with great rigor by the government, and many of them left the kingdom and settled in Holland. Finding themselves not so eligibly situated in that country as they had expected to be, a portion of them embarked for America, and were the first settlers of New-England.

Quixotic : Absurd, romantic, ridiculous ; from *Don Quixote,* the hero of a celebrated fictitious work written by Cervantes, a distinguished Spanish writer, and intended to reform the tastes and opinions of his countrymen.

Reeking : Smoking, emitting vapor.

Residuum : The remainder or part which remains.

Routine : A round or course of engagements, business, pleasure, etc.

To *Run* a seam : To lay the two edges of a seam together and pass the threaded needle out and in, with small stitches, a few threads below the edge and on a line with it.

To *Run* a stocking : To pass a thread of yarn, with a needle, straight along each row of the stocking, as far as is desired, taking up one loop and missing two or three, until the row is completed, so as to double the thickness at the part which is run.

Sabbatical year : Every seventh year among the Jews, which was a year of rest for the land, when it was to be left without culture. In this year, all debts were to be remitted, and slaves set at liberty. See Ex odus 21 : 2 ; 23 : 10 ; Leviticus 25 : 2, 3, etc. ; Deuteronomy 15 : 12 ; and other similar passages.

Saleratus : See *Pearlash.*

Sal ammoniac : A salt, called also muriate of ammonia, which derives its name from a district in Libya, Egypt, where there was a temple of Jupiter Ammon, and where this salt was found.

Scotch Highlanders : Inhabitants of the Highlands of Scotland

Selvedge : The edge of cloth, a border. Improperly written *selvage.*

Service-book : A book prescribing the order of public services in a church or congregation.

Sharps : See *Blunts.*

Shorts : The coarser part of wheat bran.

Shrubbery : A plantation of shrubs.

Siberia : A large country in the extreme northern part of Asia, having the Frozen Ocean on the north, and the Pacific Ocean on the east, and forming a part of the Russian empire. The northern part is extremely cold, almost uncultivated, and contains but few inhabitants. It furnishes fine skins, and some of the most valuable furs in the world. It also contains rich mines of iron and copper, and several kinds of precious stones.

Sinclair, Sir John : Of whom it was said, " There is no greater name in the annals of agriculture than his," was born in Caithness, Scotland, May 10th, 1754, and became a member of the British Parliament in 1780. He was strongly opposed to the measures of the British government toward America, which produced the American Revolution. He was author of many valuable publications on various subjects. He died December 21st, 1835.

Sirloin : The loin of beef. The appellation " sir " is the title of a knight or baronet, and has been added to the word " loin," when applied to beef, because a king of England, in a freak of good humor, once conferred the honor of knighthood upon a loin of beef.

Slack : To loosen, to relax, to deprive of cohesion.

Soda : An alkali, usually obtained from the ashes of marine plants.

To *Spade :* To throw out earth with a spade.

Spermaceti : An oily substance found in the head of a species of whale called the spermaceti whale.

Spindling : Shooting into a long, small stalk.

Spinous process : A process or bony protuberance, resembling a spine or thorn, whence it derives its name.

Spool : A piece of cane or reed or a hollow cylinder of wood, with a ridge at each end, used to wind yarn and thread upon.

Stamen, (plural, *stamens* and *stamina :*) In *weaving,* the warp, the thread, any thing made of threads. In *botany,* that part of a flower on which the artificial classification is founded, consisting of the filament or stalk, and the anther, which contains the pollen or fructifying powder.

Stigma, (plural *stigmas* and *stigmata :*) The summit or top of the pistil of a flower.

Style or *Stile :* The part of the pistil between the germ and the stigma.

Sub-carbonate : An imperfect carbonate.

Sulphates, Sulphats, Sulphites : Salts formed by the combination of some base with sulphuric acid, as *Sulphate of copper,* (blue vitriol or blue stone,) a combination of sulphuric acid with copper. *Sulphate of iron :* Copperas or green vitriol. *Sulphate of lime :* Gypsum or plaster of Paris. *Sulphate of magnesia :* Epsom salts. *Sulphate of potash :* A chemical salt, composed of sulphuric acid and potash. *Sulphate of soda :* Glauber's salts. *Sulphate of zinc :* White vitriol.

Sulphuret : A combination of an alkaline earth or metal with sulphur, as *Sulphuret of iron,* a combination of iron and sulphur.'

Sulphuric acid : Oil of vitriol, vitriolic acid.

Suture : A sewing ; the uniting of parts by stitching ; the seam or joint which unites the flat bones of the skull, which are notched like the teeth of a saw, and the notches, being united together, present the appearance of a seam.

Tartar : A substance, deposited on the inside of wine casks, consisting chiefly of tartaric acid and potass. *Cream of tartar :* The crude tartar separated from all its impurities by being dissolved in water and then crystallized, when it becomes a perfectly white powder.

Tartaric acid : A vegetable acid which exists in the grape.

Technology : A description of the arts, considered generally in their theory and practice as connected with moral, political, and physical science.

Three-ply or *triple ingrain :* A kind of carpeting, in which the threads are woven in such a manner as to make three thicknesses of the cloth.

Tic douloureux : A painful affection of the nerves, mostly those of the face.

Tocqueville, (*Alexis de :*) A celebrated statesman and writer of France, and author of volumes on the political condition, and the penitentiaries of the United States, and other works.

Trachea : The windpipe, so named (from a Greek word signifying *rough*) from the roughness or inequalities of the cartilages of which it is formed.

Truckle-bed or *Trundle-bed :* A bed that runs on wheels.

Tuber : A solid, fleshy, roundish root, like the potato. *Tuberous :* Thick and fleshy ; composed of or having tubers.

Tucks, (improperly *Tacks*) : Folds in garments.

Turmeric : The root of a plant called *Curcuma longa*, a native of the East-Indies, used as a yellow dye.

Twaddle : Idle, foolish talk or conversation.

Unbolted : Unsifted.

Unslacked : Not loosened or deprived of cohesion. Lime, when it has been slacked, crumbles to powder from being deprived of cohesion.

Valance : The drapery or fringe hanging round the cover of a bed, couch, or other similar article.

Vascular : Relating to or full of vessels.

Venetian : A kind of carpeting, composed of a striped woolen warp on a thick woof of linen thread,

Verisimilitude : Probability, resemblance to truth.

Verbatim : Word for word.

Vice versa : The side being changed, or the question reversed, or the terms being exchanged.

Viscera, (plural of *viscus :*) Organs contained in the great cavities of the body, the skull, the abdomen, and the chest. Generally applied to the contents of the abdomen.

Vitriol : A compound mineral salt of a very caustic taste. *Blue Vitriol,* sulphate of copper. *Green Vitriol,* see *Copperas. Oil of Vitriol,* sulphuric acid. *White Vitriol,* sulphate of zinc.

Waffle-iron : An iron utensil for the purpose of baking waffles, which are thin and soft cakes indented by the iron in which they are baked.

Wash-leather : A soft, pliable leather dressed with oil, and in such a way that it may be washed without shrinking. It is used for various articles of dress, as undershirts, drawers, etc., and also for rubbing silver, and other articles having a high polish. The article known in commerce as chamois or shammy leather is also called wash-leather.

Welting-cord : A cord sewed into the welt or border of a garment.

The *West* or *Western World.* When used in Europe, or in distinction from the Eastern World, it means America. When used in this country, the West refers to the Western States of the Union. *Western Wilds :* The wild, thinly-settled lands of the Western States.

White vitriol : see *Zinc.*

Wilton carpet : A kind of carpets made in England, and so called from the place which is the chief seat of their manufacture. They are woolen velvets with variegated colors.

Writ of lunacy. See *Lunacy.*

Xantippe : The wife of Socrates, noted for her violent temper and scolding propensities. The name is frequently applied to a shrew, or peevish turbulent, scolding woman.

Zinc : A bluish-white metal, which is used as a constituent of brass and some other alloys. *Sulphate of Zinc* or *White vitriol :* A combination of zinc with sulphuric acid.

INDEX:

ANALYTICAL AND ALPHABETICAL.

———•♦•———

AMERICAN EDUCATION:
ITS MEN, IDEAS, AND INSTITUTIONS
An Arno Press/New York Times Collection

Series I

Adams, Francis. **The Free School System of the United States.** 1875.

Alcott, William A. **Confessions of a School Master.** 1839.

American Unitarian Association. **From Servitude to Service.** 1905.

Bagley, William C. **Determinism in Education.** 1925.

Barnard, Henry, editor. **Memoirs of Teachers, Educators, and Promoters and Benefactors of Education, Literature, and Science.** 1861.

Bell, Sadie. **The Church, the State, and Education in Virginia.** 1930.

Belting, Paul Everett. **The Development of the Free Public High School in Illinois to 1860.** 1919.

Berkson, Isaac B. **Theories of Americanization: A Critical Study.** 1920.

Blauch, Lloyd E. **Federal Cooperation in Agricultural Extension Work, Vocational Education, and Vocational Rehabilitation.** 1935.

Bloomfield, Meyer. **Vocational Guidance of Youth.** 1911.

Brewer, Clifton Hartwell. **A History of Religious Education in the Episcopal Church to 1835.** 1924.

Brown, Elmer Ellsworth. **The Making of Our Middle Schools.** 1902.

Brumbaugh, M. G. **Life and Works of Christopher Dock.** 1908.

Burns, Reverend J. A. **The Catholic School System in the United States.** 1908.

Burns, Reverend J. A. **The Growth and Development of the Catholic School System in the United States.** 1912.

Burton, Warren. **The District School as It Was.** 1850.

Butler, Nicholas Murray, editor. **Education in the United States.** 1900.

Butler, Vera M. **Education as Revealed By New England Newspapers prior to 1850.** 1935.

Campbell, Thomas Monroe. **The Movable School Goes to the Negro Farmer.** 1936.

Carter, James G. **Essays upon Popular Education.** 1826.

Carter, James G. **Letters to the Hon. William Prescott, LL.D., on the Free Schools of New England.** 1924.

Channing, William Ellery. **Self-Culture.** 1842.

Coe, George A. **A Social Theory of Religious Education.** 1917.

Committee on Secondary School Studies. **Report of the Committee on Secondary School Studies, Appointed at the Meeting of the National Education Association.** 1893.

Counts, George S. **Dare the School Build a New Social Order?** 1932.

Counts, George S. **The Selective Character of American Secondary Education.** 1922.

Counts, George S. **The Social Composition of Boards of Education.** 1927.

Culver, Raymond B. **Horace Mann and Religion in the Massachusetts Public Schools.** 1929.

Curoe, Philip R. V. **Educational Attitudes and Policies of Organized Labor in the United States.** 1926.

Dabney, Charles William. **Universal Education in the South.** 1936.

Dearborn, Ned Harland. **The Oswego Movement in American Education.** 1925.

De Lima, Agnes. **Our Enemy the Child.** 1926.

Dewey, John. **The Educational Situation.** 1902.

Dexter, Franklin B., editor. **Documentary History of Yale University.** 1916.

Eliot, Charles William. **Educational Reform: Essays and Addresses.** 1898.

Ensign, Forest Chester. **Compulsory School Attendance and Child Labor.** 1921.

Fitzpatrick, Edward Augustus. **The Educational Views and Influence of De Witt Clinton.** 1911.

Fleming, Sanford. **Children & Puritanism.** 1933.

Flexner, Abraham. **The American College: A Criticism.** 1908.

Foerster, Norman. **The Future of the Liberal College.** 1938.

Gilman, Daniel Coit. **University Problems in the United States.** 1898.

Hall, Samuel R. **Lectures on School-Keeping.** 1829.

Hall, Stanley G. **Adolescence: Its Psychology and Its Relations to Physiology, Anthropology, Sociology, Sex, Crime, Religion, and Education.** 1905. 2 vols.

Hansen, Allen Oscar. **Early Educational Leadership in the Ohio Valley.** 1923.

Harris, William T. **Psychologic Foundations of Education.** 1899.

Harris, William T. **Report of the Committee of Fifteen on the Elementary School.** 1895.

Harveson, Mae Elizabeth. **Catharine Esther Beecher: Pioneer Educator.** 1932.

Jackson, George Leroy. **The Development of School Support in Colonial Massachusetts.** 1909.

Kandel, I. L., editor. **Twenty-five Years of American Education.** 1924.

Kemp, William Webb. **The Support of Schools in Colonial New York by the Society for the Propagation of the Gospel in Foreign Parts.** 1913.

Kilpatrick, William Heard. **The Dutch Schools of New Netherland and Colonial New York.** 1912.

Kilpatrick, William Heard. **The Educational Frontier.** 1933.

Knight, Edgar Wallace. **The Influence of Reconstruction on Education in the South.** 1913.

Le Duc, Thomas. **Piety and Intellect at Amherst College, 1865-1912.** 1946.

Maclean, John. **History of the College of New Jersey from Its Origin in 1746 to the Commencement of 1854.** 1877.

Maddox, William Arthur. **The Free School Idea in Virginia before the Civil War.** 1918.

Mann, Horace. **Lectures on Education.** 1855.

McCadden, Joseph J. **Education in Pennsylvania, 1801-1835, and Its Debt to Roberts Vaux.** 1855.

McCallum, James Dow. **Eleazar Wheelock.** 1939.

McCuskey, Dorothy. **Bronson Alcott, Teacher.** 1940.

Meiklejohn, Alexander. **The Liberal College.** 1920.

Miller, Edward Alanson. **The History of Educational Legislation in Ohio from 1803 to 1850.** 1918.

Miller, George Frederick. **The Academy System of the State of New York.** 1922.

Monroe, Will S. **History of the Pestalozzian Movement in the United States.** 1907.

Mosely Education Commission. **Reports of the Mosely Education Commission to the United States of America October-December, 1903.** 1904.

Mowry, William A. **Recollections of a New England Educator.** 1908.

Mulhern, James. **A History of Secondary Education in Pennsylvania.** 1933.

National Herbart Society. **National Herbart Society Yearbooks 1-5, 1895-1899.** 1895-1899.

Nearing, Scott. **The New Education: A Review of Progressive Educational Movements of the Day.** 1915.

Neef, Joseph. **Sketches of a Plan and Method of Education.** 1808.

Nock, Albert Jay. **The Theory of Education in the United States.** 1932.

Norton, A. O., editor. **The First State Normal School in America: The Journals of Cyrus Pierce and Mary Swift.** 1926.

Oviatt, Edwin. **The Beginnings of Yale, 1701-1726.** 1916.

Packard, Frederic Adolphus. **The Daily Public School in the United States.** 1866.

Page, David P. **Theory and Practice of Teaching.** 1848.

Parker, Francis W. **Talks on Pedagogics: An Outline of the Theory of Concentration.** 1894.

Peabody, Elizabeth Palmer. **Record of a School.** 1835.

Porter, Noah. **The American Colleges and the American Public.** 1870.

Reigart, John Franklin. **The Lancasterian System of Instruction in the Schools of New York City.** 1916.

Reilly, Daniel F. **The School Controversy (1891-1893).** 1943.

Rice, Dr. J. M. **The Public-School System of the United States.** 1893.

Rice, Dr. J. M. **Scientific Management in Education.** 1912.

Ross, Early D. **Democracy's College: The Land-Grant Movement in the Formative Stage.** 1942.

Rugg, Harold, et al. **Curriculum-Making: Past and Present.** 1926.

Rugg, Harold, et al. **The Foundations of Curriculum-Making.** 1926.

Rugg, Harold and Shumaker, Ann. **The Child-Centered School.** 1928.

Seybolt, Robert Francis. **Apprenticeship and Apprenticeship Education in Colonial New England and New York.** 1917.

Seybolt, Robert Francis. **The Private Schools of Colonial Boston.** 1935.

Seybolt, Robert Francis. **The Public Schools of Colonial Boston.** 1935.

Sheldon, Henry D. **Student Life and Customs.** 1901.

Sherrill, Lewis Joseph. **Presbyterian Parochial Schools, 1846-1870.** 1932 .

Siljestrom, P. A. **Educational Institutions of the United States.** 1853.

Small, Walter Herbert. **Early New England Schools.** 1914.

Soltes, Mordecai. **The Yiddish Press: An Americanizing Agency.** 1925.

Stewart, George, Jr. **A History of Religious Education in Connecticut to the Middle of the Nineteenth Century.** 1924.

Storr, Richard J. **The Beginnings of Graduate Education in America.** 1953.

Stout, John Elbert. **The Development of High-School Curricula in the North Central States from 1860 to 1918.** 1921.
Suzzallo, Henry. **The Rise of Local School Supervision in Massachusetts.** 1906.
Swett, John. **Public Education in California.** 1911.
Tappan, Henry P. **University Education.** 1851.
Taylor, Howard Cromwell. **The Educational Significance of the Early Federal Land Ordinances.** 1921.
Taylor, J. Orville. **The District School.** 1834.
Tewksbury, Donald G. **The Founding of American Colleges and Universities before the Civil War.** 1932.
Thorndike, Edward L. **Educational Psychology.** 1913-1914.
True, Alfred Charles. **A History of Agricultural Education in the United States, 1785-1925.** 1929.
True, Alfred Charles. **A History of Agricultural Extension Work in the United States, 1785-1923.** 1928.
Updegraff, Harlan. **The Origin of the Moving School in Massachusetts.** 1908.
Wayland, Francis. **Thoughts on the Present Collegiate System in the United States.** 1842.
Weber, Samuel Edwin. **The Charity School Movement in Colonial Pennsylvania.** 1905.
Wells, Guy Fred. **Parish Education in Colonial Virginia.** 1923.
Wickersham, J. P. **The History of Education in Pennsylvania.** 1885.
Woodward, Calvin M. **The Manual Training School.** 1887.
Woody, Thomas. **Early Quaker Education in Pennsylvania.** 1920.
Woody, Thomas. **Quaker Education in the Colony and State of New Jersey.** 1923.
Wroth, Lawrence C. **An American Bookshelf, 1755.** 1934.

Series II

Adams, Evelyn C. **American Indian Education.** 1946.
Bailey, Joseph Cannon. **Seaman A. Knapp: Schoolmaster of American Agriculture.** 1945.
Beecher, Catharine and Harriet Beecher Stowe. **The American Woman's Home.** 1869.
Benezet, Louis T. **General Education in the Progressive College.** 1943.
Boas, Louise Schutz. **Woman's Education Begins.** 1935.
Bobbitt, Franklin. **The Curriculum.** 1918.
Bode, Boyd H. **Progressive Education at the Crossroads.** 1938.
Bourne, William Oland. **History of the Public School Society of the City of New York.** 1870.
Bronson, Walter C. **The History of Brown University, 1764-1914.** 1914.
Burstall, Sara A. **The Education of Girls in the United States.** 1894.
Butts, R. Freeman. **The College Charts Its Course.** 1939.
Caldwell, Otis W. and Stuart A. Courtis. **Then & Now in Education, 1845-1923.** 1923.
Calverton, V. F. & Samuel D. Schmalhausen, editors. **The New Generation: The Intimate Problems of Modern Parents and Children.** 1930.
Charters, W. W. **Curriculum Construction.** 1923.
Childs, John L. **Education and Morals.** 1950.

Childs, John L. **Education and the Philosophy of Experimentalism.** 1931.

Clapp, Elsie Ripley. **Community Schools in Action.** 1939.

Counts, George S. **The American Road to Culture: A Social Interpretation of Education in the United States.** 1930.

Counts, George S. **School and Society in Chicago.** 1928.

Finegan, Thomas E. **Free Schools.** 1921.

Fletcher, Robert Samuel. **A History of Oberlin College.** 1943.

Grattan, C. Hartley. **In Quest of Knowledge: A Historical Perspective on Adult Education.** 1955.

Hartman, Gertrude & Ann Shumaker, editors. **Creative Expression.** 1932.

Kandel, I. L. **The Cult of Uncertainty.** 1943.

Kandel, I. L. **Examinations and Their Substitutes in the United States.** 1936.

Kilpatrick, William Heard. **Education for a Changing Civilization.** 1926.

Kilpatrick, William Heard. **Foundations of Method.** 1925.

Kilpatrick, William Heard. **The Montessori System Examined.** 1914.

Lang, Ossian H., editor. **Educational Creeds of the Nineteenth Century.** 1898.

Learned, William S. **The Quality of the Educational Process in the United States and in Europe.** 1927.

Meiklejohn, Alexander. **The Experimental College.** 1932.

Middlekauff, Robert. **Ancients and Axioms: Secondary Education in Eighteenth-Century New England.** 1963.

Norwood, William Frederick. **Medical Education in the United States Before the Civil War.** 1944.

Parsons, Elsie W. Clews. **Educational Legislation and Administration of the Colonial Governments.** 1899.

Perry, Charles M. **Henry Philip Tappan: Philosopher and University President.** 1933.

Pierce, Bessie Louise. **Civic Attitudes in American School Textbooks.** 1930.

Rice, Edwin Wilbur. **The Sunday-School Movement (1780-1917) and the American Sunday-School Union (1817-1917).** 1917.

Robinson, James Harvey. **The Humanizing of Knowledge.** 1924.

Ryan, W. Carson. **Studies in Early Graduate Education.** 1939.

Seybolt, Robert Francis. **The Evening School in Colonial America.** 1925.

Seybolt, Robert Francis. **Source Studies in American Colonial Education.** 1925.

Todd, Lewis Paul. **Wartime Relations of the Federal Government and the Public Schools, 1917-1918.** 1945.

Vandewalker, Nina C. **The Kindergarten in American Education.** 1908.

Ward, Florence Elizabeth. **The Montessori Method and the American School.** 1913.

West, Andrew Fleming. **Short Papers on American Liberal Education.** 1907.

Wright, Marion M. Thompson. **The Education of Negroes in New Jersey.** 1941.

Supplement

The Social Frontier (Frontiers of Democracy). Vols. 1-10, 1934-1943.